Dear Unknown Friend

DEAR UNKNOWN FRIEND

The Remarkable Correspondence between American and Soviet Women

ALEXIS PERI

HARVARD UNIVERSITY PRESS

Cambridge, Massachusetts & London, England 2024

Printed in the United States of America

First printing

Library of Congress Cataloging-in-Publication Data

Names: Peri, Alexis, author.
Title: Dear unknown friend : the remarkable correspondence between American and Soviet women / Alexis Peri.
Other titles: Remarkable correspondence between American and Soviet women
Description: Cambridge, Massachusetts ; London, England : Harvard University Press, 2024. | Includes bibliographical references and index.
Identifiers: LCCN 2024001362 | ISBN 9780674987586 (cloth)
Subjects: LCSH: Women—Soviet Union—Correspondence—History. | Women—United States—Correspondence—History—20th century. | Pen pals—Soviet Union—History. | Pen pals—United States—History—20th century. | Female friendship—Political aspects—Soviet Union—History. | Female friendship—Political aspects—United States—History—20th century. | Cold War. | Soviet Union—Relations—United States. | United States—Relations—Soviet Union.
Classification: LCC DK268.5 .P47 2024 | DDC 909.82/5—dc23/eng/20240314
LC record available at https://lccn.loc.gov/2024001362

For Hanns,
my love and my inspiration

Contents

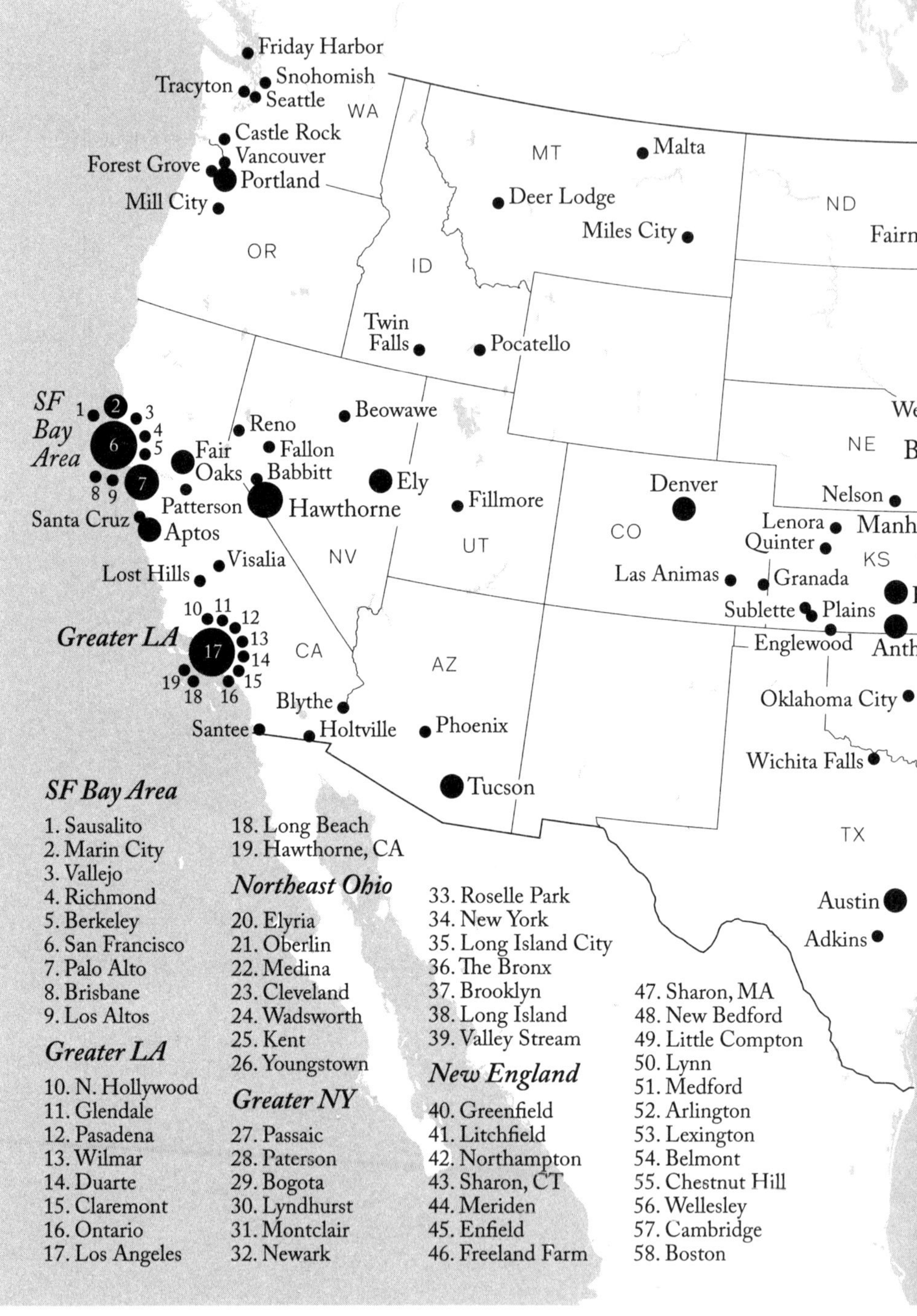

Friday Harbor
Snohomish
Tracyton
Seattle
WA
Castle Rock
Vancouver
Forest Grove
Portland
Mill City
MT
Malta
Deer Lodge
Miles City
ND
OR
ID
Twin Falls
Pocatello
SF Bay Area
1
2
3
4
5
6
7
8
9
Reno
Beowawe
Fair Oaks
Fallon
Babbitt
Ely
Hawthorne
Fillmore
Patterson
Santa Cruz
Aptos
Denver
NE
Nelson
Lenora
Quinter
CO
KS
UT
NV
Visalia
Lost Hills
Las Animas
Granada
Sublette
Plains
Englewood
Greater LA
10
11
12
13
14
15
16
17
18
19
CA
AZ
Oklahoma City
Blythe
Santee
Holtville
Phoenix
Wichita Falls
Tucson
TX
Austin
Adkins
SF Bay Area
1. Sausalito
2. Marin City
3. Vallejo
4. Richmond
5. Berkeley
6. San Francisco
7. Palo Alto
8. Brisbane
9. Los Altos
Greater LA
10. N. Hollywood
11. Glendale
12. Pasadena
13. Wilmar
14. Duarte
15. Claremont
16. Ontario
17. Los Angeles
18. Long Beach
19. Hawthorne, CA
Northeast Ohio
20. Elyria
21. Oberlin
22. Medina
23. Cleveland
24. Wadsworth
25. Kent
26. Youngstown
Greater NY
27. Passaic
28. Paterson
29. Bogota
30. Lyndhurst
31. Montclair
32. Newark
33. Roselle Park
34. New York
35. Long Island City
36. The Bronx
37. Brooklyn
38. Long Island
39. Valley Stream
New England
40. Greenfield
41. Litchfield
42. Northampton
43. Sharon, CT
44. Meriden
45. Enfield
46. Freeland Farm
47. Sharon, MA
48. New Bedford
49. Little Compton
50. Lynn
51. Medford
52. Arlington
53. Lexington
54. Belmont
55. Chestnut Hill
56. Wellesley
57. Cambridge
58. Boston

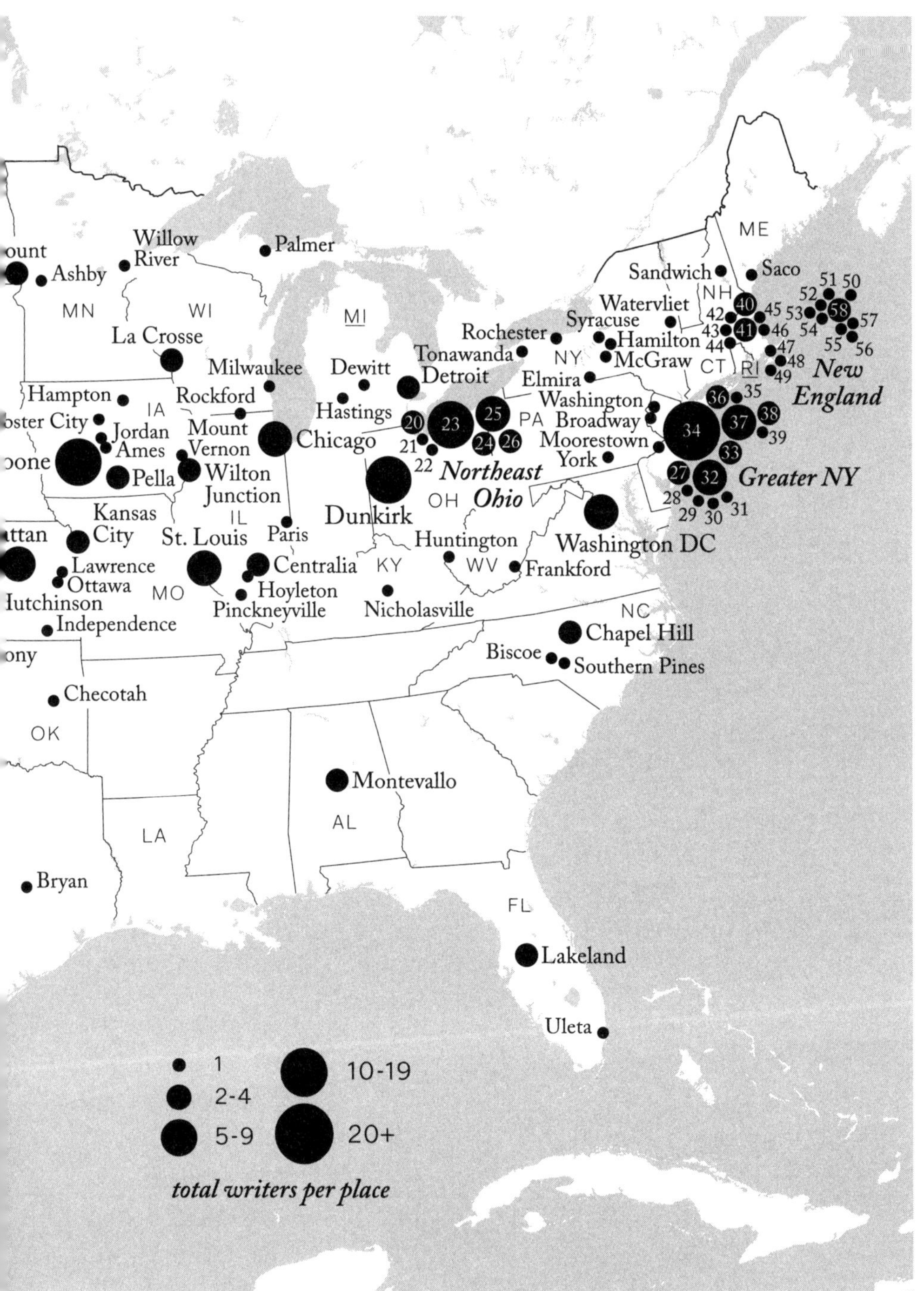

Locations of select letter writers from the United States. Not shown are several dozen American correspondents who did not share their addresses.

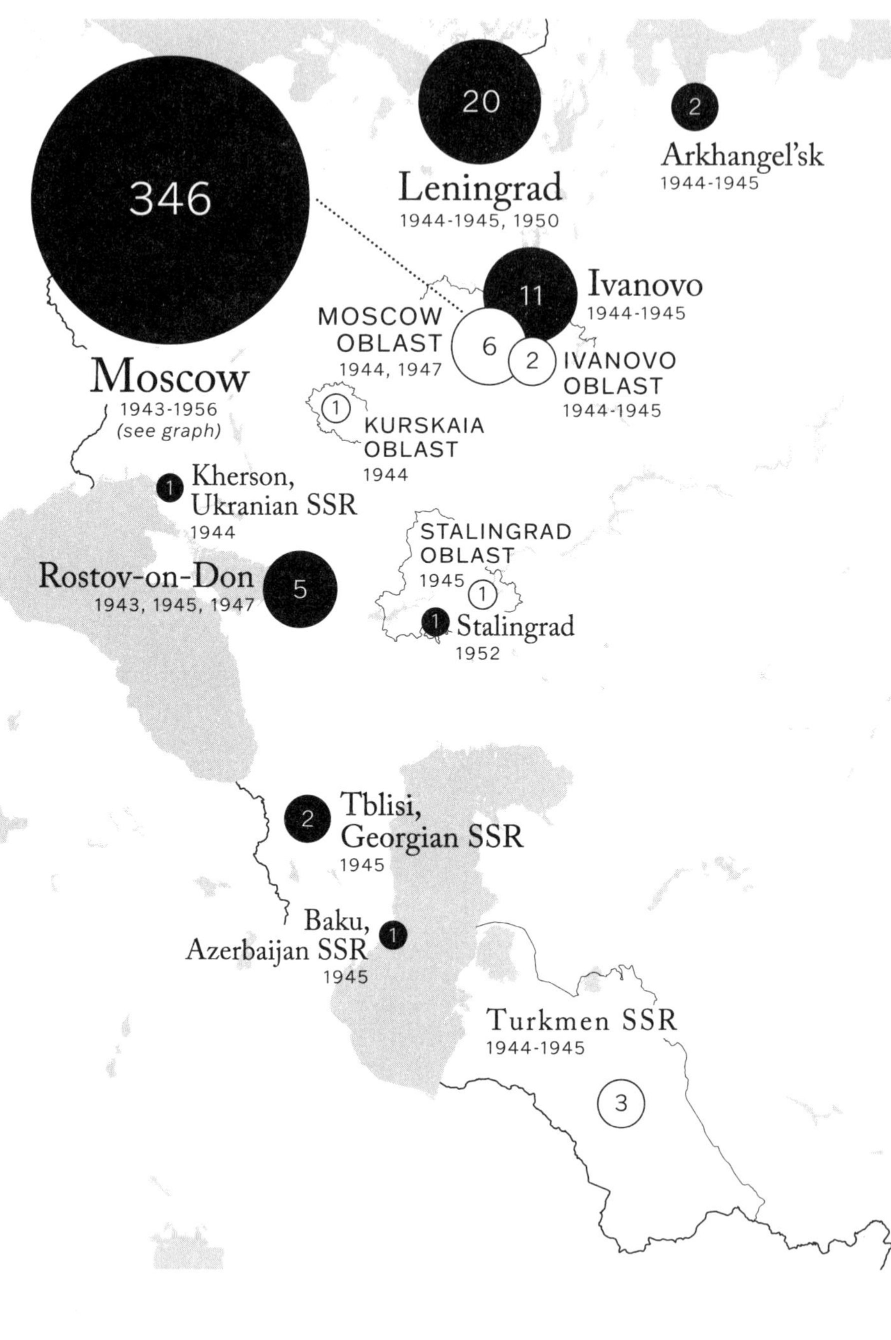

346
Moscow
1943-1956
(see graph)
20
Leningrad
1944-1945, 1950
2
Arkhangel'sk
1944-1945
11
Ivanovo
1944-1945
MOSCOW
OBLAST
1944, 1947
6
2
IVANOVO
OBLAST
1944-1945
1
KURSKAIA
OBLAST
1944
1
Kherson,
Ukranian SSR
1944
STALINGRAD
OBLAST
1945
1
Rostov-on-Don
1943, 1945, 1947
5
1
Stalingrad
1952
2
Tblisi,
Georgian SSR
1945
Baku,
Azerbaijan SSR
1945
1
Turkmen SSR
1944-1945
3

sk

Noril'skii 1
1946

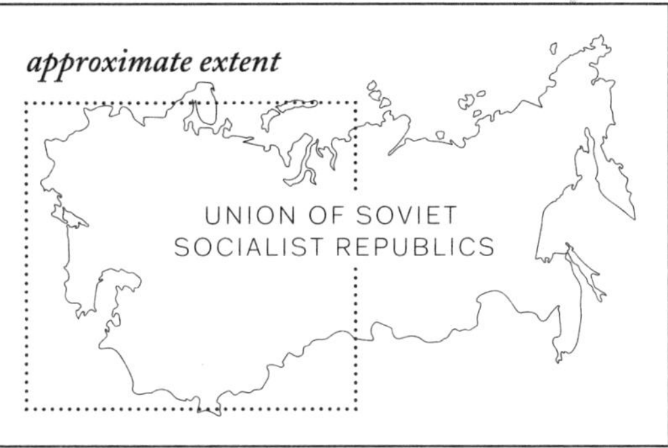

Locations of select letter writers from the Soviet Union. Not shown are several dozen Soviet correspondents for whom no address was listed.

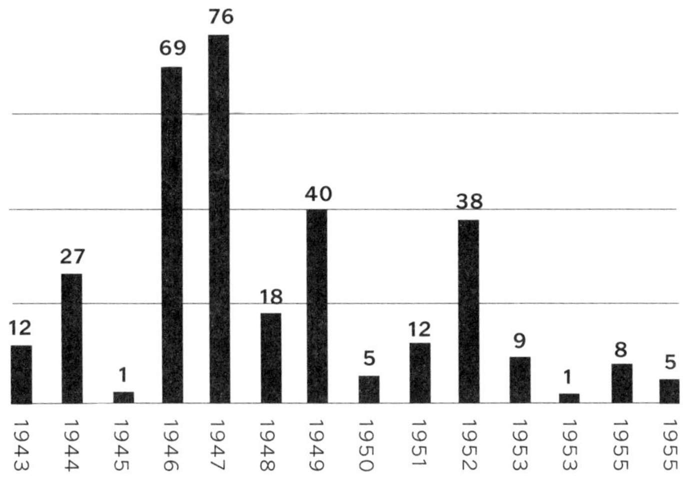

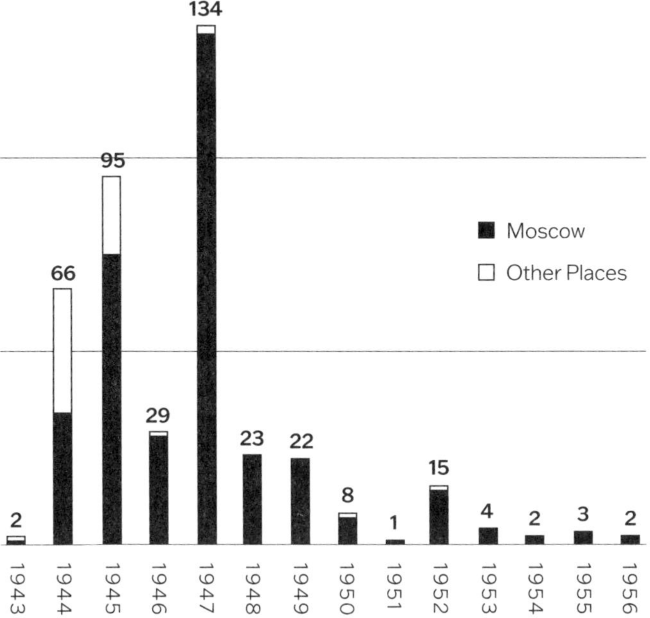

Approximate number of new correspondents who joined the pen-pal project per year between 1943 and 1953. Top: American correspondents. Bottom: Soviet correspondents.

Greeting ~

Hello to You, My Still Unknown but Already Close Friend!

"Dear Unknown Russian friend," Myrtle Park began one afternoon in September 1947, "it makes me quite happy to have the opportunity to write to you!" Park sat at her dusty writing desk, flushed with excitement and worry. She had just read about a heated exchange that erupted between American and Soviet delegates to the United Nations (UN) over communist-led uprisings in Greece. This civil war in Greece ignited one of the first proxy wars between the United States and the Soviet Union, which had still been allies when the conflict began at the end of the Second World War.[1] Park's thoughts churned as she pored over the bellicose speech delivered by Soviet representative Andrei Vyshinskii on the floor of the UN. Vyshinskii not only attacked American statesmen for helping the Greek government suppress the communist revolt, he also accused them of stockpiling weapons and preparing to attack the USSR.[2] Determined not to let official diplomats speak for her, Park's fingers flew across her typewriter. "We believe that the USA and Russia can and should be friends," she proclaimed, "but our leaders, unfortunately, do not always express such confidence. They do not represent the interests of the common people of the United States." "Common people" like her appreciated Soviet sacrifices during World War II and remembered how the United States and USSR had put aside two decades of mutual suspicion to defeat Hitler. "We do so hope that there will be no war," Park declared, "I do so hope you, Russian people, may have the

opportunity to go on with your way of doing things without ever having to fight another war. I am, sincerely your friend, Mrs. Ethan J. Park."[3]

Part distress call, part friendship appeal, Park's letter had the earnest, improbable feel of a message in a bottle, dispatched to a stranger on the other side of the world. Miraculously, a reply arrived only a few months later. It was the first of more than a dozen letters Park received from Irina Aleksandrovna Kuznetsova of Moscow. "My Dear Mrs. Park!" Kuznetsova exclaimed, "I have only just got your letter and am sitting down immediately to answer it, as I wish you to have my reply as soon as possible. I sincerely hope we will be able to keep up our correspondence and will become real friends. Dear Mrs. Park," Kuznetsova continued, "I was deeply touched by your interest to hear from far-away Moscow and the sincere sympathy that breathes in your letter," especially when it came to the Soviet war experience. More Soviets perished in the battle for Moscow than the total number of Americans and Britons who died during the entire Second World War.[4] Kuznetsova told Park about this ordeal, about running for cover as bombs exploded over her home. And she echoed Park's concern that mounting US-Soviet tensions might turn violent.[5] "I am awfully worried by all this, dear Mrs. Park. Those who have lived through the horrors of the last war cannot look with equanimity on preparations for a new war and cannot consider it other than the most horrible crime."[6] "I completely agree with you," Myrtle Park replied, "that war is the most horrible crime. I am determined that I shall do my little, tiny bit toward furthering understanding and peace on earth. World peace is based greatly on understanding, isn't it?"[7]

What Park called her "little, tiny bit," the exchange of letters, was in fact a major political act. Park and Kuznetsova went on to correspond for seven years, from 1947 until 1953. Those years bookended one of the most tumultuous periods of the Cold War, when the Soviet Union and United States fought numerous battles—armed conflicts and information wars—to expand their own spheres of influence and contain each other's. Park and Kuznetsova forged their friendship while the top scientists in their countries developed new nuclear weapons, while American politicians fanned the flames of anti-communist hysteria and the Soviet state whipped up anti-Americanism. McCarthyism and *zhdanovshchina*, as those campaigns came to be called, ruined thousands of lives and careers. At times, fear rippled through Park's and Kuznetsova's letters; they knew their correspondence was being read by government officials and that it might be used against them. "Do not be surprised if my letters stop," Park warned, explaining that some Americans who advocated for US-Soviet friendship were "already spending three months in jail."[8] And whenever a long gap elapsed between their letters, the pen pals assumed the worst, that "maybe it was true, your government didn't want you to write to me because of this awful 'cold war' our papers talk about."[9] Yet, Park and Kuznetsova kept on writing, despite the risk of being blacklisted or incarcerated. And they were one of more than three hundred pairs of women who did so. In *Dear Unknown Friend,* I bring the hidden history of this correspondence to light.[10] I uncover how these pen friendships got started, how they managed to survive, and how they changed the correspondents' lives, communities, and nations.

This is a story about the power of the personal. It casts a spotlight on that delicate dance between friendship and politics as it was performed by some 750 women in the United States and Soviet Union. These self-described "ordinary" women, like Park and Kuznetsova, held no government post nor had any foreign policy expertise. They were not culturally elite or well connected. Most of them had never even been abroad. Yet, by taking up their pens, they thrust themselves onto the international political stage at a time when women were relegated to playing minor roles.[11] Starting at the height of the Second World War in 1943 and extending through 1953, Soviet and American women reached out to each other and began to share personal—sometimes intimate—details about their lives. They discussed their aspirations and heartaches. And they began to model what they believed was a new, woman's style of diplomacy: a diplomacy of the heart. This was the idea that heartfelt storytelling and expressions of empathy could be mighty political forces, strong enough to help win wars and secure peace.[12] Throughout World War II and the early Cold War, which American and Soviet statesmen waged primarily through displays of aggression, the pen pals experimented with displays of vulnerability. They explored the possibility that opening up emotionally to one's historic enemy might be politically expedient rather than pose a political liability.[13]

The pen friends' style of diplomacy revolved around human connection rather than debate or negotiation. Instead of hashing out policy differences or discussing abstract tenets of socialism and liberal capitalism, the letter writers focused their conversations on emotional and everyday experiences, which they assumed all women shared.[14] Through these common concerns, they hoped to establish "communities of emotion" that could nourish

US-Soviet relations.[15] In every letter, they tried to emphasize what they had or *felt* in common even as they discovered how different their lives were. At the time of her first letter, Myrtle Park was a forty-six-year-old housewife who raised cattle and wheat in the remote town of Englewood, Kansas.[16] There, she confessed, "I very often feel alone and abandoned." She longed for great museums, exciting travel, and engrossing conversation. "That was a reason why I was drawn to correspondence,"[17] she reflected, "I am interested in the people of the world and what they are doing for themselves."[18] Park was delighted, therefore, to connect with Irina Kuznetsova. Kuznetsova was a twenty-three-year-old doctoral candidate in art history and a curator at the Pushkin Museum in Moscow. That war-battered but bustling metropolis was home to over four million people after the war, whereas Englewood's population hovered around 350.[19]

Peace first inspired them to write, but mutual curiosity and admiration sustained their correspondence for almost a decade. Park was in awe of Kuznetsova's "very interesting" career and "great education." "You studied much more at university than I did," she added with a touch of timidity.[20] Park grew up on a cattle ranch and taught fifth grade before she married and became "a housewife." For her part, Kuznetsova found Park's routine of riding horses and chasing coyotes through the "Kansas steppe" positively exotic.[21] "We were quite wonderstruck" to "read that you and your mother (she must be at least sixty) inspect herds on horseback! Please tell her from me that she is a wonder!" Kuznetsova marveled. "How nice it is that two people who are thorough strangers and live so far away from each other in such different surroundings can find a common language and interest each other. Each time I get a letter from you," Kuznetsova continued, "it makes me want more eagerly to get the next. The image I had of you after your first letter, as yet very nebulous and abstract, is now getting more and more real. I can now almost visualize your home, your husband, your mother, and yourself occupied with housekeeping duties or pounding a typewriter. I can't run a typewriter, nor can I ride horseback," Kuznetsova admitted. She got in the saddle once, but it was a short ride that came to "a very sorry and comical end."[22]

Kuznetsova's romantic image of Park might have come straight out of a Hollywood western, but the Muscovite claimed their correspondence was demolishing stereotypes rather than perpetuating them. "For it is quite a different thing to read about the life of American farmers in newspapers or novels," she explained, "than to be personally acquainted with an American farmwoman."[23] The caustic way their newspapers portrayed each other's societies provided another source of fascination. "What do you read about us? Something very bad? Ha ha!" Park giggled. "Well, if you ask me about them," she added, referring to anti-American articles in the Soviet press, "I will tell you what I think about them. That, truly, will be very interesting."[24] Pen friendship, they hoped, would provide an alternative source of information about life beyond the "iron curtain."

The letter writers deliberately struck a tone that ran counter to the combative discourse they encountered in the press and from government leaders. Their style of diplomacy was both highly personalized and deeply gendered. There were formal restrictions on men joining the letter-writing program, but there were informal ones too. Five men requested pen pals, but they were rebuffed because their letters read like treatises—dry, argumentative, and devoid of personal charm.[25] "I am sorry to say that it gave me no real idea of you at all," Antonina Pavliuchenko complained to her would-be pen pal.[26] The participants demanded a "personal touch," insisting that, if Americans and Soviets were to understand each other better, that shift had to occur in the heart first and then in the mind.

There were at least two reasons why the pen pals believed their approach would succeed where official diplomacy had not. The first was that they were women. Women, they assumed, were better than men at listening, forming friendships, and avoiding conflict. Some pen pals, particularly from the United States, argued that women's maternal instincts made them inherently more committed to preventing war. When articulating such perspectives, many letter writers drew on conventions of sentimentalism and maternalism, sometimes simplifying femininity to underscore the values and concerns they held in common.[27] It is not that sentimentalism or maternalism encompassed the whole of the letter writers' political thought, far from it. Rather, they drew on these discourses to make their political commitments legible to correspondents they knew nothing about—except that they were women. This approach also led them to focus not on debating current events but discussing the personal, the emotional, and the everyday. Major crises like the Greek Civil War, the Korean War, and the division of postwar Germany often provided the initial impetus for them to join the pen-pal program, but once they started corresponding, the letter writers generally avoided hot-button issues and looked for common ground by discussing recipes and childcare, housework and paid labor, books and music, sorrows and anxieties. Park and Kuznetsova's conversations ran the gamut from school systems to silk stockings. They cheered each other's successes and consoled each other in grief. And they reveled in the little things that might unlock profound understanding between them. "You must tell me every small detail about your life, work, and country," Park implored Kuznetsova. "You also must ask me questions. Everything that simply comes to mind. Please do not be embarrassed to ask direct and intimate questions."[28]

Second, the pen pals believed they could engage in such frank discussions because they were "common people," as Park put it, not politicians. The correspondents' decision to write during such a politically perilous time was nothing short of extraordinary, but they constantly emphasized their own ordinariness because it allowed them to claim their remarks were sincere, and it freed them from their governments' foreign relations failures. Thus, the pen pals not only skirted key topics of official diplomacy, they rejected its strongman rhetoric as well. They couched their political ideas in stories, compliments, and advice. They traded jokes, postcards, nicknames, and photographs. "You are a charming young woman and you have wonderful hair!" Park exclaimed upon receiving a snapshot of Kuznetsova.[29] In short, the pen pals gave their messages power not by being forceful but by being friendly. And because they privileged civility over winning any one argument, some pairs exchanged as many as thirty-six letters with each other, weathering both geopolitical conflicts and individual disagreements.

And disagreements abounded. The letter writers did not shy away from spirited debate. Even though they were determined to defuse US-Soviet hostilities, they engaged in some cold war competition themselves. In some cases, this stemmed from their emphasis on peace, as the harmonious world order they envisioned was typically based on ideals and practices espoused by their own countries. In other instances, the correspondents were drawn into competition through the act of cultural translation. As they worked to explain their nation's values and societal norms, they justified them. Still other participants were keen to boast about themselves or their children, lauding the society that made such success possible. Finally, a major reason for this competitive spirit is that the Soviet letter writers were explicitly told to promote Soviet socialism, especially the USSR's policies on peace and women's rights. They did not follow this directive blindly, however, as constant complaints from Communist Party authorities attest. Soviet correspondents were instructed to ask their American interlocutors for military aid during World War II, but they ended up seeking emotional and psychological support instead. Later, they were told to champion Soviet-backed summits and peace petitions, but only three obeyed. Irina Kuznetsova was not one of them. She did, however, probe Myrtle Park about who she planned to vote for in the 1948 US presidential election, voicing strong support for a "peace candidate" and gesturing toward Progressive Henry A. Wallace.[30] Compared to their Soviet pen pals, the American participants were much more outspoken against their own government's policies, but they, too, defended their country's core values. Park, for instance, did not need any convincing to vote for Wallace. She considered incumbent Harry S. Truman's foreign policy "reactionary" and militaristic.[31] But Park had an eye for Soviet militarism as well, and she raised questions about the Soviet Union's "enormous secret police," asking if it was true that "seven percent of the population of the Soviet Union is in penal camps."[32]

Nearly every letter contains some mixture of peacemaking and propagandizing.[33] Although Americans like Park were not under overt pressure to promote their national way of life, they often did anyway. In effect, both the Soviet and American pen pals acted as surrogates.[34] They wove their own stories into the story of the nation, propagating various cultural myths in the process. A recipe, for instance, could illuminate sharp differences in American and Soviet ideals of womanhood. The question of how to raise one's children brought out narratives of American "rugged individualism" and Soviet communalism. And their dreams of world peace evoked images of the United States as a redeemer nation and of the USSR as a multiethnic utopia built on "the friendship of the peoples." In staking these claims, the letter writers drew on their own lives as evidence, and they enveloped national ideals in a personalized "language of feeling."[35]

The letters' propagandistic qualities certainly limit their factual reliability. They cannot be taken as accurate accounts of "what life was like" in the United States or the Soviet Union at midcentury. The correspondents performed what, in their eyes, it meant to be a citizen, woman, worker, mother, and peace advocate in the United States or Soviet Union.[36] And this provides valuable insight into how national identities and ideologies are constructed—not from the top down but dynamically and subjectively, through the stories we tell ourselves and others.[37]

Even as they championed certain ideals, the letter writers' actions often told another story. Soviet letter writers, for instance, lauded socialist principles, but they also—perhaps unwittingly—identified key shortcomings of the Soviet gender policies they were supposed to trumpet. In recounting their daily routines, they pointed to the lack of reliable childcare. Irina Kuznetsova, for instance, told Myrtle Park that working mothers preferred to leave their children with a relative than in a state-run kindergarten.[38] Or, when bragging about their professional achievements, Soviet participants highlighted how misogynistic labor practices persisted in the USSR. Meanwhile Myrtle Park, who chose not to have children of her own, nonetheless pushed some middle-class American ideals of womanhood onto her pen friend. Even as she admired Kuznetsova's career, Park advised: "you should marry and have children of your own."[39] Indeed, the letters capture many areas of disjuncture between the correspondents' advocacy and their actions. They also document the struggles Soviet and American women shared as conservative gender norms took root in their countries after World War II.

The Importance of Small Talk

Skeptical readers might look at these discussions about the little things in life and dismiss them as trivial. They might chalk the letter writers' effusive prose up to naiveté or superficial politeness. Such readers will find themselves in good company with the Soviet and American officials described in this book. Thanks to their suspicion that these were just a few hundred women chattering amiably, the Central Committee of the Communist Party of the Soviet Union and the US State Department allowed the pen friends to communicate in the face of numerous restrictions. They conversed during World War II, when there were strict limits on the quantity and content of civilian post sent overseas, and they kept talking after the war, when contact across the iron curtain was considered treasonous by statesmen in both countries. Being underestimated had its advantages.

Although their conversations may seem mundane and their lives ordinary, much about this pen-pal program was new and extraordinary. It compels us to change the way we periodize and conceptualize the Cold War, and it calls us to recognize the enduring impact of the US-Soviet alliance and the legacy of the popular front. The correspondence project broke new ground as one of the first public diplomacy ventures to foster ongoing conversations between American and Soviet citizens.[40] And it was the first such initiative organized and conducted exclusively by the women of those countries. The program expanded the bounds of women's political participation, both in wartime and early cold war diplomacy.

The Soviet and American women's letter exchange was the first of its kind in many respects, but it built on a long history of Europeans and North Americans using international correspondence to strengthen cross-cultural connections. Starting in the late eighteenth century, letter writing became a favorite tool of revolutionaries, pacifists, suffragists, and others working to forge overseas alliances through a republic of letters.[41] The practice gained traction among non-elites and non-activists in the late nineteenth century, especially after the establishment of the Universal Postal Union and a common system of flat rate postage in 1874. Both the tsarist empire and the United States participated in these accords, which made it easier and more affordable to have a pen pal abroad.[42]

During the 1920s and 1930s, international correspondence flourished in the United States and made modest gains in the new Soviet Union. It became increasingly common for ordinary Americans, including children, to have a far-flung pen pal. Pen friendship became especially popular among American charities, religious groups, and educational organizations keen to cultivate Christian fellowship and friendly ties abroad. The terms "pen pal" and "pen friend" entered American English parlance during the interwar period.[43] Meanwhile, in the USSR, the All-Union Communist Party and its youth affiliates launched several letter writing schemes in the name of proletarian solidarity. They aimed to foster ties between decorated workers, revolutionaries, and young communist enthusiasts.[44] Only select Soviet citizens were permitted to have international pen friends during the USSR's first two decades, but it was very common for Soviets to engage in other forms of epistolary politicking such as crafting personalized letters of petition to convey their grievances to state and party leaders.[45]

This women's letter exchange, which was created in Moscow during the Second World War, broke with these precedents. It was one of the first Soviet public diplomacy programs to focus on women, particularly "ordinary" women who lacked any special labor or revolutionary credentials. Moreover, the program's organizers arranged for Soviet women to be in sustained contact not with socialist allies but with "bourgeois" women in the capitalist

West. Both the US and Soviet governments considered this a risky venture. Their officials read the letters and monitored the exchange but agreed that the program's potential for strengthening the alliance against Hitler outweighed the hazards it posed as a source of subversion or spycraft. When the war ended, US-Soviet hostilities quickly reignited, but the memory of the alliance was not snuffed out. Most pen pals referred regularly to the wartime partnership in a decade's worth of letters. To them, it proved that the Cold War was not inevitable, that cooperation was possible. Even so, their faith was repeatedly tested in the late 1940s and early 1950s, as both US and Soviet officials tried to shut the program down. Still, it survived. In the end, the political potential of US-Soviet friendship proved alluring, both for the individual volunteers who kept sending messages of peace and for the skeptical bureaucrats who scanned their notes for intelligence and propaganda exploits.

This pen-pal program was also remarkable for how it privileged ongoing dialogue, not one-time exchanges. Some better-known letter writing schemes from the cold war era like Letters from America, Letters Abroad, and the People-to-People Program arranged for thousands of participants to send one-off letters but seldom fostered continuous conversations.[46] And that makes all the difference. It is one thing to send a message of peace and goodwill, and it is quite another to nurture a lasting epistolary relationship, where the participants must continually model principles of reciprocity, civil discourse, and friendship, not just pay lip service to them. Moreover, compared to general letter-writing campaigns, pen friendship demanded a huge investment of resources—emotional, energetic, and financial. It took a whole team of translators, editors, censors, and couriers to facilitate this decade-long exchange of ideas between a small number of people. The program peaked in 1949 with 319 pairs of dedicated correspondents. This is a small but significant number, considering scholars estimate that the Soviet Union's All-Union Society for Cultural Relations with Foreign Countries (VOKS) hosted only fifty-seven Americans in the USSR between 1947 and 1951, and a similarly paltry number of Soviets visited the United States.[47] Moreover, the fact that this was an ongoing exchange means we can read the letters to trace how shifts in US-Soviet relations, from allies to adversaries, came to bear on "ordinary" citizens.

The pen-pal program upends the conventional historical wisdom that there was virtually no contact between American and Soviet citizens during the Truman-Stalin era.[48] This notorious period, 1945–1953, has generally been understood through the lens of those statesmen's policies of containment and isolation. Truman and Stalin restricted the sharing of scientific and military information, curtailed travel, and—in the Soviet case—banned marriages that crisscrossed their borders.[49] The United States did not even have an ambassador in Moscow in the winter of 1952–1953.[50] During these years when official diplomacy faltered, the pen friendships thrived.

Historians routinely claim that communication between American and Soviet civilians began to flow only after Stalin died in 1953 and when President Dwight D. Eisenhower and Premier Nikita Khrushchev tried to "thaw" relations between their countries. I also thought this was true until I discovered these letters, hastily bundled together and gathering dust in the State Archive of the Russian Federation. I was there to research a completely different topic but quickly changed course when I found these thousands of letters chronicling a decade of American-Soviet conversations. By the time Khrushchev and Eisenhower's first citizen exchange programs got off the ground, those conversations had been going on for ten years. They had been inspired by the 1943 "spirit of Stalingrad," not the oft-cited 1955 "spirit of Geneva," when Eisenhower met with Soviet, British, and French leaders and called for "friendly understanding" between east and west.[51] Geneva marked the expansion rather than the beginning of American and Soviet exchange. And that expansion was of a distinct, limited type. Eisenhower and Khrushchev focused on how increased contact could create more opportunities to showcase their national superiority.[52] They were more interested in exchange as a form of "psychological warfare" and "peaceful competition," respectively, and not as a way to foster a sense of reciprocity or emotional investment between their peoples—two bedrocks of pen friendship.[53]

The correspondence project suggests, therefore, that the memory of the wartime popular front was more powerful, the Truman-Stalin era was not as isolating, and the "thaw" not as radical a rupture as previously supposed.

The Personal as Political

The pen-friendship project not only blurs the lines of demarcation between the US-Soviet alliance, the start of the Cold War, and the "thaw," but also reinforces the causal link between women's midcentury experiences and the international feminist movements that crystalized in the late twentieth century. As the pen pals discovered, despite their initial expectations, the everyday lives of Soviet and American women were quite different, as was their access to higher education, career development, consumer comforts, and free political expression. Still, the years around World War II gave them some common experiences. Both Soviet and American letter writers saw their professional and public opportunities greatly expand during the war and then contract afterward, at which time they were advised to give way to returning male soldiers in the workplace and in the home. The pen pals' conversations about everyday life captured these moments of possibility and of retrenchment. They cut across the binaries journalists and politicians frequently used to juxtapose Soviet and American womanhood, and they presaged transnational conversations about women's rights that exploded in the 1960s and beyond. During the 1940s, the pen friends explored the pressures of motherhood, their desires for professional fulfillment, and the challenges of balancing work inside and outside the home. In an effort to promote their own housekeeping strategies, American participants worked to send a model kitchen to Moscow in 1946, thirteen years before US officials used the same strategy and touched off the notorious "kitchen debate." Here again, what we assume was new about US-Soviet relations during the 1950s was already a decade in the making, by women.

The pen friends' conversations about what it was like to be a woman and especially a working mother broadened the political horizons of those who participated in the program, whether by writing letters or by reading them. Many pen pals, including Park and Kuznetsova, shared their letters with relatives, neighbors, and coworkers. They read them aloud at church and club meetings, and they sometimes set up pen friendships between their children.[54] Park and Kuznetsova tried to arrange for their nieces to correspond.[55] Furthermore, both the pen friends and the project's organizers sent copies of the letters to the press. Excerpts appeared in pamphlets, newspapers, magazines, and broadcasts throughout the 1940s and 1950s, allowing many more people to participate vicariously in the conversation about gender inequality.

In this way, the program was much more than an avenue for peacemaking and propagandizing; it also became a fount of self-examination. Letter writing, it has been said, "is an opportunity for self-reflection through dialogue."[56] One of the project's most important legacies, I contend, was it raised the political consciousness of those involved by heightening their awareness of how the personal was political.[57] As the correspondents became better acquainted with one another's circumstances and convictions, they began to parse the similarities and differences. The letter exchange threw some of the legal and social prohibitions they faced as women into sharp relief. It helped them notice the norms and structures that undergirded their daily lives, to see the particular in what they had assumed was universal. The more they became aware of political alternatives, the more they reflected upon their own values and life choices. Thus, even as they idealized their national concepts of womanhood, the participants acquired a keener sense of how their routines and habits of mind were embedded in the political and the patriarchal.

With the encouragement of their pen pals, some correspondents set about making new choices. They began to read new political literature, embark on new careers, or seek out alternative forms of childcare. Myrtle Park, for instance, enrolled in a nursing program, moved to Arizona, and started an entirely new life in 1952. This was not solely because of Kuznetsova's encouragement, of course, but Kuznetsova's example helped expand Park's sense of possibility and emboldened her to revamp her life.[58] In the years after they stopped corresponding, several American participants underwent a political evolution, moving from conservative to liberal and even pro-socialist politics, and campaigning for peace and women's equality. Park was already a progressive in 1948 but became more critical of capitalism and complimentary of Soviet socialism over time.[59] While it is impossible to pinpoint a single, exact reason for these shifts, the pen friendships these women carried on for many years and at great personal risk likely had an important albeit indirect impact on their lives and attitudes.

I learned about these later developments in the letter writers' lives by tracking down their children and grandchildren. With the help of local historical associations and genealogical databases, I located a few of the pen pals' descendants. Most were shocked to hear from me, as they had never heard about the letters. "As it is said, O.M.G.!," Joanne Jahr replied when I first wrote to her about her mother's correspondence, "neither I nor my brother Marc ever knew. I am in complete and total shock and I'm in tears. Everyone keeps secrets—children from parents and parents from children. I'd love to talk to you."[60] Most of the descendants who responded to my queries were similarly intrigued. I shared the letters with them, and they shared family stories with me. They often remarked that the letters showed an unknown side of their mother or grandmother, but at the same time the experiences and relationships she described rang true to them. Joanne and Marc Jahr told me about how their mother, Jean Jahr, started a career and gained more confidence in the years after she corresponded with Ol'ga Mel'nikovskaia. The pen friendship was not the chief cause of this change. Most likely their mother reinvented her life after numerous conversations—with her pen friend, with other friends, with family members, with her husband, and with herself.

I had less success connecting with the children and grandchildren of Soviet letter writers. This was especially true of those living in Russia, where ongoing state surveillance and mounting tensions with the United States pose strong deterrents to communication, just as they did in the 1940s and 1950s. Although more Americans than Russians were willing to speak with me, the reverse was true when it came to the availability of archival sources. This project would not have been possible without the Russian state archives, which kept copies of the letters. They house the censored and uncensored versions, as well as translated and untranslated versions, all of which I compared. In US archives, I found ample documentation that the pen-pal program existed but no letters except for a published pamphlet of excerpts from them. Those extracts matched complete letters located in Moscow. Many of the files I requested about the pen-pal program from the US national archives and the FBI were heavily redacted or still classified. So, there are gaps and silences on all sides.

Although I have been unable to unearth how individual Soviet correspondents might have been impacted by their pen friendships in the years after they stopped writing, the Russian state archives do document how the women's organizations that ran the pen-pal exchange were deeply affected by it. Many of the project's American and Soviet leaders were full-time activists who simultaneously worked on other campaigns to advance peace and women's rights. Over time, they began altering their tactics based on the suggestions and criticisms contained in the letters. This was especially true of the Soviet women who ran the pen-pal project from Moscow. They marshaled the letters to demand better rights and conditions for women in the USSR—everything from stronger coveralls to greater reproductive freedom. They also drew on the pen-pal project as a model for the Soviet Union's later citizen diplomacy ventures, which proliferated in the second half of the twentieth century. Breaking with previous efforts in Soviet cultural diplomacy, they emphasized that personal bonds were a necessary precondition for political persuasion, and they insisted that "ordinary people" living in bourgeois, capitalist countries were "peace-loving" and could be regarded warmly as potential comrades, not criminals.[61] The pen friendships, therefore, are not just part of the history of World War II and the Cold War, they link to the peace and feminist movements, movements that also emphasized the power of friendship and the insight that the personal is political.

Mixing Friendship and Politics

The letter writers conducted their political work in a friendly, even effusive manner, but can they actually be considered friends if they were not able to meet face-to-face or to speak freely? Certainly, their conversations were censored and monitored by various institutions—from the women's groups who organized the letter exchange to the Central Committee of the Communist Party and the FBI. This underscores why the letters cannot be mistaken for spontaneous outpourings of their authors' innermost convictions; they are declarations of feeling and belief. Whenever I quote the letters, I note any text that was excised or altered and by whom. As it turned out, censorship was light. Typically, Soviet censors did not cut more than a phrase or two from each letter, and there are no obvious signs of censorship on the American side. Self-censorship, however, was formidable. The women who participated in the project were often candid about their emotions but careful about externals. Some concealed details about their lives or disguised their names. This makes it even more difficult to excavate their "real" lives with any certainty.

In light of all this, I treat the letters as highly personalized performances of the self, of womanhood, and of the nation. But by approaching them in this way, I am not suggesting that the pen pals were necessarily insincere in the sentiments they expressed about peace, gender equality, or national achievements.[62] The post–World War II moment was a high point of patriotism in the United States and the Soviet Union. It was also a time when people earnestly believed war would never return and life was getting better. Propaganda was certainly an aspect of the project, but that does not mean that these rich and detailed letters were crafted solely through a means-ends calculus and dashed off as "mere propaganda," or that their authors should be dismissed as templates of Soviet and American citizens.

On the contrary, the letters feel idiosyncratic and extemporaneous. The pen friends did not follow a script or parrot their leaders' (often forceful) speeches. In fact, they often neglected to pick up on conversational threads that were ripe for espionage or indoctrination. Soviet participants did not press for details when their pen pals let slip that they had a relative working at Los Alamos National Laboratory, for instance, and they seemed more pleased when their pen friends read Tolstoy than read Marx. There is no question that Soviet women had far less choice about what to write, but their notes suggest they had considerable creative leeway in *how* to write. To borrow a phrase from Miriam Dobson, they employed "a broad range of dialects and idiosyncrasies as they tried to 'speak Bolshevik.'"[63]

Genuine connection can happen even in a restricted space, even when the parties pick and choose what to share. And the truth is, all letter writers pick and choose. As literary scholars and sociologists point out, to write a letter is to create a curated version of the self, akin to a self-portrait. When correspondents put pen to paper, they all "filter" their lived experiences and they express themselves "in such a way that what they say will have an impact" on their interlocutor.[64] Even when letter writers do not deliberately invent, they live inventively on the page. True, the Soviet and American correspondents never met face-to-face, but friendships often center on heartfelt talk more than shared activities or physical proximity. This is especially true, psychologists have suggested, of women's friendships.[65] What matters most is not whether the American and Soviet participants were friends by some empirical measure, but how they posited their relationships as friendships—how they showed up to each other and how they responded to each other, year after year. Reflecting on the first three years of their correspondence, Myrtle Park told Kuznetsova: "It is so wonderful to think about you who are so far away at that end of the world and how the thought that you are my friend warms my heart. Please, write to me sooner if you can and bring us the pleasure of your letters."[66] These correspondences are brimming with symbolic gestures of intimacy and terms of endearment.

Were the pen pals really friends if they were trying to influence each other? The fact that a friendship has an instrumental component does not negate its emotional veracity. On the contrary, scholars of foreign relations have argued, emotional attachments can be powerful "agents of change in international politics."[67] They can strengthen individuals' commitments to each other and to their shared cause.[68] Such attachments need not be formalized into friendship treaties or involve high-ranking officials to be politically efficacious. They can be the personal bonds forged between civilians living across borders. Women suffragists and peace activists from the nineteenth and twentieth centuries were strong examples of this. They embraced the letter's intimate and familial qualities, acutely aware of the seminal role interpersonal relationships played in the formation of political identity. They often referred to their transatlantic political networks as networks of friends, and they couched their political arguments in an epistolary frame.[69] In sum, as Roland Bleiker and Emma Hutchison put it, "emotions can generate new and valuable perspectives on political puzzles."[70] Emotional bonds can be both political and personal, both strategic and sincere.[71]

THE CHAPTERS THAT FOLLOW trace the pen-pal project's twists and turns. The program was born amid the chaos of World War II, part of the Soviet Union's desperate attempt to solicit aid from its western Allies. But the program almost never got off the ground. Soviet organizers failed ninety-five times to generate American women's interest. This changed only after the Red Army triumphed over Hitler's troops at Stalingrad in 1943. In the wake of that victory, US citizens began to send notes of appreciation to their Soviet allies, opening up space for the women of each country to connect. They grieved together for fallen husbands and sons, compared their wartime work, and formulated ideas about how to prevent such wars from reoccurring. This first cohort of pen friends spoke of peace as anti-fascism. This was a vague, politically expedient formulation that masked their considerably different visions of an ideal world without Hitler.

The pen friends reckoned with those differences when the war ended, though they almost never got the chance. In 1945, the Soviet organizers nearly terminated the pen-pal program because its initial goal, military victory, had been achieved. They ignored the letters arriving from the United States until they recognized that such American enthusiasm was a prime opportunity to promote Soviet ideas, especially regarding peace and women's rights. In 1946, a new cohort of correspondents emerged. They took up their pens in hopeful expectation that the United States and USSR would jointly protect the new world order. They quickly discovered, however, that making peace together was much harder than making war against a common enemy. The Soviet pen pals argued that peace must be rooted in social and ethnic equality, while their American interlocutors espoused a model of peace based on Christian teachings. Though moderate, even conservative, in their political outlook, American participants from the immediate postwar years fell under the suspicion of anti-communists in the US government who began legal proceedings to prove American-Soviet friendship was a "communist front."

Thus, the spirit of internationalism that infused the correspondence of 1946 was displaced by a spirit of anxiety, which pervaded letters sent between 1947 and 1949. During those tension-filled years, Soviet and American diplomats dueled over UN governance, aid for European recovery, divided Germany, and nuclear proliferation. In 1949, the Soviet Union successfully tested its first atomic bomb, while the Truman administration proposed the development of a hydrogen bomb. Afraid war was on the horizon, new correspondents—more politically progressive ones, in the American case—wrote with a sense of urgency, determined to protect their children from bombs and battlefields. Myrtle Park was one of them. The pen pals corresponded about raising their children to be peace-loving and doing meaningful work inside and outside the home. Their ever-pressing concerns about peace mingled with a growing awareness of women's inequality and how it differed across cultures. The question of if and how women could "have it all," domestically and professionally, became a major point of debate.

As their personal connections intensified, so too did the anti-American and anti-communist movements in the Soviet Union and United States, respectively. As the 1940s gave way to the 1950s, fearful letter writers from both countries began abandoning the program. The Americans who remained were more radical than previous cohorts of letter writers, defiantly criticizing McCarthyism while defending American values. Soviet women proved even more reluctant to correspond, as numerous artists and officials around them were denounced for "kowtowing" to western ideas.[72] In 1951, the Central Committee of the Communist Party demanded the program shift its focus away from "ordinary and unimportant women" and toward prominent women activists on the far left, with whom Soviet women could collaborate on peace and women's rights initiatives. The trouble was these activists made lousy correspondents. Still, despite all these threats and challenges, the pen-pal project endured.

When US-Soviet relations began to "thaw" in the mid-1950s, Khrushchev and Eisenhower opened up several channels for exchange. This is where most histories of Cold War–era citizen diplomacy between the United States and Soviet Union begin, and it is where my story ends. Soviet women's letters to American women disappear from archival records at this point, making it impossible for me to reconstruct both halves of the conversation any further. Even so, throughout the second half of the twentieth century, these pen friendships continued to create ripples in the lives of the individual participants as well as in the peace and women's movements coalescing at that time.

The pen-pal project gave "ordinary" Soviet and American women a chance to do something extraordinary. Through the alchemy of conversation, they borrowed each other's perspectives, inhabited each other's worlds, and imagined alternative ways of living, thinking, and seeing. They also endowed the ideological and political fault lines of World War II and the Cold War with personal meaning. Taking up their pens, they practiced the arts of politics and of friendship at the same time.

1 ~

Dear Sister-Ally

"I will not describe my grief to you," Mariia Shchelogova declared to the unknown American woman she hoped would receive her letter. Yet a few lines later, Shchelogova broke this promise. Life before the war, she recalled, had been happy and comfortable. She and her husband had lived in the elite, central district of Moscow on Mantulinskaia Street, which opened up onto picturesque Krasnaia Presnia Park, once the grounds of an imperial estate. "I got married early," at age nineteen, "and I have always been a housewife," Schelogova explained. "I never strove to work in industry. I always preferred to take care of my family, keep a cozy home, and raise my children. I was happy when I saw that my loved ones were healthy and satisfied." The Shchelogovs welcomed their first son, Fedia, within a few months of their marriage. Two more children quickly followed. "When this terrible war broke out," Fedia was six and their youngest just over a year old. After her husband left for the front in the summer of 1941, Shchelogova supported her little ones by taking in sewing and relying on help from neighbors. Thankfully, little Fedia received regular meals at school. That autumn, German troops began their assault on Moscow. The children's afternoon romps through Krasnaia Presnia's sprawling lawns and along its winding canals came to a halt. Their lives became governed by air-raids and martial law.

Moscow survived—the Red Army's first major victory—but the celebration was short-lived for Shchelogova. Her husband was killed at the front during the German offensive that following summer. At the age of twenty-five, she became a widow with three young children. Her oldest had just started the first grade. Shchelogova invited her sister to come live with them. She, too, had lost a husband and a son at the front. The sisters scraped together a living to support their families. "I must live for the sake of my children," Shchelogova explained, to remain steadfast and resolute. At first, she tried to maintain that stoicism with her unknown reader, too, but she quickly relented. Writing offered an opportunity for her to release some of her heartache. As she unfolded the story of her husband's death and her children's struggles, Shchelegova imagined her unknown reader as not only a sympathetic listener but a version of herself. She asked the Soviet Women's Anti-Fascist Committee to deliver her letter to "the wife of a frontline soldier whose husband has been drafted. That kind of woman will better understand my grief, my sadness, and my hatred of the enemy who has deprived me of my husband and my children of their father."[1]

Shchelogova was one of hundreds of Soviet women who, during World War II, penned heart-wrenching notes to women in Allied countries, especially Britain and the United States. These letters were solicited and sent overseas by the Soviet Women's Anti-Fascist Committee.[2] This was one of five anti-fascist committees founded in 1941 by the Soviet Information Bureau, which oversaw the dissemination of wartime information and propaganda both in the USSR and abroad.[3] The anti-fascist committees were tasked with soliciting Allied aid for the Red Army by targeting particular constituencies. The bureau created anti-fascist committees of Soviet women, Jews, scientists, youths, and Slavs, and it ordered each one to connect with their counterparts overseas and generate money, supplies, and support. The Soviet need for aid was desperate. Just two months after Hitler's armies invaded in June 1941, they already occupied roughly half a million square miles, and Soviet troops were dying at a rate of 44,000 per day. That summer, German forces slaughtered millions of Soviet citizens as part of the genocidal plan to eradicate Jews and communists.[4] It was not at all clear whether the USSR would survive.

The mission of the Soviet Women's Anti-Fascist Committee was to get women from Allied countries to invest personally in the Soviet war effort by collecting donations, taking up war-industry jobs, and pushing their governments to open a second front in Europe. From its headquarters in Moscow, the committee produced pamphlets, organized broadcasts and rallies, and eventually spearheaded a personal correspondence project. Shchelogova joined that effort by penning a letter to an "unknown friend (*neizvestnyi drug*)" whom she imagined as the wife of a soldier. Such a reader would not know her but, she hoped, would understand her.

The letter-writing program represented a different kind of citizen diplomacy both for the Soviet Women's Anti-Fascist Committee and for the Soviet Union in that it mobilized the personal, not just people, for the sake of victory. The Soviet women who volunteered as correspondents emphasized intimacy, everyday life, the mother-child bond, and womanhood to create personal connections and emotional resonances between themselves and "bourgeois" women in the capitalist West. This was a clear departure from Soviet international letter exchanges of the 1920s and 1930s. Most earlier programs arranged correspondence between model workers or between intellectuals and activists sympathetic to socialism. Soviet youth in the Pioneers and the Young Communist League, for instance, sent letters of solidarity to German socialists in 1923, Britons on strike in 1926, and Spanish revolutionaries in 1936–1937, heralding socialist internationalism.[5] By contrast, the wartime letter exchange created an opportunity for women, including individuals like Shchelogova, who did not have impressive labor or revolutionary credentials, to represent their country and promote its interests abroad.[6]

Moreover, unlike most Soviet interwar letter-writing schemes and Soviet wartime propaganda more generally, these letters downplayed ideological and patriotic themes. Instead, they appealed to shared human emotions and stressed concerns presumed to be universal among women: motherhood, work, and gender equity. The letters were not emotive because of some false notion that women are inherently emotional, though women likely felt less culturally constrained when expressing their feelings than men did. Rather, the profound poignancy of these letters stemmed from the harrowing circumstances in which they were written, where everyday acts had life-and-death import.

By emphasizing these themes, the letter writers reoriented and reconceptualized the alliance, endowing it with personal meaning. Through the heartfelt stories they traded about their families, daily activities, and work—all dramatically altered by war—the participants worked to bridge the political gulf separating the Soviet Union from its western Allies. Like Shchelogova, the letter writers envisioned each other through the prism of their own lives and celebrated their similarities even as they discovered dramatic differences in their experiences of war and as women. The act of corresponding broadened their political horizons and expanded their sense of personal possibility. In this way, the letter-writing program empowered individual women to speak for their nations at a time when the stakes of east-west understanding and cooperation could not have been higher. By nesting their stories into national imperatives, the correspondents made the alliance their own.

Victory was their goal, but other motivations also drove them to write and keep writing. Some sent letters in search of human connection or solace from the tumult of war. Others took up their pens out of deep curiosity about a country so different from their own. Still others hoped to compare notes about their wartime jobs and work conditions. For the letter writers, pen friendship came to mean more than a way to request supplies and troops. In fact, many Soviet correspondents—including Shchelogova—neglected to raise that subject at all. Instead, they fashioned themselves into allies whose partnership was based on more than military cooperation. It was rooted in the language of friendship and grounded in shared experiences as women. Perhaps that's why the pen-friendship project significantly outlasted both the war and US-Soviet cooperation.

Allied in Grief and Empathy

When Riva Abramovna Vezumskaia's daughter Emma asked her to come along on a work trip to Brest, Vezumskaia did not hesitate. Life had quieted down in the four years since she had retired from teaching, and she looked forward to one-on-one time with Emma, who was always so busy with her young children and engineering career. Vezumskaia planned to cook and provide small maternal comforts for Emma as she put in long days overseeing the construction of a new bridge. Vezumskaia delighted in telling her American reader about her two accomplished daughters—one an engineer, the other an economist. "Dear Friend, I was a happy wife and mother. My husband, also a pedagogue, and our two daughters Rakhil' [Rachel] and

Emma made up our happy family," she began her 1945 letter, before turning to how the war had shattered their happiness.

In spring 1941, Vezumskaia left her home in Kherson, Ukraine, and traveled with Emma to Brest. Her account of their time there is notable for both its silences and its revelations. Vezumskaia never acknowledged that Soviet forces brutally invaded and annexed this Polish territory as part of Stalin's 1939 pact with Hitler, nor did she mention her Jewish heritage. She picked up her story in summer 1941, when German troops invaded and imprisoned her and Emma in a ghetto.

At first, Vezumskaia declared she was "not going to tell" about the atrocities she experienced there. Soviet citizens were immersed in a culture of stoicism, and it was not uncommon for a letter writer from the USSR to ask her pen pal for "the strength and support to suppress my personal grief," rather than for permission to share it.[7] But the intimate mode of letter writing cut against codes of self-restraint. As Vezumskaia's letter guides her reader through the world of the ghetto, it captures much of the savagery and despair that afflicted the "16,000 unfortunates" trapped inside the razor wire. Vezumskaia resolved not to discuss "all of the hunger and destruction, robberies, rapes, and murders committed by the Germans," but she did mention two scenes that haunted her: "babies murdered while still in their mothers' arms" and mothers cut down "for refusing to give up their children." This desecration of families, especially the mother-child bond, became unbearable to witness. Vezumskaia and her daughter decided to flee, even if getting caught meant certain execution. "There was no other way out. Death was better than staying there and torturously waiting for one's end." Ultimately, the pair managed to escape into a nearby forest, where they were found by a Soviet partisan unit. They survived, but the ordeals of hunger, imprisonment, and flight remained indelibly etched onto them. "No one believes I am fifty-seven because I look like a shattered old lady, eighty years old. Can a person who has been in a ghetto and escaped from there, having seen death many times, again look as she did before?"

Despite her pledge "not to tell," Vezumskaia offered her unknown American reader this intimate view of the Holocaust, told from the perspective of a mother desperate to protect her daughter. Remarkably devoid of nationalist or ideological themes, her letter is written in the universal language of grief. Even though she and her daughter survived, the letter's tone never shifts from tragedy to triumph. It does not laud the motherland or the resilience of the Soviet people, nor borrow from the wartime press in other ways. It would have been easy for Vezumskaia to draw on the narrative of heroic Brest, which was well in the making. The Soviet state had dubbed it a "heroic fortress" after 3,000 Soviet soldiers fought "almost to the last man" against 20,000 German troops before the fortress fell.[8] And by the time she sent her letter in 1945, the Soviet Union was on the verge of victory. But the letter contains no notes of celebration. Nor does it appeal for Allied aid to support Soviet postwar reconstruction—the explicit objectives of the letter exchange as specified by the Soviet Women's Anti-Fascist Committee. Instead, Vezumskaia asked her American reader, who had no comparable experience of invasion or occupation, simply to share her letter with friends and neighbors "so that they know what fascism is and who the fascists are."[9]

Stories of Soviet families like Vezumskaia's, which had been torn asunder by death and displacement, increasingly were reported in the Soviet press. During World War II, reporters and writers in the USSR began to spotlight Soviet families, elevating personal bonds to the level of patriotic commitment. Soviet citizens were battling to defend their own mothers as much as to defend their motherland.[10] One critical way the Soviet press showcased this "nexus between home and nation" was by publishing citizens' letters to their sweethearts and relatives. "The gap between official language and the language of grandmothers" narrowed significantly, historian Lisa A. Kirschenbaum observed of wartime discourse in the USSR.[11] By circulating these letters, Soviet editors and broadcasters tried to stoke the public's outrage at the enemy and strengthen its determination to fight on. However, the letters that Soviet women like Vezumskaia sent to Americans are comparatively devoid of these patriotic elements. They, too, emphasize the suffering of mothers, but without lauding the motherland. They feel more cathartic than strategic. This is particularly significant because they were directed at readers in the capitalist West.

Vezumskaia approached her "unknown friend" with a willing vulnerability and presumed intimacy quite distinct from the tepid language Soviet journalists and political leaders used when referring to the western Allies. Although Soviet press coverage of the United States and Britain increased fourfold between 1941 and 1944, much of it took the form of "dry communiques" and "technical analysis," which cast the Allies as "useful but not indispensable partners."[12] Stalin helped set that tone. In his 1942 speech honoring the anniversary of the October Revolution, he decried the western

Allies' failure to open a second front in Europe but still called for a "progressive rapprochement" with them. "It would be ridiculous to deny the differences in ideology and social system between the countries that compose the Anglo-Soviet-American coalition," Stalin remarked. "But does this preclude the possibility and usefulness of collaboration between the members of this coalition against the common enemy who threatens to enslave them? It certainly does not."[13] Following suit, Soviet newspapers began to describe Britons and Americans in more positive terms like "freedom-loving," "peace-loving," "progressive," and "democratic." These labels were hardly effusive, but they did replace old monikers like "imperialist" and "exploitative."[14]

Soviet citizens' curiosity about and admiration for their western partners warmed considerably in response to the influx of foodstuffs delivered through Lend-Lease as well as films, music, and newsreels arriving from the West.[15] A number of Soviet letter writers opened their notes with words of appreciation for the tinned meats and Hollywood flicks arriving from overseas. Thousands of copies of the magazine *British Ally* reached Soviet readers starting in 1942, and the US State Department's *Amerika* arrived in 1944–1945. The war created opportunities for the exchange not only of cultural products but of people, too—artists, academics, and chess champions who contributed to "growing understanding and goodwill between the American and Soviet peoples," as the Soviet Embassy in Washington, DC, put it.[16] Still, Soviet authorities put limits on how positively the United States and Britain were portrayed. Shining too bright a light on the western Allies might hurt Soviet ideological discipline, the Propaganda and Agitation section of the Central Committee of the Communist Party warned. In 1943 alone, 432 books and pamphlets were pulled from circulation because of this concern.[17] Official Soviet endorsements of the military alliance warmed in the latter half of the war but, on the whole, they were measured and inconsistent, to say the least.[18]

The tenor of Soviet women's letters could not have been more different. Correspondents in the USSR embraced their American readers, perfect strangers, from the outset. They addressed them as "dear unknown sisters" and "dear unknown friends," and filled their letters with expressions of fondness, giving their recipients license to respond in kind. This affectionate language marked a departure for the Soviet Women's Anti-Fascist Committee as well. Up to this point, the committee mostly used anger and shame, not appreciation or intimacy, as diplomatic tools. In general, the committee hewed closely to official discourse and, like the Soviet press, it concentrated on disclosing atrocities committed against Soviet civilians to demand that women in Allied countries send help on moral and contractual grounds. During one of its first events, an anti-fascist rally held on September 7, 1941, a dozen women—workers, soldiers, and officials—took turns at the podium condemning German troops who "shoot defenseless children, attack girls, kill old people, plunder and pillage" in order to jolt women abroad into action. "Is it possible for a mother's heart to remain calm?" demanded Klavdia Nikolaeva, a former head of the Women's Section of the Communist Party (*Zhenotdel*) and the secretary of the All-Union Central Council of Trade Unions. "Every woman regardless of her social status, political views, or religious creed must realize that Hitlerism is humanity's worst enemy," she continued, "it brings endless suffering, slavery, and oppression to peoples of all freedom-loving, democratic countries of Europe and America."[19] Other speakers similarly downplayed themes of ideology and class, implying that women everywhere had an instinctual and moral duty to stop the senseless slaughter of mothers and children. And through these universalizing, maternalist claims, they demanded supplies, troops, and a second front. "Everything for war! To destroy the enemy we need guns, aircraft, tanks, machine guns, shells, and bullets," Nikolaeva thundered from the stage. The committee delivered this message to British and American women by broadcasting the rally internationally and publishing a pamphlet of its proceedings.[20]

British women, many of whom were already working in armament plants by 1941, responded readily to the call. They penned a deluge of supportive messages to the committee—72,238 in 1942 alone—and sent individual letters to Moscow in which they described how they were laboring, fundraising, and rallying friends to support the Red Army.[21] A sense of guilt that Britons had not suffered to the same extent as Soviets tinged many of the replies. "We do not feel so brave," a group of women railway workers from Stafford, England, wrote, "we know what other countries have suffered. That has not been our lot. And we feel deeply grateful for what your armies have stood up to. We know it has saved us British people. We had a meeting, where your Russian women have spoken about the real horrors women and children have suffered."[22] Such self-reproach was elicited intentionally. The Soviet Women's Anti-Fascist Committee's events and publications preyed on a sense of obligation. While planning a second anti-fascist rally in 1942, one member of the committee declared: "we need to *attack more* on why we have the right to demand more from them," that is, from western women. "It is necessary to shame them," another member agreed, and to drive home the point: "the end of the war would come faster if you, women, strive to open a second front sooner."[23]

But what worked with Britons failed to move women in the United States, where most citizens did not feel the war's impact on such a personal level. The committee made ninety-five attempts to connect with US women's organizations in 1942; all were "greeted with silence."[24] The committee admitted to its superiors in the Soviet Information Bureau that its inability to reach American women was its main "failing" and "shortcoming." "No matter how much we appealed to them, they replied: 'we have no need for this,'" Emma Stasova, a member of the committee's executive board said, summarizing the American response.[25] She and other board members began brainstorming ways to connect with "the USA first and foremost."[26] At one meeting in February 1943, Ekaterina Leont'eva floated the idea of establishing "personal connections" with American women through "individual correspondence," much like the friendly letters the committee had received from Britons. "Isn't it possible for those of us in major, critical enterprises (I have in mind sectors of light industry, textiles, and metallurgy) to organize some cadres of correspondents—whatever you call them?" she asked.[27] Others quickly agreed, but they, too, were unsure of what to call this venture. Soviet citizens had participated in only a handful of international letter exchanges before World War II, and there was no set expression like "pen pal" in Russian. Committee members vacillated between several labels including *drug po peru* (a pen friend), *drug po perepiske* (a friend by correspondence), *drug po pis'mam* (a friend by letters), and *drug po sviazi* (a friend by connection or contact). Sometimes they just used the phrase "pen pal" in English.[28] It was not until Soviet citizens became more involved in international letter exchanges during the mid-1950s and beyond that "*drug po perepiske*" became a standard Russian phrase for "pen pal."

By creating this correspondence campaign, the committee sanctioned a type of international propaganda that was new for the Soviet Union. The committee continued to produce rallies, broadcasts, and pamphlets that adopted a crusading, strident tone, but the letters it dispatched were affectionate and sought understanding more than material aid. In other words, the committee adopted one tactic but allowed the letter writers it supervised to embrace another. It advertised for correspondents in newspapers and over the airwaves and gave them no explicit instructions or script of what to write. However, it did supervise them closely and cautioned them not to spout anti-Soviet sentiments. "You can write about everything as true patriots of your motherland," one veiled warning suggested.[29] The committee's staff translated and inspected every note, censoring a few phrases here and there. But no Soviet letter writers denounced their motherland, and the staff ultimately changed remarkably little.

The committee launched the program, but the problem remained that there was no audience for these letters in the United States. American women and women's organizations largely ignored the committee's overtures. How could it attract their attention? Why not use celebrities, Viktorina Kriger, another board member, suggested. "I was in America. I know the people there. I know what they hunger for. Americans really hunger for sensations, for [recognizable] names, and for some kind of relationship with famous people." By recruiting prominent Soviet women in the arts, sciences, and industry to send letters, "perhaps we can somehow nudge American women," and "make them our allies," Kriger proposed. The committee had connected with British women through trade unions and charity groups, but Americans required more glamor.[30] Moreover, if the committee recruited Soviet celebrities, they could promote the alliance and socialism at the same time. Accomplished Soviet citizens would model how legal equality, free education, and equal pay helped women in the USSR rise in their chosen professions. "They will serve as great, compelling examples for the women of England and America," Kavnatora, another committee member echoed.[31] This notion, that pen friendship could improve both the Soviet war effort and American women's views of socialism, convinced the Soviet Information Bureau to permit the pen-pal campaign.

Still, the program floundered. Recruitment was difficult in the USSR, too. Soviet celebrities were consumed with other wartime projects, and the committee managed to recruit only one minor writer and an artist. It did not gain traction with American women either.

It took another event to attract pen pals from the United States: the Red Army's 1943 victory at Stalingrad.[32] For the first time, an Allied army forced an entire German army group to surrender and halted the German advance. The news became a media sensation. Several US cities, including New York, proclaimed "Stalingrad Day" a holiday, and *Life* dubbed the Red Army "the World's Number One Army."[33] American journalists and Hollywood producers—prompted by the US Office of War Information—had been working to cultivate public support for the US-Soviet partnership since the alliance was formed, but they kicked that campaign into high gear after Stalingrad, saturating Americans with stories of Soviet sacrifice and bravery.[34] While the Soviet press's references to the western Allies were often tepid, many US media outlets went to great lengths to humanize Soviet people and suggest numerous affinities between them and Americans. *Look* and *Life* (the latter devoted an entire issue to the USSR in March 1943) proclaimed Americans and Soviets were kindred spirits: they were hardworking, unpretentious, and pioneering peoples with glorious revolutionary pasts.[35] At Stalingrad, one article in the *Christian Science Monitor* declared, Soviet troops were fighting against the forces of slavery and racism just as Union soldiers did at Gettysburg. "One feels that Lincoln would have entered into their triumph wholeheartedly knowing so well why it should be."[36] These pieces urged Americans to see themselves in the Soviet people and to connect with them on a human, emotional level.

This message reached its widest audience through cinema. Hollywood made twenty-five films honoring the USSR's war effort; many of their directors were later blacklisted for doing so. A common feature of these wartime films is that they make Soviet characters appealing and admirable by projecting American qualities onto them. Soviet women are portrayed as courageous workers and fighters who maintained a resolute beauty, wholesomeness, and maternalism, which aligned with mainstream US values.[37] It is no wonder that American men fell for these characters.[38] In the 1944 film *Song of Russia*, the protagonist John pays his new love Nadia the highest compliment by exclaiming, "if I did not meet you in Moscow, I would think you are an American girl!" These films and articles exhibit the same tendencies that Soviet letter writers had: to imagine one's ally as a version of oneself and to downplay ideology in favor of seemingly universal values and experiences. Steeped in such messaging, American letter writers adopted a similar approach. They began sending heartfelt notes in spring 1943. Most of the American women who wrote wanted to connect with a Soviet woman like themselves and to share their personal experiences as mothers, daughters, workers, and individuals caught in the tumult of war. They sent those letters—some simply addressed to "A woman, Russia"—

on an individual basis, not as part of a state-sponsored initiative. Once the letters crossed into Soviet territory, they were intercepted by the All-Union Society for Cultural Relations with Foreign Countries (VOKS). VOKS coordinated the Soviet Union's contact with foreigners and organizations abroad and was charged with disseminating a positive image of the USSR. It forwarded letters from American women to the Soviet Women's Anti-Fascist Committee.[39]

"To Stalingrad. To someone in Russia," Mrs. Margaret Walters began her first letter in June 1943, "Women in America salute your Red Army. I have seen pictures of them where they seem to move the whole earth. They look so powerful, which I really think they are at the present time. [. . .] I pray every day for the divine power to give your Red Army more courage and strength to carry on and stop this terrible war in 1943. Your beautiful city of Stalingrad is a debt, which can never be repaid to your people." Walters started writing in this way, addressing any Soviet citizen, but her letter gradually shifts to address a female reader, a mother and worker like herself: "I would like to hear how you working mothers care for your children while [laboring] in factories. I am fifty-eight years old, and I worked as a telegrapher on a railroad during War No. 1. I have one daughter and a grandson. He is very tall, 6 foot 2 inches, and is 16 years old. He plays the accordion very beautiful [*sic*], goes to high school, and is a very good student also. Do you have any hobbies, collect things? If so, tell me about them and let me know what they are. Write."[40] Walters's admiration for the Soviets' extraordinary victory was palpable, as was her curiosity about Soviet women's everyday affairs. Her inquiry about her reader's hobbies reveals a certain naiveté about what daily life had become for Soviet women during the war. But it also was a well-intended invitation from Walters that she and her future correspondent bring each other into their personal lives.

Walters offered more than words of support; she volunteered with her local Los Angeles branch of Russian War Relief, Inc. Backed by Roosevelt's War Relief Control Board, this national charity sent roughly forty-six million dollars' worth of clothing, medical necessities, and food to the USSR. In 1943, it began to enclose letters, like Walters's, in its shipments.[41] "Your letter will do much to strengthen the bonds of understanding and friendship between our two great nations fighting the same enemy," the organization promised in its recruitment pamphlet.[42] Most of these letters were like Walters's: short, one-page notes of encouragement scrawled across the

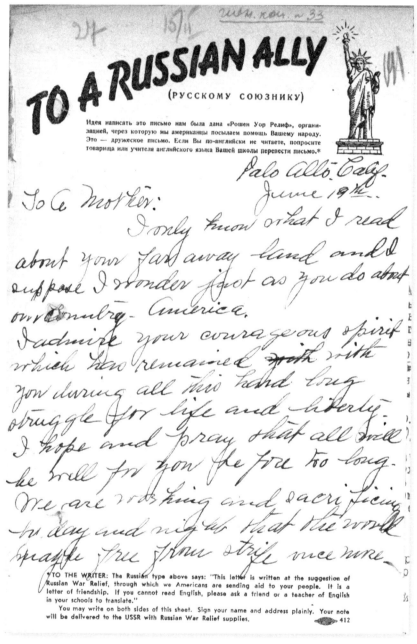

TO A RUSSIAN ALLY

(РУССКОМУ СОЮЗНИКУ)

Идея написать это письмо нам была дана «Рошен Уор Релиф», организацией, через которую мы американцы посылаем помощь Вашему народу. Это — дружеское письмо. Если Вы по-английски не читаете, попросите товарища или учителя английского языка Вашей школы перевести письмо.*

Palo Alto, Calif.
June 19th.

To a Mother:

I only know what I read about your far away land and I suppose I wonder just as you do about our country – America.

I admire your courageous spirit which has remained ~~with~~ with you during all this hard long struggle for life and liberty.

I hope and pray that all will be well for you before too long.

We are working and sacrificing by day and night that the world may be free from strife once more.

*TO THE WRITER: The Russian type above says: "This letter is written at the suggestion of Russian War Relief, through which we Americans are sending aid to your people. It is a letter of friendship. If you cannot read English, please ask a friend or a teacher of English in your schools to translate."

You may write on both sides of this sheet. Sign your name and address plainly. Your note will be delivered to the USSR with Russian War Relief supplies. 412

Letter "To a Worker," sent June 19, 1943, on the official stationery of Russian War Relief, Inc. (State Archive of the Russian Federation, f. R7928, op. 2, d. 50, l.191.)

organization's stationery, which was adorned with the Statue of Liberty and American flags. But unlike Walters, most other Americans writing through Russian War Relief did not include an address or request a reply.

That reply was slow in coming. It reached Walters roughly a year later. Its sixteen-year-old author, Nadezhda Stepanova, had asked to be paired with an "American friend" who was a girl her own age, but the anti-fascist committee matched her with Walters, the grandmother of a sixteen-year-old, instead. The image Walters sketched of her strapping young grandson, playing the accordion and acing his classes in sunny Los Angeles, is jarring next to the picture Stepanova painted of her teenaged years in war-torn Smolensk. A site of fierce fighting, Smolensk changed hands several times during the war. German troops invaded and occupied it in 1941. The Red Army retook it later that year, then lost it during a successful German counteroffensive, and liberated it again in 1943. All told, German troops occupied Smolensk for twenty-six-months, and 90 percent of the city was destroyed.[43] "They robbed us; they took our cattle, clothes, food. We almost died of hunger," Stepanova reflected. "The fascists started to destroy everything. For three days before the arrival of the Red Army, they drove all of the remaining residents of our village into a little building and locked it. They placed a guard near it. They kept us locked up there for days. We had nothing to eat, nothing to drink. Apparently, the Germans' initial plan was to burn us alive." In the end, the townspeople were not incinerated but enslaved as workers for the German Reich. Still, the soldiers set the village aflame. "During the fire, in a state of turmoil, we lost our parents. The four of us—three sisters and I—could not see mama and papa anywhere, so we decided to run on our own. Then we learned that mama and papa were taken by the Germans. I do not know where they are now. It is very hard for me to think about that." With nowhere to go, Stepanova and her sisters hid in the woods until a Red Army unit found them and transported them to Moscow, where they were placed in the Kaganovich Factory School. "I am waiting in hope," she told Walters, "that when the war ends, my parents will return to us and once again we will live as a family. I wish you all the best. I will be very glad to receive a letter from you." Stepanova closed her note by inviting Walters to call her by her nickname, Nadia.[44]

By becoming acquainted with Stepanova, Walters gained an intimate view of the war on the eastern front. This understated letter conveys the unthinkable ordeal of waiting to be burned alive. It captures the panic the Stepanov children felt as they frantically charged through the smoke, searching in vain for their parents. Stepanova offered no pledge of imminent victory, no praise for the troops who rescued her, no allusions to socialism or patriotism. She stressed the emotional, familial, and universal. Unlike the charged pamphlets and broadcasts crafted by the anti-fascist committee, Stepanova did not ask anything of Walters except for emotional support. Although the letter diverged from its rhetoric and official mission, the committee passed Stepanova's note through its censors without altering a word and sent it to Margaret Walters. They did the same with more than a hundred other Soviet letters dispatched to the United States between 1943 and 1945.

The committee did not post the letter to Walters directly or to Russian War Relief's Los Angeles office for her to retrieve. Rather, the committee sent all Soviet women's replies through a new organization, the National Council of American-Soviet Friendship, which was founded in New York City during that landmark year for American-Soviet goodwill, 1943.[45] Unlike Russian War Relief, which had mainstream and bipartisan support, the National Council of American-Soviet Friendship was on the far left of the political spectrum. A private nonprofit, its mission was to promote cooperation, friendship, and understanding by combatting "anti-Soviet propaganda" in the United States with positive information about the USSR.[46] The council touted itself as a pro-peace, not a pro-Soviet, organization, but during the war it published nary a word of criticism about the USSR and did a great deal of propagandistic work for the Soviet Union. The FBI began monitoring the National Council within weeks of its founding and, in the decades to come, the US government indicted it repeatedly as a "communist front" organization. There *were* Communist Party members in the National Council, but the group had no affiliation with or sponsorship from the Communist Party of the United States or of the Soviet Union.[47] It was a popular front organization with supporters from a variety of left-leaning groups including labor unions and the American Committee for the Protection of Foreign Born.[48]

The National Council would go down in history as a leftist fringe group, but it did not yet have this reputation during World War II, when it enjoyed its broadest public appeal and had roughly 20,000 supporters and sponsors. This was still a fraction of Russian War Relief's base.[49] Even so, the group received warm endorsements from Roosevelt, Truman, Eisenhower, and numerous congressmen as well as prominent artists, scientists, and businessmen who commended the US-Soviet alliance.[50] The Roosevelt administration sent encouraging messages to the National Council's friendship rallies in Madison Square Garden, and First Lady Eleanor Roosevelt and Marjorie Post Davies, wife of the former US ambassador to the USSR Joseph E. Davies, together sent "warm and heartfelt greetings" to the Soviet Women's Anti-Fascist Committee in an American broadcast celebrating International Women's Day, a major socialist holiday.[51] In addition, one of the National Council's exhibitions, "Two Allies—One War, One Peace," was sponsored from on high by the US Office of War Information, the US War Department, the US Army, and the Lend-Lease Administration. The exhibit opened to the public at Rockefeller Center in June 1943. Like the articles and films mentioned above, it encouraged visitors to identify with Soviet citizens by recreating the experience of the eastern front. Patrons had the chance to crawl through a Soviet trench and sit in a war-battered Soviet kitchen. At the end of the exhibit, they were invited to send a "correspondence for friendship" card to someone in the USSR.[52]

Indeed, the National Council hit upon the idea for a letter-writing project on its own, apparently unaware of the numerous overtures made by the Soviet Women's Anti-Fascist Committee. In summer 1943, the National Council began selling correspondence cards for a quarter. Like Russian War Relief's stationery, the cards were covered in American flags and only provided space for a very short message. But the National Council's cards differed in a key way: they all bore the postscript "Please write to me as soon as you can."[53] The council wanted the conversation between Soviets and Americans to be ongoing. It arranged for the New York Postal Censorship Station to review the cards and approve them for dispatch to Moscow.[54]

But the federal government quickly intervened. While Soviet authorities made correspondence an officially sponsored venture, one run by a state agency and subject to government oversight, the Roosevelt and Truman administrations did not control the National Council and were clearly suspicious of it. Not only were they wary of the council's far-left views, they regarded the letter writing project as a security threat, especially when the council began recruiting American GIs to participate. Indeed, the National Council did not limit participation to women, the way the Soviet Women's Anti-Fascist Committee did. But the US Army prohibited active-duty troops from communicating privately with Soviets, and it forwarded to the FBI the names and addresses of sixty-four American soldiers who had signed up to

Dear Friend:

Insert & Check
☐ 25c Coin
☐ Dollar Bill

Name
Address
City State

I have also contributed money to help build American-Soviet friendship in the United States

P. S. — Please write me as soon as you can

Partial list of National Council sponsors: Hon. Harold L. Ickes, Hon. Joseph E. Davies, Sen. Claude D. Pepper, Corliss Lamont, Bishop W. J. Walls, R. J. Thomas, Paul Robeson, Eugene E. Barnett, Dr. Ales Hrdlicka, Albert Einstein, Charles Chaplin, Joseph Curran.

Back side of the correspondence card created by the National Council of American-Soviet Friendship for its "Letters to Russia" Campaign, 1943. (National Archives and Records Administration, Washington, DC, RG 233, Records of the US House of Representatives Un-American Activities Committee, National Council of American-Soviet Friendship, box 626.)

be pen pals.[55] The bureau warned that "much valuable information could be transmitted to the Russian government in the guise of personal letters," and State Department officials took action.[56] When Americans contacted them about how to get a Soviet pen friend, they declined, saying it was too difficult and expensive to transport private mail overseas during wartime.[57] Russian War Relief had its own vessels (not to mention more mainstream politics), but the National Council was relying on the US Postal Service. Still, despite the State Department's discouragement, American citizens wrote encouraging notes and dropped them into their local mailboxes. The US Office of War Censorship intercepted these letters and sent the writers' names and addresses to the FBI.[58] The bureau's case file on the National Council quickly thickened. It installed wire taps in the council's headquarters and recruited informants to corroborate what it already assumed was true: the group's friendship activities were a front for disseminating communist ideas. The FBI never dropped this accusation. It was never able to prove it either.

But women found a way around these obstacles. In 1944, one of the National Council's subcommittees, the Committee of Women, reached out to the Soviet Women's Anti-Fascist Committee after the latter held another one of its Moscow rallies. The two groups quickly formed a partnership that would last for decades. By mid-1944, they were exchanging pamphlets and reports, and—thanks to diplomatic couriers—letters between their countrywomen.[59] Indeed, to get around the restrictions imposed by the US Army and the US Postal Service, the Soviet Women's Anti-Fascist Committee and the Committee of Women turned to the staff of the Soviet consulate in New York and asked it to shuttle letters between Moscow and Manhattan.[60]

Here is how it worked. The New York–based Committee of Women solicited letters from women across the United States, collected them into bundles, and brought them to the Soviet consulate located in Manhattan a few blocks away. The consular staff then forwarded those letters to the Soviet Women's Anti-Fascist Committee in Moscow. The anti-fascist committee also received American women's letters from other sources. Some arrived via Russian War Relief. Others came from individual women who were unaffiliated with an American group but simply dropped letters addressed to "a Russian woman" into their local US mailbox. When those letters made it through American postal censors and arrived in Moscow, VOKS forwarded them to the Soviet Women's Anti-Fascist Committee.[61] Importantly, the anti-fascist committee sent Soviet replies to *every* American woman's letter it received—regardless of how that note was initially sent—to the National Council's Committee of Women in New York, which then forwarded it to its intended American recipient. As a result, American women who had no knowledge of or interest in the left-leaning National Council of American-Soviet Friendship were brought into the group's orbit and became dependent on it for their pen friendships to survive. This greatly extended the National Council's reach among American women with mainstream political views.

The State Department and FBI knew that Soviet and American women were trading letters in this way but did not stop them.[62] Why not is a bit of a mystery. I did not find any direct statements as to why American women were permitted to correspond, while American men, not just those in the armed forces, were prohibited. The answer may lie in one of the classified

US government documents to which I was denied access. One likely explanation is that both the organizing women's groups and female participants themselves were of minor status. They were not well-connected to high politics. Unlike American GIs, they had no access to military intelligence, let alone state secrets. Similarly, Soviet letter writers like Shchelogova, Vezumskaia, and Stepanova were not well-known intellectuals, celebrated workers, or members of the party. The attitude, among both Soviet and American authorities, seems to have been that the letter writers were "just women" and relatively harmless. Likewise, both governments allowed another marginal and seemingly innocuous population to write to each other: children. One of the other five anti-fascist committees established in 1941, the Anti-Fascist Committee of Soviet Youth, ran a letter exchange between youngsters in the USSR and the Allied West.[63] I imagine that the Soviet and American governments allowed women and children to correspond because, at best, they might bolster public support for the alliance and, at worst, if their efforts failed, they posed little threat to national security. Later, US officials grew more concerned about American women becoming covert communist agents, especially after Soviet spy Elizabeth Bentley defected in November 1945.[64] But during the war years, the US and Soviet governments ultimately allowed a small number of women, 102 pairs of correspondents, to exchange letters under their watchful eye.

The letters were highly personalized but never private. Each one passed through at least four sets of hands between the time it left its author and the time it reached its intended reader. For instance, when an American woman sent her letter to the Committee of Women's New York headquarters, it was cataloged, reviewed, and then sent to a Soviet consular official who delivered it to the anti-fascist committee in Moscow. The anti-fascist committee's staff translated the letter, struck out any objectionable phrases, then retyped it. The committee likewise translated, censored, and typed all Soviet replies before sending them back to the Committee of Women in New York through a Soviet diplomat. Before the letters left the USSR, the Soviet Information Bureau's censors also examined them but rarely altered the contents.[65] Most of the censorship was done by the Soviet Women's Anti-Fascist Committee and, in truth, it was light. With a few exceptions, American letters were unaltered, and typically only a phrase or two was cut from Soviet ones. Most of the phrases that were cut were either boasts that the author made about her own country or potentially insulting remarks she

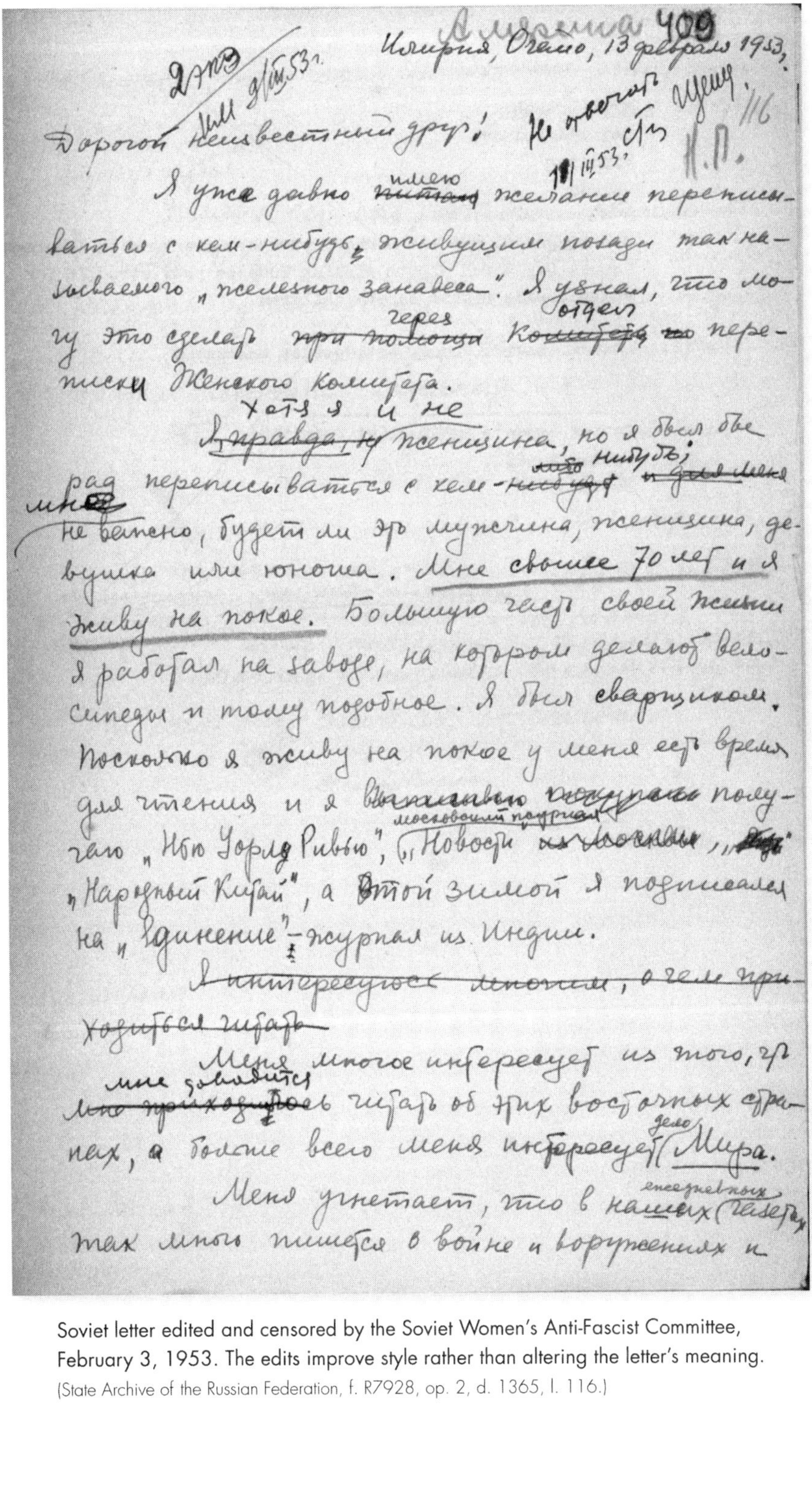

Илирия, Огайо, 13 февраля 1953.

Дорогой неизвестный друг!

Я уже давно имею желание переписываться с кем-нибудь, живущим позади так называемого „железного занавеса". Я узнал, что могу это сделать через отдел переписки Женского Комитета.

Хотя я и не женщина, но я был бы рад переписываться с кем-нибудь; мне не важно, будет ли это мужчина, женщина, девушка или юноша. Мне свыше 70 лет и я живу на покое. Большую часть своей жизни я работал на заводе, на котором делают велосипеды и тому подобное. Я был сварщиком.

Поскольку я живу на покое у меня есть время для чтения и я получаю „Нью Уорлд Ривью", московский журнал „Новости", „Народный Китай", а этой зимой я подписался на „Единение" – журнал из Индии.

Меня многое интересует из того, что мне доводится читать об этих восточных странах, а больше всего меня интересует дело Мира.

Меня угнетает, что в наших американских газетах так много пишется о войне и вооружениях и

Soviet letter edited and censored by the Soviet Women's Anti-Fascist Committee, February 3, 1953. The edits improve style rather than altering the letter's meaning.

(State Archive of the Russian Federation, f. R7928, op. 2, d. 1365, l. 116.)

wrote about her pen pal's country. Evidently, the censors were trying to smooth any potential bumps in communication. The staff of the anti-fascist committee also translated the letters faithfully from English to Russian and Russian to English with only occasional errors.

Most of the time, Soviet and American participants usually received the original handwritten letter along with a typed translation of it. In a few rare cases, the handwritten versions remain in the archive. Sometimes, it took only two months for a letter to travel from point A to point B, but during World War II, it was not unusual for six months to elapse.

Still, the letter writers were willing to wait. They commented elatedly upon receiving a handwritten letter even if they could not read it. They were moved by the feel of the note in their hands and by the sight of their pen friend's handwriting. Even though the script was indecipherable to them, it gave them a sense of authentic connection. One American letter writer described sitting with her son and poring over "the strange letters" in "such clear and pretty hand-writing" for hours "as though if we stared at it for long enough then we would be able to read it. Can you blame us? When the pages of a letter come to you from far away and at some point are in your hands, you passionately want to know and love them just as we passionately want to know and love you."[66]

So, despite the presence of censors and government monitors, the participants wrote with affection and emotional openness, trying to connect with their readers as mothers, wives, daughters, and workers. The American correspondents in particular pictured their "unknown friends" in their own image, projecting their values and experiences onto them. This fostered some naïve misapprehensions about each other's circumstances. But the letter writers made those errors in hopeful expectation that they could be understood, on a personal and emotional level, even when their pen pal's social class, nationality, religion, ethnicity, and ideological background were so unlike their own.

The American women who joined the pen pal project during the war years were quite different from their Soviet pen-friends. They also represented a fairly narrow demographic. Like Margaret Walters, most American participants were white and middle-class. They tended to live in coastal cities or urban centers in the Midwest, and their political views seemed to be left of center. A few American notes contained strong statements of Soviet patriotism—even more so than the letters from the USSR did. "May the enemy be cursed forever!" and "Long Live the Soviet Union!" New Yorker Sonia Starr declared.[67] Mildred Kres of Cleveland, a representative of the United Office and Professional Workers of America (Local 5), predicted: "Soviet women will go down in history as being the most courageous women of all time!"[68] Comparable slogans or proclamations rarely appeared in Soviet wartime letters.

Only one American woman of color wrote during these years. This was Jane E. Hunter, president of the Ohio State Federation of Colored Women's Clubs. She sent a brief congratulatory letter on behalf of that organization on International Women's Day, commending "women of the Soviet Union. The courage and bravery you have exhibited in this worldwide struggle," she continued, "has touched the hearts of the thirteen million negros in America."[69] Hunter never responded to the reply sent to her by Nadezhda Maksimova, but after the war, the Soviet Women's Anti-Fascist Committee expended considerable effort to connect with American women of color and civil rights activists in particular.

A significant number of Jewish Americans also participated in the program during World War II. Roughly one-third of the wartime letter writers were of Jewish descent, according to census and immigration records. They, too, tended to be affiliated with progressive politics, organized labor, and popular front organizations. Some may have been a part of the Jewish Council inside Russian War Relief or the United Jewish Appeal, which were created during World War II to send aid to European and Soviet Jews, though none of the participants mentioned having these affiliations.[70] Although they did not spell out their political or religious backgrounds, they undoubtedly were deeply distressed by the Nazis' mass slaughter of Jews and so were particularly invested in the Soviets' effort to stop Hitler's onslaught. This must have strengthened their sense of solidarity with the Soviet people and driven them to write. The pool of Jewish participants peaked during World War II and fell dramatically after 1945.

Two of the Jewish women who joined the project expressed a literal kinship with Soviet women. They were former subjects of the tsar but emigrated at the turn of the century when violent pogroms became rampant in the Russian empire. Anne Krich now lived in Newark, New Jersey, but she begged her pen pal, a woman who went by the pseudonym Iraida Il'inichna Fedorova, to help her locate the sisters and brother she left behind in 1913.[71] Perhaps anticipating an antisemitic response, Krich did not mention her

Jewish heritage (nor did Soviet letter writers like Vezumskaia), but she was not shy about conveying her disapproval of the Bolsheviks and her loyalty to her newly adopted country. "I began to love this country when I learned a little about its history and literature," she wrote of the United States, and she was proud that she and her husband built a "quite comfortable" life in New Jersey, purchasing a home and an automobile. Still, such political differences did not prevent Krich from empathizing deeply with Fedorova. "My hands tremble at the thought of what you people have gone through at the hands of the fascists," Krich remarked, for she had suffered "many sleepless nights" worrying about her siblings in Soviet territory. "I am sure that the time has come when you are ready to tell" about your war experiences to "those whose sympathy and understanding are with you," Krich added, coaxing Fedorova to "please write about yourself and your family" and holding space for her to do so.[72] Family and motherhood—these critical points of connection helped the pen friends identify with each other despite their radically different circumstances. "Dear Russian mothers," Mrs. J. Wise, who hailed from San Francisco's Jewish community, opened her June 1943 letter. "I wanted you to know how much we think about you, how we want to encourage you with our love and sympathy. [. . .] our hearts are with you," she promised.[73]

Many others who did not have relatives in the USSR similarly drew on the language of sisterhood to convey a sense of affection and affinity.[74] "Dear Unknown Family of Friends," Grace Burt of Greenfield, Massachusetts, began.[75] "Dear Sister," schoolteacher Aleksandra Bobkova wrote, "You are very far away from me, separated by half a world, but we all want the same things: for the war to end quickly, for Hitlerism finally to perish, and for our children to grow up in happy conditions without experiencing the horrors of war." That same goal "brings us together and makes us family [*rodnit nas*]."[76] Such statements, as well as the oft-used salutation "dear unknown friend," capture how the participants articulated a sense of intimacy and kinship even with a perfect stranger.

Women with husbands and sons in the armed forces formed a particularly strong bond. They both knew the ordeal of waiting and worrying, even though American conscripts had a slimmer chance of seeing combat than Soviet ones did.[77] Ruth Brooks of Long Beach, California, and Liusia Vdovina, who lived outside of Moscow, waited together for news from their husbands. Brooks directed her letter to someone like herself: "to a mother of a two-to-four-year-old child." Russian War Relief allotted Americans only one sheet in which to write their messages, and Brooks filled hers with details about her children. Her five-year-old son Larry had sandy blond hair and deep brown eyes. He was "a very loving child, good natured and tenderhearted" but feisty. He "put up a fight" when he wanted to do something himself without his mother's help. Carol, aged four, was "small and delicate" with "dark curly hair and dark eyes." The Brooks children spent their days skipping along the beach just four blocks from their home on picturesque Alamitos Bay. As he ran, Larry lifted his brown eyes skyward and tried to identify the planes that flew overhead. Carol tagged along behind him, clutching her doll. "All day long they are in their bathing suits. They are very tan," Brooks explained, enclosing a photograph of her little ones. These happy moments with her children helped dull the pang she felt each time her thoughts wandered to her husband, who was serving in the US Navy. Brooks had no idea where he was or how long he'd be gone. Liusia Vdovina, who lived 6,000 miles away amid the smokestacks of the Northern Railway, understood. She was awaiting word from her husband who had deployed in March 1942. Shortly before he left, Vdovina discovered she was pregnant. She described feeling utterly "alone" and without "care or affection" after he deployed. "I lived from letter to letter, cheered by them or else falling into despair if I did not receive one for a long time," she told Brooks. Then the letters "stopped coming altogether." Vdovina received the news that her husband was killed in action a few weeks before her daughter Irina was born. "She is a curly-haired, tender girl with big blue eyes. She very much resembles her father." Despite this resemblance, "with her I am able to forget my grief a bit," Vdovina reflected. Irina was "always chirping like a bird about something," and she was "affectionate and calm"—except when plying her mother for sweets. Brooks could instantly relate, noting her own son's stubbornness. She and Vdovina took solace in their children and in each other, offering each other well wishes, kisses, "lifetimes of happiness," and photographs of their children.[78] By sharing the joys of motherhood and the agony of uncertainty, they strengthened the alliance without ever discussing it.

Grief transcended national borders, political lines, and language barriers. This was the theme that Emma M. Turner of New Jersey stressed in a prayer she composed for Soviet mothers. "Thy children speak in a different tongue / their skin a different hue," Turner wrote, "But in each heart that mourns a son / the grief is so deep, wherever born." After her son Raymond died at the front in 1944, Turner felt moved to reach out to Soviet mothers, inspired by the "bond we share in the loss of our sons."[79] Letters like hers strengthened the alliance by fostering a community of feeling.

Sisters by Work

Intermingled with these sorrowful reflections were stories of empowerment and exertion. More than victims of war, the letter writers presented themselves as active fighters on the labor front, doing essential work for the military effort. Whether paid or voluntary, work provided another way for the letter writers to connect and find meaning in the alliance. Work was also a natural topic of conversation for correspondence which, as a form, tends to highlight everyday matters.

The various institutions and governments involved in the pen-pal project did not need to encourage this shop talk, but they likely would have done so. The Soviet Women's Anti-Fascist Committee's official mandate was to strengthen western support for the Red Army, in part by summoning Allied women into war-industry jobs. The committee's rallies and publications profiled exemplary female workers to inspire women in the West to greater industriousness and to assert their equality with men. "Today we are equal to any job—that is the motto adopted by Soviet womanhood," the committee proclaimed at its 1942 anti-fascist rally.[80] The committee's chairperson, Valentina Stepanovna Grizodubova, embodied this principle. She was a decorated pilot who commanded the 101st Long-Range Aviation Regiment and earned the rank of colonel before she was asked to head the anti-fascist committee.

The twin goals of Allied victory and gender equity dovetailed with the interests of the New York–based Committee of Women, which facilitated discussions between Soviet and American women on how to balance careers with motherhood and housework.[81] This distinguished the Committee of Women from the National Council of American-Soviet Friendship, of which it was a part. The council's publications and its top leaders—all men—seldom mentioned issues of women's equality. By contrast, most of the women who steered the Committee of Women had been suffragists, and many were progressives and socialist sympathizers, including chairwoman

Muriel Draper.[82] Draper and her colleagues were highly educated and well-connected with the elite of New York City, and they ran their committee somewhat independently from the National Council in terms of funding and day-to-day activities.[83]

Work talk also aligned with the interests of the US government. American labor officials worked hard to recruit female citizens to "male" jobs in order to free up men for military service. However, unlike their counterparts in the Soviet Union, US officials did so without making any proclamations about rectifying gender inequities and imbalances in the labor force. On the contrary, the US government tried to entice women to do traditionally male jobs without upending conventional gender norms and hierarchies. In 1942, President Roosevelt issued an executive order to establish the Fair Employment Practices Committee and the War Manpower Commission, which viewed American women as short-term replacements, whose stints in heavy labor would not supersede their fundamental role as homemakers and guardians of domesticity and normality.[84]

Letter writers shared these concerns about war production, but they also engaged in conversations about labor for other, less strategic reasons. Work offered them another potential point of common ground and identity. Soviet pen pals often hoped to connect with co-professionals, sometimes out of curiosity, sometimes out of solidarity for the work they were doing in tandem. Indeed, many participants derived a sense of purpose, even empowerment, from contributing to the war effort, especially as they stepped into "male" roles now accessible to them. They were excited to discuss skills they had acquired or obstacles they had overcome. And the letter writers cheered each other's labors not only because their work hastened victory but because it gave them a sense of personal fulfillment.

Imagining that they were addressing Americans just like them, Soviet letter writers directed their notes to fellow machinists, miners, or surgeons. "Dear female doctor," or "dear female engineer," they began. "Dear fellow female zookeeper," exclaimed three Soviet women with careers in wildlife.[85] A few others used the more all-purpose salutation: "Dear Sister by Work!"[86] These greetings were another sign of how the participants projected their circumstances onto their unknown friends. Soviet letter writers assumed American women were entering the same male-dominated fields and encountering similar challenges there. "You, wives and sisters of those who are fighting our common enemy, probably also have only entered the timber industry in wartime," Rosa Rait, a lumberjack in the far-northern city of Arkhangelsk, wrote on behalf of herself and seven other female loggers. "We are working in those professions that earlier were considered male. Here, in the northern port, we often meet English and American sailors, and they always say that we are doing difficult work. Ours is a timber plant that hauls wood and makes from it many needed and useful things for the front. Earlier there were few women at the plant and only in auxiliary roles. Now there are a great many of us, and we are glad to have freed our husbands and brothers for the navy and army." Rait and her female coworkers were "upholding the reputation" of the timber plant as "the best of the north," she boasted.[87]

But Rait's letter did not reach female loggers in the United States. Although millions of American women took jobs in heavy industry during World War II, the vast majority of letter writers from the United States did volunteer and service work instead. They were a privileged population, and most identified as housewives. The US War Production Board and War Manpower Commission made a concerted effort to recruit this particular demographic to the labor force, but it accounted for less than 25 percent of American women workers during the war.[88] In light of this mismatch, the Soviet Women's Anti-Fascist Committee sometimes crossed out Soviet letter writers' salutations addressed "to a worker" and replaced them with "to a mother."[89] The stark differences in Soviet and American attitudes and experiences regarding women's labor made motherhood even more important as a foundation upon which the pen pals could connect. Work talk brought home to the participants just how different their lives were despite their determination to find and bond over shared experiences.

Farmwomen were an important exception to this. They were eager to talk shop, diving into conversation about each other's methods and yields as well as how they were managing without their husbands. Hazel Mustanich and Evdokiia Vaniukova were one such pair. Mustanich, who lived in Aptos, California, initiated the correspondence after Stalingrad, offering both gratitude and condolences. "I am very sorry for you people in Russia. I guess we people here don't know how much you are suffering, but it is our prayer that someday soon Hitler will be put out of commission, and everything will be peaceful again. It looks to me that if you hadn't put up the fight you did, Hitler would have ruled the world. All of us are in it together now." "I was very glad to receive your letter from a friendly country faraway, from an

American farmer," Evdokiia Vaniukova replied from the village of Ezdotskoe, near Kursk. "You are absolutely right, noting in your letter that we are all now united in the aspiration for a final victory and for world peace. That united task has closely connected the peoples of our countries in the struggle against our common enemy."

"I am a widow operating a 22-acre apple ranch on my own," Mustanich continued. "We farmwomen have had to do men's work. I used to do only housework and cooking, but now I am operating a tractor." Her husband Jack, an immigrant from Yugoslavia, died in 1942 and, with so many male farm hands enlisting, she had little hope of hiring help.[90] But Mustanich had exceeded all expectations, including her own. She managed to grow, pick, and ship so many apples that her business was booming, and she raised enough chickens and rabbits to offset meat rationing. "I guess you people are used to that," Mustanich said of food shortages, "but it is new to us."[91] Although the comment was rather indelicate, Mustanich's tone was friendly.

In reply, Vaniukova applauded her pen pal's accomplishments, adding that many apple orchards were tragically destroyed during Germany's invasion. Vaniukova's crop was the sugar beet. She lived in the Kursk region, which had been occupied by German troops. Shortly after Hazel Mustanich dispatched her May 1943 letter from California, Kursk became the site of the biggest tank battle in history, involving thousands of armored vehicles and two million troops.[92] Vaniukova was badly wounded in the leg and developed a permanent limp, but still she tended the fields. "Every day the German planes bombed us and each time they created deep craters among the sewed beets. Again and again, I had to restore the earth. That is how I grew beets under the bombs."

The pair's cordial tone became competitive at times, especially when they compared outputs. Mustanich boasted that she had harvested so many apples that she had paid off her mortgage. She then asked Vaniukova about the interest rates Soviet banks charged farmers—clearly unfamiliar with Soviet practices of land distribution and collective farming. Vaniukova in turn bragged that her crop of beets "exceeded 368 centares per hectare," and she nudged Mustanich: "write to me about what the average harvest of beets is in the USA per hectare and what the records are," assuming Americans shared a similar culture of labor competition. "It will be interesting to know how women in the USA are doing agricultural work during the war and how they are helping our common struggle with the enemy," she noted, perhaps

Aptos Calif.
May 27- 1943.

To a Farm Woman in Russia:

I am a widow operating a 22 acre apple ranch on my own. I guess Hitler has made millions of widows out of younger women than I am, in your Country. Since the war we farm women here have had to do mens work.

I used to do only house work & cooking, but now I am operating a tractor, and in the picture you see me, driving a team of mules, picking up apple boxes, for market.

I expect a good crop of apples this yr. and prices do not look so bad at present, so hope to get my mortgage paid off this year. I hear you farmers in the Soviet Union don't have to pay six or seven per cent, interest to the banks, as we do here on our farms.

I am also raising chickens & rabbits, for meat as it is hard to get meat now, most of it goes to the army. Almost every thing is rationed here now. I guess you people are used to that. It is new to us, but farmers are lucky. They can raise their own vegetables, we have our fruit, & poultry & rabbits, and a few hogs, we can always find enough to eat.

I am very sorry for you people in Russia, I guess we people here don't know how much you are suffering, but it is our prayer that some day soon Hitler will be put out of commission and every thing will be peaceful again.

It looks to me if you hadn't put up the fight you did, Hitler would have ruled the world. All of us are in it together now, so here's to final Victory and a world of peace.

Mrs Hazel Mustabich,Rt 1,Box 225,Aptos,Calif.

Your Friend
Mrs. Hazel Mustanich

Letter and photo of Hazel Mustanich, May 27, 1943. (State Archive of the Russian Federation, f. R7928, op. 2, d. 50, l. 274.)

to soften her pointed question.[93] But the competition was subtly stoked when someone, either the anti-fascist committee or Vaniukova herself, included with her letter a clipping of a newspaper article honoring her agricultural achievements. Not to be outdone, Mustanich sent a photograph of herself driving a team of mules.[94] These enclosures and the farmers' spirited exchange helped them visualize and appreciate each other as they worked in parallel, each woman facing her own challenges.

Most pen pals could not relate to each other's work so closely, but their conversations about labor—whether paid or voluntary—fostered a sense of common purpose as allies and of efficacy as individuals. "We are fighting for the same causes—for our homes, for our personal and national freedom," Vivian Slater, a Russian War Relief volunteer, remarked to Elizaveta Vasina, "it is difficult to put into words, the deep feeling of unity and comradeship we American women feel for all of you."[95] "I have the greatest respect" for "the work of women in your country," Vasina replied. "Many of us have learned male professions during the war years, replacing the men at work," she said, referring to both American and Soviet women with this remark. Vasina worked as a tunneller in the construction of the Moscow metro, and she boasted that she had received the Order of Lenin, but she wrote nothing to diminish the labor accomplishments of American working women.[96] Other pairs similarly validated each other's activities, no matter how different they may have been, and reassured each other that they were steadfastly working for victory. Mrs. S. K. Hass of Wilmar, California, recounted her packed schedule of volunteer activities to Margarita Bendrishova, a cafeteria worker in Moscow. Hass was taking a home nursing course, serving as a block mother, donating blood, growing a victory garden, and "canning all that I can this year to help win the war." "I am writing this from my heart. All of us are doing our best to help all of our friends" in the Soviet Union.[97] Importantly, when they discovered their American pen friends were not in war-industry jobs, Soviet writers did not push or shame them into taking on such roles. That is, they did not adopt the forceful approach favored by the anti-fascist committee that inspected and posted their letters.

American letter writers were equally proud of the inroads women in the United States were making into traditionally male jobs, even if they themselves were not the pathbreakers. "Before the war, the majority of American women took part in the cultural life of the country and were busy with charity," Anne Krich of Newark, New Jersey, explained to Iraida Il'inichna

Fedorova. "But as soon as we were attacked at Pearl Harbor, the women of this country began working in the munitions factories, in the fields, in canteens, and in civilian defense. I too was drawn in to help." Krich had no need to do wage work. She and her husband owned a home and a car, which she mentioned with pride. Still, she was eager to assist. "At first, I helped at the draft board of my district. Later I was assigned to teach women how to use ration coupons and went out to stores to watch that they didn't overcharge. On Fridays, I used to work in the hospital near me. Of course, I didn't forget Russian War Relief. Whenever possible I mended, packed, and collected food and clothing. So, as you see, I am kept busy," she told Fedorova, assuring her pen friend that she was working for victory. Still, Krich craved some personal connection to give her labors more meaning. "I put my name on numerous packets" for Russian War Relief, "but I never heard from anyone." Finding Fedorova reinvigorated Krich and inspired her to double her efforts. "I will be glad to send you whatever helpful articles I can" and to "read your letter to many other women who work with me in the organization. Personal contact with you will help us to create better friendship with the Soviet Union and help us to aid you."[98] By sharing the letters with others, women like Krich hoped the stories of personal tragedy and triumph they contained would touch many more lives. Fedorova was equally enthused by the notion that an affective alliance was an effective one. "I personally would like to have a correspondence with you, to know about your life, about your work, and about your struggle," she affirmed.[99]

Soviet and American participants alike were proud of women's professional advancement, but only Soviet letter writers cast this as a victory in another battle, one for gender equality. The way they did so undercut official Soviet declarations, including those made by the anti-fascist committee, that men and women were already equal in the USSR. This principle had been enshrined in the Soviet constitution, and it helped justify the dissolution of the Women's Section of the Communist Party in 1930 on the grounds that a women-only sector was no longer necessary and that it smacked of "bourgeois feminism," not proletarian solidarity. The Soviet Women's Anti-Fascist Committee was the USSR's only union-wide all-women's organization from 1930 until 1958, when women's councils (*zhensovety*) emerged. Gender equality was a cornerstone of the anti-fascist committee's official mission, but its mandate was to help women abroad, not Soviet women at home. However, by the early 1950s, the letter writers would help change this by making the Soviet Women's Anti-Fascist Committee an advocate for Soviet women, not just an instrument of state propaganda.

But that came later. During World War II, the anti-fascist committee heralded full equality between the sexes even as the letters they dispatched pushed against those claims. Correspondents from the USSR took care to stress how they had to overcome bureaucratic hurdles and discriminatory attitudes in order to excel in "male" jobs. To be sure, the letter writers lauded the educational and professional opportunities afforded to them under socialism, but their personal accounts also testify to a more complex reality. While Soviet women were legally entitled to the same rights, education, and pay as men, in practice they made up the majority of unskilled and semi-skilled workers, so they earned lower wages and were considered more expendable. They also faced discrimination from coworkers and managers. Soviet correspondents drew particular attention to that fact, especially as the growing demand for women workers during wartime collided with entrenched misogynism. Here again, the pen pals diverged from the anti-fascist committee's idealized rhetoric, not out of an unpatriotic impulse but rather a desire to share their stories of personal triumph.

The difference between the messaging in the letters and in the anti-fascist committee's materials was especially palpable when it came to male-dominated professions like mining. The Soviet Commissariat of Labor officially classified mining as "male" in 1930 and then re-categorized it as such in 1949 after a brief hiatus on this restriction during World War II.[100] When appealing to women overseas, the Soviet Women's Anti-Fascist Committee upheld women miners as models of industriousness and of gender equality under socialism. At its 1941 rally, the committee introduced Natal'ia Fishina to drive home these points: "From ancient times, the miner's profession has been considered a man's job. But Natal'ia Fishina knew that the country needed more coal and metal, and so she descended into the mines, joined her husband's team, and is exceeding normal output."[101] According to the anti-fascist committee, Fishina's foray into this new profession was swift and straightforward.

But the letters told a more complex story. Nadezhda Makushkina, for instance, wrote with great pride about how she overcame both bureaucratic and attitudinal roadblocks in mining. Makushkina was one of many individuals who was inspired to join the pen-pal project by the influx of American cultural products to the USSR. "My girlfriends and I really like American films, only it is a pity that they do not show enough of the lives of working people. We would really like to see a film about you, dear American girlfriends, about the life of American workers." She imagined her readers were, like her, "female workers in the confectionary industry of the USA."[102] Or, that is what Makushina had been; she worked at the Red October Confectionary when the war began. But the sweets factory had to halt operations once German troops invaded the Don Basin, and the plant could no longer access its supply of coal. Local officials ordered coal deposits near Moscow be mined to supply factories like hers. The trouble was there were not enough men for the job. So, Makushkina stepped in. "When we girls came to the mine, the administration first wanted us to take up lighter work, but I had closely observed how the experienced miners worked. Summoning my strength (and I have more than a bit of it), I went to the main engineer. I told him: 'if old people work in the factories, how can it be that I, who am young and healthy, cannot manage this work?' The main engineer and the mine's director agreed but on the condition that the other girls and I work based on a lower [production] norm." The women quickly began to fill and overfulfill those quotas. Eventually, the manager was compelled not only to raise their norms but to hire more women. He assigned Makushkina's brigade the task of training the new arrivals. Makushkina unfolded her story along the plotlines of socialist realism—complete with intractable bureaucrats, environmental obstacles, and workers' triumph over quotas and societal expectations—but she infused all these tropes with feminist overtones. Makushkina's letter is a celebration of what women workers could do as well as a condemnation of enduring sexism in the Soviet Union. By her own telling, Soviet women were battling for equality at the same time that they were fighting fascism.[103]

Not every Soviet correspondent told stories of overcoming with the same flair as Makushkina, but housewives like Aleksandra Konovalova, Akulina Antonova, and Sonia Karaeva wrote about banishing the skepticism of their relatives and neighbors when they took on industrial and agricultural jobs.[104] Karaeva admitted that she herself questioned whether she could step in for her husband as a brigadier on an Ialkym collective farm in Turkmenistan. "~~As a rank-and-file collective farm worker, I am not fit for such work~~," Karaeva declared too modestly for the anti-fascist committee editor who cut this remark. When presented with the opportunity to take a leadership role on the farm, "I was overwhelmed by joy and doubt. Would I be able to cope?" she wondered. Gradually, her confidence grew, as did the success of her brigade. Karaeva was fueled not only by the mandate to grow more eggplants and cabbages but by the prospect of telling her husband about her achievements. "I have not received a letter from my husband for a long time now," she observed apprehensively. "But if he remains alive, I will proudly tell him: 'while you were fighting the fascists at the front, I replaced you and maintained order on the collective farm. I helped you and the motherland smash the enemy.'"[105] By 1943, Soviet women comprised more than half of farm brigade leaders and tractor drivers.[106] Letter writers like Makushkina and Karaeva thus cast their wartime work as both military and personal triumphs. Their stories speak to an ethos of gender equality in the USSR, but they do so by highlighting that discriminatory attitudes towards women were still in place, even when womanpower was needed most.

The picture these letters paint of Soviet women on the job clashed with the idealized images of them that circulated in both the Soviet and the American press. The former presented gender equality as a fait accompli, whereas the latter reworked the image of Soviet women laborers to reinforce more traditional gender roles that aligned with US values.[107] Before the war, the Soviet woman was a common target of ridicule in the American press, which portrayed her as plain, haggard, and exhausted—apparent symptoms of Soviet poverty and brutality. But she got a makeover during World War II. Following guidelines from the US War Advertising Council and Magazine Bureau, the American press transformed her into a role model for female labor recruits in the United States. Articles in *Newsweek*, *Woman's Home Companion*, *Saturday Evening Post*, *Woman's Day* and other outlets argued that Soviet women entered heavy industry not in pursuit of equality or ambition but out of a selfless commitment to family and nation, reassuring American readers that women's workplace integration would not disrupt gender norms in the United States either.[108] As one *New York Times Magazine* article explained in November 1944: "Here [in the Soviet Union], to a greater extent than in any other country at war, women [a]re actively fighting beside men in turning back the invader." The article acknowledges "the sacrifices they have made for victory" by reifying traditional femininity and projecting it onto them. "Russian women, like women of all countries, like new clothes and leisure time to be with their children, all that normal peacetime life offers to a woman," the article proclaims, reducing women to a singular type. "Here, in the midst of war, they have for the most part gone without new clothes entirely. They have patched and mended their old ones and repaired their shoes time and time again. The materials which go into lipsticks and other cosmetics are needed for the vital task of killing Germans, so they have for the most part gone without the beauty aids so indispensable to the happiness of women around the world." "Of course," the article continues, "the greatest importance is placed here [in the USSR] on the role of woman as a mother." In other words, Soviet women performed male roles without adopting masculine qualities. In such articles, the impulse to project oneself onto one's ally—which colored the letters—took the form of reassuring *Times* readers that Soviet women workers were feminine, not feminists; they were hardy, not haggard. It likened them to pioneer women of Kansas and Nebraska.[109] American letter writers, however, gained a starkly different view of Soviet women's work from the notes sent by their Soviet pen pals. Soviet letter writers were proud of their rough hands and steely bodies and never wrote a jot about the lack of cosmetics or clothes.

In sum, work, like grief, was a critical touchstone for the pen friends. It helped them carve out and understand their role in the war effort. And the knowledge that they were laboring in parallel with their pen pals nurtured a sense of affinity with them. This perceived solidarity played a strategic role, of course, but bound up with it were additional messages of empowerment, overcoming, and opportunity. The letter writers certainly upheld the official goal of the correspondence project—a swift Allied victory. At the same time, they transformed and expanded this objective by recasting the war effort and their allies through the prism of their own lives.

"PERHAPS WHEN YOU RECEIVE this letter, our sons will be meeting in Berlin," Faniia Shamesova mused.[110] Jeanne Platt of San Francisco wondered the same thing. She imagined her husband and her pen pal's son "taking the streets of Berlin arm-in-arm."[111] For many letter writers, the act of corresponding was something akin to a "meeting on the Elbe": a precious moment when the Soviet and American Allies embraced each other, recognizing their common struggle and common humanity. Elizabeth Johnstone was thrilled to tell Al'vina Vitovtona about her son's encounter with Soviet people. A parachutist from the Eighty-Second Division, he touched down into now

Soviet occupied territory, where he danced, sang, and celebrated with his eastern Allies. "They are a miraculous people," he told his mother, "they hugged and kissed me and brought me to tears." And that bond fortified the connection between Johnstone and Vitovtona: "I feel very close to you," Johnstone wrote.[112] "Allow me to call you dear sister," Vitovtona replied.[113] The pen pals experienced the US-Soviet partnership as a one-on-one relationship, and they represented their nations in that same intimate way.

In the epistolary space available to them, Soviet and American women practiced and personalized the alliance. Intertwined with the official goals of the pen-pal project were unexpected admissions, an array of storytelling styles, and a desire for human connection. Such connections were eased by the pen pals' eagerness to imagine each other as fundamentally similar, whether in values or experiences, and to downplay nationalism and ideology. This comforting thought offered a way for the correspondents to feel less alone in their grief, less isolated in their labors.

The 1945 meeting on the Elbe was a fleeting moment. It was not long before Soviet filmmaker Grigorii Aleksandrov set to work recasting it in dark tones as a time when Americans rejected Soviet offers of friendship and resumed hostilities with their allies. His classic cold war film, *Meeting on the Elbe,* hit Soviet theaters in 1949. Even as anti-communist attitudes swelled in the United States and xenophobic anti-westernism surged in the Soviet Union after World War II, the letter writers returned to the alliance again and again as a source of inspiration. To them, it meant more than just a military partnership or a diplomatic marriage of convenience. It was proof that their governments and communities could cooperate. By mid-1945, the military partnership between the United States and USSR began to wane, but conversations between American and Soviet pen pals were just getting started. Some 200 women joined the program in 1945 and 1946, taking up their pens to safeguard the fragile postwar peace. Like their wartime predecessors, they were convinced that connection across national and ideological lines was both possible and valuable, even though corresponding for American-Soviet friendship was increasingly looked upon as an act of subversion, not patriotism.

2 ~

I Come in Peace!

"Someday," Mary Roe Hull mused as she drew another letter to a close, "people will finally understand that not through violence but through affection, and with the help of the golden rule and the brotherhood of men, swords will be turned into plowshares." Why were governments wasting resources on bombs and weapons, Hull demanded, when they could construct housing, build infrastructure, or plant forests. "My brother, an artistic gardener, often says: 'who plants a tree does a good deed for the world!' In the Bible it says that 'the wind blows where it wants.' The same winds that blow on the USSR also blow on Wisconsin." They swept over Soviets and Americans alike as they tilled their corners of the earth. "We benefit because you are planting trees, and you benefit because we are planting them. Although we are so far away from one another in terms of distance, the winds bring us together. Isn't that a comforting thought?" With that hopeful image of "one world," popular during and in the wake of World War II, Mary Roe Hull closed "with the most heartfelt greetings to you and your daughter." She signed her name "Aunt May."[1]

Hull dropped the letter in the mailbox around the corner from her cottage, just outside of Oshkosh, Wisconsin. From there, the letter made its way to the Committee of Women in New York City. The committee's staff brought the letter from its office on East Thirty-Second Street to Pavel Fedosimov of the Soviet Consulate on East Sixty-First Street. He carried it, along with a host of other letters, to the Soviet Women's Anti-Fascist Committee in Moscow.[2]

By the time she posted this letter in summer 1948, Mary Roe Hull had already deposited a dozen such notes into that tattered blue mailbox. She composed many of them while sitting in her easy chair or on her porch, gazing out at the cottonwoods, grand elms, and wild violets that dotted the shore.[3] In 1869, Hull's father had purchased some twenty acres bordering Lake Winnebago and began to cultivate it. Soon, the property was teeming with apple, cherry, walnut, and plum trees. Asparagus, strawberries, rhubarb, and grape vines lined the farm's fences. This waterfront Eden, which he named "Lake Rest," filled Mary Roe Hull with divine inspiration for international peace and friendship.[4] Every letter to her pen pal contains a declaration of peace that was at once horticultural, spiritual, and geopolitical.

Hull's earnest, eccentric letters charmed her "Moscow niece." "Dear Auntie May," Nina Sergeevna Morozova replied, "I have never read any letters with more lively interest than yours. I am absolutely amazed and delighted with them! Your descriptions of nature are simply marvelous. I think you could write books if you tried to. Altogether, the range of your interests, knowledge, and personal qualities is, to my mind, so wide that I am quite amazed at it. I would like to be as much alive, full of energy and as young in mind at your age as you are." Hull was seventy-six and Morozova forty-one at the time. The Muscovite's pen overflowed with words of praise and agreement. "Yes, you are quite right, life is wonderful. How much joy there is in simply contemplating the beauties of nature and of the universe! And you are also right in saying," Morozova continued in somewhat awkward English, "how much more joy living people would know if only all the material resources now spent on killing would be turned to furthering the progress of civilization and technical progress, thus making them serve for the improvement of living conditions and not for hideous slaughter and devastation. How I agree with you that it is not power spent for evil, but kindness and the brotherhood of all men that are the greatest powers on earth." In this exuberant tone, Morozova affirmed Hull's statements about peace in letter after letter. And each time she sidestepped her "dear and far-away Auntie May's" religious discourse and substituted in a secular, often socialist, framework for peace instead.[5]

In her next letter, Hull cheered Morozova's declaration, but she put the bits of spiritual wisdom back in. "What is now being wasted on weapons should go to improving the quality of life, education, and work that is interesting and useful in every region," Hull echoed. We "ought to have the golden rule otherwise we will all perish. [. . .] I pray every day about peace for the whole world, so that people turn their arms into plowshares and so that there is plenty for everyone around the world."[6] And around and around they went. In this affable way, the pair continually performed their commitment to peace, all the while gently revising each other's vision of a world without war.

Morozova, Hull, and the two dozen letters they exchanged were quirky and unique. Yet, they also capture the spirit of the American-Soviet correspondence sent in the years immediately after World War II. Hull was one of roughly 200 American women who requested a Soviet correspondent during late 1945 and 1946.[7] In a sharp reversal of the war years, the demand for pen pals now emanated from the West. At first, the new volunteers were full of optimism that the United States and Soviet Union would continue working together and safeguard the postwar peace. Corresponding was their way of personally contributing to that partnership. In September 1945, 55 percent of Americans polled by Gallup agreed "Russia can be trusted to cooperate with us after the war." This assessment was even higher—71 percent—among college-educated Americans.[8] When the alliance began to unravel in the months after V-E Day and especially after the United States tested two nuclear weapons in July 1946, many more Americans sought out Soviet pen pals, their requests now tinged with anxiety. "The idea of another war just scares us all half to death," exclaimed Maxine Cryder of Boone, Iowa, "and I do think one good way to avoid it is for the common people of Russia and of the United States to get better acquainted."[9]

By opening up to each other, they aimed to succeed where their statesmen had failed. The correspondents not only called for peaceful US-Soviet relations, they modeled it by imbuing their remarks with personal stories, compliments, and terms of endearment. They avoided controversial debates about policy or nuclear proliferation and instead turned to everyday life and emotional engagement as two ways of finding common ground. "We laugh at the same things and feel moved by the same things. Close human contacts like these are even more important in my mind than a thousand diplomatic overtures," Henrietta Buckmaster declared in 1946. A journalist and civil rights advocate, Buckmaster was one of the few prominent activists who contributed a letter to the pen-pal program in the mid-1940s.[10] She, like the project's other participants, nurtured this sense of closeness by writing in an effusive tone and by frequently declaring that—as women and as allies—their visions of peace were fundamentally alike.

As they did during the war, the postwar letter writers assumed they shared common values. They took it for granted that they all wanted the same thing: a world free of violent conflict. The way they expressed that certainty, however, brought out meaningful differences in their outlooks and ethics. The participants based their commitments to peace on distinct moral codes, gendered assumptions, and political frames of reference. The particular Americans who sought out Soviet pen pals in late 1945 and 1946, including Mary Roe Hull, conceptualized peace through Christian teachings and maternalist arguments. They presented themselves as pacifists and rooted that commitment in two factors: first, religious faith in universal brotherhood and the sanctity of human life, and second, a belief that women were naturally predisposed toward peacekeeping.[11] In this way, the American letter writers drew on some traditional arguments that women peace activists had wielded since the late nineteenth century. They blended these claims with elements of emerging cold war rhetoric, which used spirituality to define Americans against Soviets and proclaim American liberal-democracy was divinely ordained.

By contrast, Soviet letter writers like Nina Morozova grounded their devotion to peace in the suffering they endured during World War II and in socialist principles. They countered that Soviet men and women were equally determined to prevent violent conflict because both knew the horrors of war firsthand. That ordeal made them more devoted to peace than peoples who had never been invaded, but it did not make them pacifists. Instead, the Soviet correspondents fashioned themselves as soldiers for peace, ready to fight oppression. Here, they echoed official rhetoric that the USSR was the world's bulwark against fascism and the champion of exploited peoples. The Soviet pen pals' ideal society was not an Eden but an earthly utopia based on a socialist model of equity and ethnic tolerance. Thus, although they seemed self-evident, the letter writers' declarations of peace were entangled in a skein of ethical, ideological, and gendered assumptions, which threaded their sense of right and wrong.

On the one hand, the pen pals repeatedly offered each other peace as a sign of their appreciation and acceptance of each other. On the other hand, they undercut that spirit of tolerance by assuming their pen pals saw matters as they did, by projecting their own values onto each other.[12] Peace talk, Petra Goedde has shown, was deceptively simple and flexible during the Cold War: it had universal, humanitarian appeal, and yet was easily imbued with ideological and political agendas.[13] The women who joined the pen-pal project in the months after Victory Day infused their letters with both.

Their conversations reinforce how anti-fascism provided a tenuous basis for US-Soviet military cooperation. It had given the Allies a shared moral imperative and common purpose, but it also opened up space for a great deal of ambiguity. Reading backward from their conceptualizations of peace, the American letter writers understood fascism primarily by its acts of unprovoked war and aggression. To be anti-fascist was to reject war altogether. By contrast, the Soviet correspondents focused on the Nazis' genocidal violence, horrifically perpetrated on the eastern front. Fascism's antithesis, they reasoned, was a system that celebrated human life in all its diversity. These definitions were not mutually exclusive, but they provided foils against which the letter writers idealized their nation's values and ways of life. Only a few women from either country acknowledged the pervasive injustices in their own societies, especially those perpetrated against Jews and ethnic minorities. And this glaring oversight cut against the Christian and socialist ethics the letter writers espoused. Their reflections on peace were dotted with blind spots.

In this way, peace talk proved to be more conceptually complex and potentially divisive than the pen pals' words about war. The same was true for American and Soviet diplomats, who had largely reached an impasse by the end of 1946. Around the time that Mary Roe Hull was requesting a pen pal, Soviet and American officials were crossing swords over Soviet troops in Iran, communist uprisings in Greece, and the right of the United Nations to mitigate these conflicts. At times, the letter writers echoed their more aggressive statesmen's views. They, too, claimed the moral high ground. However, they did so in a personal, non-combative way that kept the dialogue going. They did not accept that their differences were irreconcilable or that a "cold war" was inevitable.[14] The letter writers who joined the program in late 1945 and 1946 did so out of a sense that mutual understanding and cooperation were possible, and they were eager to contribute personally to the achievement of both goals.

Brave New World, Brave New Letter Writers

Hull and Morozova were separated by five thousand miles and a thirty-five-year age gap. They were a world away from each other in other ways, too. Born in 1871, Mary Elizabeth Roe Hull came from Puritan ancestors with deep ties to American history: three colonial governors, five minutemen, one signer of the Declaration of Independence (Oliver Wolcott), and "a plethora of Puritan ministers." The Roes were direct descendants of Nathaniel Brewster and George Phillips, and indirect descendants of Jonathan Edwards and Cotton Mather, Hull's great-grandniece Connie Roe Burtnett told me.[15] "Grandma Roe," Hull herself recalled, "was very religious, a Presbyterian that believed a mother had the right to dedicate her sons to the ministry and she did, all four of them; but none remained in the ministry."[16] Hull's uncle Edward (E. P.) Roe was a Civil War chaplain who met with President Lincoln about improving soldiers' hospitals before he became a celebrated novelist. Hull's father, John Peter Roe, had been a chaplain to the Ninety-Seventh New York Regiment under General Ulysses S. Grant during the Civil War and moved to Wisconsin in 1865 to become the pastor of Oshkosh, Wisconsin's First Congregational Church. "Father did three strenuous years" preaching in that "rough and ready" lumber town before "his health gave way—a nervous breakdown," Mary Roe Hull explained. His "doctor prescribed life on a farm."[17] From that farming business, her siblings created Roe Nurseries and Lake Rest Resort, businesses that thrive to this day. Several sites in the region still bear the family name, including scenic Roe Point, which juts into Lake Winnebago. In light of this heritage, it is no wonder that spirituality and nature featured so prominently in Hull's declarations of peace.

"I am very happy that you are going to rest in such a picturesque place," Nina Sergeevna Morozova remarked to Hull, "I am very fond of nature but have consistently live[d] in town."[18] In comparison to her pen pal, Morozova's origins are a bit of a mystery. While Hull devoted her spare time to chronicling her family history, Morozova—like many Soviet participants—was not

Mary Roe Hull picking a mango, 1958. (Courtesy of Constance Roe Burtnett.)

forthcoming with many basic details, including her husband's name or those of her parents. No doubt she was afraid. During the mass political repression commonly known as the Great Terror, which raged in the years before World War II, both personal letters and foreign contacts were presented as evidence of anti-Soviet sentiments.[19] In addition to leaving genealogical blanks, Morozova lived with over four million people in the capital city, where there were hundreds of Nina Morozovas—a common surname. By contrast, Hull resided outside a small town, where her family name was quite prominent. While Hull proudly studied her family's illustrious history, Morozova presented herself in unremarkable terms. "As for me," she told Hull, "I am an average, simple Russian woman of forty. I am busy all day with my work, household matters, and the rearing of my daughter."[20]

Morozova and her daughter shared a room in a communal apartment atop a six-storied, dust-colored building in the heart of Moscow. Though modest, the building was located just off of Tverskaia Street, a bustling thoroughfare that led to Red Square. It was in that posh though battered neighborhood that Morozova tried to pick up the pieces of her life. "My husband was killed in action at the beginning of the war," she explained, and for four years she had struggled to shield her nine-year-old daughter from bombardment and hunger. Little Svetlana's lungs were permanently damaged as "a result of war, not enough food, cold rooms, and other hardships," she told Hull in her first letter.[21] Morozova never complained, but daily life was a grind, and one she apparently undertook alone. She never mentioned relatives, neighbors, or friends. Hull, on the other hand, frequently spoke of her nieces, nephews, and throngs of neighborhood children who all called her "Aunt May."[22]

Why did the Soviet Women's Anti-Fascist Committee pair Hull and Morozova together when they seemed to have little in common? In true Soviet fashion, the committee continued to assume labor was the most important element of identity and compatibility, even though pairings based on that criterion proved impossible during the war. The committee put Hull and Morozova together because Morozova was working as a typist and Hull was once a typist—a secretary at an Episcopal church—before she became a schoolteacher. It was a feeble connection. Hull and Morozova traded only a few lines about it, noting how their fingers ached after hours of pounding away on a typewriter—"Richard," as Hull dubbed her Remington.[23] In truth, the pair seldom talked about work. Just as the wartime pen pals discovered, common employment was not necessary for common ground; neither was shared class status. The pen pals did not have to do the same activities in order to relate to the feelings those tasks elicited.

Instead of work, Morozova and Hull explored a myriad of other topics, and they folded promises of peace into each exchange. The pair swapped photographs, soup recipes, and vacation stories. They also frequently discussed little Svetlana's academic progress. "I will tell the dear boys of my neighborhood how well she studies at school, and it will drive them to study better!" Hull promised, touching off a mini "Sputnik effect" in Oshkosh a decade before the satellite's launch.[24] But Morozova tried to dispel the competition right away: "tell the fifth-grade boys Svetlana is a middling scholar. [. . .] I can't say she gets only top marks."[25] Morozova was eager for her daughter to learn English, so she welcomed the cartoons and notes Hull sent Svetlana. "The pictures and the story about Mr. Jingles are exceedingly funny!" Morozova exclaimed, apparently hyperbolically, because she immediately added: "Of course, I could understand the words in the comic strips, but I do not always understand the humor of the 'funnies' in your papers and magazines."[26] Hull not only clipped comics for Svetlana, she shared life lessons with her, ones steeped in American values. When instructing the eleven-year-old about the importance of keeping one's word, Hull advised: "our promises should be as strong as American currency."[27] To practice her English, Svetlana wrote back to her "Aunt May," asking if she liked ice-skating and chewing gum.[28]

Hull and Morozova began corresponding in 1946 and eventually wrote just for the sake of connection, even when they had "nothing new to tell."[29] Hull, who was in her mid-seventies, wrote at least once a month throughout 1947 and 1948, whereas Morozova wrote about every two months, blaming any delays on her busy schedule. Hull had far more leisure time, but she felt compelled to write for the sake of peace and understanding, not just for want of something to do. "Look how I have yammered on," she exclaimed in one lengthy letter, "but then again how could anything else I do be more important than talking to you?"[30]

Their conversation was fueled by additional goals besides peace. Both longed to travel, and pen friendship offered them a virtual way to do it. "Our dream is to go to America," Morozova declared in her first letter.[31] And she wrote these words in English, which she had been studying in earnest. "I know English not brilliantly," she admitted, "but I love this language awfully." She was one of just two Soviet letter writers who wrote in English, though the censors in the Soviet Women's Anti-Fascist Committee still checked every note she penned. Hull had been bitten by the travel bug since the Battle of Stalingrad, when she began immersing herself in the writings of war correspondents Il'ia Ehrenburg and Konstantin Simonov. In 1946, Hull wrote to Ehrenburg and asked him to find her a Soviet pen pal. It was her dream to visit the USSR, she explained, but since she had no passport, she would travel there "through books and letters."[32] Hull did not seem to understand Soviets and Americans were largely forbidden from visiting each other's countries.

It might seem audacious for Hull to ask the Soviet Union's most famous writer for a personal favor. In fact, many Americans contacted Soviet elites for pen pals in the months after Victory Day. They wrote to the Soviet Union's UN ambassador Andrei Gromyko, vice consul Evgeniia Tamantsova, and to Stalin, asking him to "be so kind as to help see that some kind of Russian woman gets this letter."[33] Other Americans contacted the US State Department or its embassy in Moscow. "Could you kindly put me in communication with educated people who would correspond and exchange stamps with me?" a Mrs. John King asked the US ambassador, "I am seventy and not after adventure."[34] Such requests reflected enduring enthusiasm for American-Soviet cooperation and optimism that both governments would continue to support contact between their citizens. But there was no longer a state-sponsored media campaign to encourage American-Soviet friendship, as there had been during the war. These American volunteers were self-mobilizing and self-motivated.

The demand for Soviet pen pals was "steadily mounting," Harry R. Warfel of the US embassy in Moscow reported to secretary of state James F. Byrnes in May 1946. Should pen friendships be allowed now that "restrictions on international correspondence no longer obtain?" Warfel asked.[35] That had been one of the US government's excuses for discouraging pen friendship in 1943, and trepidation about the program had not subsided by 1945. American officials had no illusions about the Soviet Women's Anti-Fascist Committee. It will "use correspondence exchanges with the United States as a channel for disseminating propaganda," Elizabeth Eagan of the embassy warned Byrnes in June 1946.[36] Yet, the State Department ultimately allowed women to continue exchanging letters. It even helped the program along. Eagan herself forwarded the names and addresses of several American petitioners to the anti-fascist committee.[37]

Why did the State Department facilitate the pen-pal project in this way? Unfortunately, many of the relevant documents remain classified, but available materials suggest US officials recognized that friendly ties between Soviet and American women could be advantageous for national promotion and intelligence gathering. American correspondents could disseminate positive images of the United States, while the letters they received might provide useful information about the USSR. Of course, the US government continued to set limits on this exchange. It still excluded men from the program, and the FBI kept up its surveillance of the National Council of American-Soviet Friendship. It was partly on FBI evidence that the House Un-American Activities Committee subpoenaed the National Council and cited it as a "communist front organization" in June 1946. Those proceedings were underway at the very same time that Eagan sent the Soviet Women's Anti-Fascist Committee the contact information for several Americans seeking pen friends in the USSR.[38]

The US State Department was not the only government agency questioning whether the correspondence project should continue. With Hitler defeated, the Soviet Women's Anti-Fascist Committee saw little use for the program. Its editors scrawled "no need to reply" atop dozens of letters that arrived weekly from the United States and Britain in late 1945.[39] The future of the committee itself was also uncertain. In February 1946, the Central Committee of the Communist Party sharply reduced the five anti-fascist committees except for two: the committees of women and of youth. The Central Committee gave those two more staff, bigger budgets, and the green light to keep running pen-pal programs with women and children abroad.[40] Neither the US nor the Soviet government spelled out why they limited the project to women and children—just girls in the American case—but widespread assumptions that women and kids are disarming, adept at making friends, and have minimal political power likely played a role. The Soviet Women's Anti-Fascist Committee, as US officials knew, continued its propaganda work. Now that victory had been achieved, its new charge was to establish friendly ties with women overseas and, once it had their ear, to promote Soviet socialism, especially the USSR's policies on peace and on gender equality. By the end of 1946, the committee expanded its pen-pal program to forty-two countries, including the new people's democracies in eastern Europe.[41] It also shared excerpts of the letters with Soviet audiences on the radio and in periodicals like *Literary Gazette*, *Teachers' Gazette*, and the anti-fascist committee's own magazine *Soviet Woman*.[42]

But the pool of Soviet pen pals never kept pace with the program's ambitions. From 1945 onward, American demand always exceeded supply. The anti-fascist committee was a propaganda agency, but it was the New York–based Committee of Women that repeatedly pushed for more contact, not the other way around.[43] In fact, the Soviet committee was often slow to respond to these pleas, and Soviet letter writers proved difficult to recruit. Women in the USSR were occupied with the monumental tasks of rebuilding their country and their families—usually without a husband's help. No doubt they were anxious, too. Although Soviet women stood to gain cultural cachet and to strengthen their candidacy for party membership by working with the anti-fascist committee, they often were afraid to forge ties with the capitalist West.[44] The committee admitted as much: "many Soviet women write abroad very reluctantly. In a number of cases, there is a certain fear about forming a written connection with a foreign country," it reported to the Central Committee of the Communist Party. And it is easy to see why. In addition to the repressions of the late 1930s, Stalin unleashed a new campaign of terror in the mid-1940s, which targeted those who "kowtowed" to western influence. Most of those fired and arrested were officials and intellectuals, many of them Jewish, but fear rippled through all strata of society. This xenophobic, antisemitic crusade came to be known as "the anti-cosmopolitan campaign" or *zhdanovshchina*, named after one of its notorious perpetrators, Andrei Zhdanov.[45] No wonder pen pals were hard to recruit and retain. "The [Soviet] persons to whom the letters are addressed do not respond to them," the anti-fascist committee admitted in 1946. "For example, in the last month 172 letters arrived in Moscow. But we received only fifty-one replies even after committee workers gave many reminders and made personal visits" to the letter writers' homes.[46]

Even so, the stream of letters from the United States remained steady. American women's voluntary organizations, which declined after suffrage, resurged in the wake of World War II as grassroots movements for world peace took shape.[47] Groups ranging politically from the United Council of Church Women to the National Council of Negro Women organized campaigns demanding that women be part of the postwar peace process. At the White House, Eleanor Roosevelt hosted a conference on "how women may share in post-war policy making," based on the premise women were better at conflict resolution and more invested in peace than men.[48] Letter writing was a key grassroots strategy for building international peace and sisterhood; the Young Women's Christian Association, Girl Scouts, and Camp Fire Girls all launched such programs at this time.[49]

For its own correspondence project, the National Council of American-Soviet Friendship's Committee of Women tapped into this spirit of internationalism and worked to recruit women from "influential conservative groups" that "otherwise would not be primarily interested in Soviet life": women's clubs, church societies, and the umbrella organization representing three million of them, the General Federation of Women's Clubs.[50] An unlikely advocate of American-Soviet friendship, the federation was explicitly anti-communist, but it softened that stance during the war.[51] President

Lucy J. Dickinson implored the USSR's embassy in Washington, DC, in 1944 and 1946, asking for "something definite that our three million federation members might do to promote friendships with individual women of the Soviet Union."[52] Dickinson was a Republican national committeewoman and an outspoken anti-communist. "I do not want communism here in the United States," she declared. "If people do not like our form of government and like communism, they should go to the Soviet Union." However, she was equally emphatic that "one of the most important things in the world today is friendship between the Soviet people and the people of the United States."[53] In what became a signature story—reminiscent of *One World*, Republican presidential nominee Wendell Willkie's 1943 travelogue calling for global interdependence—Dickinson described a soul-stirring conversation she had with a war widow in Stalingrad when she visited there with a Red Cross delegation in 1946.[54] The woman wore medals for heroic labor, but her fingers were bare: German troops had stolen her wedding ring. Dickinson offered the woman one of her own rings to signify her commitment to peace: "For better or for worse, for richer and for poorer, in sickness and in health, until death do us part, I pledged to her that I would do everything I could to bring friendship between our people."[55] Inspired by Dickinson, clubwomen sent letters carrying the same message. "I feel that I sort of know the [Soviet] people since she was there," Mrs. Frank Reed of Independence, Kansas, wrote to her new Soviet pen friend.[56] To reach more women like Reed, the federation advertised the pen-pal program in its magazine *Clubwoman of America*.[57]

Those who did not read about it there may have encountered the program in *Woman's Home Companion*, one of the most widely circulated women's magazines in the United States. A two-issue feature from journalist Oriana Atkinson, who had been stationed in Moscow during World War II, recounted a conversation she had with the executive secretary of the anti-fascist committee, Lidiia Petrova. The pair discussed whether "there could be friendship and cooperation between the women of our two countries." Petrova was emphatic that this was possible. "I knew that she meant it with all her heart," Atkinson observed, but the American was doubtful. Atkinson concluded that peace was impossible so long as neither the United States nor the USSR was "willing" to "abandon their form of government."[58] In response, Atkinson received "bushels" of letters from readers rebuking her skepticism.[59] Atkinson sent her critics Petrova's address, and dozens wrote to her.[60] Petrova arranged pen pals for them.

This first postwar cohort of American letter writers, therefore, by and large heard about the pen-pal program through their clubs, church groups, and the press. They tended to be more conservative and openly religious than their compatriots who wrote during World War II. The strong contingent of Jewish letter writers disappeared. Most American participants now were Methodists, followed by Presbyterians and Episcopalians, but they were highly ecumenical, downplaying denominational distinctions or omitting to mention them altogether. Mary Roe Hull was a prime example; she worshipped with Presbyterians, Congregationalists, Episcopalians, and Methodists at times. Also like Hull, these new American correspondents were overwhelmingly white, middle-class, politically moderate, and from small towns in the Midwest.

Meanwhile, Nina Morozova was typical of the postwar Soviet writers. Nearly all lived in Moscow and were ethnically Russian.[61] Like her, most were widowed or single white-collar professionals, including teachers, engineers, and scientists. Several of the Soviet women who joined were medical doctors; they were paired with Americans whose husbands were doctors. At the same time, the factory and farm women who descended into Soviet mines or operated plows during World War II were now a scant part of the letter-writing pool. In this way, the body of participants from both countries became less diverse regionally, professionally, socioeconomically, and ethnically than it had been during the war. All of the Soviet participants were vetted for their political loyalty, but anti-fascist committee records indicate that none were members of the Communist Party.[62] As with the wartime letter writers, there is no question that the new Soviet correspondents agreed to partake in the committee's propagandistic mission when they signed on as pen pals. They were instructed to champion the Soviet way of life but, as their idiosyncratic letters affirm, they were not handed a script for doing so.[63] Censorship ensured the participants upheld this agenda, but they were not held hostage to it. Nor were they prevented from quitting the program or from writing for other, personal reasons, as Morozova did.

Morozova knowingly participated in the committee's propagandistic work. No organization pushed Hull to do so. Yet both women ultimately promoted their own national ideals. They also displayed an emotional openness and earnestness to connect. The circumstances of their writing were different, but the end results were similar.

Blessed Are the Peacemakers

From the start, Mary Roe Hull declared that she had a complicated relationship to the church. She was deeply committed to Christian morality but resented organized religion for causing so much bloodshed, Hull explained when first introducing herself to her pen friend. She described herself as a woman with white hair, lavender eyes, and a French grandmother who escaped Catholic persecution for being a Huguenot. This was actually not true, her great-grandniece Connie Burtnett explained; some of Aunt May's genealogical work was faulty. "She did the best she could without the internet as well as adding some wishful thinking to the mix," Connie observed.[64] Accurate or not, Hull identified with this renegade grandmother, whereas she never mentioned to Morozova that her father, her late husband, two uncles, numerous cousins, and other ancestors had all been ministers or missionaries.[65] "A strange thing, the religious wars through the centuries," Hull mused to her pen pal. "What I think, I believe in, [is] the study of the person known as Jesus whose hometown was Nazareth. He showed how one ought to live, so that the human race could become better. If our leaders around the world had followed his teaching, then there would not have been enemies, only brotherly love and a real golden age."[66] Hull valued Jesus's teachings about peace over the doctrine of salvation. "Instead of the crucifixion of Christ on the cross, I always was inclined toward 'the Person who brought Peace.' To popularize the suffering of a great teacher of peace only burns the heart with anguish. If not, then why are religious leaders inclined to holy war?" she demanded. Then, noting the unconventionality of her views, she added: "As I wrote to you already, I do not think of myself as orthodox."[67]

Hull constantly wove spiritual reflections into her letters, whether asking about Morozova's daughter Svetlana or commenting on her neighbors. When describing a June rain after a dry spell, Hull wrote: "God cleansed this part of the world today."[68] Or, when Morozova told her about Soviet plans to expand irrigation, Hull could not help "but recall the saying from the Bible: 'and the deserts will flower like roses.'" In Hull's mind, irrigation was related to peace and so to God because it was one of many productive things that governments could do instead of expanding their arsenals. "Disarm, leave as many soldiers as you need to protect you in the service of natural disasters," she ordered the world's statesmen in the middle of one letter to Morozova. "Use your resources to improve the lives of people. Build houses, pave roads, irrigate everywhere it is needed. Use your finances for these things."[69]

Hull's religious views, however idiosyncratic, spoke to the dominant role Christianity played in American rhetoric about US-Soviet relations. The notion that the United States had a sacred mission to bring Christian ethics to the world enjoyed a revival at the end of World War II. This idea emerged in many forms and political circles, inspiring conservatives and liberals alike. On the political left, Christian pacifism rebounded and undergirded a progressive commitment to social reform in organized labor and civil rights. Half of the American letter writers during this era belonged to the Women's Society (or Division) of Christian Service, the Women's Society of Christian Endeavor, and other groups that upheld Methodism's strong tradition of social activism. They sent letters abroad and agitated at home for "a spiritual transformation of humanity that would manifest itself in a reformed social order."[70]

Christian ethics also justified hardline policies toward the Soviet Union on the political right. Presbyterians George Kennan and John Foster Dulles were among the loudest voices in the Truman administration to advocate a "get tough with Russia" attitude on spiritual grounds. They were part of a growing cohort of politicians who saw the Cold War as a religious crusade, and they both wrote sermons (as well as speeches and memoranda) preaching that individual rights and freedoms came from God and that Americans had a sacred obligation to combat godless communism.[71] Dulles not only participated in meetings of the UN General Assembly and foreign ministers' councils, he also chaired the Federal Council of Churches' Commission on a Just and Durable Peace and brought its recommendations to President Truman. A devout Baptist, Truman declared more than once: "my political philosophy is based on the Sermon on the Mount."[72] "We cannot sit idly by and see totalitarianism spread to the whole of Europe," he proclaimed, "We must meet the challenge if civilization is to survive. We represent the moral God-fearing peoples of the world. We must save the world from Atheism and Totalitarianism."[73] Dulles carried that message to readers of *Life* magazine in two 1946 articles. The United States and Soviet Union were in moral and mortal opposition, he argued. "The Soviet program threatens our way of life and our cherished political and spiritual freedoms. [. . .] The overriding and ever-present reason for giving freedom to the individual is that men are created as the children of God, in His image. The human personality is thus sacred, and the State must not trample on it." Americans, in other words, were spiritually obliged to combat communism "by conduct and example, to show the righteous way to live."[74]

Mary Roe Hull was not one of Dulles's crusaders. She and many others who joined the pen-pal program in late 1945 and 1946 shared his faith in the righteousness and universality of Christian morality, but they drew on Christ's teachings to voice goodwill and tolerance rather than cite irreconcilable differences between the United States and USSR. As Hull explained in her second letter to Morozova: "You think that your government is better now, but I think that my government is much better. I think that my government is the best, and I would not give a penny for someone who would not agree. Yours is better for you, and ours is better for us, and there is no reason for us to argue because of that."[75] This attitude stands in sharp contrast to the hardline discourse of inevitable capitalist-socialist conflict, wielded by the Truman and Stalin administrations.

No doubt Hull and many other letter writers saw it as their mission to offer peace and the gospel to Soviet women, but to model the former, they took a softer approach to the latter. Sometimes they directed their interlocutors to specific bible verses, but in general they conveyed their faith by offering blessings, not by proselytizing.[76] "We have love and good feelings in our hearts for you. We are praying for you and yours, that only good things will come to you and the whole world," Mrs. Charles L. Young of Youngstown, Ohio, declared.[77] "We love you folks, and we pray for you," echoed Blanche Lamb. Lamb was an advocate of peace and patriotism. She was active in the Women's Society of Christian Service, and she founded an auxiliary post of the American Legion in her hometown of McGraw, New York.[78] Still, Lamb addressed her unknown Soviet readers gently, even affectionately. That approach may explain why the anti-fascist committee did not censor any religious remarks from Americans. However, it did not arrange replies to evangelizing letters sent by Mormons.[79]

Letter writers like Hull, Young, and Lamb embraced the Soviet people as God's children. At the same time, they undercut that apparent tolerance by projecting their Christian ethics and worldview onto their pen pals. "Dear

Sisters of Russia," Mrs. J. N. Proctor of Twin Falls, Idaho, began in 1946, "I am addressing you as sisters because, as Christians, we are all brothers and sisters regardless of race, color, or creed, and God is the father of us all. We Christian women of America are earnestly praying for peace that will make the world all one brotherhood. And we know that the women of Russia are just as eager for that peace as we are and that there will be no more war."[80] "We are praying for a permanent peace," Mrs. Leonard Osborne of Fairmont, North Dakota, echoed in her first letter to Moscow, "We know that wives and mothers all over the world must feel the same, and we are sure our prayers are joined by your prayers."[81] Proctor and Osborne extended these messages of goodwill to build community with Soviet women, but they thrust their own beliefs upon them in the process.

How did such comments land with Soviet women who, until recently, had been living in a vehemently atheistic society? Stalin famously initiated a rapprochement with the Orthodox Church in 1943, partly to smooth relations with the Allies and partly in response to a revival of faith among bereaved Soviet citizens seeking spiritual solace. Some 1,270 churches were reopened during the war. This was a tiny percentage of the 50,000 that had existed at the time of the revolution, but it was a significant, symbolic reversal of the regime's violent assault on clergy and church properties.[82] In light of this perhaps, American letter writers wrote unabashedly about their faith, thinking that their Soviet pen friends would be receptive to it. After all, many Americans believed that ordinary Soviet citizens remained devout despite the party's efforts to promote atheism.[83] And perhaps some Soviet pen pals were religious, though none penned a profession of faith, whether due to self-censorship or to non-belief. Certainly, the wartime religious revival was weaker among their demographic—educated urban professionals—than it was among rural peasants. No doubt many Soviet letter writers were jarred by their American pen pals' prayerful prose and presumption of Christian righteousness. In their replies, Soviet letter writers continually decoupled peacemaking from Christianity, but they did so in a nonconfrontational way that fostered connection and intimacy.

When replying to a note from Dunkirk, Ohio's Women's Society of Christian Service, Moscow subway worker Anna Alekseevna Cherkasova stressed her agreement with the society's members while supplying a different conceptual framework for their claims. "Your letter has touched us dearly," she wrote, "we sincerely want peace," especially "now, after the unheard off [*sic*] hardships of the war-years. We are very happy to hail the sincere wish of American Christian women to join their efforts to ours in striving for a lasting peace between all nations." Cherkasova anchored that commitment to the story of how her eldest son, Zhenia, was permanently disabled during the battle for Sevastopol. "In our social[ist] Soviet country," she continued, "you won't find a single woman, whatever her religious beliefs and nationality, who does not wish with heart and soul for peace and happiness for all people." And Soviet people—including Cherkasova's two other, younger sons—were prepared to fight in order to secure such happiness. "We are content to bear all the present discomfort and are even ready for the hardest sacrifices in the name of the future." In this way, Cherkasova subtly rejected both Christianity and pacifism even as she praised her pen friends' spiritual work. "I am very interested in the activities of your Women's Society for Christian Endeavor," she added. "It is so interesting, and in our times it is so necessary to feel the friendship of people who are close to us Soviet women in their feelings and ideas."[84] Cherkasova's reply was so agreeable that it is easy to overlook how it decenters Christian ethics. The letter models the notion that peace could be better achieved through open dialogue than forceful preaching of either Christianity or socialism.

Nina Morozova was the only Soviet pen pal who gave any inkling that she had religious faith. That moment occurred when Mary Roe Hull asked why her daughter Svetlana had two names: Svetlana-Natal'ia. Morozova penned just one phrase in reply: "the second name was added when she was baptized according to Church rites." She then moved on to thank Hull for offering to send her daughter a doll.[85] Still, this quick reference to baptism leaps out from the page. That sacrament was forbidden during most of the Stalinist period, and eleven-year-old Svetlana was likely christened during the late 1930s, a time when tens of thousands of believers were arrested and killed as part of the Great Terror. Morozova was born in 1907. She was Svetlana's age when the Bolsheviks took power, and so she grew up under both theocratic and atheistic governments. Morozova never spoke about her own faith. Did she fabricate the baptism story to curry favor and influence with Hull? Perhaps. But she never leveraged it for this purpose. Nor did she comment on any of Hull's spiritual reflections. As a Christian, Morozova could have embraced them. As a Soviet citizen, she could have critiqued them. She did neither.

Instead, Morozova sidestepped Hull's religious remarks and drew on another moral system, one that also promised social harmony and shared Christianity's universalizing reach: Soviet socialism. In that same letter, she moved from baptism to the Arab-Israeli war, which erupted after the Israeli Declaration of Independence in 1948. This was one of the rare times that the pair touched on a current event, and they did so very briefly, each expending only one phrase about it. In rather rough English, Morozova wrote: "Yes, I quite agree with you that the war between the Arabs and the Jews is a creed [*sic*] and unnecessary thing. And always when there is bloodshed and men are killed, even in very distant countries, it tears my heart to know it. If only all nations would follow the example of the many nationalities who live in peace, cooperation, and amity in the confines of the great and united Soviet Union! They know no conflicts and labour peacefully for the good of all."[86] Substituting the Soviet family of nations for the paradigm of Christian brotherhood, Morozova offered the multiethnic, multiconfessional USSR as a model of cooperation for others to follow.

Like Hull's Christian-inspired politics, Morozova's argument had deep roots. Soviet cultural diplomats had pushed this picture of ethnic harmony overseas as a selling point of socialism since at least the 1930s.[87] It was a core tenet of Soviet ideology. The Bolsheviks envisioned the Soviet project as an anti-imperialist enterprise from the start.[88] They were intent on reversing centuries of tsarist repression of non-Russians as well as winning the loyalty of those peoples by celebrating ethnic particularism and expediting the promotion of minorities up the professional and political ladders.[89] At the same time, Soviet modernization drives—whether economic, like the first Five-Year Plan, or cultural like the atheism campaigns—assaulted non-Russian populations in ways that were ethnic in nature.[90] Despite a robust commitment to promoting local languages and leaders, discrimination endured and ethnicity remained a powerful marker of inequality in Soviet society. This became especially pronounced in the years around World War II, which led to a surge in state-sponsored Russian chauvinism. First the purges in the late 1930s and then the cleansing campaigns of the 1940s targeted certain ethnic groups as perfidious and forcibly relocated them. These included Crimean Tatars, Chechens, Greeks, Koreans, Germans, and Jews. The deportations took millions of lives, and many of those who managed to survive never regained their lands.[91] Morozova lauded the Soviet "friendship of the peoples" in the wake of these atrocities and concurrently with the anti-cosmopolitan campaign, which accused Jews of being particularly susceptible to western influence and thus disloyal.[92] Indeed, the leaders of the Soviet Jewish Anti-Fascist Committee—one of the other five anti-fascist committees formed in 1941—were brutally murdered, and the committee liquidated in 1948.[93] Nina Morozova, well-educated and living in the heart of Moscow, probably knew about this ethnic violence to a certain extent, but she never hinted at any discord in the Soviet "family of nations." Perhaps this was because, as a pen pal, she was tasked with lauding Soviet socialism. Or perhaps this was because of her position of privilege; being a Russian and a Muscovite may have blinded her to the egregious miscarriages of justice that marred the legal equality guaranteed by the Soviet constitution.

Morozova did not promote socialist tenets in the abstract but folded them into personal stories and confessional moments. "I have nothing new to tell you this time," she began one letter to Hull, "I am in rather low spirits. I miss my husband very much and often grieve for him. This hateful war has taken my man, the father of my child, and this makes me very unhappy at times. Don't you think that nobody can ever replace a child's father?" The thought that more children would be orphaned by future wars was unbearable for Morozova, as was the realization that Svetlana may never have a father figure in her life—"though they say some men grow to love other people's children very dearly," she ventured hopefully. In this moment of anguish, she beseeched her pen pal: "Dear Aunt May, write so often. I would like our personal correspondence to contribute as much as possible to creating mutual understanding and friendship between our two nations, and I think that personal contacts between American and Russian women ought to grow and contribute to this friendship and understanding." Morozova's conflation of Russian and Soviet here is notable in light of the rosy picture she painted of inter-ethnic harmony in the USSR. "Dear Aunt May," she continued, "you who have such a clear mind and love Peace, you must do all you can to help other American people to [gain] a proper understanding of the peaceful policies and aspirations of our Soviet Union and to unmask those who want to lead mankind into a new war; war means new devastation, new bloodshed, new tears."[94]

Like many wartime letter writers, Morozova confided her grief to her pen pal in this way. She appeared vulnerable rather than stoic, despite mounting pressure on Soviet people to project an image of strength abroad.[95] And this openness had both a comforting effect and political utility. Morozova turned to Hull for emotional as well as political support. In the space of those few lines, she wrapped her hatred of war in personal tragedy as well as in official discourse. Her demand that Hull "unmask" American war hawks echoes the speech given by UN representative Andrei Gromyko a few months earlier.[96] "Unmask" was a politically loaded term that the Soviet regime evoked repeatedly in its violent campaigns against enemies, both domestic and international. It is jarring to see it side-by-side with declarations of Soviet ethnic tolerance in Morozova's letter. Morozova wrote these lines at a time when Soviet UN Ambassador Andrei Gromyko and Deputy Minister of Foreign Affairs Andrei Vyshinskii repeatedly "unmasked" US politicians and businessmen in front of the international press, upbraiding them as war hawks who stoked conflict in order to spread their influence and line their pockets. Proletarian peoples had an obligation to expose them, Gromyko declared in 1946. "The Soviet people will in the future, as it did in the past, defend the cause of peace. It will continue to unmask warmongers wherever their voices may be raised."[97] Reiterating this claim in 1947, Vyshinskii called out Dulles, Kennan, and Byrnes as warmongers, and he made a motion that the UN make their kind of war agitation illegal.[98] Gromyko and Vyshinskii cast the Soviet Union as a bulwark of peace, but their rhetoric was so heated that even the National Council of American-Soviet Friendship, which tended to back Soviet perspectives on foreign policy, decried it as illustrative of how statesmen in the United States and USSR were unwilling to compromise.[99] Nina Morozova's claims echoed Vyshinksii on a substantive level, but the way she articulated them was different. She wove her call to "unmask" into admissions of grief and pledges of friendship. "I do so want us to be friends and so do all here!" she underscored as she condemned American warmongering.[100] Morozova fashioned herself on the page as both personally unguarded and politically resolute.

Hull's response was heartfelt, but it skirted her Moscow niece's request to "unmask" instigators of war. "Your husband valiantly perished for you, your daughter, and your country," Hull replied, "so that you could live freely in beautiful Moscow, go on vacation in Riga, and be yourself." And while she encouraged Morozova to "preserve his memory," Hull also urged her to remain open to new possibilities for love. "I think that if you find a person who has lost his beloved wife, he would understand you and you could be happy, loving each other." Interestingly, Hull encouraged Morozova to find a new partner, but she never mentioned her own marriage or the fact that she never remarried after her husband's death. Although they addressed each other wholeheartedly, there were clear limits on what Hull and Morozova were willing to share. Hull could have bonded with Morozova as a wife and widow, but she never mentioned her husband to her pen pal or even to many of her relatives. Growing up, Connie Roe Burtnett never heard "one word" about that marriage from any relative, nor did Connie—as the new family historian—encounter any reference to it in her great-grand-aunt's many autobiographical writings.[101] Mary Roe Hull's husband, Charles Clarence Hull, was a laborer and Methodist preacher. He entered an insane asylum in 1926 and passed away within its walls in 1936.[102] Instead of opening up to Morozova about this tragedy, Mary Roe Hull responded by linking Morozova's personal crisis to geopolitical tensions, providing spiritual grounding for both: "If I had participated in assembling the Bible," she continued, "I would not have included these words in it: 'there will be wars and rumors of wars.' I would write that life in eternal peace is a treasure. No intelligent man, woman, or child wants the world to perish in war."[103]

Hull's advice, including its religious evocations, deepened Morozova's appreciation for her pen pal as well as her concern about American militarism. "My dear, good Auntie May!" Morozova replied, "I am simply beginning to love you. You are so good, and it is such a pity you are so far away. Your letters are so sweet and warm. And every time I hear about war I think: why are there people in America who want you to thirst for my blood and me for yours? What have we to divide us, why should we fight and kill each other, our children, and those near and dear to us?" Thus, in one swoop, Morozova embraced her pen friend and took a swipe at Hull's compatriots. "I would like us to be the best of friends," she added, to "have nice chats around the tea-table about our children and our happy future, and not about war, ruin, and death." Encouraged by their ability to connect, Morozova again appealed to Hull as a mediator who could correct misconceptions about Soviet aggression. "You are good and wise, dear Aunt May, tell all your friends and neighbors that we are full of the best intentions towards the American people, as towards all other nations. Don't allow slanderous lies and misinformation about the Soviet Union to be told."

Then, to substantiate the USSR's commitment to peace, Morozova again painted her country as a harmonious family of nations: "You can judge by the happy and peaceful friendship of the many nationalities of our Soviet Union how we wish for friendship and to work in peace together with other nations. Expose these odious warmongers whenever you get a chance to. There is no word I hate more than the word 'war'! I go on living with little or no change," she continued, downshifting from the geopolitical to the personal. "You write it is time for me to leave off grieving for my husband and that I ought to find a good friend who could take his place. Yes, you are right, but I haven't found such a friend as yet. The days fly by quickly and one doesn't notice them pass in the everyday bustle of housekeeping chores . . ." And she went on, turning the conversation back to everyday matters.[104]

In this highly personalized way, Morozova and Hull modeled their devotion to peace while pressing the Christian and socialist tenets behind their commitments. The hostile language of their statesmen confirmed how easily Christian or socialist ethics could justify aggressive foreign policies, but Hull and Morozova rejected this combative approach. Rather than sermonize, they embedded their arguments in the intimate and the everyday. They tolerated each other's scriptural and socialist references without comment. And in this way, they did not seek to make each other wrong but remained open to each other, intellectually and emotionally. Ultimately, they focused on keeping the conversation going rather than on winning the debate.

What was the impact of the arguments and affections they traded? Hull convinced Morozova to look for love again, but did they change each other's political actions or attitudes? The evidence is inconclusive, but there are more clues from the better-documented life of Hull than of Morozova. On the one hand, Morozova made one, very direct attempt to influence Hull's political behavior, which failed. She tried to convince Hull to vote for Henry A. Wallace for president. Roosevelt's former vice president, Wallace ran on the Progressive Party ticket in 1948. He spoke openly about the need for peaceful, normalized political relations as well as trade with the Soviet Union, and he quickly developed a reputation as a socialist sympathizer. "How right he is in everything he says, what a clear and sound mind he has," Morozova exclaimed to Hull in July 1948, "Oh, how I wish that ninety-nine percent of Americans would think as he does and see things as he sees them!"[105] Her Aunt May did not reply, but in a separate letter Hull wrote to her grandniece Helen three months later, she declared she was voting for the Republican ticket at the opposite end of the political spectrum. "I believe Dewey and Warren are our best bet," she explained. Hull explicitly declared that she did not put much stock in the Progressives, "a new party" that "will be out in the open, strong in four years, but now it doesn't count." The party's main utility, she noted, was "to give us awareness of how we are slipping in our Democracy." Hull advised Helen to "wise up" about the decline of American freedom.[106]

On the other hand, Mary Roe Hull's growing fascination with the USSR was clear. Since her pen friendship began, she began reading the Soviet embassy's *Information Bulletin*, crafted to promote the USSR to foreign readers. And there is one other indication that Morozova made an inroad into Hull's view of the Soviet Union. In 1948, Aunt May was in the midst of saying how she longed to visit the USSR when she exclaimed: "I am just amazed when I think of the 189 different nationalities, 150 different languages [in the USSR] and how they all coexist. It is something to be proud of, Nina, and for which one ought to love your wise leaders who implemented it."[107] Notably, Morozova did not go for the jugular in her reply and condemn racial segregation in the United States—the move Soviet statesmen, journalists, and the anti-fascist committee would have made. It is equally notable that Hull, a white woman of privilege, did not point to American racism either. Illusions about freedom and equality pervaded their letters.

Hull never complimented the Soviets to Morozova so overtly again, but from around that time and until her death she began pasting into her personal scrapbook articles covering Soviet affairs, especially clippings that criticized US foreign policy toward the USSR. The fact that she collected these pieces does not mean she endorsed them, but she did annotate one saying she wanted to include positive portrayals of the Soviet Union. Moreover, Hull created an impression among her younger relations that she had leftist views. I asked Connie Roe Burtnett about her great-grand-aunt's vote for Dewey. She raised an eyebrow. "I always got the impression that she was more socialist," Connie explained.[108] "I didn't know that Aunt May wrote the letters you're researching, but it sounds like something she would do. She devoted herself to social causes later in life and I know she advocated socialism in some of her later writings."[109] Unfortunately, Connie and I were not able to find them.

Mothers and Women Warriors for Peace

While Nina Morozova associated warmongers with a particular nationality, Mary Roe Hull associated them with a particular gender. Hull assumed that men instigated violent conflict, whereas women like her "have had enough" of war and "categorically demand an end to it."[110] "We need to compel men away from their idea: 'I do what I want or else . . .' and bang! Already another senseless war is prepared. No one wins wars. They only destroy families, create want, deprivation, and suffering." Hull ordered the world's diplomats: "Return back and sit at the conference table and sit there until [you] agree to make the world a more suitable place for living." The primary way women could help foster peace, Hull suggested, was through their capacity as caregivers: "we women ought to use our influence among the goodness of the world, among small children, who are growing up everywhere around us."[111] Men emerge from her letters as natural aggressors and women as intuitive peacemakers who prioritized family over powerplay. They could raise the next generation to negotiate rather than fight.

Like Hull, more than half of Americans corresponding during this time adopted a maternalist perspective and projected it onto their pen pals, the way they did with Christian ethics. They expected their Soviet pen friends to agree that mothering and peacemaking were interconnected. They also stressed their personal identities as mothers, the way many wartime letter writers did, in order to bond with their pen pals and to justify why they, as ordinary women with children, were specially qualified to intercede in US-Soviet relations. For their part, Soviet letter writers were equally adamant about protecting children from violent conflict, but their determination did not stem from the fact that they were women. In response to Hull, Morozova raged against war, but she did not couch her outrage as feminine nor link masculinity to warmongering.[112]

Here, again, the pen pals stressed their agreement, admiration, and appreciation all while reframing each other's claims about the relationship between gender and peace. Dr. Klavdiia Soloshenko had lost both a husband and a son in the war, and she beseeched Zoe Perkins that war had to end; it simply devastated families. Perkins heartily agreed but imposed a masculine-feminine binary onto Soloshenko's plea. "Dear Dr. Soloshenko!" Perkins wrote from her Los Angeles home, "Thank you very much for the kind letter, which I received this morning. Yes, I agree with you that if a new war can be prevented, women ought to do it. Over the course of the century men have proven that they cannot do it. Mothers of the world must stop this. [. . .] I also had a son in the war, in the last war, and I do not want him to fight again." Perkins seemed confident that women would bring fresh approaches to diplomacy and avoid the mistakes made by generations of statesmen. "We ought to be cleverer and [find] more beneficial methods of solving all of the problems of this crazy world. It seems to me that after World War I, people ought to have understood that such methods are not advantageous at all."[113]

By juxtaposing feminine pacifism and male belligerence, American correspondents like Perkins drew on a rich heritage of maternalist thinking, which had colored many of the women-led peace initiatives that sprung up across Europe and North America during the late nineteenth and early twentieth centuries.[114] The letter writers followed these activists by grounding their peace advocacy in claims about "international Christian responsibility" and about women as the givers and protectors of life.[115] After dipping in popularity during the 1930s, maternalism rebounded on the American political scene after World War II in a range of forms.[116] While many used maternalism to prop up a conservative view of women's roles, others increasingly brandished maternalist arguments with, not against, feminist demands. The democratic ethos that prevailed in the wake of fascism's demise brought with it a more expansive view of human rights that included socioeconomic opportunity, not just legal equality. This milieu encouraged a new generation of women activists to recognize gender difference while demanding gender equality.[117] In this way, maternalism's purchase expanded across the political spectrum and across borders, even to the Soviet Union.

Soviet gender theorists had long criticized maternalist ideas as bourgeois and biologically deterministic. Yet they crept into Soviet discourse around the mid-1930s, when ideologues and scientists began to herald motherhood as women's primary and most hallowed calling.[118] Still, in the USSR there was no explicit association between motherhood and peacemaking until World War II, when the Soviet Women's Anti-Fascist Committee began referring to a maternal obligation to defend the innocent in its pamphlets and rallies aimed at western audiences. Through the remainder of the decade, the committee continued to cast mothers as natural peacemakers while arguing for full equality between the sexes. It relayed that message at home and overseas through its international magazine *Soviet Woman* and through the Women's International Democratic Federation (WIDF), both established in November 1945.[119]

The WIDF was founded in war-battered Paris by women who fought in the anti-fascist resistance, some of them imprisoned at Ravensbrück. The federation started with forty-one membership organizations representing 117 countries and grew into the largest women's organization of the twentieth century.[120] Its Soviet affiliate was none other than the Soviet Women's Anti-Fascist Committee. The federation's four-pronged platform combined feminism with maternalism. It was dedicated to advancing peace, women's equality, the protection of children, and social justice for oppressed minorities and colonial peoples.[121]

The organization was progressive, often pro-socialist, and consistently maternalist. "Mothers!" its 1946 "Appeal to the Women of the World," thundered, "remember that there are reactionary forces, which for the sake of their own predatory aims, seek to destroy our children. Housewives! In building a home for your family, remember that there are still people in this world who would condemn your home and hearth to devastation!" This appeal demanded that "mothers, wives, and sisters" push their governments to sever ties with Franco's Spain and aid Greek communists, clearly supporting Kremlin foreign policy in both regards.[122] The federation's pro-Soviet bent grew stronger by 1947, when it began virulently attacking the Marshall Plan and "American reactionaries" who it claimed were "urged on by an insatiable thirst for new billions of dollars and insane aspirations for world domination. [. . .] Is there a wife who will agree to her husband being killed for the sake of enriching a handful of billionaires? Is there a mother who will give up her son to enable imperialists to pile up more profits? Is there a sister who will agree to her brother becoming a cripple by defending the interests of reaction?"[123] This vitriol, all republished in the anti-fascist committee's magazine *Soviet Woman,* is a classic example of how the peace movement became a cold war battlefield by the late 1940s. Such aggressive rhetoric casts doubt on the assumption that women had a natural proclivity for resolving conflict.

The federation and its maternalist, often hostile discourse had direct import for the pen pal project because the women who ran the program were also WIDF vice presidents: Nina Vasil'evna Popova, a war widow and the new, postwar chairperson of the anti-fascist committee, and Muriel Draper. Draper was chair of the Committee of Women and president of the WIDF's US affiliate, the Congress of American Women. Popova and Draper collaborated on many WIDF statements like the ones quoted above as well as on events such as the 1946 "international children's week," which was predicated on a maternal obligation to oppose war.[124] In the United States, Draper also launched a "Mother's Crusade to Prevent War," whereby members of the Congress of American Women marched on the Capitol with their children in tow to demand that President Truman improve relations with the Soviet Union rather than prepare to fight it.[125] "Peace is a woman's business," a joint resolution of the WIDF and Congress of American Women declared, "It is the keeping together of home and family, the protection of health, education, the very lives of her children. The creator of new life, she must be the protector of all life."[126]

The Soviet letter writers could not have been more different in their language and approach. They adopted neither the anti-American nor maternalist discourse of the anti-fascist committee that supervised them.[127] The Soviet participants often related to their pen pals as mothers, and they definitely agreed that mothers were determined to establish peace, but not more so than fathers. This was the argument Mariia Korneeva of Moscow made in response to Angelina R. Checki of Lyndhurst, New Jersey. Checki described herself as "just an average American housewife with four children," a "Roman Catholic, and a confirmed dyed-in-the-wool Republican." She was one of the politically conservative participants who joined the pen-pal program after reading about it in *Woman's Home Companion* in 1946.[128] "Let us, the women of the world, form an anti-war ring," Checki proclaimed, "for we are the builders of men and only we know what an effort and what a struggle that takes. While men build only to destroy, let us see to it that we preserve the welfare of our children." In her response, Mariia Korneeva emphatically agreed war must be prevented. "If there is war again, what will happen to my daughter? So many children killed in this war! I look at my child and my soul cringes in horror when I think of a new war. This is the attitude of all who witnessed the suffering of children. Your country, on whose territory war has not been waged, cannot understand all the horrors of war." While she linked her antiwar stance to her status as a mother, Korneeva rejected her pen pal's association between masculinity with militancy. "I think that not all men in your country want war," she told Checki. "The majority are honestly working and have no wish to hear again the dying groans of men on the battlefields."[129] Refusing to employ a male-female dichotomy, Korneeva evoked what historian Anna Krylova has called the "nonoppositional though still binary" Soviet understanding of masculinity and femininity. It was not considered transgressive for Soviet women to take up arms and fight for peace even if combat was still considered a largely masculine domain.[130]

This is how the handful of female soldiers who contributed letters to the pen-pal program explained their war service: they were driven by a devotion to family, to country, and to peace. Between 520,000 and 800,000 uniformed women, including the first head of the Soviet Women's Anti-Fascist Committee, Colonel Valentina Grizodubova, served in the Soviet armed forces during World War II. There were also some 28,500 women partisans or guerilla troops.[131] Tat'iana Lagunova was one of them. She explained to her pen pal that she hated war but also opposed pacifism. Lagunova joined the partisans in July 1942 after German troops murdered her father and tortured her brother. She took up arms, she said, not in search of revenge or bloodlust but a quicker end to the war. "I was terribly afraid of shooting," she admitted, "I was fighting, but I did not like war. I killed enemies because I wanted war to be over sooner. It was hard for me physically and still harder morally."[132] But these acts were justified, Lagunova explained, by the greater good of destroying fascism. In mounting such claims, Soviet letter writers like her may have been drawing on Leninist arguments that proletarians had a moral imperative to crush exploiters and that pacifism was a form of bourgeois hypocrisy, a ruse that leaders in capitalist societies used to discourage the oppressed from rising up against them.[133] From this point of view, pacifism was nothing more than passivism. By contrast, the Soviet letter writers fashioned themselves as warriors for peace. "I am still suffering the aftereffects of shellshock," another soldier, Serafima Antonova, told Mrs. Fred Nay, "and there are scars left on my soul, which have not healed yet." Nevertheless, Antonova proclaimed she would sacrifice it all again if it meant defeating the Nazis.[134]

ONE THING THAT ALL THE SOVIET and American letters have in common is that they begin with a pledge of peace. The letter writers voiced these declarations confidently and in full expectation that, as former Allies, their interlocutors shared their views. However, the way they made these peaceful proclamations brought their different moral, spiritual, ideological, and gendered understandings to the fore. The Americans who joined the program in 1945 and 1946 pushed Christian and maternalist arguments, whereas their Soviet interlocutors pressed ideas of just warfare and ethnic harmony, inflecting both with socialist principles. Anti-fascism proved to be a vague and tenuous foundation for American-Soviet partnerships, big and small. War brought the correspondents together, but peace alerted them to how different they were.

It is not surprising that the letters capture these opposing views, many of which appeared in the press, in politicians' speeches, and in publications from women's transnational organizations. What is striking is not what the letter writers said but how they said it. Rather than deploy socialist tenets or cite scripture abstractly, they couched their assertions in well wishes, admissions, and personal stories—especially as mothers. They reframed each other's claims rather than attack them. Their words derived power not from their forceful tone but from the feelings behind their expression. Even if they did not convert each other to socialism or to Christianity, they raised each other's awareness of their values in a non-confrontational way. And the amiable, often intimate manner in which they presented their ethical codes probably did convince their pen pals that they were deeply committed to friendly US-Soviet relations. Some expanded their advocacy work beyond pen friendship. Zoe Perkins, who so warmly comforted Dr. Klavdiia Soloshenko over the loss of her son, also wrote letters to the *Los Angeles Times* and the *Daily News* in the years after their pen friendship ended, calling on her generation to teach young people that they must make "Peace on Earth, Goodwill to Men" not an "idle phrase but a reality."[135] Perkins became an outspoken critic of Kremlin politics, but her appreciation of Soloshenko did not dim.[136]

Nor did disagreement mar the friendly rapport between Mary Roe Hull and Nina Morozova. "My affectionate regards to you, dear Aunt May," Morozova wrote to Hull. "It is so nice to have someone so far-away, a dear friend who writes such interesting letters. I wish you the best of health and many long happy years, Your Moscow Niece, Nina."[137] In contrast to their political leaders, the pen friends modeled ways to disagree without sowing resentment or distrust.

Letter writers like Hull and Morozova who joined the pen pal program in late 1945 and 1946 did so in the hope that the cooperative spirit of the wartime Alliance would continue. That optimism began to fade by summer 1947, when some of the key weapons of the Cold War, including the Marshall Plan and the Cominform, were up and running. That year, the Truman administration established the Federal Loyalty Board to screen all federal employees for disloyalty or communist tendencies. Even "sympathy" with an organization or cause that the government deemed subversive was considered proof of perfidy.[138] The US State Department also required all Soviet visitors to the United States to register as government agents when they entered US territory. Meanwhile, the Soviet Union became closed off to nearly all western visitors. Stalin criminalized many forms of information sharing through the new State Secrets Act, and he curbed circulation of the State Department's promotional magazine *Amerika*, which Mary Roe Hull had recommended to Morozova. "Honor courts" in universities and state organizations tried Soviet citizens for insufficient patriotism or vigilance against foreign influence. The Kremlin even made it illegal for Soviet citizens to marry foreigners.[139] Moreover, the other anti-fascist committees were severely circumscribed; most would not last through 1948.[140]

By 1947, some scholars assume, "Soviet patriotism could not coexist with any form of sympathy for the West, especially not for the United States."[141] But sympathy and empathy were the pen pals' stock-in-trade. Despite this political climate of hostility and isolationism, the pen-pal project continued. In fact, it expanded to almost three hundred pairs of writers, including Americans from nineteen US states.[142]

Though peace always remained a central topic, the most prolific pen friends opened up more aspects of their lives for discussion: their families, their professional aspirations, and their desire for fulfillment from both. Their letters were part of growing national conversations about women's roles in the wake of postwar normalization. The Women's Division of Christian Service, to which so many of the American correspondents belonged, became a wellspring of feminist activity by the 1960s.[143] The more the pen pals shared with each other, the more they glimpsed the limiting structures and systems that undergirded their lives as women. Next, I explore how the letter exchange drew the pen friends into each other's worlds and invited them to imagine alternative perspectives and ways of living.

3 ~

What Do You Do for Work?

"I don't understand why you can't go to work," Ol'ga Mel'nikovskaia probed Jean Jahr, "Because it is hard to get work, or because there is no need for you to work, or because you must take care of your children?"[1] These queries were sparked by something Jahr, a mother of two and a self-described homemaker, had written in her previous letter. "I would be very happy to have some kind of work," Jahr had remarked, "but, of course, one cannot speak of that."[2] Jahr accepted this as a foregone conclusion, but her pen pal pressed her to say more, replying: "I can't imagine life without work, without my 'collective' of fellow-workers." At the time, Ol'ga Nikolaevna Mel'nikovskaia was a junior researcher in archeology at the Soviet Academy of Sciences in Moscow.[3] Though her career was just beginning, Mel'nikovskaia made work the center of her life. It was her source of fulfillment and of social belonging.

Jahr understood Mel'nikovskaia's enthusiasm. She, too, had found tremendous gratification when she worked for the Bronx House, a settlement home that helped the poor of New York City find their feet. Jahr was no stranger to financial hardship herself. Born in 1919, Jean R. Jahr (née Saidi, which the family changed to Sardy) grew up on the Lower East Side in a working-class, Sephardic household. The family of seven lived in a cramped two-bedroom apartment. Jahr's father was a longshoreman; many of her relatives worked in the garment industry. She had dreams of going to

Jean Jahr with her children, Marc and Joanne, circa 1953. (Photo by Bert Jahr. Courtesy of Joanne and Marc Jahr.)

college, but after her father suffered a back injury and was put on bedrest, Jahr began working as a secretary at the Bronx House. At just sixteen years old, she was now the breadwinner for her parents, sisters, and brother. "Her mom gave her only one dime from her salary every week," and this was to pay for subway tokens, Jahr's daughter Joanne explained. It was at the Bronx House that Jahr met and fell in love with its arts coordinator, a charismatic performer seven years her senior, who called himself Bert. "Her striking beauty enchanted my father," their son Marc recollected.[4] Jean Jahr left her job not long after she married Bert in 1940.[5] Joanne was born in 1943 and Marc in 1946.

A young mother of two, Jean Jahr's days were filled, but not always fulfilling. "There is almost nothing to say about my activities in the capacity of a homemaker," she wrote to Mel'nikovskaia. "I am busy with such problems that occupy all housewives: tedious housework, constant care to make sure that there is enough of everything, especially in light of price increases, the constant need for good medical and dental care for the kids, etc."[6] I sent this letter to Joanne and Marc, so they could read it nearly seventy-four years after their mother penned it. "I think the letter-writing was an outlet from what must have been the boredom of being a full-time mother and not having a job," Joanne reflected. "It gave her something to think about besides wrangling two small children and dealing with their needs."[7]

Ol'ga Mel'nikovskaia's reaction to Jahr's situation was one of confusion. "I don't quite understand," she replied, "why can't Joanne go to [after-school] classes?" Could Marc be sent to a nursery school?[8] No, Jahr replied, because "classes for young kids are so expensive." She needed more income to afford daycare, but she could not go out and earn it without someone to look after the kids. She explained this "economic situation" to her pen pal, calling it "an issue for the majority of mothers" and "a problem for which there is no solution."[9] At the same time that she longed for paid work, Jahr adored her children and loved looking after them. And this was something Mel'nikovskaia understood. She, too, had wanted marriage and a family, but the war had robbed her of that dream.[10] "I am very sorry I have no children," she told Jahr, "but even if I had children, I would go on working, because I can't imagine life without work."[11]

The question of if and how women could make space in their lives for careers, children, and housework—to say nothing of improving US-Soviet relations—occupied most of the 319 pairs of women corresponding during the late 1940s. After initially focusing on peace, the letter writers broadened their conversations to discuss everyday matters like work and parenthood. This was peace talk by other means. Most pairs believed that understanding and appreciating each other's way of life was prerequisite for defusing US-Soviet hostilities. As the letter writers described their day-to-day affairs, they spoke to prevailing gender norms. At times they upheld those ideals, presenting their lives as affirmations of them. At other times, and often inadvertently, they testified to the difficulty of achieving them. Taken together, their conversations point to distinct yet overlapping views of what roles women should play in society and how they should prioritize them.

These discussions took place at a time when expectations for women in the United States and the Soviet Union were expanding. The imperatives of military victory and then of postwar recovery pulled women in opposite directions. Intense, back-to-back campaigns urged them first to tackle "male" jobs and then to be devoted mothers and homemakers. This mixed messaging strengthened both personal aspirations and social pressures to "do it all."[12] So even though the Soviet Union and the United States were very different in terms of gender ideology, the letters capture key convergences in gender practice. So far, these convergences have largely gone unstudied: scholars rarely examine Soviet and American women's lives in the same analytical frame, and cold war assumptions that women in the United States and USSR embodied two opposing ways of life continue to hold sway.[13] The pen-pal project, however, provided an opportunity for the correspondents to compare their lives and connect their stories. Letter by letter, they discovered both what they had in common and how their circumstances diverged. They meditated on the joys of motherhood, the gratification of meaningful work, and the difficulty of allotting time to both. And, unlike the combative public discourse of the era, the pen friends did not make each other wrong at every turn. They acknowledged each other's struggles, validated each other's aspirations, and offered encouragement and advice—even when they disagreed.

The letters cut against emerging cold war stereotypes that Soviet women were so haggard and overworked that they had little time or energy for their children, or that American women were so absorbed in homemaking that they did not look far past their manicured lawns and local parent-teacher associations to make larger contributions to society. In fact, the vast majority of the American and Soviet correspondents understood "women's work" to mean some combination of the domestic and the professional.[14] Where they differed was in how they prioritized those realms and justified their life choices. The majority of Americans who corresponded between 1946 and 1949 heralded motherhood as their main, most rewarding vocation, and they embraced paid labor insofar as it was another way to serve their families. By contrast, Soviet participants during these years focused their remarks on personal fulfillment and insisted that women needed satisfying work to be happy and raise happy kids.

The pen pals explained their decisions in this way, but how much choice did they actually have? Without question, they were under considerable social, ideological, legal, and financial constraints with limited room to maneuver. They had heavy responsibilities, which pulled them toward the home or the job site. Yet, in their narratives, most participants downplayed external pressures and drew on their countries' values and gender norms to explain why they had taken a particular path. This is especially true early on in their correspondences, when they introduced themselves and their national way of life in quite idyllic terms. Over time, however, the pen friends admitted to frustrations and dreams deferred. It became clear that they did not always choose the roles or adopt the strategies that had become convention. In this way, their letters both idealized and undercut prevailing ideals of womanhood. They propagandized and they problematized. All told, their correspondence gives a complex, dialectical picture of the relationship between societal norms and individual actions. They underscore how difficult it was for Soviet and American women to navigate the challenges of the postwar moment, especially when they strove to "have it all."

These conversations presage major debates of the feminist movements that crystalized in the United States during the 1960s and 1970s and in the Soviet Union during the 1980s and 1990s. The letters affirm scholarly claims that the postwar 1940s were a critical juncture in the formation of these movements by setting the agenda that true equality for women meant personal liberty, not just equal rights, and the opportunity to "have both satisfying family lives and good jobs."[15] The pen pals did not identify as feminist activists—yet. The American participants were not part of the organized initiatives for equal pay, an Equal Rights Amendment, or a Women's Status Bill during the late 1940s.[16] The Soviet correspondents had no opportunity for such social protest, though some later appealed to the Soviet Women's Anti-Fascist Committee to advocate on their behalf. Still, at the time of their pen friendships, letter writers from both countries acknowledged policies and pressures that constricted them, and they tried to find workarounds. The act of corresponding heightened their awareness. The American writers grew more expressive about the obstacles they faced after they read about their pen pals' careers and childcare options. Soviet women had stronger legal status than women in any other country, but letter writers from the USSR wrestled with some unintended consequences of opportunity, such as the "supermom" ideal and the double burden. When their feminist movements later gathered steam, some Soviet women demanded the right to stay home with their children and cut back their hours on the job. By contrast, American women tended to focus their efforts on achieving equity in hiring, education, and pay.[17] In short, women in both countries wanted similar things, and their feminist movements moved in opposite directions toward obtaining them.

Pen friendship was one setting where the seeds of these later struggles germinated, where women looked across borders to imagine alternative choices and circumstances. They could see their own situation more clearly against the backdrop of another way of life. In this way, their letters raised the pen pals' consciousness about the politics that shaped their everyday routines and the systemic inequalities they faced. Such discoveries were at the core of the international feminist movements of the late twentieth century. At the same time, the pen pals also tended to defend their own circumstances as choices and to perpetuate the unrealistic expectations that beset Soviet and American women alike.

Let Me Introduce Myself

"My unknown American friend!" Ol'ga Mel'nikovskaia began her first letter, "I like America, and I would like to know more about this country and about American people. It seems to me that the American radio-broadcasts for the USSR—I always listen in—only prevent us from getting a correct impression about the United States and the American people. I shouldn't think the voice of the American people is really 'the Voice of America.' That is why I would like to hear from a real, 'live,' American who would tell me about the life of your people, what they really think and feel. And I also would like you to tell me about your own life, about what you do, your thoughts and aspirations."

By the time she sent this in 1948, hostilities between the United States and Soviet Union had sharply escalated. Between the Marshall Plan in the West and the communist takeover of seven countries in the east, Europe was deeply divided. The US and Soviet governments intensified their information war against each other. The same week Mel'nikovskaia penned her letter, Secretary of State George C. Marshall urged Voice of America—now under State Department control—to step up its attacks on responses to Soviet misinformation.[18] Meanwhile, the Kremlin began jamming Voice of America broadcasts to keep individuals like Mel'nikovskaia from tuning in. Likewise, the Foreign Policy Department of the Central Committee of the Communist Party (to which the Soviet Women's Anti-Fascist Committee reported) chastised news agencies for not being vigilant against "American reactionaries" and ordered them to strengthen their anti-western campaign and discredit the Voice of America.[19] Additional decrees soon followed, demanding anti-Americanism in plays, books, and even the circus.[20]

Although she stopped well short of acknowledging her own country's propaganda campaigns, Mel'nikovskaia declared that only by cutting through the noise and connecting on a personal basis could Soviets and Americans make peace. "I deeply believe in your nation. A nation, the ordinary people, cannot want war with its countless sufferings, bloodshed, privations, and hunger." Like most Soviet pen pals, Mel'nikovskaia insisted her compatriots knew "what war means" "much more so than Americans" because of how they "greatly suffered in this last war." However, she moved on from that point quickly. "No need to mention how awful it was for us," she remarked. Instead, she set about becoming acquainted with the "do[ings], thoughts, and aspirations" of a "real 'live' American."[21] It was through the personal and the everyday that international tensions could be eased.

Jean Jahr echoed Mel'nikovskaia's hopes that pen friendship could provide an alternative source of information and thus of understanding. "My dear friend Ol'ga! With deep comradely feelings I read your warm and friendly letter of October 15. I have long wanted to correspond with someone in the USSR. I am curious and want to learn more about your country, about your way of life, and the mutual relations of the Soviet government and Soviet citizenry. Here, we have gotten so many sensationalized messages about Russia—all repeating each other and almost completely slanderous—that I wanted to learn the other side of the matter from a Soviet citizen." The "average American," she explained, was being "flooded" with "'cold war'" propaganda designed "to force him to forget our alliance during the war." But Jahr was not the average American. "The circles with which I associate myself look at the peoples of the USSR with great respect because we know that, if it were not for your suffering and valiant struggle, we also would have had to endure the violence of the fascists on our soil."

Jahr was one of many left-leaning American letter writers who joined the pen-pal project in the late 1940s. Although many of the politically moderate and conservative women who joined right after World War II kept writing, around 1947 the pool expanded, mostly to the left. Although Jahr never revealed this to her pen pal, her husband Bert was in the Communist Party, and she was a progressive and a fellow traveler, according to her children, Joanne and Marc.[22] They remember "visitors" coming by for years, even after the Jahrs moved house, just to show Jean and Bert that the FBI knew where they lived. "Mother and Dad—especially Dad—were fairly certain that our phone was being tapped," Joanne remarked.[23] Jean Jahr likely began to develop a strong sense of social justice and progressive politics from her days at the Bronx House, and her views may have moved to the left after she fell in love with Bert, her children suggested. Bert, born Benjamin Norman Jahr, was from an Ashkenazi Slovak family with socialist leanings. In 1918, he and his mother emigrated from what was becoming Czechoslovakia to New York City, where he became an accomplished singer, actor, and artist.[24] During World War II, Bert Jahr worked for the USO's arts program and for the National Council of American-Soviet Friendship.[25] Jean Jahr was his unofficial, unpaid assistant for both positions. She no doubt heard about the letter exchange program from her husband's contacts at the National Council, and she also volunteered for Progressive Henry A. Wallace's presidential campaign in 1948.[26] In her letters, Jahr stressed her admiration for America's tradition of radicalism, citing Thomas Paine, Frederick Douglass, and John Brown, but also more conservative figures like Thomas Jefferson and Andrew Jackson. She described herself as a "true American patriot."[27]

Jahr let her husband be the star of her letters and introduced herself in modest and thoroughly domestic terms. "About me: my name is Jean Jahr, I am married, and I have two children: Joanne is five-and-a-half and Marc turns three this week. Bert, my husband, besides working for the cause of peace, is also an artist and a singer. He is even travelling to Chicago this month (a big city in the Midwest) to sing the part of Ostap in the opera 'Taras Bul'ba'," Jahr noted before turning to discuss the "tedious housework" that occupied her days. With her husband frequently away, she often shouldered all the parenting duties. By contrast, when Mel'nikovskaia first offered "a few words" about herself, she described her studies at Leningrad and Moscow State Universities and her archeological research.

In fact, all of the participants introduced themselves according to these patterns. The Americans began by describing their marital status, children, and living conditions in that order of priority, whereas their Soviet interlocutors stressed their educations and occupations. Some, like Mel'nikovskaia, did not mention family life until a second or third letter. Conversely, American letter writers often did not indicate their level of education until well into the correspondence.

Typically, we do not give much thought to how we introduce ourselves, especially when communicating in a formulaic mode like letter writing. We offer a few customary details about our lives. We gloss over complexities and fall back on convention. And this is precisely why introductions reveal so much about prevailing social and gender norms. The correspondents began to encounter such norms the moment they read each other's names. Americans like Jahr always used a title like Mrs. or Miss to indicate their marital status. Very often, they used their husbands' first names. "My dear friend Leonard!" Klavdiia Andreeva began her note to Mrs. Leonard Osborne, unaware of this custom. Equally confused, Serafima Antonova repeatedly called Mrs. Fred Nay "Fred" in her letter.[28] Americans in turn felt uneasy about the Soviets' patronymics and disregard of titles. "Dear Russian Friend!" wrote Dorothea M. Bush, "You did not write to me if you are married or not, so I do not know how to address you, Mrs. or Miss Mendeleeva." "I have been married," Serafima Mendeleeva replied, "but it makes no difference. Here we call all people 'comrade' be they married or not."[29]

Naming conventions were just the first indicators of how the letter writers situated themselves socially. After mentioning their husbands and children, most American participants then gave detailed descriptions of their homes, down to the square footage and "flowers and pink bulges" on the upholstery.[30] "Dear friend in Soviet Russia, Although we live on opposite sides of the world, we have many things in common," Mrs. Alfred I. Maile cheerfully pronounced at the start of her first letter. "I am a homemaker in a small city in Montana in the northwestern part of our big country. My husband is a telegraph operator for one of the large railroads that cross our country. His elderly mother lives with us. We have a small, comfortable home with every modern convenience such as a telephone, electric lights, and many electric appliances including a radio, vacuum cleaner, and electric washing machine. We have hot and cold water in our bathroom and kitchen and do our cooking on a gas stove. Our home is heated by a gas furnace. For recreation, we take drives out into the country in our new automobile." Maile delighted in making her home so comfortable. "Most of my early life was spent teaching young children in rural and city public schools. That was very interesting work, but I find more happiness and have a greater feeling of security as a housewife in our little home."[31]

Perhaps Maile and other American participants took such care to describe their homes at the start of their first letters so their pen pals could picture what their day-to-day lives were like. At the same time, these letters—mostly from middle-class white women like Maile—sent a clear message about American prosperity. The US economy boomed and its middle class doubled after World War II. Family incomes increased by 24 percent on average and so did buying power, despite a postwar spike in prices.[32] After suffering through the Great Depression, American letter writers took pride in having a high standard of living. Jean Jahr was an exception in that she did not take Ol'ga Mel'nikovskaia on a virtual tour of her home, yet even she referred to the affluence of her family and country in her very first letter. "In comparison to the rest of the world, we live very well. Our quality of life is rather high."[33] When she married Bert, Jahr "escaped the gravitational pull" of her working-class roots, her son Marc observed, and acquired a comfortable middle-class lifestyle.[34] Hers was a classic story of American upward mobility. In general, the pen pals' introductory remarks were the most formulaic parts of their letters as well as the most idealistic. Most participants worked to create a strong first impression of success, both personal and national.

Moreover, by putting their belongings and their families' comfort on display, the American participants underscored their patriotism and their effectiveness as homemakers.[35] Consumerism had long been associated with choice, freedom, democracy, and security in the United States.[36] Ideals of womanhood had been intensely commercialized since at least the turn of the century. And the post–World War II years ushered in new opportunities and pressures for women to consume. As their families grew, they needed more stuff and more living space.[37] American homeownership grew by a whopping 71 percent over the course of the 1940s, despite a persistent housing shortage.[38] The emerging Cold War raised the political stakes of these purchases. Advertisers, politicians, and even the director of the FBI called on housewives to stave off the threat of communism by creating stable, comfortable homes, which constantly reminded their occupants of capitalism's superiority. If a mother failed to provide "a hot meal ready to serve" or to be "fully dressed and ready to receive not only her own children but their friends," J. Edgar Hoover observed in *Woman's Home Companion*, she was essentially "driving them to [. . .] clandestine places, where there may be hospitality but decency is unknown."[39] Obviously, the Americans who requested Soviet pen pals were not the type to be easily convinced that a poorly provisioned home was a hotbed of communist thought. Nevertheless, by describing their homes in such detail, the participants sent their pen friends a strong message about their social status and national values. As they introduced themselves, they introduced the American Dream.

Given Soviet attitudes about excessive materialism under capitalism, correspondents from the USSR must have been jarred by these descriptions of electric appliances and colorful couches. But they did not comment on them, critically or complimentarily.[40] Nor did they describe their own living conditions, even when their interlocutors implored them to do so. For one thing, housing was not commercialized in the Soviet Union in the way it was in the United States, so it was not a benchmark of success to the same degree. More importantly, the war had plunged Soviet citizens into abject poverty. Cities and farms lay in ruins; a quarter of the country's physical assets had been obliterated; and at least twenty-five million people had no roof over their heads.[41] The human losses were even more astounding. Some twenty-seven million people perished, and much of the surviving population was emaciated, injured, or ill. This created an acute labor shortage which, when combined with brutal agricultural policies and drought conditions, unleashed a horrific famine in summer 1946. Between one and two million more lives were lost. Hunger devastated the countryside but also gripped cities, reaching the pen pals in Moscow. It did not abate even after rationing was lifted in December 1947.[42] Stalin kept the famine a secret, posturing to his western rivals about the Soviet Union's strength and war readiness. Likewise, the pen pals concealed the extent of their suffering—the opposite of what they did in the letters they sent during World War II.

But rather than adopt Stalin's aggressive stance, Soviet participants engaged in evasive maneuvers. "We have a small apartment," Ol'ga Mel'nikovskaia wrote to Jean Jahr, "two rooms, a kitchen, and bath." She did not explain that this was a communal apartment, where the kitchen and bathroom were shared by half a dozen households. "My room is small. I am very fond of it, it is cosy [*sic*] and agreeable to work in. "Cozy" was the descriptor of choice for many Soviet letter writers; it put a positive spin on the dearth of living space. The average Muscovite had 4.4 square meters of living space between 1946 and 1953.[43] By comparison, the average American family that owned or rented a home—as the vast majority of US letter writers did—occupied between ninety-one and one hundred square meters during those years.[44] Ol'ga Mel'nikovskaia was clearly trying to impress her new pen friend, for even "room" was an exaggeration. In a memoir she published after the USSR's collapse, Mel'nikovskaia revealed she did not have her own room but a seven-meter "nook, fenced off" from her parents' living space. Mel'nikovskaia was one of the few Soviet pen pals who enumerated her possessions, but they were a far cry from the labor-saving devices or mechanized comforts American volunteers highlighted. "In my room, I have bookshelves, my desk, my bed, dressing table, and several chairs," she told Jahr. In fact, this list included all the furniture her family owned. In her memoir, she explained that her partition contained "just a bed, a table, and a window."[45]

These exaggerations aside, Soviet participants did not convey their status or their values through ownership. They highlighted their education and occupation instead. Six weeks after Mrs. Alfred I. Maile dispatched that first note detailing the amenities of her home, she got this reply: "Dear Mrs. Maile, I was very pleased to have your letter. I in turn want to tell you a few words about myself. I am a scientific worker in one of the institutes of the Academy of Sciences of the Soviet Union. Not so very long ago I was just an ordinary 'factory-hand' in one of the Moscow factories. Wanting a university education, I went to a 'school for young workers' in the evening. After graduating, I went on to Moscow University [. . .] and earned a master's degree in chemistry. I am passionately keen on my work," she stressed. "Accept my most sincere wishes of happy and merry days in the coming New Year—1949. Your unknown friend, S. Bratskaia."[46] Bratskaia, like Mel'nikovskaia and most postwar Soviet letter writers, was ethnically Russian and a white-collar professional living in her country's most elite city. These women were proud beneficiaries of educational and labor policies that gave them "the opportunity to take an active part on equal terms with men in all branches of the public, industrial, and cultural life of our country," as another letter writer put it.[47] Charged with promoting socialism rather than the wartime alliance, the Soviets who joined the pen pal program after World War II were less forthcoming than their wartime counterparts about enduring inequality for women in the workplace, especially when introducing themselves and trying to create a positive first impression. Bratskaia stressed how she had gone from "ordinary factory-hand" to professional chemist; Mel'nikovskaia, the daughter of a radio technician, had become an archeologist and was busily working on her doctorate. They wove the Soviet Dream of upward mobility into their correspondence from the very start. Others flagged their humble beginnings by referring to themselves as "a daughter of a factory worker" or "a daughter of a farmer." These were the first, and sometimes only, gestures toward family in their inaugural letters. They were also clear references to social class and a way to show their humble or proletarian roots. Of course, stories about social mobility were integral to American national mythology too. And roughly half of the American letter writers had some post-secondary education, which they could have mentioned.[48] But they did not reach for this fact in their first letters. They emphasized other markers of status like marriage and home ownership instead.

Soviet women mentioned work before family not just because they were ideologically committed to labor or personally enamored with their jobs. Family was a painful subject, and the Soviet letter writers seemed reticent to discuss it. Ol'ga Mel'nikovskaia had been trapped in besieged Leningrad during the war, and she held the details of that ordeal in reserve until she and Jahr had become better acquainted. "In my first letter, I told you very little about my life," she acknowledged after several months, "I was married and very happy." She met Vladimir Alymov at Leningrad State University. "We got married when we were both eighteen, and a year later war began, and we had to part. He was on active service at the front, and I volunteered for the civilian militia and remained behind to defend Leningrad," the city "which had given us so much happiness." She also worked as a medical assistant until she became too weak from hunger and consumption to continue on.[49]

World War II was replete with tragedies, but the Leningrad blockade was one of the most horrific. For nearly 900 days, Finnish and German troops cut the city off from the rest of the Soviet Union, bombing and starving the civilians trapped inside. About one million died. Hundreds of thousands more perished at the Leningrad front. Mel'nikovskaia did not know these staggering figures; Soviet officials concealed the full death toll, even when presenting the siege as a war crime at Nuremberg.[50] Jahr could not have known that more people died in the battle for Leningrad than the total number of Americans who died in all wars combined between 1776 and 1975.[51] Still, the New Yorker got a glimpse inside the moribund city from her pen pal. "Helping to clear away the rubble and bearing away [*sic*] dead and wounded, for the first time I saw the real face of war clearly. I will always see this tiny tot with his little swollen tummy bare, his mouth full of dirt, and his awful staring eyes," Mel'nikovskaia recalled. By a major stroke of luck, Mel'nikovskaia and Alymov managed to survive and were separately evacuated to the same hospital in the city of Saratov. "Half dead from hunger, I nursed him, never leaving his side." In 1942, he returned to active duty. "He fought all the way from Stalingrad to Belorussia and was killed in action in spring 1943."[52]

That was one version of events, the one she shared with Jahr. A different, equally tragic version appeared later in Mel'nikovskaia's memoir. She and Vladimir Alymov—engaged, not yet married—were separately evacuated to Saratov and reunited there. When she found him there, she discovered Alymov was different, mentally shattered. Mel'nikovskaia chalked this up to his physical injuries and waited patiently. But each time she brought up marriage, he put her off. After the couple relocated to Moscow, he ended things. "Only now in my old age do I understand," Mel'nikovskaia reflected. "I was humiliated, I cried. I could not believe that he had fallen out of love with me, that, psychologically, the nerves of a soldier change after the front (as is the case now with those fighting in Afghanistan and Chechnya). Then, fool that I was, I insisted on explanations and tried to justify everything by the nature of his rather severe thigh wound, that he had no time for a woman, no time for loving emotions." She had survived the Leningrad blockade and been given a second chance to pursue her "dreams of love only to have them crushed after the war." Mel'nikovskaia was certain she would never love again, never have a family. She repeatedly contemplated ending it all. "I kept a razor blade under my pillow."[53] Did her parents, sleeping several feet away, know that she—who had already come so close to perishing—still teetered on the brink of death? The story she told Jahr, of her marriage, her husband's heroic return to the front, and his death during battle, was what she must have wished had happened. To be a widow would make her less alone, make her part of a community of millions who loved and lost through heroic sacrifice, not the stigmatized shame of post-traumatic stress disorder.

Back at home with her parents, Mel'nikovskaia threw herself into archeological work. And this is where the details of her memoir sync up with what she told Jahr, although she concealed its darker edges from her pen friend. At age twenty-seven, she felt she had lost her love and her independence in one fell swoop. "The world of my parents seemed, after all I had been through, uninteresting and narrow." In addition, the trauma of acute starvation continued to take a toll. Mel'nikovskaia recalled in her memoir, but not in her letters, how she ate obsessively, whether or not she felt hungry, and how her parents—wracked with guilt—insisted that she eat their portions too.[54]

But Mel'nikovskaia found salvation in her archeological work and in her supportive colleagues. She explained this to Jahr, wrapping her remarks in sorrow and in national pride. "I am very happy, Jean, to be living in the Soviet Union. I can't imagine how I would have been able to bear all I've had to bear if I had lived in any other country. Here, we are never left by our lone [*sic*] self. [. . .] We have a very united collective at our lab. We all help each other."[55] For Mel'nikovskaia, such collectivism was a coping mechanism as well as a socialist principle. She was a dutiful student of Marxism-Leninism and her patriotism surged during wartime.[56] Even though she concealed from her pen pal much about the specific nature of her suffering, Mel'nikovskaia showed Jean Jahr some of her scars: grief, loneliness, and a loss of independence. This later letter, in which she recounted the war years, gave Jahr critical context for understanding Mel'nikovskaia's initial declaration that she "could not imagine life without work." That ideologically inflected remark had profound personal meaning too.

In sum, these introductions provide a glimpse into prevailing social and gender norms as well as show how the letter writers envisioned their roles and responsibilities during the late 1940s. Material conditions made a big impact on those perceptions. In light of their privileged circumstances and the strong state of the US economy at mid-century, it is no wonder that the American participants framed their lives in terms of affluence. Given the utter devastation of the USSR and its people, it is understandable that Soviet letter writers situated their lives around the professional, not the domestic or material. Yet, as their conversations continued, a more complicated picture emerged of the personal, practical, and cultural considerations behind why the pen pals structured their days the way they did. After introducing themselves, they began to recount their daily routines—which Mel'nikovskaia did right down to the "coffee, bread, and butter" she had for breakfast—and to share their aspirations for a fulfilling life.[57]

The Idea of "Having It All"

"To my friend whom I have never seen, May I call you just Nina? I am sure that I will not be able to correctly pronounce your surname." So Mrs. Oscar King began her first letter to Nina Rozdevich. King was eager to get acquainted and share the details of her life in Kent, Ohio, with her new Moscow friend. Like many American participants, King joined the pen-pal program through the Women's Society of Christian Service. She explained she was devoted to "peace and harmony" between "all the different peoples of the world" and read widely about world affairs. And she was a critical reader. Not trusting the translation from the anti-fascist committee, King took Rodzevich's letters to a Russian-speaking member of her congregation to confirm their accuracy. King's routine was a busy one, filled with church work and helping her four daughters and seventeen grandchildren. "We mothers think first and foremost about the wellbeing of our children," she wrote in this first letter to Rodzevich, underscoring her priorities. In reply, Nina Rodzevich underscored hers. "I am not just a mother, I am a woman-engineer," Rodzevich wrote, "I worked a lot during the war" and now "I want to work even more in order to hasten the restoration of normal life, to work for the happiness and good of our people."[58]

After introducing themselves in this typical way, King emphasizing motherhood and Rodzevich work, the pair wrote on and soon discovered that their aspirations were not as far apart as they first seemed. "Thanks for your great letter, it is very good to learn about the work of women in other countries," King replied. "In my youth I also dreamed about receiving a good education and I wanted to become a teacher, but my mother died when I was very young and, when the last of my three sisters got married, I was seventeen years old." Because she was not yet married and keeping house for a husband, "I had to do the housework for my father, and that ended my studies." King was determined that her own daughters would not have to make similar sacrifices. "All four of my daughters studied in college and received some of the advantages that I did not manage to have, and now my granddaughter is in college."[59] It is unclear if King's daughters pursued careers, especially considering they had seventeen children between them, but King clearly wanted them to develop their minds and expand their knowledge even if they did not apply them to a specific occupation. King's devotion to motherhood, which she had declared in her first letter to her pen pal, came across in how she supported her daughters—as educated individuals and as mothers.

In reply, Nina Rodzevich began by heartily congratulating King on the birth of her latest grandchild and affirming her pen friend's emphasis on motherhood. For Rodzevich, the greatest fulfillment came from nurturing one's career and one's children in equal measure. "At present I am again hard at work, but my work affords me great moral satisfaction. For work well done I often get premiums over and above my ordinary wages. Having both work I love and a happy family makes my life a very full one, and I begin to understand and appreciate better and better the beauty of life." It was only in this, her third letter, that Rodzevich opened up to King about her family, echoing that helping one's children develop their intellect and interests was one of the most gratifying aspects of motherhood. Rodzevich was delighted, for instance, that her twelve-year-old son was following in her engineering footsteps. He loved to build model planes and gliders and even won a prize for one at a children's exhibition, she boasted. Her fourteen-year-old daughter was "clever," "a good student," and dreamed of becoming a film director.[60] Charmed by this description of the Rodzevich household, King exclaimed: "What a wonderful world God has given us. If only people of different nations tried more to understand each other and to believe each other and to live by the 'golden rule': 'treat someone else as you would want to be treated,' how happy life on earth would be! We here in the USA, like you, are passionately interested in the success of our children." From there, the pen friends began comparing the school systems in the United States and USSR, their Soviet translator struggling a bit with the different grade structures and stumbling over terms like "4-H."[61]

King and Rodzevich were from different generations and cultures; their circumstances led them down divergent paths. Yet, over the course of half a dozen letters, they found common ground and agreed that fulfillment came from some combination of motherhood, education, and professional work. The vast majority of letter writers voiced similar views. Out of the 319 pairs of women corresponding during the late 1940s, only three Americans presented themselves as devoted mothers with no interest in paid work. Two of those three were newlyweds, like Marjorie Crouse of Boone, Iowa. "My life is full and brimming over. I enjoy keeping house and I could spend all of my time in the kitchen trying out recipes," she exclaimed.[62] But Crouse was in the minority. Most of the American participants voiced a strong interest in work outside the home, sometimes tinged with regret or embarrassment that they did not have careers like their pen friends. The level of support that American letter writers expressed for paid work was markedly higher than the rate indicated by public opinion polls in the United States, which may reflect the particularity of the letter-writing pool or the possibility that their Soviet pen friends provided some measure of inspiration.[63]

Reciprocally, over ninety percent of the Soviet participants did jobs outside the home, yet all but two Soviet participants declared that they treasured being a mother or that they wanted children of their own. This is notable considering that more than half of them did not have husbands.

King and Rodzevich felt a dual pull towards career and motherhood long before World War II. The war amplified that feeling for many pen pals. Even women who did not take on war-industry jobs, as was the case with many American correspondents, were presented with new possibilities for working outside the home, which their governments urged them to accept. Dorothy McDade and Pava Grinval'd were one of many pairs to compare how wartime opportunities and pressures impacted their work.

While King and Rodzevich had taken distinct paths, McDade and Grinval'd marveled at all the parallels in their lives. They both came from poor families. They hustled and grinded. They started off as domestic servants, moved into the textile industry, became representatives in their local trade unions, and found white-collar professions during the war. For McDade, as for millions of working-class women and people of color, the enduring American ideal of the male breadwinner and female homemaker was a practical impossibility. A native Chicagoan, McDade came of age during the Depression. "In the years before the war I had many kinds of jobs. Work was not easy to find, and often a job did not last long. I worked in a laundry, a clothing factory, once worked as a chambermaid [. . .] I eventually ended up as a stenographer."[64] McDade struggled with job insecurity, low wages, and discrimination, which confined her to the "pink collar ghetto" of feminized industries.[65] Despite such obstacles, the number of American women in the workforce steadily increased to 26 percent by 1940.[66] Stable employment and reliable income were the motivations driving McDade, by her own telling.

Grinval'd connected to McDade's story but assigned different meaning to a similar set of experiences. "I, just like you, began my working life as a maid, and thanks to my character—not being a fan of submission, slavery, and constant dependence—I went to work at a sewing factory. It was only after joining in this work that I understood clearly how noble, interesting, and good it is to be a free and organized citizen," she declared, evoking the Soviet notion that women must be freed from domestic labor to do "socially useful" work and cultivate their proletarian consciousness.[67] Grinval'd joined the factory trade union committee and, though she did not have children herself, she used that position to demand that plant managers provide childcare for their women workers. Soviet leaders had promised to socialize housework, but cafeterias and daycares were always in short supply, forcing many female employees to scramble.

Grinval'd's attention to childcare reflected a larger development in Soviet ideology during the mid-1930s, which placed a premium on motherhood, even for working women. With the threat of war looming and the goal of raising birthrates in mind, ideologues and policymakers began to herald motherhood as women's natural calling, laying the groundwork for Soviet maternalism. At the same time, they continued to champion women who did "productive" labor outside the home and recruit them throughout the second Five Year Plan of 1933–1937. The number of women in the Soviet workforce steadily climbed to roughly 40 percent.[68] This divergent messaging, which called women to both the factory and to the nursery, was enshrined into law. The year 1936 saw the promulgation of both the new Soviet constitution, which guaranteed equal rights, pay, and education for women, as well as the "Law of Happy Motherhood," which banned abortion, restricted divorce, and paid mothers for having large families.[69] Thus, on the eve of World War II, Soviet letter writers like Grinval'd were immersed in both revolutionary and traditional ideals of womanhood.

Soviet and American gender ideals did not change dramatically when the war began, but gender *practices* were stretched to meet new demands for women's labor in the USSR and the United States.[70] The aspiration to "have it all" melded with new pressure to "do it all." And women in both countries answered the call. By 1945, American women comprised 36 percent of the labor force in their country and Soviet women 55 percent in theirs.[71] The biggest change, however, was not the sheer number of women workers but their shift into "male" jobs that were better paid and—according to McDade and Grinval'd—more gratifying.[72] "When my husband went into the army," McDade explained, "I went to work in a war plant" where she helped "hot metal be poured into forms and turned into planes to be used against the enemies of our country. It made me feel that I was doing my part in the long and terrible war." She seemed almost sorry to leave the shopfloor when the Congress of Industrial Organizations (CIO)—the "most progressive union in the world"—tapped her as a union instructor. Five thousand miles away, Grinval'd also found fulfillment by tackling a "male" profession: medicine. Thousands of women entered Soviet medical schools during World War II to meet an urgent demand for doctors. They comprised 41 percent of frontline doctors and 43 percent of surgeons. These figures reached 70 percent by the 1960s.[73] So continued Grinval'd's journey toward self-actualization, made possible, she claimed, by Soviet policies regarding equal opportunity and education. "Only in our country, where infinite attention and care is given to improving a person's life, lifestyle, and cultural development, can one easily turn from a dark, domestic worker into a cultured person in any specialty."[74] Meaningful work had taken her out of the darkness and into to the light.

The fact that both Soviet and American discourse continued to identify these new roles as "male" underscores how gender hierarchies endured even as practices shifted. Indeed, while McDade and Grinval'd tackled their new positions, state-backed campaigns painted them as dedicated wives, mothers, and daughters temporarily taking the place of their husbands, sons, and fathers out of devotion to family and to nation.[75] Advertisements in the United States, created with direction from President Roosevelt's War Advertising Council, reassured the public that women workers were eager to return to domestic bliss once the war ended. A 1944 Briggs Home Appliance ad, for instance, featured a woman in coveralls fantasizing about her dream kitchen—the reward for her labors. A Thermos advertisement from the same year pictured a grease-spotted woman pouring coffee for male coworkers and dreaming about the day when she could put on a dress and serve coffee to her husband and friends in her tidy living room. "This is what I am working for," she says, "the carefree home parties we used to have."[76] In actuality, the Women's Bureau in the US Department of Labor found that three out of four women workers they surveyed during the last year of the war planned to stay in the workforce once hostilities ceased. Fifty-seven percent were married women.[77] The Soviet press similarly took care to stress that women who entered male domains in industry or the military were still mothers at their core. "In the Red Army," one March 1945 pamphlet echoed, "women very energetically showed themselves as pilots, snipers, submachine gunners [. . .] but they don't forget about their primary duty to nation and state, that of motherhood."[78] During World War II, a "woman's place" was not just at home but everywhere.[79]

In many ways, these dual demands on women only intensified in the years after the war when Grinval'd and McDade began corresponding. Female workers were needed by both the United States' booming economy and the Soviet Union's devastated one. In addition, the need for "womanpower" was fed by emerging cold war hostilities and growing demands that all human and natural resources be leveraged for the sake of national strength.[80] Women in the United States and Soviet Union generally stayed in the workforce but were relegated to "female" jobs as discriminatory hiring returned with force. Some Americans briefly left but returned due to the high cost of living.[81] Although the number of Soviet women workers outnumbered men by 12.8 million, new protective labor laws in the USSR recategorized certain jobs as "male" and "female."[82] In the United States, wage gaps, marriage bars, and social pressures combined to reestablish prewar patterns of gendered employment by 1947.[83] "The activities of women in this country are very limited," Jean Brand explained to her pen pal. "In general, women are either housekeepers or, if they work for wages, they do unskilled factory or routine office work such as typing or filing. [. . .] During the war, women were given opportunities to do more skilled and interesting work—not equal opportunities with men, but still it was a great advance. Now that the war is over, most women are fired and wherever they go, they are refused jobs that use their newly acquired skills." Brand was a marine engineer. She designed power plants for cutters and aircraft carriers, but now she had to look for work in more feminized sectors of the economy.[84]

Though needed in the workforce, Soviet and American women were also summoned home to raise children and comfort husbands returning from the front.[85] They were charged with mending the war-torn fabric of society, worsened by the spiking divorce rate in the United States and severe social displacement and gender disparities in the Soviet Union. There, women outnumbered men one hundred to twenty-eight on average.[86] Millions of Soviet women were widowed or single and unable to find husbands. But married or not, the state pressed them to repopulate the USSR. A new family law code, the most conservative one in the country's history, reaffirmed the ban on abortion, made divorce difficult, and taxed childless adults. It expanded maternity leave and financial benefits for mothers, giving state honors to those with seven or more kids. The code also enshrined childrearing as a woman's duty by shielding men from paying child support for children out of wedlock. Unmarried mothers were even forbidden from giving their children the surname of their biological fathers.[87]

McDade's and Grinval'd's letters reflect this postwar moment and its messaging. McDade was working as a CIO instructor, but she said almost nothing about that to Grinval'd. Instead, she wrote excitedly about how she could quit her job now that her husband had been demobilized. The couple moved to Durham, so he could attend the University of North Carolina. Just as Grinval'd praised free Soviet education, McDade heralded the GI Bill for paying "his tuition and our living expenses." So ended her decades of hustling and scraping by.[88] "At the present time I am not working. We are expecting a child. We are very happy that the war is over, and we can begin building our family." Like Grinval'd, she presented her life as a journey towards fulfillment, but one that culminated in matrimony and motherhood. Her Soviet pen pal, by contrast, had no husband or child of her own, but she found another maternal outlet. Grinval'd became a pediatrician, so that she could help "to raise future healthy, vital, and brave generations, who will continue to build and create an even happier life. Every day of my life is (now consciously) full of striving to give my country, my people as much as I can and, if my labor and efforts do not fail, then I will receive enormous satisfaction from that."[89]

So, despite their countries' distinct gender ideologies, despite their starkly different material circumstances, Soviet and American women experienced expanding opportunities and pressures to be mothers and paid workers, to "do it all."[90] McDade's and Grinval'd's letters testify to this. They also demonstrate how differently Soviet and American pen pals assigned meaning to their experiences. No doubt, a host of reasons drove them to paid employment, including poverty, but they overwhelmingly justified their actions using the same societally acceptable explanations that Grinval'd and McDade evoked. The Soviet participants stressed individual purpose and community service, whereas the Americans emphasized familial devotion. "My work isn't just a means of earning my living, but the first, essential [part] of life," chemist and war widow Ekaterina Slavianskaia proclaimed. "I just can't imagine life without work, without using my knowledge, my experience, and my skills for my work every day. Even if my share is small, it still is a part of the big common labor, and this makes it joyful, inspired, and I would like to go on forever living and to work on and on."[91] This exalted view of work cropped up in so many Soviet letters. And while there is no reason to doubt the sincerity of these testimonies, it is important to note how curated they were. Slavianskaia was a chemist; Grinval'd a doctor; Mel'nikovskaia an archeologist. They were not doing backbreaking labor; they had professions, not just jobs. Indeed, the antifascist committee likely recruited them as pen pals because they exemplified

Soviet socialism's promise to lift up the disadvantaged and help them realize their potential through work.

These Soviet paeans to labor were clearly inflected with ideology. So, too, were American letter writers' assertions that paid work was their way of putting family first.[92] "Dear Friend, I am a mother, housewife, and assistant to my dentist husband," Clementine Jordan Goulart of New Bedford, Massachusetts, began by way of introduction. "Currently I work very diligently," she added. While her kids were young, she had stayed at home, but she returned to the office now that "my two children study at college, which means that we have big expenses."[93] Other American letter writers also worked before starting families, so that their children would be in good stead. "We have big plans to have a home and a family but have not yet realized either dream," Maxine Cryder wrote from Boone, Iowa.[94] An active member of the United Methodist Church and supporter of the American Legion, Cryder was working as a school bookkeeper while she waited for her husband, a sergeant on the North African front, to return and take over as breadwinner.[95] She presented her job as a form of homemaking. "One reason I am working is to get money to help furnish our new home. Prices are still too high when it comes to buying things for our home." They shot up 8 percent on average in 1946 and 14 percent in 1947.[96] Still, Cryder was making headway in equipping her dream house. "So far we have purchased an electric refrigerator, bottled gas stove (for cooking), electric vacuum sweeper, and electric food mixer."[97] It was her devotion as a wife and future mother that drove her to work outside the home. This rationale was widely supported in books, magazines, and films, which honored the mother who tried to earn more for her children but vilified the careerwoman as narcissistic and emasculating.[98] American letter writers did not frame their work in terms of ambition or empowerment, just as Soviet participants neglected to mention they had to work out of financial necessity. Both sides wrote themselves into national narratives and validated national values and gender expectations, even those that constricted them.

In sum, many "Rosies" lost their wartime positions but not their sense of what was possible. "The baby boom at war's end was real enough," historian Dorothy Sue Cobble explained, "but so too was another phenomenon: the rise of the Working Wife and Mother." American women after World War II were having more children and spending more time in paid jobs."[99] This shared expectation provided another basis for connection between pen friends. And the letter writers themselves seemed to feed those expectations by encouraging each other to "do it all"—or at least to do more.

Ways to "Do it All"

The letters capture these heightened expectations, but they also document the difficulty of juggling motherhood, homemaking, and paid employment. The pen pals traded ideas about how to prioritize and strategize those multiple callings. The opportunity to discuss this balancing act was one reason many joined the pen-pal program in the first place. When trying to recruit American correspondents, the Committee of Women of the National Council of American-Soviet Friendship surveyed clubs and church groups, asking: "what do American women want to know about the Soviet Union?" The most popular topics were: "employment (outside the home) of mothers with young children. Working hours for mothers in peacetime. Solutions to housework problems for working mothers." "Do Soviet women feel any conflict between their family life and their work?" Americans asked.[100] After the committee dispatched the survey results to the anti-fascist committee, it heard back that those concerns were mutual.[101] When Jessica Smith, a Communist activist and member of the National Council of American-Soviet Friendship, traveled to Moscow in 1946 to deliver this "long list of questions [. . .] about women, children, and family life in the Soviet Union, Muscovites replied: 'why these things are just the things we want to know about you—can you get together similar material for us?'"[102]

Both the pen pals and the women's committees recommended solutions that they knew, that aligned with their national norms, and that they had been socialized to adopt since at least the 1920s. The American participants favored two strategies: they opted for paid work only before or after raising their small children, and they streamlined housekeeping through smart consumption. The United States Information Agency, a propaganda organ that promoted America's image overseas, also stressed that these two strategies would allow American mothers to work without neglecting homemaking—"still the goal of most American girls," one of its pamphlets insisted.[103] By contrast, the Soviet correspondents touted a different solution: state-subsidized or free daycares, cafeterias, and kindergartens. Yet, letters from both countries reveal major problems with the advice their authors doled out. Some participants acknowledged those issues explicitly; others made this point through their behavior, acting in ways that ran counter to social norms.

Many American letter writers tried to "do it all" in phases by timing their years of paid employment around their childbearing ones. This would ensure they were home and present when their children were little. Dorothy McDade and Maxine Cryder worked before starting families, while Clementine Goulart went back to work as her children were completing high school. "Since my son grew up and moved out, I have not had enough to do at home," Zoe Perkins told Dr. Klavdiia Soloshenko, so Perkins decided to return to her job as a dressmaker, which she had before marrying. Back then "I never was actually able to do all that a seamstress does, and now I am going to a part-time school to learn the mastery of dressmaking as a profession."[104] And Soloshenko applauded her decision: "This is very good! I think all women ought to know how to sew"—a reaction that embraced both professional and domestic aspects of femininity.[105]

Soviet participants cheered when their American pen pals returned to work outside the home, and they pled with them to reconsider when the Americans quit jobs or college to become full-time homemakers. When Patsy Pfeiffer of Provincetown, Massachusetts, matter-of-factly explained she had to drop out because she and her fiancé could not afford both his college tuition and hers, her pen pal Tamara Borodavkina, a medical student, seemed genuinely distressed at what she assumed was an act of self-sacrifice.[106] "I am so sorry you could not go on with your education and go to a teacher's college, that it is so hard for you to do as you wish. But don't lose hope."[107] Likewise, when Jeanne A. Woolf decided to quit her part-time job as a reporter so she could help her husband and care for their two sons, Ekaterina Andreeva urged her to reconsider: "Dear Jeanne, please don't give up your work in the newspaper. I am sure your articles must be good, judging by your letters. Couldn't you let me have some of them? Couldn't you manage to do both: help your husband and go on with your own work?" Though pushing her pen pal to change course, Andreeva's tone was encouraging rather than judgmental. She ultimately helped convince Woolf to keep her job, reinforcing the expectation that women "do it all."[108]

By contrast, American correspondents did not urge their pen friends to quit their jobs and become housewives, but they may have increased the pressure on Soviet women to "have it all" by emphasizing what women in the USSR did not have: labor-saving appliances. Indeed, the second solution that letter writers from the United States emphasized was to manage the time crunch between housekeeping, parenting, and paid labor with the help of the right equipment. "Technology has come to the relief of many working mothers," Gladys Brown told A. Fedosova, "in America many married women have work outside the home. Some of them have housekeepers, others get by without it because they have many electronic appliances: vacuums, washing machines, refrigerators, electric irons, etc."[109] This was the same consumer-based approach to homemaking that many American letter writers heralded when they first introduced themselves to their pen pals.

Echoing the American correspondents whom they oversaw, the Committee of Women argued that women could "do it all" if they had the right gear. This was the gist of several exhibits that the committee dispatched to Moscow. The first exhibit, sent in 1944, was of a model nursery outfitted with "everything from a crib to a perambulator."[110] The committee's officers, several of whom resided in posh areas of New York City, presented the items as "moderately priced" and "representative of what is within the reach of average American families."[111] But the baby clothes they displayed, for instance, cost up to thirty-five dollars (roughly equivalent to $516 today) and were prohibitively expensive for many Americans, let alone Soviets. Muriel Draper and the other women at the committee's helm insisted that they assembled this model nursery in good faith, not as a show of American affluence. Still, they took it for granted that Americans were superior homemakers and mothers. "Soviet women are eager to learn everything possible about American methods of childcare, housekeeping, and other matters of special concern to women," the committee declared in one pamphlet. "Such information will have special value in connection with the immense problem of the reconstruction of devastated areas" of the USSR after World War II. Despite this note of recognition, the nursery showed tremendous ignorance about what was possible for ordinary women given the state of the Soviet economy. It was a showpiece, displayed at McCreery's department store on Fifth Avenue before traveling to the Mother and Child Institute in Moscow.[112]

The Committee of Women sent two other exhibits in 1945 and 1946 that further tied good mothering to shrewd consumerism. The first was a display of books on childrearing and the second of women's clothing.[113] In 1946, the Committee of Women launched an even more ambitious plan to send "a complete model kitchen." Also intended for a "family of moderate income," the kitchen became more lavishly stocked over time, at considerable cost to the committee.[114] However, when it learned, "with great distress," that the anti-fascist committee never received its earlier shipments of clothes and books, the Committee of Women decided not to send the kitchen.[115] Did the Soviet government confiscate those earlier shipments, or was the cargo lost amid wartime chaos? It is unclear. Even so, messages about superior American technology and consumer choice still reached Soviet letter writers through their pen pals. The Committee of Women has often been dismissed as a "communist front," but its advice for Soviet women in the mid-1940s came straight out of a capitalist playbook.

The American letter writers, however, proved more ambivalent about this consumerist solution. Even as they recounted the appliances they owned or hoped to buy, some American participants admitted over time that the right equipment did not remove the burden of housework. Iowan Maxine Cryder, as I mentioned, had been steadily accumulating appliances to help with cooking, cleaning, and laundry, but she constantly felt the nag of unfinished chores when she was working as a bookkeeper or writing to her pen pal. "Here I sit writing letters," Cryder declared in her third note to Natal'ia Popova, "with my house in real need of cleaning. Also, I have a large basket of clothes to be mended." Cryder set aside Saturdays for housework, but it often spilled over into the work week. She suggested to Popova that they share recipes as a timesaver.[116] But Popova did not reciprocate. She shared neither her recipes nor her thoughts about housekeeping. This was quite typical. American correspondents frequently brought up housework as a central part of their days: those who worked outside the home reproached themselves for having little energy left for adequate housekeeping, whereas those who were housewives felt overwhelmed by the constancy and quantity of their chores. "I often think about how you manage to cope with housework and laundry when you also work," a letter writer from Kansas admitted to her pen pal, "I got so tired that I fell ill."[117]

This feeling of being overwhelmed reflects what some scholars have characterized as a mid-century American obsession with cleanliness, a phenomenon fed by conservative gender norms and by intertwined fears about dirt, illness, and national security. Home economists and advertisers bombarded American women with the message that devoted mothers safeguarded the nation by keeping immaculate homes. Filth was a sign of maternal carelessness and patriotic indifference.[118] "Good housekeeping," one US Federal Civil Defense Administration official declared, "was one of the best protections against an atomic blast."[119] After World War II, American women spent significantly more time, fifty-two hours a week, on housework. Women who worked outside of the home condensed this to roughly twenty-six hours a week. But their husbands spent just 1.6 hours on domestic tasks.[120] And those coveted appliances? They made matters worse by discouraging husbands from helping their wives at all.[121]

Even though their American pen friends repeatedly invited them to talk about housekeeping, all but two Soviet participants avoided the subject. And the two who mentioned their chores—both "heroine mothers" of seven children—did so without the sense of guilt that so often permeated letters from the United States.[122] In truth, all Soviet letter writers were just as swamped with housework. No pen pal from either country ever mentioned a husband lending a helping hand. Perhaps they dodged conversations about housekeeping because of longstanding views of it as unproductive "drudgery" in Soviet society.[123] Or perhaps they avoided the subject because to talk about their domestic tasks would reveal their low standard of living. Even the well-educated Moscow professionals who joined the pen-pal program frequently lacked electricity or hot running water; they had to queue and navigate the ration system for basic necessities; they prepared meals on crude stoves in crowded communal kitchens. When it came to laundry, they took turns scrubbing clothes by hand in the wee hours of the night—the only time when communal kitchens were empty. "We'd sit tired, dozing, and wait for everyone to go to sleep and then we'd begin to wash," one Muscovite recalled about the late 1940s.[124] Or perhaps Soviet pen pals did not respond to comments about housework because they did not conflate good housekeeping with good mothering. Soviet public discourse put less pressure on women to keep immaculate homes. Articles in *Woman Worker*, the most widely read Soviet women's magazine, noted that the apartments of exemplary female workers "were not always tidy."[125] In truth, letters from both countries suggest that the authors were often overwhelmed and overworked, but rather than encourage each other to reset expectations, the pen friends focused on ways to get more done, reinforcing the idea that "doing it all" was achievable and advisable.

Another solution the pen pals discussed was childcare. None of the American participants voiced objections to working mothers sending their children to daycare on principle, despite prevailing norms against it. Indeed, when the US government provided some subsidies for public childcare during World War II under the Lanham Act, many women chose not to use them. Assumptions that only poor women used such facilities and that they provided inadequate care remained widespread. However, there is also evidence that public perceptions toward childcare began to warm at the war's end, the moment when it was being phased out.[126] The US government rescinded the Lanham Act in 1946 on the grounds that it was a temporary emergency measure and not—as one school official scoffed—"a convenience for women who want to make a little extra money."[127] "There are only a few nursery schools run by public agencies for working mothers," Rose Freedman, a mother from Bogota, New Jersey, explained to her pen pal in June 1946, "and with the end of the war, even some of these have been disbanded. Most married women in this country are forced to give up their work when they start raising a family." In response, Freedman decided to establish her own nursery school, so she and her clients could be mothers and earn a living simultaneously. "We rented a large house with a half-acre of ground. We moved into the house (occupying the second story) and turned the downstairs into a school. As for myself, I find the work more and more interesting and, while it keeps me very busy, I do feel a great deal of personal satisfaction in being able to do something useful."[128] This was one of the only times a correspondent from the United States praised her paid work as deeply meaningful but, like most American letter writers, she made maternal devotion her main goal. Her business was to care for children, including her own daughter who attended the school.

Rose Freedman's initiative in creating her own childcare solution was admirable. Yet one could imagine other American letter writers viewing her facility as just another expensive private nursery school. While the American correspondents clearly identified the cost of daycare as an obstacle, they stopped short of arguing for permanent, government-subsidized childcare for all children in the United States. Still, a few curiously asked about this system in the Soviet Union. So did the Committee of Women. The committee's leaders resided further to the political left than most of the letter writers they oversaw, and they included radical feminists, progressives, and socialists. Many of them, like chairperson Muriel Draper, had been drawn to Soviet ideals since the Bolshevik Revolution, which offered an exciting new vision of women's legal and social equality. Draper traveled to the Soviet Union several times in the interwar period. She was one of many "American girls in Red Russia," as one journalist put it, who wanted to see the socialist experiment at work. And this fascination did not dissipate under the pressure of the Cold War. The Committee of Women and the pen-pal project are testaments to that.[129] So, at the same time that the Committee of Women mounted exhibitions showcasing what Soviet women should purchase to make their lives easier, it asked the Soviet Women's Anti-Fascist Committee to prepare an exhibition about the USSR's welfare programs for employed mothers.[130] That exhibit arrived in New York in June 1945.[131]

Entitled "Mother and Child Care in the Soviet Union," the exhibition was structured around the lifecycle of a Soviet child to show that, from conception through adolescence, his development was nurtured by state institutions such as medical clinics and summer camps. Photographs vividly drove that point home. One pictured an expectant mother gushing over the tiny baby clothes she purchased through government subsidies. Another showed a decorated "heroine mother" of seven children helping her latest take his first steps while a nurse looks on attentively.[132] Out of the exhibit's thirty-four photographs, only two featured fathers. The glowing picture the exhibit painted of the solicitous Soviet state cast a faint but dark shadow across the postwar USSR as a virtually fatherless society.[133] The exhibit traveled to museums and libraries in New York City, Washington, DC, New Orleans, Cleveland, St. Paul, Durham, and Baton Rouge. It also made special stops at women's colleges like Vassar and Bryn Mawr.[134]

A handful of Soviet letter writers hewed closely to the exhibition's message by heralding state facilities and professional caregivers. Mariia Pasynkova proclaimed that public daycare succeeded where she struggled. When she first started her factory job, she left her son in her mother's care. "Everything was fine," until he "became naughty, started to act rudely to me and grandma, and did not want to do anything to help out around the house. My girlfriend, who has two kids, convinced me to send him to a kindergarten in our factory. I sent him there, and the boy became completely different." He found the kindergarten so "interesting and fun" that he forgot to make mischief. He also learned good habits like washing his hands and tidying up. "The main thing is that he has become polite and obedient and started to take a completely different attitude towards adults. I work calmly knowing that my child is not only receiving food and care but also [a good] upbringing." When her second child was born, Pasynkova did not hesitate to enroll him in the school. "He is growing up into a healthy and cheerful child, to everyone's delight," she declared to her pen pal.[135]

No doubt Pasynkova was sincerely grateful toward these caregivers who made her day-to-day life easier, but the idyllic picture she, and the exhibit, painted was not widely replicated in other Soviet letters. Most were candid that the surge in fatherless children made public childcare a necessity.[136] "Very many children have been orphaned during the war, losing both parents or only their fathers," Raisa Mikhailovna Kopylova explained to Mrs. Paul A. Walter of Fairmont, North Dakota. "Our factory," the Mikoyan shoe plant in Rostov-on-Don, "has opened a nursery and a kindergarten where working mothers can leave their children. The children are well looked after, get regular and nourishing meals, and there are doctors in attendance to supervise their health."[137] These included the children of widows like Fima Petrovna Dashevskaia. She told a Mrs. Fridley (whom she mistakenly addressed as "Mistress Friday") that she only made ends meet with the help of a widow's pension, free kindergarten and summer camp, and state subsidies for her two children. "I have been left alone in the world by the death of my husband, but notwithstanding that, I feel strong and hopeful that I can bring up my children, with the help of our Government, to be Soviet citizens worthy of the name."[138] Dashevskaia's letter certainly extols socialism, but it also captures the struggles of a single mom in need of financial help.

The USSR's public childcare system was the most extensive in the world at that time, but it was not a sure fire solution to "doing it all" any more than time-saving appliances were. At the war's end, Soviet authorities doubled down on the promise that every factory, every town would provide food, shelter, and education to needy children through the Family Law of July 1944. But they could not keep this promise. Schools and nurseries were in short supply and poor condition; thousands had been requisitioned for military use, bombed by the enemy, or otherwise rendered inhabitable. The number of childcare facilities did not reach prewar levels until 1950 while demand for them soared, as some 8.7 million Soviet children were born to single mothers in the ten years after World War II.[139]

In this way, the struggle to find dependable and good-quality childcare was something American and Soviet pen pals shared. For every Soviet letter writer who touted state daycares, twice as many left their children in the care of relatives or neighbors instead. One of them was Ol'ga Mel'nikovskaia, Jean Jahr's correspondent. After she gave birth to her daughter Antonina in

1953, Mel'nikovskaia turned to relatives and hired nannies for help. Even the wartime chairman of the anti-fascist committee, Colonel Valentina Grizodubova, opted to leave her son with her mother rather than in a state-run facility.[140] "If there is a grandmother or the parents have the possibility to have a nurse, they sometimes prefer to keep the child at home," Irina Kuznetsova explained to Myrtle Park. "If there is nobody to look after the baby when the mother isn't at home, as is the case of one of my close friends, there are kindergartens that have long become one of the usual conveniences here."[141] Kuznetsova made it sound, perhaps inadvertently, that home care was preferable to public childcare, despite the anti-fascist committee's insistence to the contrary.

Moreover, when children fell sick and had to stay home, their mothers skipped work and civic activities to care for them. In fact, one of party officials' major complaints was that Soviet women were not reaching the top of professional and party hierarchies because they deferred so much of their time and energy to their families.[142] This attitude put undue blame on women who were already severely overtaxed. It also was indirect confirmation that state welfare facilities had certainly fallen short of liberating Soviet women from domestic tasks.

Thus, when it came to childcare, or a desire to work outside of the home, the pen friends were not really so different even though the contrasts between their countries' ideologies and between their material circumstances remained stark. It was an American, Betty Oberstein, who touted the merits of affordable childcare, while her pen pal Natal'ia Aleksandrovna Chudovskaia, a factory worker, widow, and mother of three, preferred that her mother babysit.[143] In making their case, neither Oberstein nor Chudovskaia criticized their nation's gender ideals, but they did not strictly conform to them either. What shines through the letters are stories of women coping the best they knew how and explaining their choices through a combination of pragmatic considerations and cultural conventions.

The Soviet Women's Anti-Fascist Committee knew full well that state welfare programs were not the simple solutions it purported them to be. It regularly received letters from Soviet women complaining about the shortage of daycares and asking the committee to help or at least not to glorify those facilities in its magazine *Soviet Woman*.[144] At one 1948 meeting, members of the committee's presidium admitted they were torn between wanting to help Soviet women through these postwar challenges and their propagandistic mission to promote socialist policies on gender equality. How could *Soviet Woman*, which targeted both domestic and foreign readers, reconcile these two goals? "We are enduring colossal difficulties," presidium member O. P. Mishanova remarked. "Everyone knows that we have a very serious struggle between societal problems, women's employment, and everyday life. A woman herself remains privately responsible for matters of everyday life," and this, Mishanova admitted, was "the biggest contradiction" of Soviet gender policy. "Women suffer terribly from it." Even though "we are building more laundries" and canteens, they were not enough. Mishanova blamed the male-dominated party elite for "taking too little care of women." "Why do we hide from [readers] abroad the fact that we have this difficulty?" she asked. Another member of the presidium, T. V. Fedorova, agreed that *Soviet Woman* should champion state welfare programs but that the magazine must stop "embellishing" them. "Woman will work and she will look after her home," Fedorova said, accepting as fact that Soviet women had to "do it all." "We need to say how we plan to resolve those everyday-life issues."[145] The committee brainstormed ways to walk this line between promoting Soviet policies and acknowledging their shortcomings. They concluded at that 1948 meeting, in the words of committee chairperson Nina Popova, that *Soviet Woman* should "provide rich material showing the state and party's care" for working mothers but "raise criticisms of negligent individual leaders and organizations."[146]

In this way, the two women's committees overseeing the pen-friendship project offered starkly different advice at the war's end but began shifting toward each other's positions slightly but significantly by the late 1940s. The New York–based Committee of Women became increasingly curious about how social welfare policies could help American women. It began hosting conferences and published pamphlets that explored the possibility of instituting socialist welfare policies for women in the United States.[147] As a state agency, the Soviet Women's Anti-Fascist Committee had comparatively less room to maneuver, but its messaging shifted too. Not only did it temper its idealism in *Soviet Woman*, it expanded the recommendations it made to women in the USSR by discussing what consumer goods to purchase and ways to shop better. During the early 1950s, *Soviet Woman* began publishing articles about pressure cookers, ice cream makers, and washing machines that "make housework easy." It advised Soviet working mothers to use grocery delivery, and it added a regular feature called

"Dear Young Housewives."[148] At the same time, the anti-fascist committee began to advocate for better social services for Soviet working mothers through the All-Union Central Council of Trade Unions. Because Nina Popova was both chair of the anti-fascist committee and secretary of the council of trade unions, she was uniquely positioned to coordinate women's demands with policy changes.[149]

In short, both the Soviet Women's Anti-Fascist Committee and the Committee of Women upheld the notion that women could and should "do it all." When it came to the question of how women could manage this, both organizations made recommendations that reflected their national norms. Yet, they also showed increased receptivity to each other's strategies over time. Many of the pen friendships followed a similar trajectory. They idealized their day-to-day affairs and overall way of life when first introducing themselves to their pen pals. Yet, as they continued to exchange thoughts about work and family life, they discovered the aspirations and obstacles they had in common and contemplated the alternative ways that women on the other side of the world were attempting to "do it all."

IN 1959, Vice President Richard Nixon and Premier Nikita Khrushchev had their famous "kitchen debate." Standing beside another model American kitchen bound for Moscow, they argued over whether socialism or liberal capitalism offered women a better life, mapping their countries' geopolitical rivalry onto ideals of womanhood. Women figured into that notorious debate as symbols of national achievement, but they were conspicuously absent from the conversation.[150] In an interview with *National Business Woman*, Patricia Nixon described how she and the wives of top Soviet officials "sat in silence for six hours" at the Khrushchevs' dacha while their husbands continued to debate a few days later. "We women did not say a word the whole time" until finally Mrs. Nixon "said jokingly to the women: 'they ought to let women settle this.' Quite earnestly, Mrs. Kozlov [the wife of Russia's deputy premier] said: 'Yes. They should let women do it.'" As she chatted on with Kozlova and Khrushcheva, Mrs. Nixon "was planting important seeds of peace and friendship," the article's author claimed. Would these seeds "bear fruit in the homes of the men who will meet around conference tables?" the author wondered.[151]

Though they, too, were kept out of boardrooms and summits, these little-known letter writers tackled the same issues a decade before Nixon and Khrushchev did. Unlike the combative kitchen debate, their discussions were not a onetime stunt but an ongoing exchange of ideas. Even when disagreeing, they acknowledged each other's achievements and struggles, believing they were planting "seeds of peace and friendship." In truth, the pen pals may have reinforced the pressure to do more, as the Soviet pen friends encouraged, or to *have* more, as the American participants suggested. Still, their conversations were a far cry from the hostile discourse of their political leaders. American letter writers did not judge Soviet women as neglectful mothers, nor did the Soviets belittle their interlocutors' more modest occupations or ridicule their "materialistic attitudes" as Khrushchev did to Nixon. Theirs was a different kind of rhetoric, one that created space for openness and overlap. That type of dialogue was also prerequisite for the international feminist movements of the late twentieth century. By looking across borders and comparing experiences, the participants grew more aware of the political factors that shaped their daily routines. They could imagine alternative ways of living and identify some of the common challenges that women faced regardless of nationality or ideology. The letter writers were doing on an individual level what feminist activists were doing and would continue to do on a national and international scale, especially during the 1970s and 1980s.[152]

The expansion of women's roles during the years around World War II set off alarm bells in both the United States and the Soviet Union about how well children were being raised and prepared for citizenship. "Some mothers *have* to work to make a living. Usually, their children turn out all right," Dr. Benjamin Spock observed, rather skeptically, in 1946. "But others grow up neglected and maladjusted. [. . .] think of it this way: useful, well-adjusted citizens are the most valuable possession a country has, and good mother care during early childhood is the surest way to produce them."[153] As Spock's remark suggested, the pen pals' decisions about how to prioritize their work had implications for how they were raising their children. Could they bring them up to become upright citizens who could establish peaceful relations between the United States and Soviet Union?

4 ~

How Are You Raising Your Children?

"Please don't be astonished to get a letter from a complete stranger," Ekaterina Andreeva begged in her first note to Jeanne A. Woolf. Andreeva was not Woolf's usual correspondent, but she had been reading Woolf's every word. "I am one of the translators working for the Soviet Women's Anti-Fascist Committee," Andreeva explained, "and it has been my pleasant duty to translate your letter to Helen Posse. I liked your letter so much and was so interested that I decided to write and ask you to be my pen-friend as well." Andreeva was full of enthusiasm for Woolf, but she had to admit "there is another reason why I want to be your pen-friend. I have 'fallen'—and hard—for Don. I liked his picture. Such a nice, clean, typically American boy! And most of all, I liked what you wrote about him." Donald Woolf was sixteen and the older of Jeanne Woolf's two sons. Andreeva was so smitten she dropped her own pen pal, the civil rights activist and journalist Henrietta Buckmaster, and jumped into the conversation between Woolf and Posse.[1]

"Would Don care to correspond with a Soviet girl of his age?" she asked. "I have two candidates for him to choose from: my niece Marina who is sixteen and her friend Mela (Amelia) who is fifteen." Marina was a blonde, Amelia a brunette—"so he can choose according to his taste," she wrote as though arranging a blind double date. Andreeva was more reticent when forming an impression of Woolf's younger son, however. "I don't think

Cameron's picture does him justice," she remarked. "It is hard to make out what he is like, but he seems to be clever and resolute. Is he?"[2] Andreeva cajoled Woolf into sending another photo of Don, this time for Marina. "I can't very well ask Helen [Posse] to give up hers," she explained.[3]

Pen friendship soon became a family affair. At first, both girls wrote to charming Don, but gradually he and Marina became pen pals, as did Amelia and Cameron. Jeanne Woolf supplied a new photo of her younger son, which seemed to ease matters.[4] The teens began chatting about the high school band and drama club as well as books and music. They shared clippings of starlets like Deanna Durbin and Sonja Henie as well as snapshots of each other. The teenagers also told jokes, which were terribly lost in translation.[5] "Do tell me about the firefly whose tail got caught in the lawnmower," Marina asked Don with concern, "I can't understand, why was he so de-lighted?"[6] Meanwhile, Jeanne Woolf and Ekaterina Andreeva's correspondence was just as lively. Woolf replied within hours of receiving Andreeva's first note, saying she was "overjoyed" to receive Andreeva's "friendly letter." The pair went on to exchange thirty letters between 1947 and 1949. Even though Andreeva worked for the anti-fascist committee, her letters to Woolf were still subject to its censorship, but the changes were negligible. As she and Woolf became absorbed in conversation, Posse was edged out of the picture.[7]

Woolf and Andreeva bonded quickly because of the teenagers in their care. All of the American and Soviet women who enlisted as pen pals enjoyed hearing and telling each other about their children. Motherhood continued to provide a solid foundation for the letter writers to connect. Andreeva was technically Marina's aunt, but their relationship was like that of a mother to a daughter. "I have brought her up since the cradle, living on and off with [her] through the whole seventeen years of her life," she reflected. Andreeva became her niece's primary guardian after the girl's father died in 1937.[8] Andreeva loved Marina and her two brothers Vladimir and Yuri "as if they were my own" and referred to them as "my children" in her letters.[9]

The pen friends' conversations about the joys and heartaches of parenting took place amid lively, nationwide debates about how best to bring up the first postwar generation. As Soviets and Americans took stock of the damage inflicted by World War II, they looked to the family to stabilize and strengthen their societies. In households and halls of government alike, young people became a focal point of growing apprehension about the security of the nation and stability of the international order. The deterioration of US-Soviet relations after World War II ratcheted up the stakes of moral upbringing and patriotic education. On one side of the spectrum were policymakers, pedagogues, and parenting experts concerned that young people lacked the self-discipline and mental fortitude to defend their nation when the next war came. "Proper childrearing" was understood to be "the basis for good citizenship, the first and last line of national defense."[10] Americans and Soviets were similarly apprehensive about the wartime spike in broken homes, the decline of birthrates, and the rise in juvenile delinquency. After World War II, they stiffened penalties for young criminals and tried to bring youngsters back into the fold through new school curricula, youth programs, and parental coaching.[11]

On the other side of the spectrum were individuals like the letter writers who were intent on raising young people committed to not only their nations but international friendship and nonviolent conflict resolution. As one American letter writer put it: "We want our children to be brought up for peace. Peace in their own country and peace around the world. Our hope is to correct the mistakes of the past and for our heavenly father to teach us how to lead our children on the right road."[12] The question "how do you raise your children?" animated larger discussions about "what kind of world do you want to live in?"

Below, I focus on how two sets of letter writers tackled these questions: Jeanne Woolf and Ekaterina Andreeva as well as Celia Wesle and El'ga Koff. Their discussions of upbringing took them into deep ideological debate, but they unfolded from blithe beginnings—a polite query or a compliment about each other's children. They followed that up with praise, more questions, or advice. And they quickly discovered from each other's replies that what they assumed to be the best, most natural methods of childrearing were imprinted with their core values and national myths.

Their investment in upbringing was deeply personal and profoundly political. Drawing on their own experiences as well as on their national literary canons, they found themselves translating for their pen pals some of the core tenets of American liberal capitalism and Soviet socialism, casting both through the framework of their lives. Wesle and Woolf drew on notions of America as a land of opportunity and of self-made men, whereas Andreeva and Koff stressed stories of wartime solidarity—part of the emerging myth of the Great Patriotic War, as the Soviet people called World

War II. By evoking these narratives, the letter writers gave voice to the American and Soviet ways of life and how their philosophy of parenting fit into them. These narratives also led the pen friends to homogenize and idealize the complex social landscapes of the postwar United States and USSR, to downplay pervasive inequality and discord at home. They generalized from their experiences as members of the dominant ethnic group—white and Russian, respectively—and as relatively privileged individuals from the middle and professional classes. Neither El'ga Koff nor Ekaterina Andreeva were members of the Communist Party but both fiercely defended its values. Celia Wesle and Jeanne Woolf both voted Progressive in 1948 and consistently Democratic after that.

At the heart of their discussions about raising children were age-old questions about the relationship between the individual and society. Soviet and American correspondents alike wanted their children to realize their full potential as individuals, to take initiative, and to develop their personalities and talents fully. They also wanted their kids to be cooperative, socially well-adjusted, and service-oriented. What set the Soviet and American letter writers apart was how they prioritized the individual and the social, and how they understood the causal relationship between these realms. Jeanne Woolf and Celia Wesle privileged individual agency, entrepreneurship, and freedom of choice which, they argued, comprised the foundation of civic-mindedness. By contrast, Ekaterina Andreeva and El'ga Koff extolled social responsibility and communalism as necessary preconditions for individuals to become self-actualized. Soviet letter writers, following pedagogues and ideologues in their country, embraced individuality (*lichnost'*)—or the development of one's unique abilities and personality—but rejected individualism, the pursuit of economic and political self-interest.[13] Their American correspondents, however, did not draw this distinction between individuality and individualism but assumed that political and economic freedoms went hand-in-glove.

In this way, the Americans' and Soviets' attitudes clustered near the far ends of a continuum between individualism and collectivism. Still, their letters also show how those value systems overlapped, especially in light of shared concerns about their children and the future. The relationship between an individualist ethos and a collectivist one proved more dynamic than dichotomous. And this made for lively discussion. The pen friends were like-minded enough to appreciate each other's frames of reference but held sufficiently divergent views to discuss the differences passionately. Still, at every turn they reiterated their friendly regard and admiration for each other. They encouraged each other as parents, and they infused their arguments with expressions of empathy and warmth.

Raising Individuals or Nurturing Communities

"I am so happy to have you as my pen-pal," Andreeva exclaimed to Jeanne Woolf, "you are exactly the type of American woman I am most interested to know and understand and to have understand us. You are intelligent, cultured, and interested in everything. I think your sort is 'the salt of America,' and I sincerely hope we are going to be good friends." This was only Andreeva's second letter, but her impression of Woolf was spot on. The Kansan was a devoted mother and wife, voracious reader, active member of the League of Women Voters, dedicated Sunday school teacher, and ardent pen pal. She corresponded with women in Norway, Holland, England, Poland, and West Germany besides the USSR.[14]

Francis Jeanne Austin Woolf, who went by Jeanne, was born in 1909 and grew up in rural Missouri. Her parents were farmers and teachers who later became psychiatric nurses.[15] Woolf followed somewhat in their footsteps. Before her sons were born and after they finished high school, she worked as a teacher, for a time in a one-room schoolhouse, where she "did everything from building the fire in the winter to sweeping the floors, to carrying water from the well."[16] Eventually, she went on to become a published psychologist and practicing clinician, but her letters of 1947–1949 capture a time when Woolf identified primarily as a wife and mother. She met her husband Maurice at Northeast Missouri State University, and they married when she was nineteen. She moved with him as he earned his doctorate at the University of Missouri and joined the faculty at what is now Kansas State University. She even coauthored several of his publications—all while raising her boys, keeping house, hosting university functions, working at a local newspaper, organizing a study club, and teaching tap dance.[17] But Woolf longed for more. She dreamt of continuing her education and studying Russian, "but to my shame I have not yet found time to take these courses. Life is so filled

Jeanne A. Woolf, *Pittsburgh Press*, July 28, 1957, 60. (University of Pittsburgh Archives Personal Files, University Archives, Archives & Special Collections, University of Pittsburgh Library System.)

with housework, and it demands to be done every day, so that I do not have enough time for studies."[18] Like other American pen pals, this remarkable woman cast herself in modest and mostly domestic terms.

Ekaterina Andreeva was equally understated in how she presented herself—so much so that it took me some time to realize her true identity. Born in 1894, Andreeva was fifteen years older than Woolf, but she hoped this would not pose a barrier between them. Age was "a matter of temperament, not years," the Muscovite declared.[19] Like so many Soviet participants, she was a widow. She and her late husband had actually divorced, but she neglected to mention this to her pen pal.[20] Andreeva also was rather vague about her parentage. "I am from an artistic and literary family. My mother was a famous actress," she wrote but did not elaborate. Andreeva studied to be a historian but left this passion during World War I to become a nurse.[21] "In our country everybody does first and foremost the work that is needed," she explained wistfully, "and in the first years after the revolution there were very few people with good knowledge of languages." But Andreeva knew several. Her mother and stepfather, who were staunch supporters of socialist revolution, fled the tsarist police in 1906 and stayed abroad for seven years. During that time, young Andreeva learned French, German, Italian, and English, and these skills led her to become a translator.

Gradually, I pieced together a family tree from the names strewn across her letters: her brother, Yuri; her husband, Abram; and her father, Andrei, a tsarist railway official. The biggest clue was the name penciled across the header of her letters by the anti-fascist committee: Zheliabuzhskaia. This was Ekaterina Andreeva's real surname. Suddenly, I realized who her father Andrei Alekseevich Zheliabuzhskii was and, moreover, who her mother was. She was none other than Mariia Fedorovna Andreeva (née Iurkovskaia), one of the most fêted actresses of her generation, a one-time partner of Konstantin Stanislavskii, a favorite of Anton Chekhov, and a leading lady of the Moscow Art Theater.[22] That meant that Andreeva's stepfather was Maxim Gorky, the most celebrated writer of the early Soviet period. But the pen friend only gestured toward him once when referring to her favorite armchair. Above that chaise, wrapped in Ukrainian embroidery, hung "framed photographs of Mother, dad, Aleksei Maximovich (my stepfather; we call him Aliosha)," she wrote.[23] Andreeva never let on who these towering cultural figures were, but she took her mother's stage name as her nom de plume. To be sure, pen pals from both countries hid parts of their names, and many described themselves as "ordinary," "typical," or "average." But none downplayed their social standing quite like Andreeva did.

Over the course of the thirty letters they exchanged, Woolf and Andreeva covered numerous topics, from art and politics to fashion and gardening. No subject was too small. Woolf talked about her husband's dust allergies and Andreeva about her "iron-grey cat" Moorzik. Both women shared recipes.[24] Given their loquaciousness, I was surprised that certain topics yielded no conversation. For instance, Woolf let slip that her brother-in-law was in the army and now worked for the atomic commission in Los Alamos, but Andreeva never asked any follow-up questions about this or seized it as an opportunity to gather intelligence, even though she worked for the Soviet Women's Anti-Fascist Committee.[25] By contrast, the topic they returned to again and again was how the teenagers in their care—and the youth of their nations more generally—could grow up with sound morals and a commitment to peace at a time when so many spoke of war.

The thought of another conflict made Woolf feel sick. "Dear, sweet Katia," she wrote in 1948, "practically every family feels the impact of the last war now and then, and I know of none who want a new war. Children who suffered from the absence of their fathers, wives who lost husbands, and mothers who lost sons, are only now beginning to build their lives anew. Many young mothers I know are suffering from a constant affliction brought on by the current tensions and threats to their safety." A few months before she wrote this, President Truman sent B-29 bombers to Europe in a show of force to help lift the Soviets' blockade of Berlin, and he publicly endorsed the use of nuclear weapons "promptly and effectively" if it was "in the interest of national security."[26] Mothers like Woolf were sick with worry about that possibility. This illness "acts on us in strange ways," she explained. One manifestation was "compulsively caring for our children and trying to keep them safe." Others suffered from insomnia and body aches, which were triggered "if something reminds [them] of the unstable situation in the world. [. . .] We all are trying this or that to promote the cause of peace throughout the world, but each of us on our own feels so helpless. We read and try to learn to understand other nations, to fight for the means to secure peace," and to teach younger generations to do the same, "but this process of moral upbringing is so slow." Still, Woolf averred, "one needs to believe that it is possible, otherwise it is not worth living."[27] It was with this determination to deescalate tensions that Woolf launched into conversation with Andreeva about the welfare and wellbeing of their children.

The pen pals loved to boast about their youngsters, and they loyally echoed each other's praise. Jeanne Woolf gave regular updates about Don and his musical pursuits on piano, bass tuba, and cornet. Cameron excelled at math, sang in the choir, and was an accomplished athlete.[28] And Andreeva cheered the Woolf boys on, sending Cameron sports magazines and Don sheet music.[29] Andreeva in turn boasted that Marina was a straight A student, the best artist in her class, and the leading lady in the drama club play. "Marina looked lovely in her stage costume (of course this is her adoring aunt speaking)," she admitted.[30] "I am awfully interested to know what you think of Marina's photograph," Andreeva fished on another occasion.[31] "Marina is getting prettier and prettier (it is not only her adoring aunt who says it). And she promises to become almost as great a beauty as my mother was. There is a portrait of Mary, Queen of Scots, that Marina looks very much like, and she was considered one of the loveliest women of her time, wasn't she?"[32] And Woolf was quick to voice her admiration. "We find Marina's picture to be terrific! Her eyes are very expressive. She looks very serious for a young girl. Don plans to send her movie magazines."[33]

In the course of complimenting each other's children, the pen friends began to promote the core values that guided their parenting. One such discussion, which began in their second and continued through their fifth letters, centered on Don's music studies. It all started with an exciting announcement: Don "has been awarded a scholarship" for "six weeks of special instruction in music" at Kansas State College, Woolf wrote proudly. The grant covered "about a third of the cost of instruction," she explained, "but the amount left for us to pay is considerable, so my husband told Don that he would pay half of the remainder if Don would earn the rest. Today, Don drove an automobile to the country for a man, worked on another man's shrubs, mowed a lady's lawn, and washed dishes to earn money. He has even promised to stay with some neighbors' children while their parents go to a wedding. If he earns as much every day as he did today, he will be able to take the [music] lessons."[34]

Woolf was proud of her son's initiative and industriousness, and Andreeva applauded "his love of music" and his determination to earn his tuition, but she had a different take. "I've been telling all my friends about Don and all say 'oh, what a shame that a gifted boy can't get his training for free!' Here he would have been given all faculties [*sic*] to train. We have special schools for gifted children where they are given an ordinary school education plus training in the art that they love."[35] In the years leading up to World War II, the Soviet Union established special schools, scholarships, and contests to cultivate prodigies in the arts. It was part of an overall shift in Stalinist culture toward honoring individual achievements and, conversely, assigning individual responsibility when it came to poor academic performance or youth delinquency.[36]

Woolf began her next note appreciatively. Don's music school had been a great success! He won a prize as the best tuba player out of all the young sousaphoners in Kansas. But he was also rewarded by the experience of "earning room and board." "He was completely gratified by and learned a lot" from all of the hard work he did to earn the tuition money. "It was heavy work, but out in the air he got very tan and became strong thanks to it. His appearance even improved, and he developed a wolfish appetite."[37] The experience of earning his own way had done Don a wealth of good.

This conclusion may have seemed natural for Woolf, for there was a huge influx of American "teenagers"—a new coinage—into the labor force during and after World War II; nearly half of all high-schoolers had at least one part-time job by 1950.[38] Woolf's younger son Cameron was just as enterprising, doing odd jobs "for small expenses, for candy, ice cream, and theater tickets. They mowed lawns, washed windows, looked after kids, and did whatever was needed." In helping themselves, Woolf added, Don and Cameron were doing essential services for the community. "These tasks used to be done by odd-jobs men, but since so many of them served in the military, they were now enrolled in college and went on to do 'white collar' work in any industry. They do not have time for small jobs around the house, doors and windows, etc., so they rely on schoolboys for those jobs." While Andreeva touted free Soviet schools, Woolf praised the GI Bill for allowing veterans to move from blue-collar jobs into the service and professional sectors.[39]

Andreeva was skeptical. Financing one's musical training was one thing, but why should the boys earn money to spend on themselves? Somewhat taken aback by this query, Woolf penned a considered response, which distilled some of the values and narratives that undergirded this parenting decision. "I thought a lot about how to explain to you our view of the fact that the boys work during the day, after school, and during vacation," she began. "First, they spend fewer hours in school than boys and girls in Europe, so they have time left to work." Perhaps they should have a longer school day, "so they would know more," she mused, but at least these jobs kept them occupied. "The second reason," was that the boys were learning how gratifying it was to earn one's way and help others. "This work provides service, goods or beauty, promotes the common welfare and gives the worker a pleasant feeling, at the same time giving him something in exchange for goods, which he needs. In the spring, Don dug up the flower beds for a neighbor. She paid him for it and he bought himself some kind of clothing. Now her flowers are blooming and we all enjoy them. Don was satisfied because she approved of the way that he did the work and he felt that he worked well." Cameron, too, was "happier when he goes to work than when he has nothing to do at home. He can put the money they pay him towards repairing his watch, some kind of clothing, or going to the movies." Such work bettered the individual, body and mind, and it served the community. Woolf extolled both even if she gave more weight to the former.

Woolf defended her boys further by arguing that individual integrity was forged through hard work and frugality. To make the point, Woolf drew on the national ideal of the self-made man and presented Maurice as an example. Both Woolf and her husband grew up "very poor," and that shaped their approach to parenting.[40] "From a very early age, my husband paid his own way in life."[41] Upon graduating from high school, Maurice worked for three years as a teacher "and saved money for continuing his education. His father did not help him." He worked as a school principal the whole time he did his doctoral studies.[42] Full-time employment significantly slowed Maurice's progress towards earning his PhD, and it delayed the Woolfs' financial growth. "In that time we did not accumulate a lot of property." During the Depression, Woolf taught tap dance, a quarter a lesson, so she could buy clothes for her boys.[43] Eight years after Maurice graduated, the Woolfs still could not afford a house. "Despite the fact that our means have increased," she reflected in 1948, those lean years continued to "influence" their attitudes toward money and hard work.[44] The Woolfs did not lavish extras on their sons, out of principle and out of necessity. What started as a chat about afterschool jobs thus unfolded into a larger meditation on individualistic ethics and the social benefits of entrepreneurship, which Woolf linked to the ideal of the self-made man.[45]

But it was more important for Woolf to stay connected with Andreeva than to change the Muscovite's mind. After making her case, Woolf immediately reaffirmed her commitment to friendship. "But we will not start to argue about this or any other topic, right, Katia?" she asked, "People's beliefs are shaped by their needs and conditions as well as influenced by the history of their countries. I am trying to understand you." Even as she confronted their different opinions, Woolf reiterated her faith that Americans and Soviets held fundamental values in common. "Each time I feel the difference in philosophy, I remind myself that people all over the world are more-or-less the same." "May I call you Katia?" Woolf suddenly asked, "I came to the conclusion that it is a name for close friends." And she signed off in the same vein, using the nickname her pen pal had given her: "Affectionately Yours, Jeanne Woolf (Zhanna)."[46]

"I am very pleased you've begun calling me Katia," Andreeva replied, "all my friends call me that and you are my friend. Of course, we'll never quarrel over difference of opinion. We are both civilized women and can understand each other's opinions even if we don't always share them."

Andreeva explained that she did not object to the boys working; she placed a high value on labor. Although she did not mention it, Soviet wartime policies had mandated that teens do agricultural or industrial labor while not in school.[47] What Andreeva questioned was whether the boys should pocket the earnings. "I didn't say it's wrong for the boys to earn money," she clarified, "I only said it seems strange to us they earn money to spend on themselves. Here schoolchildren also often work: in summer they help on collective farms with the crops or work in their school's vegetable patch. That produce goes to school lunches. [. . .] but this work is done only as 'community service' and not for money."[48] Andreeva applauded the Woolf boys' industriousness but not the individual entrepreneurship, which their mother had praised.

Like Woolf, Andreeva also drew on national mythologies to showcase this communalist ethos. "During the war, there was a movement of schoolchildren called the 'Timur Movement'," she explained. "Timur is the name of the hero in Arkadii Gaidar's novel *Timur and his Team*. Schoolchildren belonging to the movement set themselves the task of helping the families of soldiers and war-industry workers. The boys would split wood, draw water, [. . .] do all sorts of repairs, and harvest. The girls washed and dusted, mended clothes, kept young children entertained [. . .] helped them with their homework. But they didn't want anything for what they did; that was their share in the common effort to liberate their country."[49] Such work should be a social service, an act of gratitude, rather than a source of income. Andreeva's view of this phenomenon was rather fanciful, even more so than Woolf's of the self-made man. Still, after the Timur stories appeared during the summer of 1940 in *Pioneer Pravda*—the newspaper for young Soviet scouts—some real life *timurovtsy* began to form gangs and do good deeds in secret, never accepting credit or payment. The regime tried to expand this movement after the Nazis invaded. On July 1, 1941, *Pioneer Pravda*'s front page outlined "The Patriotic Duty of a Pioneer," and instructed youth to follow "the example of the splendid Pioneer Timur." Gaidar was given just fifteen days to produce a sequel to Timur's adventures to mobilize more young Soviets.[50] Andreeva sent clippings from this newspaper to Woolf.[51]

But Andreeva, too, softened her tone, wrapping her protestations in praise for the Woolf family. "I can quite understand that you are happy about Cameron's work on the college agronomy farm and also his liking of the work," Andreeva remarked. "Perhaps this will awaken in him an interest for agrobiology? Anyway, it is much better than the senseless amusements your teenagers indulge in."[52] After firing this parting shot at the frivolity of American youth, Andreeva closed with an affirmation of friendship, asking Woolf to make a pact with her to write every month "without waiting for an answer. Now that we have begun to know each other better, we will never be short of subjects, don't you think so? I often read passages from your letters to Anne and my other friends. We all have a lively interest in everything that goes on in the world and in the USA in particular. And, like you, our greatest wish is World Peace. [. . .] Well, goodbye for the present, darling. Cordial regards to Maurice, Don, and Cameron, and love to you from your affectionate friend, Katia."[53] Thus Katia and Zhannochka, as they now called each other, laid to rest their debate about afterschool jobs.

Nevertheless, the subject of upbringing cropped up again and again, such as when Woolf asked Andreeva to trade thoughts with her about their school systems. "If you are interested in any specifics related to the education system or teaching in schools and those who did not finish their education, ask and I will answer," Woolf coaxed. As a former teacher and coauthor of several pieces in educational psychology, Woolf was invested in how schools prepared youngsters for citizenship. She was "much concerned" that "students here should think more about social and political matters and international relations. [. . .] One of our foundational educational tasks is to teach people how to use their democratic privileges, so that they can learn how to vote for an honest candidate. Community politics require time and the study of questions, and many people have not learned this."[54] Woolf volunteered some of her spare time to teaching a class for teens on "life in different countries and about world problems."[55] Her husband Maurice, now a college dean, likewise organized events for students to learn about world affairs and the political process "so that they will be ready to participate in the self-government of the country [. . .] It will allow them to develop self-confidence, the ability to express their thoughts, and to develop other areas of their individuality as well as compel them to think about the good of society."[56] The balance between individual and collective interests was integral to the Woolfs' thinking about upbringing.

The Woolfs made sure their boys learned these civic habits at home. They sent Cameron to a summer camp where "international relations and world affairs" were taught alongside "sports, crafts, and Bible study."[57] Meanwhile, Don's high school offered courses like "Freedom and Responsibility" and

"The Person in the Social World," where he studied "the structure of society, industry, economic problems and laws, and the role of individualism in the structure of both." In one 1948 letter, Woolf even sent her pen pal one of Don's compositions on this topic "for which he received the highest mark in the class."[58] As before, Andreeva was full of praise for Don. He had developed "quite a colony of well-wishers" among the friends with whom she shared Woolf's letters.[59] Don's coursework likely reflected curricular changes encouraged by President Truman's 1946 Commission on Higher Education, which placed a premium on citizenship preparation. Roughly a month after the Truman Doctrine and Federal Loyalty-Security Program were announced in 1947, Congress approved the commission's Zeal for Democracy program. It was designed to teach pupils to cherish individual liberties and prepare to defend them against "the evil character and tactics of communism."[60] Somewhat contradictorily, it called on youngsters to be both autonomous and obedient in the name of national security.[61]

Meanwhile, a similar recalibration between self-interest and social duty was taking place in Soviet classrooms. New rules of conduct and curricular changes demanded greater patriotism, self-discipline, and compliance from students. Yet the emphasis on helping each pupil cultivate "a spirit of independence and a sense of his own personality" remained.[62] "While we are desirous of cultivating in pupils the spirit of collectivism," a 1946 Soviet teacher's manual explained, "we pay due attention to the personal tendencies, needs, and interests of each child. [. . .] Only by means of a careful approach to the pupil and a complete development of his individuality is it possible to educate him in collectivism."[63] In fact, these principles were not so distant from the values espoused by American pedagogues, even though curricular changes in the Soviet Union and United States were often conceived as defensive measures against each other.

Andreeva gave less thought to the classroom setting than Woolf, a former teacher, did, but Andreeva raised the topic of upbringing while she was coping with a personal tragedy, one that led her to reflect on individualism and collectivism. "These past two months have been shockingly bad ones for me," Andreeva began in June 1949. "First, mother is ill all the time—I think I wrote you about it already. Then, I suffered a big loss. One of my best and closest friends Sarah—my late husband's cousin, by the way—has died quite unexpectedly, and I feel terrible about it." Though they had been friends for twenty-seven years, Sarah hid the fact that she had cancer until just two months before she died. Andreeva was overcome with pain and shock. "I feel so sorry for myself and for her daughter, Nadia, who has been left all alone in the world at seventeen, for Sarah was also a widow like me. Of course, it isn't as bad as in another country," she reflected, shifting from the theme of personal grief to community support. "Nadia will be given a pension until she finishes school and then she will have a stipend to live on while she is in college. And we, Sarah's friends and relatives, have formed a sort of committee of guardians to look after her daughter. [. . .] I think I must tell you more about Sarah's illness, for it is a good example of our way of life." Andreeva explained how the trade union committee at the Architect's Union where Sarah worked had raised extra funds to support her while she was on medical leave and arranged for her coworkers to take turns visiting her, bringing her food and flowers. "And they are now taking care of the official side of providing a pension for Nadia. You see, in this country nobody is ever left alone, they always have their 'collective'—meaning all their fellow workers (or fellow students)—to fall back on. The collectives help their members in everything, both at work and at home."[64] Trade unions also assisted with continuing education and childcare, but—Andreeva neglected to say—they served state interests first and focused more on maximizing productivity and disciplining workers than providing social services.[65] Andreeva also did not reveal that she had joined a trade union in 1920, when she began work as a secretary for the USSR's Supreme Council of National Economy Trade Delegation—a job she did for fourteen years but never mentioned to Woolf.[66]

Even as Andreeva touted this spirit of camaraderie, she was profoundly lonely in her grief for Sarah and turned to Woolf for comfort. When no reply arrived, Andreeva began to despair that she had lost her pen pal, too. "My dear Jeanne, I haven't had any letters from you for about four months and am very worried. I keep thinking what could have happened. All the more so because Don hasn't written Marina [. . .] I haven't been well this whole winter," she admitted, and "Mother is very poorly at present. It is thrombosis and she has terrible pains, so my heart just breaks looking at her suffering, and I am horrified at the thought of what the end will be. Oh Jeanne, you don't know what a wonderful, wonderful person my mother is! Beauty, intellect, genius—she had everything, and has lived a great and interesting life. It is so hard to see her helpless and ill [. . .] If you like, I will tell you Mother's life story sometime, but at present I am not sure you want to go on being pen friends." Andreeva's confidence in their bond was badly shaken. "I would be very happy to hear from you, Jeanne dear. I have come to think of you as a very dear friend and am sorry to know nothing [new] about you, your boys, and Maurice. Give them all three my kindest regards, and please do write! Warm Greetings, Katia."[67]

"Dear and sweet Katia, I apologize that I did not reply to you for so long," Woolf responded. "I did not think that it was so long. When a person is so busy, time flies unbelievably quickly." Woolf filled several pages explaining why she had no time to write. In addition to housekeeping, work as a reporter, and writing projects with her husband, Woolf had been doing numerous tasks for friends. One was confined to her bed because of back pain. Another was on bed rest due to complications from pregnancy. "I stop by when she needs to change the bed clothes and I did that and combed her hair and that of her little girl. At another friend's, I tidied up the room and did the laundry. Sometimes, when my friends' children are fussy, I stop by to read to them." Woolf was also overwhelmed with housework. "Right now, there is a load of laundry in the washing machine, and I have been cleaning the windows, doors, and all the wood [trim]. I also plan to mop the floors. [. . .] However, I understand that I ought to find time to write to my dear friend across the sea, and I will try to be better from now on," she pledged. "I really value our friendship and love to receive your letters." "If you do not get letters from me," she added, "please trust that this is the result of carelessness and busyness. I never could be angry with you."[68] Their style of diplomacy was built on emotional openness, a sense of presence, and reciprocity.[69]

"You are such an active soul," Andreeva replied, relieved by Woolf's reassurances. Still, not to be outdone, Andreeva added: "the things you are doing for your friends are usually done here for people not only by friends but by their neighbors too. This is another advantage of living in a big house (*dom*), and not in small isolated homes like in England and in your country. There is always somebody near who will help you."[70] Here again, Andreeva valorized Soviet communalism. Yet she undercut it a few lines later when she asked Woolf to send all future letters to the anti-fascist committee's headquarters, not to her apartment building. "The people who live there are rather unpleasant and were exceedingly nasty," she wrote. Her neighbors had refused to give her one of Woolf's letters. When they finally handed it over, "the envelope was torn and dirty and had been laying about in the kitchen for god knows how long. So do write care of the Women's Anti-Fascist Committee til I am able to give you a new address."[71]

But Woolf wrote less and less as the 1940s ended and the 1950s began. Then tragedy struck. Her son Cameron, now a young air force recruit, was hit by a car while riding his motorcycle a few miles from home and killed.[72] He was just twenty-two years old. At this point, Woolf went completely silent. Her profound grief, it seems, brought to light other reasons for her unhappiness: her marriage and her unfulfilled dreams. Within a year after Cameron's death, Woolf divorced her husband and struck out on her own. She moved to Chicago and began earning her doctorate. She continued to pursue questions about how best to guide young people, but now as a professional psychologist.[73] No doubt a multitude of experiences and conversations propelled Woolf to transform her life in this way. And there are small signs that the thirty letters she traded with Andreeva may have been among them. There are also echoes of her pen friend in the advice that Dr. Woolf gave to her patients. As a psychologist, she made it her mission to help young people "find meaning in their lives" rather than to follow "the standard formula for success": "go to college, get married, have kids," and make money. Instead, Woolf instilled in her patients the importance of doing work or service that was meaningful rather than lucrative. It was based on this principle that Andreeva urged Woolf not to quit her job as a journalist to help her husband in 1947. "I have found it so satisfying to work hard for something I really want and to do it well," Woolf explained in an interview two decades later. "Even if I didn't need to, I would want to work now," she remarked in a manner distinctly reminiscent of her pen pal.[74] Woolf never remarried. She remained in private practice for twenty-six years, and she died in 1996 at the age of eighty-six.[75]

The question of individualist versus collectivist ethics also wove in and out of the correspondence between Celia Wesle and El'ga Koff. Childrearing and values instruction were even more explicit themes in their exchange. Wesle and Koff similarly drew examples from parenting, education, and literature to make a case for their own national traditions. In other respects, they were quite a different pair. Woolf and Andreeva wrote frequently and shared many quotidian details of their lives. By contrast, only seven letters between Wesle and Koff are preserved in the archives, but they are long and detailed, especially on the subject of upbringing. Their correspondence was heavily edited and circulated by the New York–based Committee of Women in a 1949 pamphlet of letters entitled *Dear Unknown Friend.* But nearly everything I quote below, especially on the subject of individualism and collectivism, was omitted from that publication.

"My Dear Unknown Russian Woman," Celia Wesle began in October 1947, "On our radio I hear, as I write, Russian music being played. This must have been the stimulus that affected me, unconsciously, to take my typewriter" and compose a letter. Otherwise, the impulse to write to a Soviet stranger seemed rather out of character for her. "My mother never mentioned Russia or any special interest in Russia or the Soviet Union. I was surprised when you first wrote about a Russian pen pal," Wesle's daughter Marguerite told me when I shared this letter. However, Marguerite noted, her mother was deeply interested in other cultures and an avid letter writer. In that first letter of 1947, Celia Wesle framed her decision to write as an expression of her appreciation for Russian culture, including the soaring music playing on her radio. "It made me try to picture what your life is like. [. . .] If your music is a true picture of your people, then they must be full of great courage, ready to do what they are taught is right and good. ~~Unless their teachers are false and betray them,~~ the goal they attain will be good."[76] Already in this first paragraph of her first letter, Wesle conveyed, along with feelings of admiration, some doubt about values instruction in the Soviet Union. An editor at the anti-fascist committee struck out the comment, perhaps not wanting to offend Wesle's prospective "unknown friend."

"But now to get to the purpose of this letter," Wesle continued, "which is to try to tell you about one small life, which is mine, in this country."[77] Like so many letter writers, including Woolf and Andreeva, she presented herself as average and ordinary. And like them, she was anything but. Wesle was a multi-passionate, deeply resourceful, and thoughtful individual who loved "to dance, to play the guitar and sing" as well as paint. She later exhibited her work and published a collection of her paintings and poems.[78] But at the time of her letters, 1947–1950, she presented herself mostly as a wife and mother, highlighting her husband's artistic pursuits ahead of her own. When she posted her first letter, the twenty-three-year-old had been married for less than a year to John H. Wesle, and the couple was just beginning their life together. Their means were modest, but their affection was plentiful. "I live with my curly-brown-haired husband who has a dimple in his chin, on the second floor of an old, large carriage house, which kept horses and carriages in the days before automobiles were used." The building now housed a hardware store and four apartments on top. The Wesles rented one of them, but Celia Wesle dreamed of owning a home—another of numerous similarities between her and Jeanne Woolf.[79]

Like Woolf, Wesle also grew up in the Midwest. She was raised in Milwaukee in "a clapboard house with a little garden." Her parents were hard-working German immigrants who arrived in Milwaukee in 1921. Her father was a master saddler and craftsman. Like Woolf, Wesle met her husband in college and, when he left to serve during World War II, she taught third and fourth grade in Beloit, Wisconsin. After her husband was demobilized, they moved to Pella, Iowa, where he taught painting and drawing at Central College. "Besides laundering, shopping, cooking, sewing, and keeping our rooms clean and in order, I spent twenty hours a week as a librarian at the college library," she explained.[80] It was there, her daughter Marguerite Wesle Franklin suggested, that Celia Wesle heard about the opportunity to correspond with a Soviet woman. Also like Woolf, Wesle devoted considerable time to college-related events, to the League of Women Voters, and to reading. "This tells you something about me," she concluded as she wrapped up her first letter. "Is it enough to encourage you to tell me about yourself? I already feel as though you were my friend, though I don't know you. I hope soon to have a letter from you. Sincerely Yours, Celia Wesle (Mrs. John H. Wesle)."[81]

It took six months for Wesle to receive a reply. That letter is missing from the archives, but I can imagine why Wesle exclaimed she was "so, so happy" with the correspondent whom the anti-fascist committee found for her.[82] It was El'ga Grigor'evna Koff, an accomplished film editor and producer for the USSR's premier studio, Mosfilm. Koff worked on a staggering 170 films over the course of her career, including hit musical comedies like *Circus* (1936) and *Volga-Volga* (1938), which brought some levity to audiences during the tumultuous years of Stalin's Great Terror. Koff worked with some of the most famous directors in Soviet cinema, including Sergei Eisenstein, Ivan Pyryev, and Mikhail Romm, and with her husband, the legendary art director Georgii Aleksandrovich Grivtsov. But Koff never mentioned these associates. She, too, downplayed her personal accomplishments and, unlike Wesle, barely referenced her husband at all. The couple lived with their son Alik in an outer district of Moscow just across from Mosfilm studios.

Born in 1914, Koff was ten years older than Wesle, but the age difference proved immaterial; the pair quickly bonded over their love of art and of

El'ga Grigor'evna Koff, circa 1950. (The Darwin State Museum of the Russian Federation, Moscow.)

reading. It was Koff's job to research the little details for historically themed films—from the proper furnishings to the right hairstyles. When it came down to it, both women spent much of their time in libraries.[83] But it was not art or literature that formed the crux of their correspondence. Rather, questions of individualist and collectivist ethics, and how to impart them to children, became their main topic of conversation.

Wesle's letters were infused with references to American values and foundational narratives from the start, beginning with how she introduced Koff to the Iowan town where she lived. "I came here to a town of 3,000 in population called Pella, which means 'city of refuge.' It was so called by a particular group of people who settled it after they left Holland a few hundred years ago because there they were not allowed to do what they believed was right and good. Most of America is made up of such people who left other countries, their friends, and homes, so that they could come to an unsettled place where they could at least live their lives as they felt was the right and good way." Just as Woolf pointed to her husband and the concept of the self-made man to teach Andreeva about American individualism, Wesle used Pella to describe the United States as a land of individual freedom, especially in terms of worship and expression. "That is why people here are allowed so many different ideas, are allowed to say them as they wish, and why it often takes a long time for the whole country to come to an agreement of purpose on a particular subject," Wesle continued. "Their mothers and fathers and their grandfathers and great-grandfathers left their homes forever and risked their lives just to have this right to decide for themselves, and we respect it."[84] Wesle likely had her own parents in mind as well as her relatives in Ostritz, Germany, who survived the Nazi regime only to find themselves living in a socialist dictatorship. She stressed that individual rights, including the freedom to choose one's values and beliefs, were the bedrock of the American way.

Wesle began meditating on how to impart these values to children long before she became a mother. "It was while I was teaching that I discovered definitively that virtues (like, for example, the wonderful and generous ideals of communism) cannot be forced upon either children or adults, for virtue itself arises from personal goodness, and that virtue which is forced by other persons and demanded by law is not a virtue anymore but only looks like it for a while."[85] Children, in other words, must be taught morals by example. Wesle extolled American classrooms for allowing children to develop their ethical consciousness freely rather than drilling it into their young minds. Wesle did not recognize, at least on the page, the state's heavy involvement in shaping civics and social studies curricula, nor did she comment on the centrality of rituals like the pledge of allegiance, which sixteen US states had recently mandated for all citizens, regardless of their religious beliefs.[86]

When Wesle first raised the subject of values instruction, in the abstract, it elicited no response from Koff. But once they shifted to discussing their own children, the pair became engrossed in conversation. Personalizing matters raised the stakes of their discussion. And that discussion started off pleasantly with a compliment and a confidence. "It seems Alik is a good boy," Wesle remarked about Koff's son in August 1948, "I hope that we also will have happy children—we expect the first on 10 September. I am telling you about this in advance!" Wesle exclaimed. And Koff was overjoyed. This happy news sparked a number of earnest conversations between them, which ran the gamut from practical matters like breastfeeding to moral upbringing. Wesle asked Koff how Alik "absorbs the ideals of communism from his surroundings. Please tell me more about this. What does he learn and how does he apply it? Does he have playmates who do not absorb these ideals? Can they remedy that? How?" "Here in America," Wesle reiterated, freedom

Celia Wesle with daughter Marguerite, 1948. (Courtesy of Marguerite Wesle Franklin.)

of choice was built into the school curricula, as young children learned to pick their own books, games, and activities. "I hope that our correspondence will continue for many years," she added. "For me it is very important that our countries understand each other and work together." She closed "with heartfelt greetings to your family, from my heart, Celia."[87]

"Dear Celia, by the time you get this letter you will already be a happy young mother. My most cordial congratulations, dear, on this happy event!" Koff exclaimed. "Do tell me please what you think of motherhood? I know by my own ~~example~~ *experience* how motherhood does enrich a woman's life and makes it really full." Koff implored Wesle to keep her apprised of baby Marguerite's developmental milestones like her first steps and first word. Koff also seized the opportunity to press Wesle about "doing it all" and championed Soviet policies for working mothers. "How will you work now?" she asked. "Who will look after the baby during the time you are away at work? Here all women get thirty-five days of paid leave before and forty-two days after the birth of a baby. Lying-in-homes are free, as is all medical care in this country."[88] Thus Koff made the same heartfelt yet strategic move that Ekaterina Andreeva did when applauding Don Woolf's musical talents. She adhered to the anti-fascist committee's mission to promote socialism and did not acknowledge how scarce Soviet childcare was during those postwar years or how Soviet maternity centers were garnering a reputation for being unsupportive and inadequate.[89]

Koff then tackled Wesle's question about how children internalized communist ideals. When publishing excerpts of Koff's letter for American readers in 1949, the Committee of Women removed nearly all of the text I quote below, including her arguments for Soviet collectivism and against American individualism. Koff began by making the same point as Wesle: "no ideals can be forced on a nation." Alik and his classmates, she contended, adopted Soviet socialism organically just "as children usually assimilate everything that is good and noble. They drink it in through their pores, like flowers drink in water," by witnessing and emulating the model communists around them. "Every day they see convincing examples of the purity and justice of this great doctrine. For children, same as for their parents, this doctrine is the basement stone [*sic*] of their life."[90] In other words, children like Alik were not blindly obedient but discerning judges of moral character. This was the same quality that Wesle ascribed to her American pupils. The pen friends had fundamentally similar views of how children internalized ethics because those ethics, they insisted, were inherently correct. What Wesle and Koff cast as natural assimilation in their own countries they scorned as indoctrination elsewhere.

Koff may have well been sincere when she championed Soviet tenets in this way, but she had a complex relationship to the Soviet regime. She never mentioned to Wesle that her father was a revolutionary in the twilight of the tsarist era and served a long sentence of hard labor before being exiled to Siberia, where Koff was born and spent her early childhood. While he and Koff's mother (a doctor and much sought-after balneologist) thrived in the early decades of Soviet rule, the family narrowly escaped Stalin's purges of the 1930s, during which numerous "old Bolsheviks" and socialist activists were arrested and killed. "Many of father's friends and associates fell victim to it," Koff explained in a 2012 interview. During that terrifying time, her father lay in the hospital, receiving treatment for various medical conditions he developed during his incarceration and exile. "I think it was only that circumstance that saved us from Stalin's repressions," Koff remarked.[91] Terror passed the Koffs by, but it had been "very, very close."[92] Of course, she mentioned none of this to Celia Wesle. This family story does not invalidate Koff's professed commitment to socialism, which she likely learned at a young age from her father. It does, however, stand at odds with her assertions about individual liberty and choice in Soviet society.

Because, she claimed, communist ethics were natural and just, Koff could not accept Wesle's declaration that Americans unanimously embraced individualism. "You say individualism is the ideal of 'Americans' and that 'the ideas of communism mustn't be enforced, but must arise from the goodness and wisdom of the people,'" Koff wrote, modifying Wesle's original words. "Is individualism the ideal of <u>all</u> Americans? Then how is it there are [*sic*] a Communist Party, strikes, trade-unions and all other forms of <u>collective</u> effort in America?" Americans had different points of view because they belonged to different classes, and class identity superseded national identity. This principle of Soviet socialism propelled Koff's claims. "Workers all over the world tend to unite," she paraphrased Karl Marx, and "this tendency comes from the very character of their work. In this way, one cannot speak of a nation as an entity. Do you suppose that the ideas and aspirations of a millionaire and of an unemployed person are the same? Or of a mill-owner and of his workers? No, of course they are exactly the opposite," she declared. "If individualism were an ideal, it would be the main obstacle to achieving universal happiness, for when each struggles alone by himself, happiness is achieved only by a few. Whereas if millions are to be happy, they must fight all together, shoulder to shoulder, one for all."

And Koff had a literal fight in mind. For her, the ultimate proof that Soviet people were genuinely committed to communism and its communalist ethos was their sacrifice during World War II. While Wesle reasoned that free and self-interested individuals formed the basis of a moral society, Koff countered that selflessness was prerequisite for social harmony. "Here, in Soviet Russia there are popular sayings: 'no warrior is any good if he fights as one' and 'one for all and all for one.' [. . .] Collectivity and unity—these are the main principles of my nation. If we didn't adhere to them, we would never had been able to achieve the great political and economic progress we have achieved, we would never had been able to defeat the enemy."[93] This claim that the 1945 victory was the ultimate vindication of Soviet values was a cornerstone of the myth of the Great Patriotic War, a narrative that began taking shape even before the war had ended.[94]

Koff's impassioned discussion of Soviet solidarity during World War II and during postwar reconstruction was the only part of her argument that the Committee of Women published in *Dear Unknown Friend*. It also printed the following passage: "If you had seen, dear Celia, all this grief and ruin, and afterwards the enthusiasm, the ardour with which people worked—you would understand that only the great, holy, and beautiful friendship of people, only the powerful, undefeatable collective can perform such wonders."[95] The committee published this image of wartime solidarity but cut the very next sentence, in which Koff leveraged the USSR's war record to argue that communism was popularly supported. These edits suggest that, while the Committee of Women was propagandizing US-Soviet friendship in this publication, it stopped short of promoting Marxism-Leninism. Koff continued to argue: "Our leaders don't try to enforce ideals on our people. On the contrary, they only help the people to realize their ideals, for the ideals of communism are born in the hearts of the toiling masses and their leaders are just the best sons of the people, who are more clever and see further than the rest, and <u>help</u> their people to find the best and shortest way to the realization of these ideals of universal happiness."

Koff contrasted this idyllic picture with one of political manipulation, which took place "in other countries" where individualism reigned supreme. In communities where "each wants to think only about his own small prosperity," Koff argued, power "isn't in the hands of the <u>whole nation</u> (though nominally it may be so), but in the hands of a privileged minority. [. . .] Those people buy some [people] off (by offering them prosperity, a well-paid job), deceive others (with lies about the aggressive intentions of other nations), and as to the rest—the upright and brave fighters for truth—they send them to prison." Triumphant individualism left American society fragmented and easily manipulated by the rich. "The ideals of democracy are beautiful—but only in the case if [*sic*] they are applied in real life and not just on paper."[96] In this way, both Wesle and Koff praised each other's principles as theoretically democratic but undemocratically enforced. Wesle argued for individual freedoms of choice and expression, whereas Koff championed collective solidarity and class struggle as the best avenues for democracy's achievement.

All of this discussion—of individualism, collectivism, and democracy—stemmed from the letter writers' initial conversations about how they were raising their children. While discussing their parenting choices, they acted as cultural translators, explaining national narratives and defending their countries' claims to exceptionalism. Both pairs also turned to literature for illustrations of the values that young people must be taught in order to become good citizens.

National Canon, National Character

A country's literary canon typically offers a vivid repository of national heroes and honored traits, so it is easy to see why official propaganda agencies like the USSR's All-Union Society for Cultural Relations with Foreign Countries (VOKS) and the United States Information Agency avidly sent books and libraries overseas.[97] As one Soviet pen pal put it: "Literature plays a big societal role in our country. People consider it a military weapon as well as a matter of education."[98] Literary characters and narratives were central to how the pen-pals imagined their own societies and each other's. "I think it is very important for people in this country to read stories about Russian life which will make them feel identified with the characters in the stories," Jeanne Woolf observed.[99] Books connected disparate cultures as well as far-flung pen friends. Celia Wesle quickly bonded with El'ga Koff over their shared love of reading. "Because your work is also connected with books, I am sure you will understand me," she wrote.[100]

Like conversations about parenting, discussions of literature surfaced benignly but generated much reflection on Soviet and American values, especially individualism and collectivism. The letter writers routinely asked each other about their favorite authors because it was an easy way to get acquainted, and they complimented each other's canon as an expression of goodwill. "Generations of Russian children have been raised on Fenimore Cooper, Bret Harte, and Mark Twain," Ekaterina Andreeva exclaimed to Jeanne Woolf.[101] Such compliments cut against the rising anti-Americanism of the Politburo, the highest political body in the Communist Party of the Soviet Union, which a year earlier issued a directive to limit Soviets' exposure to foreign literature in order to shield them from "subversive" western ideas.[102] The letter writers also gave and asked for reading recommendations. This was another opportunity for them to influence each other politically, but they treaded lightly. Woolf's two pen pals, Elena Posse and Ekaterina Andreeva, suggested masterworks by Pushkin and Tolstoy as well as Soviet classics by Konstantin Simonov and Maxim Gorky, but never tomes of Marx or Lenin.[103] In fact, when American letter writers mentioned they had read Marx, their Soviet pen pals said nothing in response.[104]

Of course, the correspondents had very limited exposure to each other's literature, just as they had a selective knowledge of each other's culture more generally. Most American letter writers admitted they knew some Russian novels but few Soviet ones. Soviet women, by contrast, were overconfident in their knowledge of American literature even though they had only read a subset of authors who were critical of capitalism and thus published in the USSR. These included Jack London, Mark Twain, John Steinbeck, Sinclair Lewis, Upton Sinclair, and Theodore Dreiser.[105] London was the top seller. By the 1950s, over twenty million copies of his works, translated into thirty-two Soviet languages, had been sold in the USSR. Twain was next highest with eleven million copies and Sinclair with four million. Those two authors' works were available in twenty-five Soviet languages.[106]

Ekaterina Andreeva and Jeanne Woolf wavered between accepting literature as a fount of cultural values and cautioning each other against confusing fact and fiction. When she learned her pen pal loved Sinclair Lewis, Woolf recommended *Aerosmith*. But then she had second thoughts. Some members of her church group to whom she read Andreeva's letters warned Lewis's satire might give the Muscovite a negative impression of Americans. "Several of them were worried you might think that we are all like the heroes of *Main Street*," Woolf explained, reminding Andreeva that American and Soviet societies were extremely diverse. "Both countries have all different kinds of people with a wide variety of occupations, climates, and locales. Some of us are so different from each other, even more so than from people of other countries."[107] Andreeva echoed her view. "Tell your church women that it can never be that we (meaning the Soviet people) could think all American people are '*Babbits*' or 'people from *Main Street*,'" she wrote good-humoredly. "We know it takes all sorts to make a nation."[108]

Although she reassured Woolf she would not mistake literary types for a complex reality, Andreeva did turn to fiction—mostly cheap bestsellers—to criticize the habits of young Americans. "I must say I begin to think that your magazines and popular novels give a libelous picture of Americans," especially of young women, she wrote in 1947. Andreeva then recounted several popular novels about soldiers' wives who were more preoccupied with finding romance than with the war. She pounced on Kathleen Norris's *The*

Mink Coat (1946). Norris sympathetically portrays a young woman who divorces her husband while he is fighting in the Pacific and becomes seduced by a playboy armed with a mink coat. She has a whirlwind romance and neglects her children before realizing the error of her ways. Andreeva also derided Christine Weston's *The Dark Wood* (1946). It depicts a young war widow who misses her husband so much that she takes to stalking another man—in her best clothes and makeup—because he reminds her of her spouse. "They all paint American women as helpless, unprincipled, spoilt, with no feeling of their responsibility as human beings and citizens," Andreeva declared. "I don't believe American women are like that. I know you aren't, and I am sure there are very many like you. [. . .] If there weren't many American women like you, if all American women were talking puppets, like the heroines of 'popular' novels, the American people wouldn't have become a great nation."[109] The danger of such books was that they both reflected and shaped the character of young readers.

Mindful of this, Andreeva recommended several Stalin Prize–winning novels to her pen pal, which she claimed spoke to the character of young Soviets. Like the American novels she spurned, these were set during World War II. One was Vera Panova's 1946 *Fellow Travelers* (*Sputniki*). It follows the lives of young Soviets who make extraordinary sacrifices for their country while working as medics on a hospital train.[110] Their patients are also exemplary. Andreeva stressed one particular scene, which lauded collectivism and satirized self-interest. "When asked why he volunteered for the Army, one battered soldier quips: 'I am a wealthy man and went to defend my property—'" meaning the Soviet motherland. Andreeva explained, "each of us feels that everything in our country belongs to every one of us. [. . .] People in America don't seem to understand that here, in the Soviet Union, the people and the government are one." Panova's novel was "a beautiful expression of this feeling," which Soviet citizens sought to instill in young people.[111] "You probably know from Russian classics like Turgenev and the rest that our Russian youth have always been earnest and civic-minded. The Soviet youth are no less."[112] Unfamiliar with Panova's novel, Woolf was not able to offer her interpretation of it, but Mark Twain was one author they had both read and discussed eagerly.

In fact, Mark Twain surfaced in many pen friends' letters as an author beloved by Soviets and Americans alike. "I know of the United States only through literature," writer Margarita Sengalevich explained to her pen pal, "our children know about a wonderful boy called Tom Sawyer."[113] Twain's stories and novels underwent 250 printings in the Soviet Union between the 1920s and 1950s, and they became central to how Soviets imagined the United States.[114] The writing duo Il'ia Il'f and Evgenii Petrov served as major interpreters of American culture for Soviet readers during the interwar years. When they took their famous road trip across the United States in the 1930s, they spent extra time in Hannibal, Missouri, where Twain spent most of his childhood. They scoured the streets for "Twainian types" and visited sites from the storied lives of Tom and Huck, which they proclaimed were "the dearest and jolliest adventures that ever existed in world literature."[115]

American and Soviet letter writers alike accepted Twain's stories about Tom and Huck as iconic images of American boyhood.[116] But the ways they interpreted these novels illuminate their distinct views of childhood and upbringing. They all recognized Twain as a humorist, but most American pen pals cast his novels as odes to individual freedom and carefree youth, whereas Soviet letter writers read them as critiques of poverty, instability, and racism in America.[117] Many Soviet citizens knew Twain met with Maxim Gorky in 1906 and that American anti-communists and segregationists campaigned to ban *The Adventures of Huckleberry Finn*. As such, they assumed Twain was sympathetic to socialism.[118] By debating the novel in this way, the pen friends were participating in a classic dispute about the political implications of Twain's stories, one that continues to this day. For some, *Huckleberry Finn* enshrines "childhood as a bucolic time of freedom, untainted innocence, and self-discovery." For others, it exposes the "underside" of American life, where children are abused and impoverished. "Huck Finn has served as a remarkably malleable emblem of childhood, [. . .] a lightning rod for popular fantasies and anxieties about childhood," historian Stephen Mintz has argued.[119]

These two views of the novel emerged in Celia Wesle and El'ga Koff's ongoing discussion of upbringing. Koff praised *Huckleberry Finn* in her very first letter to compliment American culture. Koff commended "the sympathy of Twain for all who labor and are oppressed," including African Americans and the poor.[120] "I am very glad that you love humor and the vision of Mark Twain," Wesle replied, but she wasted no time in telling Koff that she had misinterpreted the novel by viewing it through lenses of class and race. "You must forgive me, dear El'ga, if I ask you a question which seems controversial," she began, "you mentioned 'the sympathy of Twain for all who labor and are oppressed.' I understand that this ought to mean 'for workers' (the difference between our languages ought to create a pretext for several interesting questions. Please do not hesitate to ask me questions about everything that might interest you)." After this acknowledgment that cross-cultural understanding was difficult, even with great literary works to mediate it, Wesle pressed on that Koff had mischaracterized the novel's message. "Twain, as you know, wrote about life in the Mississippi Valley, which at that time represented a kind of border because behind it there were relatively few cities. Here there was no one who could have oppressed its residents. There were people who preferred a happy-go-lucky life, sometimes working, sometimes just enjoying life—and Mark Twain wrote about them with humor and understanding. One of the reasons behind the high quality of Mark Twain's writings is that he was able to objectively observe and delight in any type of person."[121] For Wesle, Twain had created a tender snapshot of rural life, and she drew on the myth of the open frontier and the ideal of a carefree childhood to make that point.

By Wesle's reading, the novel was about freedom, specifically Huck and Jim's freedom to choose a new, unstructured life for themselves. "That is why individualism is such a great ideal for Americans," Wesle continued, "present-day leaders impose on them only the least number of limitations, which are needed so that people can live together justly and calmly and not be refused equal opportunities. Here, people can do almost anything that they want, as long as it does not prevent someone else from achieving their desires. That is perhaps the fundamental difference between the philosophies professed in each of our countries. Am I right when I say that in your country your leaders—having the very best intentions—try to direct you to what is right, good, and worthy? Many Americans think that communism is a great ideal but that it ought to emerge voluntarily from the goodness and wisdom of the people themselves in their daily lives and not be forcefully introduced by a strong group of leaders, no matter how good their intentions or how great their thoughts are." Children, too, she reiterated, must be free to choose their own values rather than have them thrust upon them by politicians, parents, or teachers. Wesle then paused, marveling: "All of these thoughts have flowed from the idea that Mark Twain saw people as they were and delighted in and wrote objectively about their individual characters!"

Wesle argued her point of view firmly but gently, determined not to jeopardize her pen friendship or the larger goal of peaceful US-Soviet relations.

"My dear friend El'ga, because I recognized you as such right away, I am prepared to do all that I can so that you would remain that [a friend]. Are you angry that I started to talk about our discord so immediately? I hope not because, of course, I cannot be sincere if I do not write to you in a timely fashion and say I disagree. However, I do not want you to be angry and resentful."[122] Wesle tried to strike a balance between friendliness and frankness, between converting her pen pal to a new way of thinking and simply connecting with her.

Koff replied with equal parts courtesy and candor. "We have agreed to be perfectly frank with each other," she affirmed, "and I want to speak as fully as possible about the problems raised in your letter, so that we could understand each other better and could become really close friends. I am very grateful to you for your long and exceedingly interesting letter. It made me think about many things, remember a lot."[123] Koff held firm that class- and race-based inequality were integral to the novel. "Dear Celia, you write that Mark Twain's heroes chose a carefree and easy existence because they liked it. But I am sure that nobody would choose to wander about the country with no ready means of existence like some of Twain's heroes (I don't speak about the boys; for whom everything is just play) if they had a good job providing them with a steady income." While Wesle saw Huck and Jim as embarking on a great adventure and free to make their own destinies, Koff argued that they were desperate to escape Huck's abusive alcoholic father and Jim's mistress Miss Watson. Where Wesle saw individual choice, Koff saw social ills. "When I re-read Mark Twain's works (and I do so often)," Koff continued, "I see in him only a passionate, irreconcilable champion of those vagabonds he describes so well. I mean especially a champion of the negroes he speaks of with such compassion and with such indignation to[ward] their tormentors. A great master as Twain was, he can't write without expressing his views. And Twain vented very actively his disgust with those who didn't consider Negroes to be human. It is for this humanity, for this vivid quality of his sympathy and antipathy that Twain is so greatly loved in this country."[124]

Koff then turned to Aleksandr Fadeev's popular 1945 novel *Young Guard* to demonstrate how Soviet youth similarly fought for social justice. The film producer may have had this work on her mind since it was made into a movie the same year that she sent her letter, 1948.[125] *Young Guard* follows a group of teenagers in the Young Communist League who fought the German troops occupying their mining town in Krasnodon. Most were tortured and executed. The novel was based on real events. Fadeev interviewed locals and gathered other materials for it. "The heroes of this film are not fictitious characters—most of them met their death heroically during their struggle against the Nazis. Some are still alive, at college or at work. I don't know if this novel has been published in America. If so, do read it and then you will understand what it means to have communist ideals at work." The youngsters' initiative, comradeship, and self-sacrifice were all traits Koff hoped her son Alik would cultivate. "Though they could have kept quiet and waited for the Red Army to deliver them," she said of the youths in the novel, "they preferred to form a fighting organization; children became fighters for liberty. [. . .] I would like my boy to grow up as upright and brave as these boys and girls." Upon revisiting the novel, Koff exclaimed, "I have again felt proud—a feeling you must know also—proud for my own country. I felt happy to be a Soviet citizen."[126] Drawing on this literary work, Koff thus reasserted her argument that youngsters in the USSR voluntarily embraced Soviet values and took the initiative to act on them. But the latter point was stressed only in the first version of the novel. Less than a year before Koff's letter, literary critics and party officials attacked Fadeev for overemphasizing the independence of these teen martyrs and underemphasizing the party's role in guiding them. He was forced to revise it.[127] Koff likely heard about this, so it is interesting that her 1948 letter to Wesle seems to praise the original novel and not the rewrite. Together, the plot and reception of *Young Guard* capture how both individual initiative and deference to authority were prized in the Soviet war myth, as well as how the merits of these qualities were reassessed during the postwar period.

As always, the pen friends interlaced their literary reflections with affectionate remarks, particularly about their children. Koff confided to Wesle that she had always wanted a daughter, even though Alik brought her so much joy. "Please do write how old Marguerite is when she begins to say her first words and at what age she begins to walk," she asked.[128] Wesle obligingly replied with photos and details about her little girl's progress.[129] "Each time I see one of your letters in my mailbox," Wesle wrote in fall 1950, "I fly down the stairs and then back up again [to read it]. It is always such a pleasure to feel connected to you who live so far away."[130]

But Koff's letters stopped coming. Wesle wrote a few more times in 1950, admitting she was "a little impatient to receive a reply" to her "unanswered letters."[131] She would never get the chance to tell Koff about her other two daughters nor the changes in her marriage, professional ambitions, and political views—a story I turn to later. Koff not only missed the chance to witness her pen pal make these bold life changes, she also did not get to ask Wesle for help with Soviet films set in the United States. In particular, she needed help identifying what American brands were typical and would make convincing props in Soviet productions about life in the United States. As Koff explained in a 2012 interview, the dearth of information about Americans' everyday affairs made her job much harder, for these cold war-edged films were "made at a time when our 'our people did not go abroad'," when "the country lived behind an Iron Curtain." That characterization suggests Koff had since become doubtful of the proclamations she made to Wesle about individual liberty and autonomy in the USSR. In 2012, Koff gave a more doleful reading of her "beloved and long-suffering Russia."[132]

THE QUESTION OF HOW TO RAISE children to be upright citizens was a lively topic of conversation for the pen pals and a pressing issue of the postwar moment. After World War II, leaders in both nations sought to restore family values, reign in rebellious youths, and cultivate their love of country and willingness to defend it. Upbringing became a cornerstone of the national security edifice in the United States and the Soviet Union.

Jeanne Woolf and Ekaterina Andreeva as well as Celia Wesle and El'ga Koff fell into debate about upbringing not during combative moments but congenial ones, when they were complimenting each other's children or literary canon. And, when it came to the question of young people's moral development, the pen friends actually held a good deal in common. They supported a similar matrix of values and strategies that promoted individual autonomy on the one hand and a social commitment to service on the other, but they prioritized them differently. Andreeva and Koff argued that self-actualization stemmed from subjugating individual interests to the collective, whereas Woolf and Wesle stressed that individual rights, freely expressed, led to the betterment of the community. Where Woolf and Wesle saw liberty, Andreeva and Koff saw selfishness; where the Soviets saw sacrifice and service, the Americans saw coercion and conformity.

In order to explain what they assumed were commonsense practices of childrearing, the correspondents had to reflect anew on the relationship between the individual and society and make explicit the cultural beliefs and practices that were implicitly woven into the fabric of their lives. They looked for examples from personal experiences, literary models, and national myths. And while they passionately defended their views, they did not engage in the gamesmanship that characterized cold war discourse. Moreover, they seemed genuinely hurt when their pen friends stopped writing—a phenomenon that happened more and more by 1950.

That was the year that Koff stopped writing to Wesle. Koff probably ended her association with Wesle in light of escalating US-Soviet tensions, not a lack of genuine concern about her pen friend. "I think that in order to live long and happily on earth, one must not be false, neither in relationships with loved ones, nor in work, nor in friendship. I didn't fake it," Koff reflected in 2012.[133] "I wish everyone around me the utmost kindness and goodness. That is what I stand for."[134] But around the time her pen friendship ended, Soviet authorities were kicking the USSR's anti-American campaign into high gear. The Central Committee of the Communist Party ordered the Soviet Women's Anti-Fascist Committee to intensify its agitation against the United States and Britain.[135] The pen-pal program was on the chopping block, assaulted from both sides by American and Soviet authorities. But it proved difficult to kill.

5 ~

You May Not Hear from Me Again

"As you probably know, there is rather a lot of hysteria in this country, and the time may come when I cannot write to you," Gladys M. Kimple warned at the end of one 1947 letter, "but no matter what happens, I know that I have a friend in Rostov and you understand that you have a friend in America."[1] As she penned these lines, Kimple worried that the surge of anti-communist sentiment in the United States would cut her pen friendship short. As it turned out, Kimple ended up participating in the pen-pal program longer than any other American, but her family paid a high price for her involvement.

Kimple sent her first note to the USSR in January 1946, expressing her gratitude for Soviet sacrifices during the war and her curiosity about "the great experiment" of socialism. She asked the unknown woman who would receive her letter to tell her all about it—"not about affairs of state but the simple little things like how you live, what you think, and what constitutes your hopes and dreams."[2] Antonina Dmitrievna Viazovskaia was eager to do so. "I hasten to tell you that I want to be your pen-friend!" she exclaimed. "As women and mothers, we are sure to find much to tell each other about our experiences." Viazovskaia began by explaining that she had "lost so much in the war." Her father was killed during the bombing; her mother starved to death under occupation. "I myself lost my health. I was a blooming young woman before the war. Now I am an invalid." On top of these tragedies,

Friday Harbor Wash.
Oct. 27- 1947

19

Soviet Women's Anti Facist Committee,
Pushkin Street 23
Moscow. U.S.S.R.

Dear Friends,

Please find enclosed a letter to:

Antonina Dmitrievna Vyazovskaya.
Rostov on Don - New Town
Institute of Railway Engineers
Residential Bldg. of Faculty - App. 12-

Will you please interpret and mail to the above address. I appreciate your kindness and the fine work you are doing toward furthering internation understanding.

I wish I could read the original Russian script of the letter I very recently recieved through your office from the lady of the above address.

I know you are very busy but would certainly enjoy a letter from any one of you. There is so much I'd like to know about life in Russia-- and the personal touch is lost a little when translation is necessary.

I have read the recent letter recieved, to my friends and will continue to do so. It is a small thing I can do toward furthering peace and understanding- but every little thing helps.

These are critical times and each of us

P.T.O.

Letter from Gladys Kimple to Antonina Viazovskaia, Oct. 27, 1947. (State Archive of the Russian Federation, f. R7928, op. 2, d. 245, l. 19.)

Viazovskaia was mourning lost opportunity. Kimple wanted to know about her "hopes and dreams," but the war had robbed Viazovskaia of the chance to complete her graduate degree and make her "dreams and hopes come true."[3] Her story drew Kimple in immediately. "I barely slept the day your letter arrived," she confessed. "I almost know it by heart. [. . .] When the pages of a letter come to you from far away and finally end up in your hands, you avidly want to know and love them just as fervently as I want to know and love you."[4]

From the start, theirs was one of the most effusive correspondences. No doubt this is why the Committee of Women quoted them more than any other pair in its 1949 pamphlet *Dear Unknown Friend*. Viazovskaia, who lived in the port city of Rostov-on-Don, told Kimple about her son and daughter, her aspirations to become a scientist, and her fondness for American literature. "My son and I, and even my husband often laugh to tears over the adventures of Tom Sawyer and Huck Finn," she wrote. The spirited characters of Mark Twain, Jack London, and John Steinbeck had taught Viazovskaia to admire "the average American. I like him for his fundamental traits. He is hardworking, businesslike, honest, and generous—traits the American people have in common with us." Inspired by that familiarity, Viazovskaia invited Kimple into her home, promising succulent fish stews and hearty bowls of borscht.[5] Kimple was elated. This pen friendship struck her as "something of a miracle." "All that distance between us amounts to nothing, really. So it is, if all the little people all over the world could know each other, they would discover that we are all fundamentally the same in our hopes and desires. The knowledge that you, too, have travelled down the Mississippi with Huck Finn and Tom Sawyer, have read so many of the same books and dreamed the same dreams, have heard the same music, and are building for the same freedoms that we struggle to attain and cherish, all these things tear away the miles and the language differences. Antonina, my friend, I salute you!"

This faith that ordinary Soviets and Americans were "fundamentally the same" fueled their correspondence as it did so many others. Kimple told Viazovskaia about her five children, her thoughts on Marx and Tolstoy, and her family's salmon fishing business in Friday Harbor, Washington, then a village of about 650 people.[6] For one wild moment, Kimple contemplated sailing halfway around the world, from Puget Sound to Rostov. "I never could make it to you on my little boat," she had to admit, "it is just 19 feet

Gladys Howard Pearmain Kimple, circa 1927–1928. (Courtesy of Roy Pearmain.)

and has a plywood cabin, which gets wet in the slightest rain, so there is no hope that I could take advantage of your kind hospitality and of all the miraculous food that you wrote about."[7] Although disappointed that they could not "sit together over a cup of tea, laughing and chatting about all kinds of small personal matters," Kimple and Viazovskaia used the written word to nurture a bond that they hoped would transform relations between their countries. "Russia and the United States are miles apart in actual space as well as in ideology. To decrease that span we must get to know each other as friends and neighbors," Kimple observed.[8] And Viazovskaia heartily agreed. Nations "can have different systems yet live in friendship. We all think like that."[9]

It was a promising beginning. But that was all it was. Only a handful of letters in, mounting opposition to American-Soviet friendship struck forcefully from both sides. By the time the pamphlet *Dear Unknown Friend* came out in 1949, publicizing excerpts from their correspondence, Viazovskaia had stopped writing. That year marked a steep escalation of cold war hostilities with the formation of NATO, the establishment of the Federal Republic of Germany, the communist revolution in China, and the Soviet Union's successful test of the atomic bomb. It was also a landmark year of so-called McCarthyism and *zhdanovshchina*, when eleven American Communist Party leaders were convicted of conspiring to overthrow the US government and state and party officials from Leningrad were imprisoned and executed for treason.[10] During this fraught moment, Viazovskaia vanished. Kimple "almost lost all hope" of "receiving another letter from the Soviet Union" when another, also orphaned correspondent reached out to her.[11] This was none other than Ekaterina Andreevna Zheliabuzhskaia, who went by Ekaterina Andreeva when she was Jeanne Woolf's pen pal. Zheliabuzhskaia and Kimple exchanged two dozen letters between 1950 and 1953. This time, Zheliabuzhskaia wrote under her own name, but all the other details she shared about her life were consistent with what she had told Jeanne Woolf, who left the program in 1950.

Gladys Kimple began this new pen friendship excitedly, but at great personal risk. The hazards she had foreseen in 1947 were coming true. The pen-pal program and the Committee of Women that oversaw it from New York City were condemned, first by the House Un-American Activities Committee (HUAC) and then by the Justice Department's Subversive Activities Control Board. In the face of intense scrutiny, the Committee of Women worked to shield the pen-pal program and its participants, like Kimple, from prosecution. The committee kept the identities of nearly all the letter writers a secret, but Kimple had put herself in the spotlight by sending copies of her letters to local newspapers. During the early fifties, Kimple told Zheliabuzhskaia how her son lost his job and how her brother-in-law was hauled before the Weld Committee on Un-American Activities in Seattle—all because of the Kimple family's progressive politics and alleged communist sympathies. In 1951, Zheliabuzhskaia's letters began to arrive previously opened. By this time, the Soviet consulate in New York City had been forced to close, and the pen-pal program commenced using the regular postal service, not diplomatic couriers, to exchange letters. Also by this time, 1951, the CIA started to inspect Americans' mail to and from the USSR.[12] Aware she was under surveillance, Kimple began censoring her remarks but did not hide her disdain for her new, uninvited readers. As the campaigns against communism intensified, she wrote more frequently and defiantly. So, too, did the other remaining American pen friends. They reached out to Soviet correspondents in peace as well as in protest against McCarthyism, as it came to be known by 1952.

Miraculously, neither Kimple nor any of the other participants were prosecuted for the letters they had written. This is due in large part to the Committee of Women. When its leaders were attacked by anti-communist officials, they protected the pen pals by playing into their accusers' assumptions that these letter writers were ordinary women of no consequence—"little people," as Kimple had called them. This was the same assumption that led American and Soviet authorities to allow the correspondence program to begin in the first place and to continue after World War II. Ordinariness remained a useful political cloak, one the remaining American letter writers donned over and over again. They championed peace and condemned US foreign policy more forcefully than the previous cohorts of pen friends had done. They wrote daring, defiant letters during the early 1950s. But almost none of them received replies.

That is because at the precise moment the Committee of Women bravely stood by the pen-pal project, the Soviet Women's Anti-Fascist Committee was dismantling it. Like many in the US government, Soviet officials also considered the pen-friendships a political liability. They, too, were concerned about the costs of the program but for opposite reasons. While American anti-communists worried that Soviet pen-pals would push American women leftward, Soviet authorities worried that its pen pals were weak, ineffective, and failing to improve American women's views of the USSR. The Central Committee called for more "important and influential" women to take their place. In other words, the notion that these letter writers were "ordinary," "little," and unimportant saved them from prosecution in the United States, but it was the very reason why the Kremlin deemed the program a waste of propagandistic resources. Under this dual assault, the number of American-Soviet pen friendships dwindled from 319 in 1949 to twenty by 1952.[13] Kimple was one of the few who was allowed to continue corresponding but, unbeknownst to her, the woman who answered her letters after 1952 was not Ekaterina Zheliabuzhskaia but another member of the anti-fascist committee in disguise.

Politically Gullible Women

During the first decade of their existence, there was hardly a moment when the National Council of American-Soviet Friendship and its subcommittees, like the Committee of Women, were not under attack as "communist front" organizations. That is, the National Council was accused of championing peace and friendship in order to trick Americans into backing a communist agenda.[14] Technically, it was not illegal to be a communist in the United States, but a slew of laws made it possible to bar communists from certain professions, government service, travel, elected office, and labor unions on the premise that they advocated the overthrow of the US government.[15] The FBI began to surveil the National Council of American-Soviet Friendship as soon as it formed in 1943, and HUAC indicted the group in 1945, just three months after V-J Day.[16] The Department of Justice followed by adding the National Council to the attorney general's list of subversive organizations in 1947 and brought charges against it in 1948 and 1950.[17] Next came the Subversive Activities Control Board, which tried the group as a foreign agent in 1953. All of these charges were eventually dropped or overturned for lack of evidence, but they devastated the group's finances and membership rolls.[18]

Most of the National Council's other subcommittees disbanded during those tumultuous years, but the Committee of Women survived. It faced the same accusation that it spread communist sentiments through its publications, events, and programs. It, too, lost the bulk of its sponsors and eventually had to scrap its newsletter and other planned publications, like a second edition of the pamphlet *Dear Unknown Friend*. Still, the Committee of Women emerged from the Red Scare relatively unscathed for the same reason that the program had been allowed to exist in the first place: it was a small enterprise of "ordinary" women who—from the investigators' point of view—were politically naïve but relatively harmless. "Ordinariness" proved advantageous. So did the deeply gendered way anti-communists conceptualized subversion. This led prosecutors to fixate on certain transgressions and overlook others.

Anti-communist crusaders in the US Congress, the Justice Department, and the American press often condemned communism and reified postwar gender norms in the same breath. They frequently turned to psychosexual explanations and cast women sympathetic to communism as deviants who flouted America's political values and sexual norms.[19] Sometimes, these suspected communists were depicted as mannish and emasculating.[20] Paradoxically, others were cast as femme fatales who lured men into doing the party's bidding.[21] Still others were painted as naïve fools, sheep "seduced" by "the Moscow wolf" as one *McCall's* article put it.[22] Such women swallowed the nefarious ideas of charismatic men like ready-made packaged foods from the supermarket, another publication alleged.[23] When investigators began to build a case against the longtime chairperson of the Committee of Women Muriel Draper and her successor Virginia Epstein, they put them in this last category. Both women were derided but ultimately dismissed as gullible and emotionally weak individuals who lacked real political convictions and therefore posed little serious threat. Draper never squared off with her attackers on the stand, but Epstein did, and she leveraged suppositions about the foolishness and fragility of her sex to shield the Committee of Women and its correspondents from further reprisals.

By the end of the 1940s, both the FBI and HUAC had compiled extensive evidence against the Committee of Women.[24] Investigators marked up copies of *Dear Unknown Friend* and the committee's newsletter, *The Women Report*, underlining in red pencil potentially incriminating passages in the letters printed there.[25] However, they never brought charges against the committee's sponsors, who were conveniently listed on the committee's stationery. Nor did they subpoena the committee for the letter writers' names or addresses. Instead of prosecuting the committee, HUAC aimed to discredit it by accusing its chairperson, Muriel Draper, of becoming communist in order to attract male attention. The focus on Draper was to be expected in the sense that HUAC's general strategy against the National Council was to take down its chairmen, including Dr. Corliss Lamont (who served as chair from 1943 to 1947), Reverend William Howard Melish (chair 1947–1949 and 1971–1978) and Dr. John A. Kingsbury (chair 1949–1956). "The key to an understanding of the National Council of American-Soviet Friendship as a Communist Front organization is the identity of its officers," one 1946 HUAC report explained. But the way anti-communists characterized these men stands out sharply from how they approached women like Draper and Epstein.

The distinct way Corliss Lamont and Muriel Draper were treated is particularly revealing. Considered a prize catch, Lamont was repeatedly called to testify before the House of Representatives and the Senate for alleged communist activities. What made him so dangerous, both houses of Congress agreed, was his deep-seated ideological commitment to communism. "There are American friends of the Soviet Union whose friendship is based exclusively on military considerations" and the United States' partnership with the Soviet Union against Hitler, that 1946 HUAC report continued, but "there are other American friends of the Soviet Union whose friendship stems first and last from their own devotion to or sympathy with communism. Corliss Lamont belongs among the latter. He has tagged along faithfully through all the sharply divided periods which have characterized Communist policy and tactics. His financial contributions to the communist front movement have made him a darling of the Communist Party."[26] The Senate's Internal Security Committee echoed that Lamont was dangerous because he was a conscious believer, not an "outright dupe."[27] Still, some FBI agents and journalists wondered if Lamont hadn't been led toward radical politics by a nefarious seductress or an overbearing mother.[28] Although he continually escaped conviction, Lamont was stripped of his passport and right to travel. The Internal Revenue Service audited him in 1951 and 1952, and he was forced to resign his lectureship in philosophy at Columbia University.[29]

Muriel Draper had much in common with Lamont. She, too, was a writer and had been intrigued by communist ideas since the 1920s. Like him, she twice visited the Soviet Union, and she served as a patron for left-leaning causes. Draper hosted a salon for fellow travelers and intellectuals, including Pablo Picasso and Henry James, first in her London home and then in New York City. She was extremely active politically. She had been a vocal proponent of suffrage, and in the late 1930s she hosted NBC's radio show "It's a Woman's World" as well as participated in various progressive causes. During the forties, she served at the head of both the Committee of Women and the Congress of American Women, the US affiliate to the Women's International Democratic Federation (WIDF).[30]

What inspired her to take on all of these activities? According to HUAC, it was unrequited love and a desire for male attention. The groundwork for this conclusion was laid in Draper's thick FBI file. It portrays her as a divorced (i.e., bad) wife and a negligent mother—common tropes in the indictments of "Red" women who allegedly put the party ahead of family.[31] FBI agents made hay of one instance where she left her boys home alone with only servants to supervise them. The children had to fend for themselves "as far as entertainment was concerned," the headmaster of the Draper children's school told the FBI when he heard about what happened.[32] Using minor incidents like these, the bureau's agents created a dossier on bad mothering.

Rather than prosecute Draper, HUAC worked to discredit her on psychological and sexual grounds. In 1949, HUAC published a pamphlet excoriating the Congress of American Women, calling it a "Communist hoax" that "ensnared" "politically gullible women" like Draper. According to the pamphlet, Draper's interest in communism was actually a reaction to her husband's infidelity and incessant gambling. This "embittered and hardened her" and ignited her "desire for importance, fame, even adulation." Draper eventually divorced and moved to New York City. She arrived "a bored and disgruntled woman suddenly deprived of opportunities for the satisfactions of the ego, condemned to 'the relative bareness of life' in the US—shorn of her position, her importance, and significantly, her audience, artistic cliques. She turned elsewhere for an outlet—to the pro-Soviet artistic circles in New York City." In short, Draper was a jilted wife who longed to "bolster her feeling of self-importance," HUAC psychologized.[33]

By this analysis, Draper's interests in women's rights, peace, and socialism stemmed from psychosexual neurosis rather than political conviction. HUAC claimed she was "confused" and "inconsistent" about Marxism-Leninism and performed "frequent ideological summersaults." The authors simultaneously vilified and trivialized her. "Muriel Draper might be discounted as harmless were it not for the fact that the Communists have succeeded in shrewdly exploiting her social standing for their own conspiratorial plot." Even communists "view this woman with undisguised contempt and ridicule," it alleged.[34] In other words, HUAC's staff considered Corliss Lamont a "darling" of the Communist Party for his support and patronage, but they assumed the party "ridiculed" Muriel Draper for allegedly fulfilling a similar role. This psychological reading was as dismissive as it was humiliating.

Certainly not all women accused of having communist leanings were considered political simpletons, but such disregard was common. "Most opponents of the Communist Party tended to ignore its women," historian Ellen Schrecker observed. During hearings, HUAC "operated on the assumption that these women knew little about politics and cared only about their homes and families. It questioned them as much about their husbands' activities as their own."[35] HUAC never brought charges against Draper, but she stepped down from her leadership roles. When the Department of Justice ordered the Congress of American Women to register as a foreign agent in October 1949, the organization's members voted to dissolve rather than fight an expensive legal battle. Draper's health deteriorated, and she died in 1952 at the age of sixty-six.[36]

The assumption that women were less politically sophisticated or threatening also colored political witch hunts in the Soviet Union. During the

Great Terror of the late 1930s, men made up the majority of individuals arrested and executed for counterrevolutionary activities, while a special article of the criminal code further gendered these so-called "enemies of the people" male by making provision for the incarceration or exile of "their wives and children." The law did not acknowledge there might be husbands of state enemies too.[37] Likewise, there were fewer female victims of *zhdanovshchina,* the terror that transpired in the years after World War II. Of course, this same assumption that women were less politically dangerous had helped sway Soviet and American authorities to allow them, not men, to correspond during the war and Cold War.

The US Justice Department's Subversive Activities Control Board operated on a similar set of gendered assumptions when it tried the National Council of American-Soviet Friendship for failing to register as a foreign agent in 1953–1954. The government's case was argued by Troy B. Conner Jr. and Oliver J. Butler Jr. before the board's representative David J. Coddaire Jr. Conner and Butler called only one female defendant from the National Council to testify: Virginia Epstein.[38] Virginia Epstein and Dr. Eslanda Goode Robeson succeeded Draper as co-chairs of the Committee of Women. Goode Robeson was a prominent anthropologist and civil and women's rights activist as well as the wife of famed performer and dissident Paul Robeson. Goode Robeson was best known for her pan-Africanist views and her work for racial and gender equality through the Council on African Affairs (also placed on the attorney general's list of subversive organizations) and the National Council of Negro Women, which she helped found. The Subversive Activities Control Board did not call Goode Robeson to the stand perhaps because she testified, and quite masterfully, before the Senate in 1953. While under cross-examination, she condemned American racism, called out demeaning questions like whether she had written her book, *African Journey,* "all by herself," and returned probes about her husband's politics with the defiant refrain: "why don't you ask him?"[39]

Epstein did not have Goode Robeson's activist pedigree, but she had participated in various popular front groups during World War II as well as in the ill-fated Congress of American Women. But the Subversive Activities Control Board did not acknowledge any of these activities. It treated Epstein as a political naïf. In its final report on the case against the National Council of American-Soviet Friendship, the board listed everyone who testified by their occupations and political affiliations. Epstein, then sixty-nine years old, was described merely as a former kindergarten teacher and camp counselor.[40] During the hearings, Epstein played into that assessment of her, ultimately convincing prosecutors that the Committee of Women was a minor, volunteer organization that operated separately from the National Council and was not worthy of much attention.

Before Epstein testified, two of the National Council's chairmen, Reverend William Howard Melish and Dr. John A. Kingsbury, took the stand. Here again, the treatment of them was strikingly different. Melish was a Christian socialist, a supporter of the American Labor Party, and an Episcopalian rector. He chaired Russian War Relief's Interfaith Committee during World War II.[41] Kingsbury was a social worker, educational administrator, former commissioner of public charities in New York City, and an independent socialist.[42] He, too, joined Russian War Relief during World War II. Like many hearings of this type, the atmosphere was tense. Melish was interrogated six to seven hours a day for three weeks. Kingsbury was questioned for three days after him. The lawyers acting for the Justice Department, Conner and Butler, asked both witnesses to provide minute details and accused the defendants of being recalcitrant when they could not recall them. They ridiculed Melish when he failed to recount all the organizations he had supported, lectures and sermons he had given, and May Day parades he attended over the past decade.[43] Butler sneered when seventy-year-old Kingsbury claimed he could not remember at which hotel a particular National Council event was held three years prior. "Why must I necessarily remember?" Kingsbury retorted, "I am an old man," but Conner and Butler pounced on every failed recollection and denial.[44]

The lawyers tried to prove Melish and Kingsbury were communists not just through their associations but also their beliefs. They asked Kingsbury to give a definition of communism and declared that any approving remark he had made about "communal ownership of property" meant he was a "communist in that sense." "I am not a communist in any sense," Kingsbury shot back.[45] They also tried to gauge his communist sympathies by asking for his interpretation of the Korean War and whether "China was the aggressor." "I am not an authority on that," Kingsbury rejoined, but "I will be glad to review that history for you."[46] Conner and Butler's examination of Reverend Melish descended far deeper into intellectual abstraction. They asked him to define communism, totalitarianism, Christianity, and progressivism, and then to explain which labels best fit his views. When Melish was not succinct in his response, they accused him of dodging. Melish countered that such complex questions required complex answers. "Are you through?" Butler retorted, "May I compliment you on your artfulness in evasion and ask you to please answer my question."[47] Butler reared up again when Melish refused to give a simple "yes" or "no" in answer to the question of whether the USSR was a totalitarian dictatorship:

> Melish: I just refuse to be forced into the use of these conventional terms, which are nothing but labels and are emotional in their content and are simply inadequate to describe a social fact.
>
> Butler: You are not a very conventional person, are you? [. . .] I am perfectly willing to stay here, with the chair's permission, for as long as is necessary to get an answer to the question which I have put to you. Now will you please answer the question.[48]

In the end, the board concluded Melish and Kingsbury were communists by resemblance. Even if Kingsbury was not "an actual, formal member of the Party," the final report admitted, his actions were "in concert with Party members and functionaries." Regarding Melish, the board also settled for affinity, saying he had "at least some predisposition towards communism."[49]

The fact that the lawyers were combative with Melish and Kingsbury is hardly remarkable. Most hearings of suspected communists proceeded this way. Nor is it surprising that Conner and Butler posed abstract questions to draw out Melish's and Kingsbury's alleged pro-communist beliefs. What is remarkable is that Conner and Butler questioned Virginia Epstein a few days later as if she had no political convictions at all. They grilled Melish for weeks but examined Epstein for one afternoon.[50] They did not sexualize her, the way HUAC did to Muriel Draper, but gendered assumptions shaped the questions they asked and answers they accepted.

Conner and Butler had been scornful when Kingsbury and Melish claimed not to know or remember something, but when Epstein repeatedly said "I don't know" or "I don't understand," they accepted her proclaimed ignorance without protest. Epstein let her apparent confusion reign, but a careful reading of the hearing transcript shows she seized upon vaguely phrased questions to protect the Committee of Women and its letter writers.

The first question Conner and Butler put to Epstein was, unsurprisingly, whether she was a member of the Communist Party. Epstein denied this, and Conner and Butler simply accepted her answer. They made no effort to prove she was a communist by resemblance.[51] Later, in the board's final report, Epstein was the only defendant listed without any political associations or sympathies.[52] Conner and Butler next asked Epstein whether other women in the National Council, including the late Muriel Draper and Epstein's co-chair Eslanda Goode Robeson, were party members. Epstein responded ambivalently that she did not know them to be but added that she never heard the Communist Party discussed nor encountered any party officials at committee meetings.[53] And Conner and Butler accepted this statement.

Next, the prosecutors tried to connect the pen-pal program to the Soviet state and Communist Party. They asked if the letters were sent through the Soviet Embassy. Epstein denied this. After all, they were sent through the Soviet Consulate in New York City until it closed in 1948.[54] A few initial packages of correspondence were sent via the embassy but that was before her time as co-chair.[55] Of course, she did not volunteer any of this information. Epstein also downplayed the scope of the project, claiming that the total number of letters exchanged were in the hundreds, not thousands. Conner and Butler expressed surprise that the number was so low, and she replied tentatively, "I should say so, but I can't be accurate."[56] When questioned about how the American correspondents were recruited, Epstein replied that the Committee of Women advertised for pen pals in the magazine of the General Federation of Women's Clubs. It was a safe publication to mention because, at the time of the hearing, its two million subscribers tended to be politically moderate and, moreover, the federation was actively preaching anti-communism through its Department of Americanism.[57] In truth, the pen-pal program had not been advertised in *Clubwoman* for years, whereas two years earlier Epstein published a promotional article in the pro-Soviet *New World Review*. Conner and Butler had that article and submitted it into evidence, but they did not use it to link Epstein or the pen-pal program to communism. This was a glaring abstention since investigators repeatedly cited the fact that Corliss Lamont, John A. Kingsbury, and other National Council leaders had published in far-left periodicals as proof that they had communist sympathies.[58]

Like others brought before the Subversive Activities Control Board, Epstein did not name names, and she took the lion's share of responsibility onto herself. She claimed she alone selected the excerpts of the letters published in the pamphlet *Dear Unknown Friend* even though a team of women did this work.[59] In order to ascertain the identities of the letter writers, the attorneys asked if Epstein had the original letters with the authors' names and addresses on them. She said no. This was true. The committee had sent the originals to their intended recipients. However, it later asked the letter writers and the Soviet Women's Anti-Fascist Committee for copies, so it could publish them in *Dear Unknown Friend* and the newsletter *The Women Report*.[60] "You don't have copies of them?" asked Coddaire, who presided over the hearing. "Not of the originals," Epstein replied misleadingly.[61] She had copies of copies. No one probed how it was, then, that the committee had access to letters sent between 1943 and 1948 for publication in 1949.

Trying a different tack, Conner and Butler asked for a list of the Committee of Women's members and sponsors. This should have been simple, as the committee printed the names of its sponsors on its stationery. Instead, this request dragged them into a quagmire, which Epstein helped muddy. Conner and Butler found themselves thwarted by two stumbling blocks. The first was the exact relationship between the National Council of American-Soviet Friendship and this subcommittee, the Committee of Women. Since 1943, the National Council had structured itself as a "loosely knit" organization with local branches and subcommittees. It had no regular membership rolls, nor did it collect dues until the 1950s, when hearings like this one almost bankrupted it.[62] The second sticking point was the distinction between being a member of a group and being a participant in it. The confusion began when Epstein offered a basic timeline of her activities in the Committee of Women and the National Council, which she constantly referred to as separate entities. She volunteered for the Committee of Women in 1945 after meeting the charismatic Muriel Draper, but she became involved in the National Council only in March 1950.[63] When Conner and Butler posed questions about the National Council, Epstein declined to answer, saying she did not know about its operations before she joined its executive board in 1953—only a few months before the hearing started.

Epstein continued in this way, repeatedly differentiating the Committee of Women from the National Council. Soviet pen pals sent their letters to the Committee of Women, not to the National Council.[64] The staff who handled those letters were not National Council personnel.[65] "Once again, you are distinguishing here between the Committee of Women and the National Council itself?" Conner inquired. "Yes," Epstein answered. "You think that is a fair distinction?" "That is the way it is, and I don't know what else to do," she replied.[66] Thus Epstein extricated the Committee of Women from the charges against the council.

Even the presiding David J. Coddiare intervened to try and pin down the relationship between the National Council and its subcommittee. Was Epstein appointed by the National Council to run the Committee of Women? No. How did she become a part of the Committee of Women without first being a National Council member? "I expressed the desire to work with the Committee of Women," and Muriel Draper "just accepted my work. I don't know," Epstein replied. In this timid register, Epstein insisted she was a volunteer, not an employee or appointee of the committee. Coddaire probed another way: if the National Council was found guilty and forced to register as a foreign agent, would the Committee of Women register separately or would "the registration of the National Council cover it?" Again, Epstein pled ignorance: "I don't know. I am not qualified to answer that. I don't understand these legal questions, so I don't know. And I am not trying to evade."[67]

Perhaps Epstein was genuinely befuddled. Perhaps she was being cleverly obstructionist. Either way, she derailed the proceedings into a tedious discussion of the legal relationship between the Committee of Women and the National Council. Rather than pressure her, the attorneys and the board representatives accepted her ignorance and spoke of it in front of her. "I think probably we are lost because this witness does not quite understand the term 'membership,'" Conner commented. "Probably," Coddaire agreed. "The witness has testified in such a way [that] there has been no positive statement," Butler added with a touch of exasperation. After several more pages of testimony, the Committee of Women's status was still opaque.[68] Epstein explained that she and her co-chair Eslanda Goode Robeson did not take direction from the National Council or report to its board of directors. However, they sometimes *chose* to submit reports to them. Coddaire decided they needed a recess.[69]

After the break, Conner and Butler continued to search for connections between the Committee of Women, the National Council, and the Kremlin. But the committee's lack of clear membership criteria and its informal chain of command hampered these efforts. Epstein claimed that it was "almost impossible to answer" even simple questions like "approximately how many people make up the Committee of Women?" "It is a very informal [*sic*]—at the present time, and it has been since about 1950—it has been a very informal organization. We do not have any membership lists. Volunteers come—." "You have no membership list?" Butler interjected. "No, we do not. [. . .] We have lists of women who have volunteered to work with us from time to time," Epstein stated. "They are not considered members?" Butler asked. "Not necessarily at this time," she hedged. But one only had to glance at the back cover of the committee's newsletter *The Women Report*, which prosecutors had submitted into evidence, to see that the Committee of Women asked readers if they wanted to become members. In the end, the only people whom Epstein admitted were members of the Committee of Women were individuals who held titled positions within it: herself, her co-chair Eslanda Goode Robeson, and the vice-chair Jessica Smith. All three were already known to anti-communist investigators, so this was not helpful information. Epstein protected the other participants from scrutiny. After another hour of queries, Coddaire admitted: "I haven't got the Women's Committee clear in my mind yet."[70]

When the cross-examination of William Howard Melish and John A. Kingsbury had descended into circular questioning, Conner and Butler reacted by pushing the defendants harder. Not with Epstein. They simply excused her from the stand. Why harp on about a minor subcommittee of the National Council, especially when its chairperson seemed unable to answer basic questions? Moreover, all the queries they had posed were organizational, not conceptual. They did not probe Epstein's ideological beliefs. In one last dismissive act, the Subversive Activities Control Board used nothing from Epstein's testimony in its final report, where it concluded that the National Council of American-Soviet Friendship "is substantially directed, dominated, and controlled by the Communist Party of the United States" and "primarily operated for the purpose of giving aid and support" to the Soviet Union.[71] The board ordered the National Council to register as a foreign agent. The National Council appealed in 1956 and lost, but a second appeal in 1962 succeeded.[72]

Ultimately, the National Council proved resilient against anti-communist litigators, but it was a pyrrhic victory. Reverend William Howard Melish was forced out as rector of the Church of the Holy Trinity in Brooklyn. Dr. John A. Kingsbury died a year after the board's ruling. The National Council was nearly bankrupted by legal fees. It lost its tax-exempt status, most of its supporters, many subcommittees, and all but three of its regional branches. Venues refused to host its events; libraries rejected its publications.[73]

By comparison, the Committee of Women and the pen-pal program were relatively unscathed. True, the committee lost most of its supporters and letter writers. Some of the most dedicated correspondents like Mary Roe Hull, Jean Jahr, Celia Wesle, and Jeanne Woolf stopped participating in 1949 and 1950, but others like Gladys Kimple kept sending letters. The Committee of Women discontinued *The Women Report* and dropped plans to publish a sequel to *Dear Unknown Friend* due to a lack of funds, but it maintained a modest slate of conferences and outreach events.[74] It had always done most of its own fundraising and got creative with raffles, Christmas bazaars, and even musicals to make money.[75] The FBI continued to monitor the committee's leaders, including Epstein, whom they tracked until she was eighty-four years old.[76] Despite such scrutiny, the Committee of Women stayed devoted to the pen-pal program.

In fact, the hearing seemed to embolden the Committee of Women and its letter writers to be more outspoken against cold war consensus politics. Several prominent leftist activists, all of whom had testified before anti-communist investigators, joined the committee's leadership in the 1950s. Jessica Smith, a Communist Party member and editor of *Soviet Russia Today* (renamed *New World Review*) became the committee's vice chair. Elizabeth Moos, a well-known fellow traveler and cofounder of the Peace Information Center, became committee secretary and, of course, Eslanda Goode Robeson, a core member of the Council on African Affairs and the National Council of Negro Women, co-chaired with Virginia Epstein. This new cohort brought more radical political views and stronger international connections to the committee. Ironically, under their guidance, the Committee of Women shifted further to the left and closer to what anti-communists had accused it of being.

Likewise, the remaining American pen pals, including Gladys Kimple, became more radical and vocally critical of the US government in their letters. Some subscribed to leftist magazines like *Soviet Russia Today* or *Soviet Woman* and wrote to these outlets in search of a pen friend.[77] Whether because of her pen friends' influence, her run-ins with anti-communist crusaders, or some other factor, Kimple's stated political views shifted leftward by the early 1950s. By contrast, her letters from 1946 and 1947 contain rather ecumenical statements on the gulf between American liberal capitalism and Soviet socialism. These were merely "two different kinds of life. I live under one system and you under another." "The system that offers the purest good to us, to the greatest number of people," Kimple reflected, "that provides them freedom and progress, that system will absolutely be victorious."[78] Although she had only an eighth-grade education, Kimple joined several book groups and read works by Marx and Stalin, though she did not find the experience "pleasurable."[79] Notably, Viazovskaia ignored those statements and instead wrote how "pleased" she was that Kimple tackled Tolstoy's *Anna Karenina*.

Around 1948, there were signs that Kimple was drifting leftward. The Committee of Women cut all indications of this when publishing from her letters—a most uncharacteristic move for a so-called "communist front" organization. It removed Kimple's announcement that she supported Progressive Party candidate Henry A. Wallace for president, and it struck out her speculation that "in the future the whole world will come to socialism," though given the popularity and comforts of capitalism, it would be a long time before socialism took root in the United States, she remarked. Despite such occasional pronouncements, Kimple shied away from overtly political talk and preferred to focus on everyday life. "I do not at all plan to make a political speech, at least not intentionally," Kimple reflected in another comment the Committee of Women cut, presumably to soften the sharp edges of political debate in *Dear Unknown Friend*.[80]

Yet, by the 1950s, political speeches were the main feature of her letters. Outrage against anti-communist crusaders fueled Kimple's tirades about the hypocrisy of American liberalism and made her more accepting of Ekaterina Zheliabuzhskaia's idealized descriptions of life under socialism. Kimple seized upon those rosy pictures as ammunition she could use to "slay the dragon" of anti-communism.[81] Her affectionate remarks towards Zheliabuzhskaia intermingled with cryptic comments about what she could not write and asides directed at eavesdropping American officials: "I want to write so much about international events and about things at home, but in a letter I must limit myself. I cannot express myself as freely as I would like." This was because she did "not agree with the politics of the US government" and such a stance was "incredibly unpopular with some people who may or may not read this before it reaches you," Kimple explained, "I want to say to them, as to you, that I love my country. There is no treachery in my heart."[82] "I love my country," she reiterated in another letter written aboard her fishing boat, "and I believe in the final word of the people. I do not much respect an economic system based on the suppression of the majority by a small group, whether in my own or in another country," she declared and then added: "I am on the lists of 'leftists,' which the 'rightists' are compiling here."[83]

Kimple had reason to believe she was being targeted by the US government during the 1950s. First, Zheliabuzhskaia's letters were arriving open.[84] Second, her youngest son David, a pilot stationed at Spokane, Washington, was "honorably discharged" from the US Air Force and subsequently lost his license to fly. Kimple unpacked what "honorable discharge" meant so Zheliabuzhskaia could understand. "Translated into everyday language it means that because of my—not his—beliefs he is considered insufficiently trustworthy for military service."[85] "He never had bad marks for behavior, and they really loved him. He loved his comrades as well as the officers. That means that this was done because of his progressively minded relatives, and they do not trust him anymore."[86] Among those relatives were his aunt and uncle Charlotte O. and Merrill D. Kimple. They were active in the Progressive Party, and Merrill lost his job after participating in the well-known 1948 strike against Boeing. In 1954, he was named as an underground organizer of the Communist Party in Washington's South King region.[87] As a result, he was tried for un-American activities and fired from his forestry job. "All of this is a sad commentary on the current limits of our freedom," Kimple observed.[88]

Kimple's marriage may have been another casualty. She never said so in her letters, for she stopped corresponding during the time when she and Dillon Kimple parted ways, but her grandson, Roy Pearmain, told me that politics may have been one reason for the split—or so it was rumored in the family.[89] What is clear is that Gladys Kimple became increasingly afraid for her own safety. After Dwight D. Eisenhower was elected president in 1952 on a platform of fighting "Corruption, Communism, and Korea," Kimple sent a panicky letter asking Zheliabuzhskaia for her "faith, encouragement, and belief." "Things may become difficult so that I can no longer write you," she added ominously. "If my letters should stop, it will only be because I cannot get them through to you."[90]

In fact, Kimple's notes were among the few letters from the United States that prompted a response from the Soviet Women's Anti-Fascist Committee. Ninety-four percent of the American letter writers—some 290 individuals—were dropped from the program during the early 1950s. The committee sent no explanation, no words of farewell. Jilted American pen pals like

Kimple assumed their own government was to blame. In fact, the decision to end these correspondences came from Moscow.

Politically Influential and Important Women

"I do not know what happened," one American pen pal despaired, "she just stopped writing to me, and right before that she promised to send a photograph of her little son."[91] When letters stopped arriving from the Soviet actress Tat'iana Ivanovna Guretskaia, Rebecca Kalmus implored the Soviet Women's Anti-Fascist Committee: "Please write to me a few words of what became of her. She was so nice to me, and now I don't hear from her at all, and I feel uneasy about her silence. Is she sick? Or is she traveling? At any rate, a word from you 'ladies of peace' about Tat'iana Guretskaia would be most refreshing." Eager for contact, Kalmus asked for someone at the antifascist committee to trade letters with her: "I am appealing to you again, my friends, that henceforth you correspond with me, as I am willing to write to you, and exchange words, thoughts, and ideas on any subject you like. Please answer this letter."[92]

Kalmus and other Americans were "bewildered" by the disappearance of their pen pals, members of the Soviet Women's Anti-Fascist Committee's presidium admitted during one meeting.[93] The Committee of Women was also confused. It kept advertising for pen pals in *New World Review*, but those new volunteers never received replies.[94] "We will be happy if Soviet women reply to the letters because such responses help us in our work to strengthen friendship with the people of the Soviet Union," Virginia Epstein gently pressed. "We plan to protect and expand this program. It has very great meaning for those few American women who continue to correspond, and they are eagerly awaiting replies." Members of the anti-fascist committee read Epstein's note aloud during one 1951 meeting, but they could not bring themselves to tell her the truth: American women were dropped from the program because they were no longer considered "important and influential" enough to participate.[95] That was not their assessment; it came from the USSR's top party organ, the Central Committee of the Communist Party.

The anti-fascist committee's use of the pen-pal program had been "improper."[96] So said investigators from the Central Committee's Foreign Policy Commission after auditing the program in May 1950.[97] The commission found the Soviet letter writers weak and ineffective in promoting socialism and the Soviet way of life, and it called for them to "be replaced by stronger ones."[98] The anti-fascist committee defended its work, claiming that the Soviet correspondents were "presenting the advantages of the Soviet system" by writing about "their lives, work, and families" as well as "every meaningful event inside the life of the USSR and international affairs. This is not achieved by chance." The committee told the Central Committee that it had been "working with the correspondents" and instructing them to champion Soviet-backed initiatives like the Stockholm Appeal—a petition to ban the use of nuclear weapons—and the World Peace Council, the international though Soviet-dominated body that put forward that petition in 1950.[99] But based on my own reading, I would have to agree with the investigating commission that these themes were very weakly developed. No doubt the anti-fascist committee advised the letter writers to include these events, but only three obeyed and with little enthusiasm.[100] One of them was Ekaterina Zheliabuzhskaia, but she merely asked, "what is being done [in the United States] about the World Peace Council?" and Gladys Kimple gave an even shorter reply: nothing. The topic generated no conversation.[101] Indeed, one of the many ways these letters contribute to our understanding of the peace movement is that they don't focus on these high-profile institutions but show us the antiwar movement through the personalized politics practiced by individual women.[102] The anti-fascist committee was right in saying that "Soviet correspondents try to actively influence their overseas friends so that they avidly work in the defense of peace," but they did so by discussing their own lives rather than promoting official institutions or campaigns.[103]

That method of persuasion did not satisfy party investigators. Going forward, the commission ordered, the letter exchange needed to be controlled tightly and Soviet letter writers had to be instructed on how to grow support for their state's policies and peace initiatives. Moreover, the anti-fascist committee should stop wasting resources by facilitating long, meandering conversations between women of little importance. Henceforth, the commission ordered the anti-fascist committee to end politically useless pen friendships and arrange them only between women who were "prominent" or "influential" and ideally both "famous and influential."[104] Following the commission's directive, the Soviet Women's Anti-Fascist Committee agreed to "remove all uninteresting and irregular correspondence" and exert tighter control over the remaining Soviet participants. In spring 1952, it set up mandatory briefings for Soviet correspondents to come and learn about the latest Soviet policies or peace initiatives to promote in their letters.[105]

The investigative commission gave the same directive to the other remaining anti-fascist committee, that of Soviet youth. But in that case, the driving concern was not that youngsters were bad propagandists but that they were being exposed to "hostile" letters containing "provocative questions" and "slander" against the USSR. The youth pen-pal program continued but, going forward, only "the most politically trained leading officials of the Komsomol (Young Communist League)" were allowed to write letters and then under close observation.[106] Thus, just as it did during World War II, the party continued to use women and children as friendly Soviet emissaries, but in 1950 it tightened its grip over who could participate and what they could say.

The anti-fascist committee made no effort to save the pen-pal program at this time. In fact, its meeting minutes from the early 1950s capture a sense of relief. The practical difficulties of translating, editing, censoring, and transporting the letters dogged the committee's small staff. The process became more time-consuming as the committee extended its pen-pal programs to many new countries in eastern Europe and East Asia.[107] It took longer to process the letters, and the conversations stalled as a result. On top of this, the same difficulties remained with recruiting and retaining Soviet letter writers. "As a rule, prominent Soviet women who participate in correspondence delay in replying to the letters of their friends overseas or else do not reply at all, despite our repeated reminders," V. E. Busygina, a member of the small staff that processed the letters, admitted to the committee's presidium during a 1951 meeting. "Very often we receive requests in which women ask to be freed from correspondence." No doubt the risk that Soviet participants took in maintaining contact with women in the capitalist West weighed on them, but the reasons they gave for wanting out were busyness and boredom.[108]

And so, the committee slashed its pen-pal programs with women in the capitalist West. In the first half of 1950, the committee received 809 letters and arranged responses to only 618 of them. In the second half of the year, it received another 907 letters but arranged replies to just 282.[109] Reductions continued into 1951 and 1952, and the deepest cuts were made to pen pals from Britain, France, and the United States, so the committee could grow its programs with women in the eastern bloc, in socialist East Asia, and elsewhere in the developing world.[110] This was such a sea change from 1943, when the committee chased after correspondents among its western Allies. Atop nearly every letter that arrived from the United States between 1951 and 1953, an anti-fascist committee staff member scrawled: "do not reply."[111] And what of those who did receive replies? The bulk of the women retained from Britain and France were members of the Communist Party. By contrast, anti-fascist committee records claim none of the American letter writers were in the party. Ultimately, the committee allowed seventy-five French and forty-one British women to keep corresponding, but it shrank the American pool to twenty.[112] Those with strong communist sympathies, like Gladys Kimple, made the cut.

Despite this liquidation, letter writing still had a place in the Soviet Women's Anti-Fascist Committee's mission. The investigative commission instructed the committee to focus its energies on exerting more influence over transnational women's coalitions, which were becoming increasingly powerful in global politics. In particular, the committee was ordered to concentrate on arranging for Soviet women to attend gatherings of the WIDF and the UN Commission on the Status of Women, to network with "important and influential" activists there, and to invite those colleagues to the Soviet Union where they would see the benefits of a socialist way of life. Such in-person meetings promised to be a more efficient and effective way to establish friendship and influence. "After their departure," some of the Soviet women they met would, "by way of correspondence, sustain friendly ties with them and send them new material and information about life in the Soviet Union" as well as on their common goals of peace and women's rights.[113]

In this way, it was not simply separation imposed by an "iron curtain" or fear engendered by so-called McCarthyism or *zhdanovshchina* that killed the American-Soviet pen friendships. It was also the rise of international women's coalitions for peace and equality, which created face-to-face opportunities to form partnerships. Despite the notorious isolationism of the late Stalin era, women affiliated with the Soviet Women's Anti-Fascist Committee began to travel abroad multiple times annually, at least three times each year to attend meetings of the WIDF's executive committee and secretariat and additional times to participate in its perennial International Women's Congresses. These gatherings, along with meetings of the UN

Commission on the Status of Women, gave committee members much larger platforms for championing Soviet approaches to peace, women's rights, and socialism. By 1951, the WIDF claimed to represent 135 million women from sixty-four countries, making it the largest women's organization in the world.[114]

The Soviet Women's Anti-Fascist Committee poured time and money into the WIDF and succeeded in exerting considerable influence over it. The committee's propaganda sector supplied the federation with a steady stream of pro-Soviet materials, while chairperson Nina Popova secured extra funds from the Central Committee of the Communist Party to support the publication of the federation's *Bulletin* and its newsletter, *Women of the Whole World*, created in 1951.[115] The WIDF did vote down some Soviet proposals, but the anti-fascist committee remained a dominant force within it—so much so that British and American delegates in the UN convinced the General Assembly to strip the WIDF of its consultative status in 1954 on the grounds that it was effectively a Soviet propaganda agency.[116] The State Department also instructed US consulates and embassies around the world to send an alert if the WIDF tried to recruit women living in their region.[117]

But State Department officials seemed even more threatened by the work that the anti-fascist committee was doing to champion Soviet policies of gender equality in the UN Commission on the Status of Women. Several high-ranking anti-fascist committee members also served as delegates to that commission. They arranged for the committee to prepare an exhibition called "Soviet Woman: Actively Participating in Socialist Construction" for the UN Commission in 1952, and for it to host a special UN seminar on gender equality in Moscow in 1956.[118] These campaigns set off more alarm bells that the commission was becoming another site of Soviet cold war grandstanding. The US Department of Justice set to work developing a strategic plan to curb Soviet influence over the UN commission, and some members of Women United for the United Nations founded a new women's letter-writing program in response.[119]

Calling themselves the Committee of Correspondence after the epistolary networks formed by American revolutionaries, the members of this new group set up shop in New York City, a few blocks away from the Committee of Women, in 1952. It got to work sending letters and pamphlets around the world, which promoted American democracy and liberal-capitalist models of peace and women's rights. Through these efforts, it aimed to "offset the Soviet Women's [Anti-Fascist] Committee."[120] Although Committee of Correspondence members certainly penned some personalized letters, I found little evidence that there were many committed pairs who corresponded over several years. Much of the committee's outreach work consisted of newsletters and training brochures, which instructed readers on how to organize their own campaigns to champion American-style democracy.[121] The group's motto, "the Truth Shall Make You Free," was taken from John 8:32 and reflected the organizers' larger claim that, unlike the anti-fascist committee, theirs was a truly voluntary civic organization, independent of government interference.

But this was not true. One of the group's founders, Dorothy Bauman, had appealed in 1948 to the State Department and in 1951 to the CIA—which displayed the same motto in the lobby of its headquarters—about the need to sponsor voluntary organizations among American women and train them to combat Soviet women's peace campaigns. Bauman then got together with Rose Parsons, who had launched the correspondence initiative, and they collaborated on the Committee of Correspondence.[122] They accepted significant funding from the CIA, some $587,500 between 1954 and 1966, and they delivered copies of all of their publications and letters—both sent and received—to the CIA. Similarly, the United States Information Agency even gave the committee a certificate of merit for its work and willingness to share "confidential information received from our correspondents with the US Department of State."[123] The committee's leaders kept these government affiliations a secret from many of its members, but the story broke in the *New York Times* in 1967. The group folded two years later.[124] In truth, both the Committee of Correspondence and its rival, the Soviet Women's Anti-Fascist Committee, relied on a combination of energetic volunteers and state support. And both groups had to contend with male government officials who financed and monitored their work.

Gatherings of the WIDF and the UN Commission on the Status of Women created opportunities for members of the anti-fascist committee to meet foreign activists face-to-face and connect with them more quickly than through pen friendship. At meetings throughout the early 1950s, they shook hands, laughed, shared meals, and sang songs with women from around the world. This physical proximity fostered an intimacy seemingly worth thousands of words about friendship.[125] It made the pen-pal program seem even more improvident. During the meetings, representatives of the Soviet Women's Anti-Fascist Committee invited many western delegates to visit the USSR and see Soviet life firsthand. With the permission of the Central Committee of the Communist Party, the anti-fascist committee hosted between six and twelve delegations of foreign women annually during the late 1940s and early 1950s. Small groups of four to eight American women arrived in 1947, 1949, 1950, 1952, 1955, and so on. Scholars estimate that the Soviet Union's All-Union Society for Cultural Relations with Foreign Countries (VOKS) hosted only fifty-seven Americans in the USSR between 1947 and 1951.[126] The anti-fascist committee's records suggest a significantly higher number of sojourners during this period were women who visited at the committee's request.

The Americans who came circumvented the State Department's travel restrictions by journeying to another destination for a women's conference or peace gathering and then arranging a "layover" in the USSR. Once in the Soviet Union, they were wined and dined. They toured schools, clinics, and factories. They chatted with (carefully vetted) workers, and they met with high-ranking Soviet officials, usually the deputy heads of the ministries of health, education, or social welfare. At night, they attended the ballet, opera, or theater. Of course, the anti-fascist committee crafted these itineraries to showcase the bright spots of Soviet society and to shield the visitors from the poverty and enduring patriarchy that Soviet women confronted daily. While a few visitors voiced skepticism or asked pointed questions, most were delighted by the experience. As activists committed to organizations and causes on the far left, most saw what they hoped to see.[127] Many shared their positive impressions with the press, and this solidified the Central Committee's position that hosting groups of prominent women was a more efficient way to promote Soviet socialism than arranging individual correspondence. Still, the anti-fascist committee saw to it that its visitors received letters from one of the "important and influential" Soviet women they had met in the USSR.

Pauline Tailor of Youngstown, Ohio, was one such visitor. She was still waxing poetic about her "layover" in the Soviet Union four years later. "Dear Ekaterina! Thank you for the lovely card, which reminded me of what I saw in December 1950. Those were unforgettable days. [. . .] My trip to your country and the great Congress of the Supporters of Peace in Poland left me with terrific memories, which I will share with others until the end of my life. The people, the new way of life, the buildings, metro, and great movement for peace in your country gave me such rich information as well as inspiration to struggle with all my strength, because time is short, to make our country a sanctuary of peace and brotherhood."[128]

As a civil rights activist, member of the Progressive Party, supporter of the Committee for the Protection of the Foreign Born, and woman of color, Tailor was typical of the new kind of active, well-connected American the anti-fascist committee now targeted. "I always will do all that I can for peace and try to enlighten those with whom I talk and tell them about what I saw in your country and about your people," she pledged to her pen pal, Ekaterina Vasil'evna Sheveleva. One of the committee's new "important and influential" recruits, Sheveleva was a poet, journalist, and member of the Communist Party. She later served on the Soviet Peace Committee. In subsequent letters, Tailor continued to reminisce about how "life in the USSR is lovely" with Sheveleva, and she did the same in person with fellow civil rights activists Ada Jackson and Eslanda Goode Robeson. Tailor also shared her travel experiences at events held by the National Council of American-Soviet Friendship.[129] She joined the National Council's board of directors in 1952. In 1956, she was summoned to testify before HUAC.[130]

Halois Moorhead Robinson also received several letters after she met members of the anti-fascist committee who came to New York for a meeting of the UN Commission on the Status of Women in 1953. A major though understudied civil rights activist, Robinson was the recording secretary of the National Negro Congress and worked tirelessly against the wrongful imprisonment of Black Americans like Rosa Lee Ingram and her sons, who were arrested in 1947 and initially sentenced to death.[131] Robinson also became a member of the National Council of American-Soviet Friendship in the early fifties and spoke at its events. Robinson was less diligent than Tailor about corresponding with her Soviet contacts, but she received several notes from Nadezhda Khimach. Khimach was one of a handful of staff members in the anti-fascist committee who translated and edited letters from the United States. After the committee made drastic cuts to the pen-pal program and focused on hosting foreign delegations instead, Khimach became the point person for British and American visitors as well as a delegate to the UN Commission on the Status of Women. As a result, she was tasked with initiating correspondences with many of the activists she hosted or met overseas. She went from translating letters to authoring them.

One might assume such fascinating individuals as Tailor and Robinson produced fascinating letters, and that their shared political goals forged a strong bond between them and their Soviet interlocutors. But their correspondences fizzled after just a few letters. Why? Of course, these women were extremely busy with advocacy work, but there is another culprit to blame. Michel de Montaigne once said, "there is no conversation more boring than the one where everybody agrees." That sentiment encapsulates this correspondence between Soviet and American activists during the fifties.

In the 1940s, letter writing provided a way for women who had never met to build connections, hash out political differences, and cultivate mutual understanding. During the 1950s, however, it was repurposed to help the antifascist committee maintain ties with likeminded activists. In the 1940s, the letters themselves had been the site of connection, the only basis upon which the "unknown friends" knew each other. But the letters written by prominent women during the 1950s mostly contained updates about ongoing political campaigns, words of mutual encouragement, and reminiscences about time spent together.[132] No doubt Soviet and American activists became friendly and perhaps even friends during the weeks they traveled or conferenced together, but they never really became pen pals.

The letters between Halois Moorhead Robinson and Nadezhda Khimach were full of fond recollections, but they were referential letters, placeholders for a relationship on hold until the next face-to-face meeting. "I shall never forget the treasured moments spent with you and the other fine women who were in our country," Robinson wrote in 1953, "I truly hope that the occasion arises for us to repeat these moments in the not too distant future."[133] "I must say," Khimach replied, "that these lines made me relive in my memory all our meetings and friendly talks."[134] Anticipating heart-to-hearts to come, the pair never had one on paper, and their correspondence stalled. Letter writing did not advance their relationship or drive their exchange of ideas forward, perhaps because they always agreed that another peace conference or petition was a good idea.

Although affectionate, these letters were also far less personal than those penned by earlier cohorts of pen friends who never met in person but knew all about each other and each other's children. By contrast, the activists rarely shared anything personal, and their political discussions were cursory. Rather than debate ideas and policies like the "unknown friends" who came before them, these new letter writers gave short updates on their advocacy work or exchanged clippings summarizing it. Eslanda Goode Robeson, who also met Nadezhda Khimach at a conference in New York, did send the Muscovite a picture of her baby granddaughter, Susan, and several of her articles, but her accompanying letter was only three lines long.[135] And Khimach was the worst offender of all. In the dozens of letters she penned, she never wrote a jot about herself. She focused on anti-fascist committee matters and the peace movement, and she offered a line here and there about the weather, Moscow skyline, or Soviet new year's traditions, never her own year-end celebration.[136] Despite their generic quality, her letters were censored more heavily by her colleagues at the anti-fascist committee than any letters sent by "ordinary" pen friends—even though the uncensored versions of Khimach's notes felt rather perfunctory from the start.[137] In nearly every case, correspondence between "important and influential" women faded after just two or three letters.

One thing Khimach did mention, repeatedly, in her notes was that she was tired—not just from traveling and hosting but from her overstuffed inbox. The old problem of absentee Soviet pen pals continued. It was Khimach's job to wrangle them into responding or, if necessary, write replies herself. Throughout the early 1950s, Khimach's supervisors scrawled across the top of letters sent by the few remaining American letter writers instructions like: "arrange a reply," "reply based on your schedule," and "we

Members of the Soviet Women's Committee with former First Lady Eleanor Roosevelt at the gravesite of President Franklin D. Roosevelt, Hyde Park, New York, 1959. (State Archive of the Russian Federation, f. R7928, op. 3, d. 326, l. 88.)

absolutely need to answer, connect her with a sensible correspondent."[138] By hook or by crook, Khimach provided a reply. When writing with activists whom she met, Khimach signed her own name. When writing on behalf of one of the twenty remaining "unknown friends" who often deserted their American pen pals, Khimach impersonated them. So, after Ekaterina Zheliabuzhskaia stopped replying to Gladys Kimple in 1953—the year when Zheliabuzhskaia's mother died and Zheliabuzhskaia began to go blind—Khimach replied on her behalf. By the mid-1950s, this situation became so common that two other committee workers, O. N. Shchelina and S. S. Gilevskaia, were tasked with procuring replies to American letters, even if they had to create them themselves.

In this way, the Soviet letter writers disappeared from the project in the 1950s. By 1953, the Soviet letters disappeared too. They are missing from the anti-fascist committee's archive. Perhaps they were lost? Or perhaps the committee staff now wrote the bulk of the replies and stopped keeping copies? Gladys Kimple wrote on, but after 1953 I could find no trace of Soviet responses, either from Zheliabuzhskaia or someone writing on her behalf.[139] The conversation—insofar as I can reconstruct it—became one-sided. Kimple finally stopped writing in 1956. That was the year she got divorced and moved to Seattle to start a new life.

ALTHOUGH THE ARCHIVAL record dries up, the demand for pen friendship did not. In fact, it was quite difficult to suppress. Despite—or perhaps because of—the accusations that US officials levied against the letter writing program, a whole new group of defiant American women sought Soviet correspondents in the early 1950s. There were only a few dozen of them, but from 1953 onward, especially after Senator Joseph McCarthy met his political demise in 1954, the number of Americans who contacted the Soviet Embassy in Washington, DC, with a pen-pal request steadily rose.[140] In 1954, the All-Union Society for Cultural Relations with Foreign Countries (VOKS), which managed the USSR's overseas contacts, received 260 requests from Americans, both men and women, who wanted a Soviet correspondent. Nearly four hundred such requests arrived in 1955.[141]

By January 1956, the Soviet Women's Anti-Fascist Committee—which changed its name to the Soviet Women's Committee—called an emergency meeting to discuss this heavy volume of letters from overseas.[142] It appealed to the Central Committee of the Communist Party asking if it should once again exploit this propagandistic opportunity by reviving the pen pal program and if, this time, it could outsource some of the work by inviting local party and trade union representatives to correspond.[143] In essence, the committee was in the same situation in 1955 as it had been in 1945. It had been ordered to end the exchange, but American eagerness for conversation was too opportune to ignore.

So much had changed in US-Soviet relations, leadership, and strategy since 1945, and yet—when viewed through the lens of women's pen friendship—there is striking continuity between 1945 and 1955. Scholars of US-Soviet citizen diplomacy invariably focus their attention on the second half of the twentieth century and link the proliferation of exchange initiatives to the death of Stalin as well as to the "thaw" and "spirit of Geneva" touted by Khrushchev and Eisenhower. But, as this little-known pen-pal program reveals, the "spirit of Stalingrad" was just as powerful in sparking this impulse for contact between Soviets and Americans, which, despite numerous geopolitical twists and turns, endured.

In fact, it grew. In 1955, the Central Committee of the Communist Party expanded the Soviet Women's Committee staff, so it could run two new commissions. The first was tasked with hosting more delegations of foreign women. Between 1954 and 1955, the committee welcomed seventy-nine groups of activists, and it sent Soviet women abroad to sixteen countries. To maintain those in-person ties, the committee was sending regular, albeit cursory, letters to fifty recent visitors by the end of 1955.[144]

The second commission was charged with recruiting new Soviet pen pals—this time from trade unions and party cells. That gave Nadezhda Khimach and her team a reprieve from penning so many notes themselves.[145] This commission focused on facilitating pen friendships with women in the eastern bloc, East Asia, and the global south, where socialism and communism were expanding. Still, a few Americans remained in the mix. By the early 1960s, the committee processed and dispatched an average of sixty-five letters a month. The cost of the now global pen-pal project continued to demand a huge amount of resources—nearly double what the committee spent soliciting articles for its magazine *Soviet Woman*.[146]

Although it was almost killed in 1945 and thoroughly gutted in 1951, the pen friendship program between Soviet and American women lived on.

Closing ~

The Heart Is the Main Source of Our Actions

"Let's write to each other frequently," Verena G. Koehler urged Zinaida Semenovna Duvankova at the end of one 1950 letter, "it seems so important for people in our two great nations to get to know one another better—not on state matters but smaller domestic details, which so touch the heart. Because in the end it is the heart, and not the head, that is the main source of our motives, of our actions."[1] Winning hearts and minds. So often scholars reach for this phrase to summarize the aim of cultural and citizen diplomacy during the Cold War. But Verena Koehler prompts us to interrogate this pat formulation. For Koehler, a fifty-one-year-old clerk at J. L. Hudson department store in Detroit, the key to strengthening relations between the United States and the Soviet Union lay in the emotional more than the analytical, in everyday practices more than policy. By shifting priorities, she and so many other pen friends hoped to succeed where cerebral analysts and headstrong politicians—all men—had failed. Pen pals like her set about modeling what they believed was a new kind of diplomacy, a diplomacy of the heart.

When Koehler made this appeal to Duvankova, 750 Soviet and American letter writers had been practicing that style of diplomacy for nearly a decade. Whether inspired to defeat fascism or to safeguard the postwar peace, the pen friends shared the "smaller domestic details" of their lives as well as their personal aspirations and anxieties in order to connect—on an emotional level and as women. Their approach to foreign relations was both highly personal and deeply gendered. It was based on the notion that during times of war, hot or cold, being emotionally open, empathetic, and even vulnerable could be politically expedient rather than pose a political liability. The pen pals frequently argued points of view that aligned with those of hardline politicians. The difference was they wrapped their disagreements in a mantle of shared humanity and common concern. They altered the method, not the message. And this enabled them to write through disputes and misunderstandings and to exchange dozens of letters during an era when official diplomacy between the United States and the Soviet Union was often at an impasse. Later, after the two countries signed a cultural exchange agreement in 1958, dozens of letter writing campaigns emerged in which Soviets and Americans participated.[2] What stands out about the program arranged by the Soviet Women's Anti-Fascist Committee and the Committee of Women is that these were not one-off letters but enduring pen friendships that lasted several years.

No one expected these conversations to last so long. They were initially permitted as a temporary measure to strengthen the wartime alliance. When Soviet or American authorities later tried to silence them, by terminating the program, as the Central Committee contemplated in 1945 and 1951, or by proving these conversations were subversive, as the Justice Department attempted to do between 1945 and 1954, the letter writers kept the lines of communication open with their persistence and enthusiasm. At a time when "ordinary" women like them had few opportunities to engage in foreign relations, the pen friends commanded a role for themselves on the political stage. The act of corresponding bolstered their sense of agency. It broadened their political horizons and opened up new vistas of possibility—both for geopolitics and for them as women. Through their wide-ranging conversations, the pen pals charted intellectual pathways that were more varied than the limited itineraries of the privileged few who actually sojourned across the "iron curtain" during the late 1940s and early 1950s. US-Soviet relations rapidly deteriorated, but the letter writers continued to draw strength from the memory of the wartime alliance as proof that their nations could cooperate. The light of the popular front dimmed drastically during *zhdanovshchina* and McCarthyism, but it was not snuffed out and would burn bright again with the rise of the New Left in the 1960s.

There was not just one type of woman who braved the risks and volunteered as a pen friend. Each stage of the program brought in different participants. And while they were never representative of Americans or Soviets as a whole, they did come from many walks of life. When the project began during World War II, the Soviets who took up their pens were laborers and farmers from a variety of regions including Ukraine and Central Asia. After 1945, the anti-fascist committee replaced these munitions workers and collective farmers with well-educated, urban professionals from Moscow, nearly all of whom were ethnically Russian. The new recruits were selected to be "great compelling examples" of women's advancement under socialism, and they comprised the bulk of Soviet letter writers for the duration of the project.[3] Although they were not in the party, these individuals were carefully vetted and often coached on what to write when they picked up their letters at the anti-fascist committee's Moscow headquarters.

The American pool of letter writers fluctuated over time. The initial group included individuals with a personal investment in the Soviet war effort; many had husbands and sons at the front or were of Jewish descent. But after 1945, the American women who requested Soviet pen pals were predominantly white, middle-class, Protestant, and from the Midwest. They tended to be moderate conservatives and liberals who were deeply inspired by Christian teachings on peace. The number of corresponding pairs grew to about two hundred. Then, around 1947, the pool expanded and changed again, as an influx of self-described progressives took up their pens. Most were still from the Midwest, but the number of Californians and New Englanders rose steadily. Their conversations expanded beyond peace to the topics of motherhood, moral upbringing, housework, paid employment, and how to balance these responsibilities for the greatest personal fulfillment. The number of active letter-writing pairs peaked at 319 in 1949, then sharply declined. The Americans who kept writing were noticeably radicalized by anti-communist hysteria, and their letters acquired a defiant edge. Professional activists, often writing in the same tenor, also joined the program during the early fifties. They were more racially diverse, but nearly all were well-educated and middle-class, and lived in coastal American cities. The Soviet Women's Anti-Fascist Committee decided that these "important and influential" advocates of peace, women's equality, and civil rights were its ideal partners for promoting socialism, but they proved to be poor correspondents. Meanwhile, Americans who lacked political stature were mostly cut from the program. Some, including Verena Koehler, kept on writing even though they got scant replies likely penned by someone other than their pen friend. The flow of letters to Moscow remained steady and, by the mid-1950s, the anti-fascist committee was appealing to its party supervisors to expand the pen-pal program once more.

The program proved remarkably resilient. It rode the waves of shifting US-Soviet relations, from enemies to Allies, back to enemies, and then to "frenemies"—a term coined in 1953 to describe the countries' new approach of congenial competitiveness towards one another.[4] In this way, the letter-writing project provides an important window onto how shifts in the relationship between the US and Soviet governments were felt and often resisted by some individual citizens.

Both the participants and their views changed over time, but their political approach remained consistent. They practiced this diplomacy of the heart in the hope that "regular exchanges," conducted "in a spirit of mutual understanding," could "contribute significantly to the betterment of relations between the[ir] two countries"—or so the first American-Soviet cultural exchange agreement put it fifteen years after the pen-pal program began.[5] This perceived link between the personal and the political, between individual connection and international transformation, inspired correspondents to share their letters with their families, friends, coworkers, clubs, and local newspapers. It is also why the organizations overseeing the exchange disseminated snippets of the letters in print and over the radio.

Of course, all of these excerpts were carefully chosen. The organizations had agendas extending beyond peace and goodwill. The Committee of Women cut the most pointed ideological language of the letters before publishing them in *Dear Unknown Friend* or *The Women Report*, which gave American readers an inflated sense of US-Soviet compatibility. The committee also endeavored—through pamphlets and exhibitions—to persuade Soviet women to adopt what they claimed were superior American methods of childrearing and household management in order to help their war-torn families in the USSR. Meanwhile, the Soviet Women's Anti-Fascist Committee had an explicit mandate to promote socialism and Soviet gender policy to Americans, whether through letter writing, mounting exhibitions, hosting delegations, or agitating at meetings of the WIDF and UN Commission on the Status of Women. The organizations' ulterior motives cut against the pen-pal project's celebration of frank conversation, but they embraced its founding premise that heartfelt connections could spark political change. Win the heart, Verena Koehler suggested, and you win the mind.

Whether they were compelled to do so or they did so voluntarily, correspondents from both countries did a great deal of promotional work. The pen-pal project revolved around two objectives: peace and propaganda. The first aim hinged upon understanding, the second on exerting influence. These goals consistently melded together, as the pen friends argued that the best hope for achieving peace resided in the policies and ideals championed by their own countries. Even correspondents who criticized their governments at times passionately defended their national values and promoted narratives of the American Dream, Soviet upward mobility, the self-made man, the myth of the Great Patriotic War, and the friendship of the peoples. All letter writers idealized, all had blind spots. All tried to create a positive impression of themselves and their communities before their foreign readers, downplaying racial and ethnic strife, poverty, political repression, and gender-based inequalities, which impinged on their own freedom. Soviet participants were certainly under overt pressure to propagandize, but that does not mean that their enthusiasm was fabricated. Flushed with the pride of victory, the pen pals wrote during a postwar moment when American and Soviet patriotism bounced back from some of the deep divisions sewn by the Great Depression and Great Terror.

The letter writers were always trying to convince as well as connect, but they were never in lockstep with the interests of policymakers or even of the organizations facilitating their exchange. Soviet correspondents failed to adopt the anti-fascist committee's anti-American rhetoric, to articulate its demands for US military aid, or to promote state-sponsored peace petitions and conferences. Neither the Soviet nor the American participants adopted the hostile discourse that permeated their press and halls of government. They did not shy away from spirited debate so long as it was conducted in the service of understanding and with empathetic intent rather than a desire to make each other wrong. "I like it when you get into your feelings and begin to talk (or write) personally about these things that are close to your heart," Verena Koehler told Zinaida Duvankova. "It does not bother me at all when we do not completely agree. I only get really angry at someone when he does not speak sincerely."[6]

But how could Koehler trust that Duvankova was sincere? In truth, we can never be certain of the participants' "real" intentions, or how accurately they presented their lives. The writers concealed a great deal about themselves, whether to protect their identities or their countries' reputations. Their highly mediated letters, which passed through the hands of so many officials, translators, and censors, do not provide an avenue into their innermost thoughts. What the letters do demonstrate is how their authors built a *sense* of intimacy on the page. They constructed a friendship by weaving stories, confidences, and affections into each note, by trading photographs and developing nicknames. They walked through each other's homes and watched each other's children grow. Although we might question whether theirs was a "real" friendship, what is important is that they construed their relationship that way. Friendship provided a productive, durable framework in which they could disagree, challenge misconceptions, and confront each other without being confrontational.

And so, the program generated thousands of effusive letters penned by total strangers. Koehler's and Duvankova's are a perfect example. Zinaida Semenovna Duvankova was a state official. She worked in the Soviet Ministry of Grain Products and had elite privileges like access to a car.[7] She was one of the "important" Soviet women the program organizers recruited, with difficulty, after 1951. By contrast, Verena G. Koehler was one of those "unimportant" Americans whom the Soviet organizers tried to shake off. But she just kept on writing. At first, Koehler seemed intimidated by her pen friend. Her own education and occupation were comparatively modest, and she joked to Duvankova that her "undignified" job as a department store clerk "required the presence of a strong back and the absence of a large brain."[8] But Duvankova dismissed Koehler's self-deprecation and applauded her pen pal's "choice of vocation because every kind of work is both honorable and dignified."[9] Although they seemed an unlikely match, the pair found lots to talk about.

Their topics of conversation were often mundane but unfolded into consequential discussions about peace, freedom, personal fulfillment, and women's equality. For example, Koehler and Duvankova decided to exchange recipes. Not only were they curious about each other's cuisine, they recognized right away that, as women, they shouldered work inside and outside the home. "When women work and also do the housework, they usually demand recipes that are very simple or can be prepared quickly," Koehler observed.[10] Their explanations of how to make piroshki (small savory pies) and Mexican-style beef thus touched off a discussion about the challenge of balancing housework and paid work. Even as a state official, "I have no help at home," Duvankova explained. After a full day at the office, she did all the housekeeping for her husband and her thirteen-year-old daughter. "You are a woman," she wrote to Koehler, "and can well understand what it means to attend to a family of three."[11] And Koehler did. She worked six days a week and had "very little time to take care of the apartment, to have some kind of entertainment, and even to do the shopping."[12] Their letters capture key differences in their lives but also how they struggled with analogous pressures.

The recipe exchange also opened the door to pointed questions about national stereotypes. Koehler followed up Duvankova's recipes by asking did "Russians eat only black bread and borscht?" Did they "typically drink a lot of vodka until they are drunk?" "Do Russians really lack a sense of humor?" Koehler went on to pose more indelicate questions about Soviet women's physique and appearance, adding that American women "were always worried about getting fat."[13] Duvankova did not respond to these unflattering insinuations or fire back in kind. Despite her busy schedule, she insisted, she "still managed to get to the hairdresser and manicurist." Koehler explained that she meant no offense; she was just trying to get past the surface-level accounts of Soviet life that circulated in the press.[14] "Our customs are very different, and therefore it is very easy to understand each other incorrectly, isn't it?" Koehler reflected. "I think it is so necessary that our two great peoples understand each other, especially with regard to small things, because the majority of us live by our emotions and are incapable of more than that." She closed "with the best wishes to you and your family and with hope in my soul that our two great countries never will fight each other."[15] By reaffirming that connection and understanding were their highest priorities, Koehler and Duvankova modeled ways to disagree without forfeiting their relationship. They went on to exchange seventeen letters.

A simple recipe exchange thus became a consciousness-raising moment—about the struggles that united the pen pals as women and about the misconceptions that divided them. The pen-pal project may have revolved around peace and propaganda, but between understanding each other and changing each other lay a middle ground: expanding each other's political awareness. That middle ground proved the most fertile. It is where, I argue, the project had the clearest success on the individual participants. Whether discussing strategies for career-building, parenting, or peacemaking, the pen pals came to recognize the systems that undergirded their pen friends' daily lives as well as their own. The insight that the personal was political surfaced repeatedly in the letters. Conversation invited comparison and competition, but it also fostered self-examination. "Our interests are pretty close," Koehler told Duvankova, "so that we can, for the most part, understand each other, but they are also different in many ways, which awakens the work of the mind and breaks up the self-congratulatory calm and satisfaction, which is [*sic*] born of laziness and the sense that 'everything has always been like this.'"[16] This was a remark that the Soviet Women's Anti-Fascist Committee underlined, and it jumped out to me too. Even as they championed their own ways of life, the pen pals were jolted out of their assumptions and feelings of "self-congratulatory satisfaction" by peering into the life of another.

The letter exchange helped heighten the participants' political awareness and broadened their sense of the possible, but did it lead to specific changes in the correspondents' actions and attitudes? That is harder to answer. The question of whether citizen diplomacy actually changes hearts and minds is much studied but inconclusive, to the frustration of policymakers and scholars alike. There are no empirical measures of whether citizen diplomacy "works" on its target audience, but there is ample evidence that citizen diplomacy feels meaningful and impactful to the participants, which might explain why individuals continue to volunteer for such programs and why governments continue to sponsor them.[17]

When I started reading the letters, I found myself constantly wondering about whether they pushed the pen friends to think and act differently during the years after they stopped writing. Dear Ms. Koehler, I wanted to ask, was it Zinaida Duvankova's example that eventually inspired you to leave Hudson's and start a new career? Dear Zinaida Semenovna, were you impressed by how openly Verena Koehler criticized the press and political establishment in her own country? What might you have written if given that freedom? I had a lot of questions but few answers.

After composing letter after letter like this in my mind, I sent actual letters to as many of the letter writers' descendants as I could, trying to unearth any traces that corresponding might have left on their lives. Suddenly I was the one writing hopeful, earnest notes to complete strangers whom I somehow felt I knew. I sent these pleas into the digital ether and through the regular mail until March 2022, when the US Postal Service stopped allowing Americans to send mail to Russia, part of US sanctions on the Russian Federation in protest against its invasion of Ukraine. During this current war, the US and Russian governments have returned to limiting contact between their citizens, both through travel and correspondence, and I find myself wondering, like the pen friends did, if closer communication wouldn't be a more expedient way to deescalate tensions and resolve conflicts.

Only a few descendants replied to my notes. I sent them copies of the letters—fragments of a lost family history they never knew existed—and together we thought through ways that pen friendship might have made an enduring impact on their mothers, great-aunts, or grandmothers. After all, the letter writers took considerable risks to correspond and devoted several years of their lives to it. It seemed unlikely to me at least that the experience left no imprint whatsoever.

Winning Hearts, but Changing Minds?

Reviewing the letters together, we noticed small ways that the pen pals shaped each other. They cracked open new books, tuned in to new radio programs, and nosed through new periodicals at the suggestion of their pen friends. Although it's possible Zinaida Duvankova would have cooked Mexican-style beef, Celia Wesle would have broken out that Stravinsky record, El'ga Koff would have reread *The Adventures of Huckleberry Finn*, Mary Roe Hull would have subscribed to the Soviet Embassy's *Information Bulletin*, or Nina Morozova would have picked up a copy of the US State Department's *Amerika* on their own, it was encouragement from their pen pals that prompted those actions.[18] Some pen friends inspired bigger changes, too. Recall how Mary Roe Hull persuaded widow Nina Morozova to start dating after years of mourning her husband, or how Ekaterina Andreeva convinced Jeanne Woolf not to quit her job as a journalist when she was overwhelmed with domestic obligations. Perhaps these women would have made those decisions anyway, but their pen friends helped plant the seed. They nudged each other toward new ideas by offering pointed questions and gentle advice. And indeed, their pen pals sometimes made decisions that were consistent with, though not solely caused by, their suggestions.

Some descendants also alerted me to potential shifts in the letter writers' political views. None of the pen pals declared that they were converting to either Soviet socialism or American liberal capitalism—much to the disappointment of the Central Committee of the Communist Party, which hoped American women would turn communist, and to the dismay of the Justice Department, which tried to prove the program was subversive. Yet, there are hints that the pen friends may have exerted some political influence, which was slow to emerge and perhaps unconsciously felt. The letters of Mary Roe Hull, for instance, contain as many laudatory remarks about conservative American politicians like Thomas E. Dewey as they do about Soviet policies. Yet, in the years after she corresponded, Hull began pasting newspaper articles that covered the Soviet Union positively into her scrapbook. She also garnered a reputation in the family for being left-wing. Hull's great-grandniece Connie Burtnett could not put her finger on why, just that "I always thought of her as more socialist-minded." It seems likely that the two dozen letters Hull exchanged with Nina Morozova played some role in Hull's political shift, even if they were not the only cause of it.

Gladys Kimple of Friday Harbor, Washington, also gained a reputation for being left-wing, which, her grandchildren Becky and Roy remember, was sometimes mentioned at family reunions. Recall that Kimple displayed the clearest political shift in her letters. She went from expressing rather agnostic political views to pro-socialist, pro-Soviet ones, which her grandson Roy Pearmain speculated might have triggered her divorce.[19] Gladys stopped sending letters to the USSR when she left her husband, but the family continued to experience repercussions for her Soviet sympathies. "In about 1963, when I was considering joining the Army and going into Army intelligence," Pearmain explained, "my father cautioned me that my grandma Gladys had been a Communist 'when that was popular.'"[20] That political taint was also why Gladys Kimple's son had been discharged from the US Air Force. Still, it cannot be definitively proven that Kimple's move leftward was due to Ekaterina Zheliabuzhskaia's letters. It may have been the result of other contacts Kimple had or materials she read.

The challenge of reconstructing the project's propagandistic success is even greater when it comes to the Soviet letter writers. Decades of repression and censorship taught them to be careful. While they confided personal feelings of grief and triumph to their pen friends, Soviet women omitted the full names of their relations, precise dates, exact locations, and other data, which I could have used to trace them genealogically. World War II rendered many of them refugees with unstable addresses, which the Soviet

Women's Anti-Fascist Committee started withholding in 1947. In addition, the vast majority lived in Moscow, which had a postwar population of between four and five million. The current war between Russia and Ukraine, the corresponding spike in American-Russian hostilities, and Russians' heightened concerns about state surveillance have made it difficult to convince relatives of the letter writers to speak with me. They ignored or politely declined my interview requests. Like the late 1940s, the 2020s have become a time when US-Russia connections are regarded with suspicion and when the prospect of friendship between their citizens seems dim.

The individual letter writers are difficult to trace, but there is clearer evidence of how the pen-pal project impacted the well-documented organizations that ran it. There were already signs of mutual influence during the program's heyday, when both groups became increasingly receptive to each other's strategies for helping women "do it all." The New York–based Committee of Women began advocating for social welfare programs to assist women, and they circulated Soviet exhibits and pamphlets advising women on how they could launch careers without neglecting motherhood. Meanwhile, the Soviet Women's Anti-Fascist Committee began including consumer-based solutions, such as shopping tips and appliance recommendations, in the advice it gave to working mothers in *Soviet Woman*. This trend increased in the mid-1950s, when some of the magazine's articles started to echo American advertisements. One piece, covering the Mikoyan food plant, celebrated the emergence of canned and processed foods as "labor-savers for the busy housekeeper" who could now "fix dinner in a jiffy."[21] An article from 1954 described how textile worker and mother-of-three Nina Averina did all the cooking and shopping and even managed to make special Sunday dinners for her family thanks to "her modern kitchen equipped with a garbage disposal chute, hot and cold running water . . ." and so on.[22]

Such cross-pollination continued after the pen-friendship project declined but, again, the data I have is asymmetrical. I know more about individual American letter writers' lives after correspondence, and I have more information about the Soviet Women's Anti-Fascist Committee than the New York–based Committee of Women. This is in large part because the Committee of Women's activities shrank considerably. Throughout the 1950s, it organized talks on peace and hosted Soviet women delegates to the UN Commission on the Status of Women, but by the mid-1960s, it was no longer the active committee it once was, no longer represented on the National

Council's Board of Directors.[23] The National Council of American-Soviet Friendship went on to arrange some correspondence between young people, working with the Soviet Youth Committee (formerly the Anti-Fascist Committee of Soviet Youth) as its partner, but from the late 1950s onward, the council shifted its focus to in-person exchanges.[24] It hosted visiting Soviet artists; organized tours for Americans to visit the USSR; and selected counselors and campers for the Soviet youth camp, Artek.[25] The National Council's Committee of Women faded into obscurity, while its Committees of Education and of Youth became the most active.[26]

Unlike the Committee of Women, the Soviet Women's Anti-Fascist Committee's programming, budget, and influence grew over time as the flagship women's organization in the USSR. In the late 1980s, the committee was granted seventy-five seats in the new legislature, the Congress of People's Deputies, and, during perestroika, it spoke out against enduring gender inequality in the Soviet Union.[27] Many feminist leaders who rose to prominence during the final years of the Soviet regime had cut their political teeth as members of the committee but grew increasingly weary of its propagandistic activities.[28] In 1990, the committee separated from the state and, after the Soviet Union's dissolution in 1991, it was renamed the Union of the Women of Russia. Its new platform centered around helping women—who comprised eighty percent of the country's unemployed—to survive the financial collapse that accompanied the collapse of communism. It also campaigned for and won several seats in Russia's first post-Soviet parliament.[29]

But long before the USSR's final decades, when the committee became an outspoken critic of Soviet gender policies, it did push state and party authorities toward reforms that would improve Soviet women's lives. Moreover, it drew on its work facilitating pen friendships and hosting foreign visitors in order to do so. The driving force behind these campaigns for change was the committee's chairperson, Nina Vasil'evna Popova. Though barely studied in her own right, Popova was one of the most influential women in the Communist Party and state bureaucracy. An orphan, Popova started working at age fourteen, and by age seventeen she was the head of a regional Pioneer bureau. From there, she quickly moved up the party ranks. When her first husband was arrested during Stalin's Great Terror, Popova successfully fought for his release. In World War II, she was responsible for evacuating people and factories from Moscow as well as for helping organize the city's defense. Popova remarried, but her new husband died at the front. She took over as chair of the Soviet Women's Anti-Fascist Committee in 1945.[30]

Popova's efforts to advocate for Soviet women during the 1950s suggests that the Soviet Women's Anti-Fascist Committee—the most explicitly propagandistic participant in the pen-pal program—was also the most transformed by it. The contacts and conversations that the anti-fascist committee arranged between women in the United States and USSR triggered some critical changes in Soviet policies in two areas: women's rights and citizen diplomacy. Popova was crucial in spearheading this.

From reading the letters and from hosting delegations, the staff of the Soviet Women's Anti-Fascist Committee became acutely aware of Americans' criticisms about the hardships Soviet women faced. Among them was the fact that Soviet women were toiling, often in heavy industries, with little protection or support. Starting in the mid-1950s, in the more relaxed political climate that emerged after Stalin's death, Popova began leveraging that negative image in order to advocate for Soviet women. "Foreigners often blame us for the fact that our women work at construction sites, in road construction" and other dangerous jobs, Popova proclaimed at one meeting in 1956, and she demanded better protective coveralls and other safeguards for women doing heavy labor.[31] When she made this speech, Popova was drawing on information gathered by the Soviet Women's Anti-Fascist Committee—renamed the Soviet Women's Committee—but she was speaking in her capacity as a secretary of the All-Union Central Council of Trade Unions. This was the second of several major administrative hats she wore. Soviet trade unions notoriously prioritized workers' productivity over their well-being, but Popova stressed that the council was obliged "to intensify its care with regard to bettering women's working and living conditions, paying special attention to women-mothers."[32] From the mid-1950s onward, the Soviet Women's Committee continued to share the perspectives of women in the West with the Central Council of Trade Unions in order to advocate for women in the USSR. And it used this strategy until the Soviet Union's collapse. Indeed, the council's secretariat always included at least one leader from the Soviet Women's Committee from World War II until 1988.[33]

Popova also drew on the committee's exchanges with letter writers and visitors from the capitalist West to advocate for Soviet women at the highest echelons of the party. In 1956, Popova became a member of the

Central Committee of the Communist Party. Later that year, she delivered a report to it about an international seminar on women's equality, which the Soviet Women's Committee had just hosted in Moscow. In her report, Popova shared with the Central Committee a litany of criticisms made by foreign visitors about the harsh realities of Soviet women's lives. Rather than dismiss these critiques as capitalist slander, Popova raised them as legitimate concerns that needed immediate redress. "Given the existing flaws in women's working and living conditions, with consideration of the critical comments of the Seminar participants," she concluded, "some suggestions are attached and submitted for consideration by the Central Committee of the Communist Party of the Soviet Union and the Soviet Ministers of the USSR. We ask you to agree [with them]." And a special commission set to work on her recommendations, which included an expansion of childcare facilities and the creation of classes to advise women on household management. In this way, Popova "continued in the tradition of early Soviet Bolshevik feminists rather than bury it," historian Alexandra Talaver argues.[34]

The Soviet Women's Committee never wavered from its mission of promoting Soviet socialism abroad but, in this way, its leaders also campaigned for domestic change. Until recently, most historians have stressed the committee's former role and overlooked the latter, arguing that it did more harm than good to Soviet women by glossing over their struggles for propagandistic purposes. Some scholars allege the committee was never seriously committed to women's rights at all but merely used the rhetoric of gender equality to promote communism.[35] Others argue it only developed a domestic program for women's emancipation during perestroika.[36] The letters and visits the Soviet Women's Committee arranged offer an important counterpoint to these claims. They reveal how this state agency walked a fine line between championing Soviet policies and pushing for them to be reformed.

The committee not only acted upon the criticisms that foreigners voiced in their letters and visits, it also responded to notes it received from aggrieved Soviet women—some five thousand a year by the mid-1950s and forty thousand annually by the 1970s. As the only union-wide Soviet women's organization, the committee became a landing place for those who had nowhere else to turn. Some Soviet women sent letters of complaint to the committee's magazine *Soviet Woman*. Several had the same first names and last initials as Soviet pen friends, though it is impossible to ascertain if these were the same individuals. Soviet pen pals also may have shared grievances with the committee when they stopped by its office to pick up their interlocutors' letters. Committee records document thousands of walk-ins who came in seeking help.[37] Whether expressed in person or through writing, Soviet women's main complaints pertained to housing, childcare, poor working conditions, and restrictions on divorce and abortion. At a meeting of the Soviet Women's Committee in 1957, executive secretary Lidiia Petrova and chairperson Nina Popova pushed *Soviet Woman* magazine to acknowledge and offer "practical advice" to Soviet women regarding these challenges, again noting how foreigners whom the committee hosted were beginning to comment on the disconnect between the idealized Soviet life they read about and the conditions of life they witnessed.[38] "It is necessary for us to show the drawbacks" of Soviet policies, Popova admitted, "but at the same time it is necessary to do so very skillfully."[39] When making plans for future issues of *Soviet Woman*, Popova implored the magazine's staff: "Please criticize, but do not touch the foundation. You need to show the advantages of this [socialist] system."[40] The committee kept its commitment to propaganda but—inspired by the conversations it arranged between Soviet and American women—it began speaking more openly and honestly about Soviet women's struggles.

Soviet Woman did not dare touch reproductive rights in its 1950s issues, but Popova did. She worked with the Soviet Minister of Health (who was also a member of the Soviet Women's Committee), Mariia Dmitrievna Kovrigina, as well as with legal experts to propose that abortion be decriminalized and—Popova particularly stressed—for nurseries, kindergartens, and contraceptive alternatives be expanded.[41] Popova argued that inadequate social programs often led women to have abortions, and not promiscuity or a callous attitude toward motherhood, as her opponents often claimed.[42] Popova focused her report on how to improve women's lives, not on pronatalism. In this campaign to decriminalize abortion, letters played a key role. In drafting their arguments, Popova and Kovrigina drew heavily on Soviet women's correspondence—some of it held by the Soviet Women's Committee, some of it sent or forwarded to Kovrigina. "Women's voices became a key force" in reforming abortion law, historian Mie Nakachi noted.[43] The Central Committee of the Communist Party examined Popova and Kovrigina's proposal in October 1955 and put it into law one month later.[44] Of course, the correspondents and contacts the women's committee accumulated were not the sole cause of this turnaround. Other officials and journalists also played major roles. Still, the committee's repository of letters was an important data set, which Popova marshaled. Whether they helped Soviet women obtain better coveralls or access to abortion, the letters left an imprint on the lives of numerous individuals in the USSR who never served as pen pals.

The foreign contacts that the committee arranged also impacted Soviet approaches to citizen diplomacy. In 1958, Nina Popova stepped into yet another major role and became the chairperson of the new Union of Soviet Societies for Friendship and Cultural Relations with Foreign Countries (SSOD). SSOD replaced the All-Union Society for Cultural Relations with Foreign Countries (VOKS) as one of the key organizations responsible for forging ties and strengthening Soviet influence overseas. It remained a pillar of Soviet citizen diplomacy through 1992, and Popova ran it until 1975. She brought her expertise on letter writing and her focus on personalized diplomacy to SSOD.[45] While VOKS had focused on attracting cultural elites to communism, SSOD sought to establish friendly ties with "ordinary" Americans and Europeans who held mainstream political views. Under Popova's leadership, SSOD operated under the assumption that also undergirded the pen-pal project: "the bourgeois public" in the capitalist West was not comprised of enemies or warmongers but of people who shared basic humanist values including peace.[46] They need not agree with Soviet people on everything to be partners for the improvement of east-west relations.

To help forge these connections, Popova recommended SSOD start a pen-friendship program at the organization's first meeting in February 1958. "International personal correspondence," she declared, was an "especially promising" way to "awaken sympathies" for the USSR. Praise of Soviet life would be far more persuasive if it came "with a personal touch" in the form of "letters from Soviet citizens to pen pals abroad." Historians have remarked on the daring and experimental quality of Popova's 1958 proposal because it seemed so out-of-character with the prevailing view of Stalinist isolationism. Some scholars suggest she got the idea from Eisenhower's 1956 People-to-People program, which launched a number of exchange initiatives including letter writing.[47] In fact, Popova was drawing on the pen-pal project she had overseen for more than a decade. This time she was proposing a larger operation that would include men and would benefit from SSOD's bigger budget and greater visibility.

During the Stalin era, Popova's staff struggled to recruit Soviet correspondents. But by the late 1950s, the public's enthusiasm for pen friendship was mounting. De-Stalinization and Nikita Khrushchev's promise to thaw relations with the United States dispelled some of the trepidation Soviet citizens had about forming contacts with the West. Their enthusiasm was stoked by the International Youth Festival held in Moscow in 1957, when Soviet citizens were encouraged to chat with foreign visitors and even trade addresses with them for the sake of "international friendship." Shortly thereafter, Eleonory Gilburd has shown, a veritable "flood" of Soviet letters arrived at SSOD and "every conceivable institution" requesting foreign pen pals.[48]

In the end, SSOD did not arrange these pen friendships. Popova's new colleagues cited numerous security concerns, including the challenge of regulating the letters' political content and the potential danger of sharing Soviets' personal addresses with foreigners.[49] Curiously, Popova had addressed these obstacles with the women's pen friendships, but she did not push for the same solutions to be applied for this new venture. Later, SSOD did coordinate pen friendships and exchanges with young people but primarily those in socialist countries. It also established friendship societies around the world, hosted delegations of visitors, and arranged for film screenings, exhibitions, festivals, and a magazine, *Culture and Life*, to expose Soviet citizens to aspects of foreign cultures.[50] SSOD remained an arm of the Soviet propaganda machine, but it departed from its predecessor VOKS by emphasizing bilateral exchanges to cultivate "friendship, mutual understanding, and trust" between everyday citizens.[51] It remained a key player in the thawing of east-west relations for the duration of the Cold War.

SSOD's hesitancy to establish pen friendships between Soviet and western citizens in 1958 underscores how unique the women's pen-pal program really was. It also reinforces how the program was allowed to exist because of its small scale and because it involved female participants who posed little security risk. Indeed, the program has gone unnoticed by scholars, overshadowed by a deluge of citizen diplomacy programs that emerged later. By the late 1950s and early 1960s, international pen friendships were all the rage in the United States and Soviet Union. Pen-pal kiosks were set up at American fairs and theme parks. They appeared at Freedomland in 1962, at the World's Fair in New York in 1964, and at the US pavilion at the 1958 exposition in Brussels, where the Parker Pen Company presented its miraculous "pen-pal picking" computer. Moreover, the World Pen-Pal Program worked with the United States Information Agency and the Peace Corps to match thousands of Americans with pen friends abroad.[52] A crop of international pen friendship groups sprung up concurrently in the Soviet Union. Most were arranged through schools, youth programs, and Clubs of International Friendship, which focused on forging epistolary ties with individuals from socialist countries and the developing world.[53] Of course, as travel restrictions between the United States and Soviet Union eased, in-person exchanges also proliferated. Thousands of Soviet and American citizens visited each other's countries during the 1950s.[54]

Throughout these later developments, the Soviet Women's Committee remained the primary conduit for Soviet women to connect with American women, right up until the collapse of the USSR. During the 1980s, amid renewed fears of nuclear war, women in the United States launched numerous initiatives aimed at working with Soviet mothers to safeguard children from war. The Soviet Women's Committee was their main point of contact and their interlocutor, whether around the conference table or during overseas visits. These highly publicized encounters, which attracted tens of thousands of television viewers and readers, helped sway public opinion in both countries toward de-escalation, David Foglesong argues.[55] They also compelled General Secretary Mikhail Gorbachev and President Ronald Reagan to take notice of "how deep the hope of peace was [. . .] in the heart of every American and Russian mother," as Reagan remarked before the two leaders met in Geneva to discuss disarmament in 1985. "The international women's movement," Gorbachev reiterated in 1987, "has markedly reinforced the potential of peace and goodwill. It has forced people to listen to it. It is a real factor in politics."[56] For fifty years, the Soviet Women's Committee facilitated critical conversations between Soviet and American women about women's rights and about peace. The pen-pal program was just the start.

These are some of the policies and processes to which the pen-pal project contributed—more obvious for the organizations involved than for the letter writers. I cannot definitively show that pen friendship "won" over individual minds, but I do suspect it captured some hearts.

The Power of Memorable Conversation

Good conversations stay with us. They can linger in our memories even if they do not spur us into action. While the evidence of the pen-pal project's propagandistic success is mixed, I believe the correspondents' exchange of ideas and affections did broaden their horizons and make them more aware of the political forces that governed women's everyday lives—their own and others. For some, this heightened consciousness was an explicit aim of letter writing. "I hope that in our correspondence we will be able to describe to each other how our different types of government are reflected in our personal lives," one letter writer exclaimed.[57] "In all likelihood, I will learn more about my own country thanks to the questions you ask me about it," another echoed.[58] Or, as Verena Koehler put it, corresponding "awakens the work of the mind and breaks up self-congratulatory calm and satisfaction."[59] The experience of pen friendship compelled the participants to look anew at the patterns, choices, and constraints that structured their lives, to reckon with one another's questions and critiques. The act of corresponding exposed them to alternatives even if it did not compel the participants to adopt them. This aspect of the pen-pal project, as a consciousness-raising experience, is a critical part of the program's legacy.

The participants' political awareness grew in a variety of ways—some of them ominous. For instance, between their letters arriving open and the nightly news, the American pen friends became increasingly conscious of government surveillance and the limits of free speech in the United States. By 1950, Gladys Kimple had learned to cloak her remarks in euphemism and inuendo. Mina Miller had learned to keep carbon copies of her letters in case she was falsely accused of disloyalty. And Jean Jahr had learned to greet FBI agents politely when they came to her door but never to let them into her home. These were some of the darker ways that the pen-pal project made itself felt in the letter writers' lives.

I imagine that the pen friends' conversations remained in their memories in more ethereal ways, too. It does not seem too much of a stretch to suppose that in 1968, as El'ga Koff scoured libraries for clues about what brand of American champagne to feature on a film set, her mind drifted to Celia Wesle, who could have been such a help to her.[60] Or when the details of Stalin's mass repression of the Soviet people was exposed by Nikita

Khrushchev in 1956, Gladys Kimple may have longed to ask Ekaterina Zheliabuzhskaia if these charges were true or if her pen pal could again "slay another dragon," this time of Khrushchev's De-Stalinization.

The pen friends' prolonged conversations about "women's work" might have come to mind, especially as their opportunities and obligations expanded in the latter half of the twentieth century. Scholars of gender and women's history have noted how conversations between female friends were powerful incubators of feminist consciousness. "The women's movement brought female friendship into a position of honor," equal to if not more important than marriage, Linda Gordon observed.[61] Friendship—whether face-to-face or in the form of correspondence—helped raise women's awareness that their struggles were common struggles, that their aspirations were shared. Such awareness likely grew for Jean Jahr and Ol'ga Mel'nikovskaia in the years after they stopped corresponding. As pen friends, they wrote extensively about individual fulfillment and how to balance family life with a career. Those questions became even more pressing for them later on, when Mel'nikovskaia, an archeologist, started a family and Jahr, a housewife, embarked upon a career. As their circumstances became more similar, the former pen pals may have recalled each other's points of view and perhaps appreciated them more in hindsight.

Mel'nikovskaia was just beginning work as an archeologist during the years she corresponded with Jahr. She was one of many Soviet women who moved into scholarly careers in the years after World War II. By the late 1960s, women comprised roughly 40 percent of the USSR's scientific and technical employees and well over 70 percent in some fields like medicine and economics.[62] During the 1940s, Mel'nikovskaia threw herself into archeological work. It was her life's passion, especially once her fiancé was gone. She was convinced she would never find love again, but she did. In 1952, a colleague and old school friend, Erast Alekseevich Symonovich, revealed himself to be her "long-awaited prince." He shared her fascination with antiquities, and he simply adored her, putting her before his own health and career.[63]

Her life with Symonovich was happy but difficult, Mel'nikovskaia recalled in her memoir. When she was corresponding with Jahr, Mel'nikovskaia had been living with her parents, so she was free of the financial worries and housekeeping tasks that plagued her pen pal. That changed when she and Symonovich married two years later. They moved into cramped university housing, which they could barely afford on their student stipends. It was a "hovel," Mel'nikovskaia admitted, but also "a really sweet heaven."[64] Though they were in love, the couple was shabbily dressed and often hungry. A daughter, Antonina, arrived in 1953, and there was no space to rock her or even set her down. When Antonina was a newborn and up at night, Mel'nikovskaia walked her up and down the streets of Moscow, "and in the morning, I had to go to work."[65] During those exhausting months, did she recall Jean Jahr's protestations that she did not have enough energy to care for her two children, keep house, and hold down a paying job? Mel'nikovskaia had struggled to identify with Jahr then but now, two years later, her pen friend's predicament may have hit home.

Mel'nikovskaia dismissed the challenge of juggling work, housekeeping, and childcare in her letters, but she discussed it at length in her memoir. She pointed out cracks in the system of social welfare she had once touted to Jahr. During those early years when Antonina was too little to attend a state-subsidized kindergarten, Mel'nikovskaia scrambled to find someone to watch her. "We both worked," she wrote of herself and her husband, and "grandma and grandpa lived in an old apartment far away from us." Even after Antonina began going to kindergarten, its hours did not coincide with her parents' work schedules. "Who could bring our child to and from school, and feed her?" When Mel'nikovskaia went on a dig, she left Antonina in the care of her husband and a nanny, but this, too, was a hardship because nannies had to be given meals, housing, and pay. Moreover, Mel'nikovskaia felt guilty leaving her daughter behind, especially when Antonina fell ill in her absence.[66] Once, when Antonina was a teenager, Mel'nikovskaia unwittingly left her home alone at a time "when depression had pushed her to the brink of death."[67] Mel'nikovskaia berated herself for not being more present for her daughter. (Happily, Antonina Erastovna Symonovich recovered and became a major poet who is still prolific today.) In this way, during the twilight years of her life, Mel'nikovskaia reflected on some of the concerns she discussed with Jahr, now seeing the other side of the issue. Ultimately, with help from her husband, nannies, and state-subsidized childcare, Mel'nikovskaia found balance between family and career. She published over forty scholarly articles and two editions of her memoir before passing away in 2008 at age eighty-seven.

The challenge of "doing it all" also intensified for Jean Jahr in the years after her pen friendship ended. Jahr's daily tasks expanded in the opposite direction, from the home to the workplace. Jahr once vented to Mel'nikovskaia that she had little time or opportunity to earn a paycheck. But her chance came when her husband Bert reached a crossroads in his career and decided to go back to school. He enrolled at Brooklyn College, and Jean Jahr went to work. Her decision reflected a nationwide pattern; the number of married women in the US labor force shot up by 42 percent in the 1950s.[68] "The postwar realities of women's lives—combining caregiving and breadwinning—were here to stay," historian Dorothy Sue Cobble observed of midcentury America.[69] Jahr became the family breadwinner, which allowed Bert to stay in school and earn his PhD from New York University.[70] Like many other American letter writers, Jahr took on full-time employment only once her children were older—Joanne was fourteen and Marc was twelve—to minimize the conflict between family and career.[71] But that trend was also changing. By 1960, 39 percent of American mothers with school-aged children were also in the labor force.[72]

Jean Jahr found a job as a secretary at the International Paper Company, and she showed great savvy in avoiding some of the pitfalls that befell women in the corporate world. Aware of the tendency to hire pretty, young women, "she knocked ten years off her age and did the same for us," her daughter Joanne told me. "She knew that if HR knew her real age she'd never be hired. Once on the job, she made certain she was always called 'Mrs. Jahr' and not Jean." Dressed in high heels, with her ebony, knee-length hair swooped into an elegant bun, Jahr accentuated her femininity and her maternity: she was attractive but off-limits to male coworkers. Jahr's keen organizational and communication skills allowed her to move quickly up the ranks—from a secretary in sales and marketing to an administrator in corporate communications. "The men in those openly misogynistic times respected her," Joanne reflected.[73] "She enjoyed her work immensely," her son Marc added, but "it wasn't until the women's movement emerged that International Paper gave her a title to accompany the respect accorded to her."[74]

The letters she wrote to her children during that time conveyed the same exuberance for work that Ol'ga Mel'nikovskaia expressed about archeology.[75] International Paper saved Jahr from what she had described to Mel'nikovskaia as the "tedium" of being a housewife, but it did not rescue her from housework. Jahr continued to do all the housekeeping. I asked Joanne and Marc if their mother's professional identity altered the dynamics of her marriage. They were unaware of any conflicts but noticed their mother was more

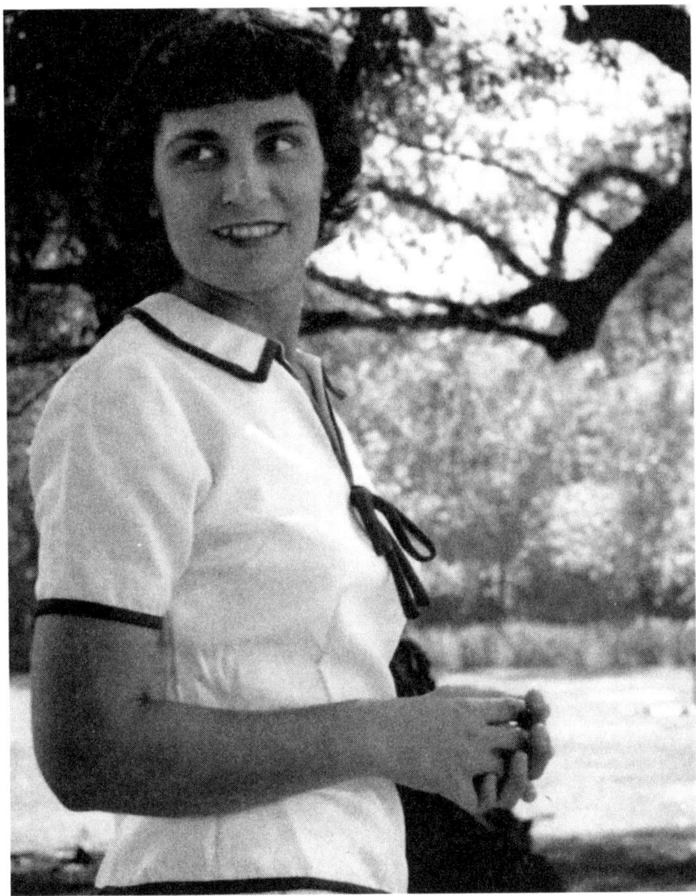

Jean Jahr circa 1953. (Photo by Bert Jahr. Courtesy of Joanne and Marc Jahr.)

confident and much busier. In her letters to them, Jahr described her life as a "rat race of working, trying to keep up with chores at home, and an occasional recreational diversion."[76] With working a full day, cooking, cleaning, and commuting an hour each way from East Flatbush to Manhattan, "I'm just so tied down with too darned much to do," she wrote.[77]

After nearly thirty years with International Paper, Jahr reluctantly retired in 1987 when the company moved its headquarters out of New York. "When she left IP, she lost the challenge of her work and the relationships beyond our families that enrich our lives. She missed that," Marc remarked.[78] And, "when it came time for her to retire and she had to give her real age to

HR, they nearly fell off their rolling chairs," Joanne added, "that tickled her to no end." By then, Bert had learned to vacuum and boil water, but the housework was never evenly divided. Jean became Bert's caregiver when his health faltered in the 1990s. She died in 2015 at the age of ninety-six. The joys and challenges of motherhood, the constant demands of housekeeping, and the importance of professional fulfillment and recognition—Jahr's and Mel'nikovskaia's lives converged in all of these respects in the years after they stopped writing. This overlap brought them closer to each other's perspective and may have created more junctures of understanding between them.

Pen friendship, together with many new experiences at home and on the job, helped raise the letter writers' consciousness of what was possible for them to achieve as women and what constraints prevented them from realizing their potential. Such awareness was integral to the women's liberation movements, which crystalized in the United States during the late 1960s and in the Soviet Union during the 1980s. The trajectories of Jahr's and Mel'nikovskaia's lives aligned with national trends; their struggles and aspirations were widely shared. Many (especially middle-class) women in the United States, like Jahr, pushed for more professional and educational opportunities, whereas women in the Soviet Union often sought greater freedom to spend more time at home, like Mel'nikovskaia. Equal wages, steady employment, and access to childcare and contraception were major demands of both movements.[79] Neither Jahr nor Mel'nikovskaia described themselves as feminists, but they certainly named the unequal demands on working mothers and claimed greater fulfillment for themselves.

Other letter writers similarly made major changes to their lives in search of greater independence and satisfaction. Their experiences as pen friends did not cause these changes, but they did foster reflection on achieving self-actualization. Again, the American participants are easier to trace. Of the five main American letter writers featured in this book—Mary Roe Hull, Jean Jahr, Celia Wesle, Jeanne Woolf, and Gladys Kimple—one, Hull, died in the 1960s, and three of the remaining four shed their lives as housewives and began careers. Three also divorced their husbands, and two actively supported feminist causes. Celia Wesle did all three.

When I left off with Celia Wesle's story, she was a model mother and wife. The local newspaper ran features emphasizing this.[80] Shortly after she sent her last letter to El'ga Koff in 1950, the Wesle family left Pella, Iowa, for Normal, Illinois, so John could take a job at what became Illinois State University.[81] At the time, the Wesles' daughter Marguerite—whom Koff gushed over from afar—was three years old. The couple soon welcomed Maria, born in 1953, and Janet, born in 1956. The eldest daughter, Marguerite Wesle Franklin, remembers Celia as a devoted, loving mother. More than one article in Normal's newspaper *The Pantagraph* lauded her "storehouse of talents." She was a Brownie troop leader and a Sunday school teacher. She hosted numerous faculty functions, and she was part of the League of Women Voters.[82]

Wesle gave much of herself to her children, her husband, and her community. At the same time, she increasingly sought opportunities for personal fulfillment. She began by teaching local art and dance classes and working as a part-time librarian. When her youngest, Janet, started the first grade, Wesle resumed her job as a schoolteacher and enrolled at Illinois State to earn her master's degree. It is possible that Wesle was partially inspired by El'ga Koff's career and advice about the importance of doing stimulating work. Their conversations likely layered upon other soul-searching discussions Wesle had with friends and with herself, which together drove her toward these pursuits.

The question of how to balance one's family and one's career became a pressing concern for Wesle by the late 1950s, as it did for Jahr and Mel'nikovskaia. Wesle applied for a job at an advertising agency but was rejected because the firm did not hire women. "She was frustrated by the lack of good career opportunities" open to her, Marguerite told me, and "she urged her daughters to train for a career, like teaching, so we could support ourselves and our children if needed."[83] Education, independence, financial freedom—Wesle began taking steps to live these principles. When she landed a job in the state of Illinois's Office of Education in Springfield a few years later, she resolved to take it. Her husband John did not want to leave Normal. So, after twenty-six years of marriage, the couple parted ways.[84] "She enjoyed having a career," Marguerite reflected. "Maybe she thought she would find a more ambitious, successful husband who would appreciate her more. She wanted to work in Springfield and to be on her own. She never remarried."[85]

Concerns about women's inequality remained at the forefront of Wesle's life, personally, professionally, and creatively. In her new post at the Office of Education, Wesle began to see and combat gender-based discrimination in Illinois schools, especially after the passage of Title IX in 1972.[86] Marguerite recalled that her mother was too busy to be a feminist activist, but she read *Ms.* magazine and joined the National Organization of Women, one of the largest feminist groups in the world.[87] Wesle took Marguerite to a rally demanding the Illinois state legislature pass the Equal Rights Amendment, and she spoke with her daughters about the injustices that women were paid less than men, had fewer career opportunities, and had to rely on their husbands to access financial credit.[88]

In Springfield, Wesle joined Brainchild, a community of women with whom she could share stories and creative work. Founded in 1972, Brainchild's mission was to nurture female authors and celebrate the "deeply personal" nature of their writing, which was often shunned by the male-dominated literary establishment.[89] Such support groups, historians have noted, were instrumental in allowing women to reflect on the unequal systems and structures that shaped their lives, to see how the personal is political.[90] One of Brainchild's anthologies, *All the Women Were Heroes*, lauded "women's work" of comforting children, tending the sick, and building community around the dinner table. Celia Wesle, who had written many letters to Elga Koff from her attic kitchen in Pella, Iowa, chose the kitchen as the setting for one of her contributions to the volume. Her poems were featured in other anthologies, and she published her own book of poems and paintings in 2007.[91] She also won a creative writing award from the University of Illinois in 2008. Celia Wesle died in Springfield in 2011 at the age of eighty-seven.

THE CORE PREMISE and discovery of the pen-pal program, that the personal is political, was a foundational insight of the feminist movements, antiwar campaigns, and citizen diplomacy ventures, which thrived in the latter decades of the twentieth century. All three phenomena were rooted in the notion that we can see ourselves in each other's struggles—whether for equal pay or to shield children from war—and that those struggles, which are so personally felt, stem from structures and practices that cut across national lines. All three movements also centered on a belief in the power of individual storytelling to raise awareness, mobilize, and effect social change.

This small and overlooked pen-pal project helps connect women's midcentury views on gender equality and on citizen diplomacy to the mass movements of feminist and peace activism. Those who participated in the correspondence program were part of a groundswell of new attitudes about women's rights and about the power of citizens to prevent war. From their letters, we can glimpse how they tried to make history, to shape women's lives and foreign relations. And we can see history flow through them. Their conversations created ripples, and those ripples streamed into the currents of thought that helped define an age.

Archives and Interviews

Archives

Bancroft Library, University of California, Berkeley, California

Beinecke Rare Book and Manuscript Library, Yale University, New Haven, Connecticut

Chicago Museum of History, Chicago, Illinois

Dwight D. Eisenhower Presidential Library, Abilene, Kansas

Gosudarstvennyi arkhiv rossiiskoi federatsii (State Archive of the Russian Federation, Moscow)

Hoover Institution Library & Archives, Stanford University, Stanford, California

Kheel Center, Catherwood Library, Cornell University, Ithaca, New York

National Archives and Records Administration, Washington, DC, and College Park, Maryland

Rossiiskii gosudarstvennyi arkhiv literatury i iskusstva (Russian State Archive of Literature and Art, Moscow)

Rossiiskii gosudarstvennyi arkhiv sotsial'no-politicheskoi istorii (Russian State Archive of Socio-Political History, Moscow)

Sophia Smith Collection, Smith College, Northampton, Massachusetts

Swarthmore College Peace Collection, Swarthmore College, Swarthmore, Pennsylvania

Tamiment Library / Robert F. Wagner Labor Archives, New York University Libraries, New York, New York

Tsentrali'nyi gosudarstvennyi arkhiv literatury i iskusstva Sankt Peterburga (Central State Archive of Literature and Art, St. Petersburg)

University of Pittsburgh Archives and Libraries, Pittsburgh, Pennsylvania

University of Wisconsin Oshkosh Archives and Area Research Center, Oshkosh, Wisconsin

Wisconsin Historical Society Archive, Madison, Wisconsin

Interviews

Most interviews were conducted over Zoom and via email unless otherwise noted.

Constance Roe Burtnett

Joanne Jahr

Marc Jahr

Jennifer Kimple

Roy Pearmain

Marguerite Wesle Franklin (interview conducted in person)

Abbreviations

Archives

GARF	Gosudarstvennyi arkhiv rossiiskoi federatsii (State Archive of the Russian Federation)
HILA	Hoover Institution Library and Archives, Stanford University, Stanford University, Stanford, California
NARA	National Archives and Records Administration, Washington, DC, and College Park, Maryland
RGALI	Rossiiskii gosudarstvennyi arkhiv literatury i iskusstva, Moskva (Russian State Archive of Literature and Art, Moscow)
RGASPI	Rossiiskii gosudarstvennyi arkhiv sotsial'no-politicheskoi istorii (Russian State Archive of Socio-Political History)
SSC	Sophia Smith Collection, Smith College, Northampton, Massachusetts
TAM	Tamiment Library / Robert F. Wagner Labor Archives, New York University Libraries, New York, New York
TsGALI SPb	Tsentrali'nyi gosudarstvennyi arkhiv literatury i iskusstva Sankt Peterburga (Central State Archive of Literature and Art, St. Petersburg)

Archival Notations

d. (plural: dd.) file

f. collection

l. (plural: ll.) sheet

ob. obverse

op. inventory

Notes

Greeting

1. Chapter title from State Archive of the Russian Federation (GARF), f. R7928, op. 2, d. 50, l. 162, dated Oct. 23, 1944 (when a letter is undated, I note when it was sent or received); John O. Iatrides and Nicholas X. Rizopoulos, "The International Dimension of the Greek Civil War," *World Policy Journal* 17, no. 1 (Spring 2000): 87–103; André Gerolymatos, *Red Acropolis, Black Terror: The Greek Civil War and the Origins of the Soviet-American Rivalry, 1943–1949* (New York: Basic Books, 2004), 207–209, 230–231.

2. A. Y. Vyshinsky, *For the Peace and Friendship of Nations, Against Instigators of a New War,* Sept. 18, 1947 (Washington, DC: The Embassy of the Union of Soviet Socialist Republics, 1947).

3. GARF, f. R7928, op. 2, d. 245, ll. 65–66, dated Sept. 24, 1947.

4. Chris Bellamy, *Absolute War: Soviet Russia in the Second World War* (New York: Alfred A. Knopf, 2007), 350.

5. GARF, f. R7928, op. 2, d. 483, l. 263, dated Oct. 15, 1948; GARF, f. R7928, op. 2, d. 361, l. 34, dated Feb. 23, 1948.

6. GARF, f. R7928, op. 2, d. 483, ll. 263–264, dated Oct. 15, 1948. This was Kuznetsova's second letter.

7. GARF, f. R7928, op. 2, d. 480, l. 4, dated Dec. 1, 1948.

8. GARF, f. R7928, op. 2, d. 985, ll. 77–80, dated Mar. 18, 1951.

9. GARF, f. R7928, op. 2, d. 480, l. 4, dated Dec. 1, 1948.

10. On other pen-pal exchanges run by the Soviet Women's Anti-Fascist Committee, see Olga Kucherenko, "A Fleeting Friendship: Anglo-Soviet Penpalship in the Second World War," *Diplomacy & Statecraft* 32, no. 4 (2021): 692–719;

Alexis Peri, "Operation Friendship: Soviet and British Women Discuss War, Work, and Womanhood," *The Russian Review* 82, no. 3 (July 2023): 453–469; Christine Varga-Harris, "Between National Tradition and Western Modernization: Soviet Woman and Representations of Socialist Gender Equality as a 'Third Way' for Developing Countries, 1956–1964," *Slavic Review* 78, no. 3 (2019): 758–781.

11. Key research on Soviet and American women's transnational political work during this era includes Cynthia Enloe, *Bananas, Beaches, and Bases: Making Feminist Sense of International Politics* (Berkeley: University of California Press, 2014); Emily S. Rosenberg, "A Roundtable Explaining the History of American Foreign Relations: Gender," *The Journal of American History* 77, no. 1 (June 1990), 116–124; Jacqueline Castledine, *Cold War Progressives: Women's Interracial Organizing for Peace and Freedom* (Champaign: University of Illinois Press, 2012); Kate Weigand, *Red Feminism: American Communism and the Making of Women's Liberation* (Baltimore: Johns Hopkins University Press, 2001); Helen Laville, *Cold War Women: The International Activities of America Women's Organizations* (Manchester: Manchester University Press, 2002); Glenda Elizabeth Gilmore, *Defying Dixie: the Radical Roots of Civil Rights, 1919–1950* (New York: W. W. Norton, 2008); Erik S. McDuffie, *Sojourning for Freedom: Black Women, American Communism, and the Making of Black Left Feminism* (Durham: Duke University Press, 2011); Keisha N. Blain, *Set the World on Fire: Black Nationalist Women and the Global Struggle for Freedom* (Philadelphia: University of Pennsylvania Press, 2018); Dayo F. Gore, *The Work of Radicals: African American Activists in the Cold War* (New York: New York University Press, 2010); Kristen Ghodsee, *Second World, Second Sex: Socialist Women's Activism and Global Solidarity during the Cold War* (Durham: Duke University Press, 2018); Francisca de Haan, "Continuing Cold War Paradigms in Western Historiography of Transnational Women's Organisations: The Case of the Women's International Democratic Federation," *Women's History Review* 19, no. 4 (Jan. 2010): 547–573; Melanie Ilic, "Soviet Women, Cultural Exchange, and the Women's International Democratic Federation," in *Reassessing the Cold War*, ed. Sari Autio-Sarasmo and Katalin Miklossy (New York: Routledge, 2011).

12. The rich scholarship on the history of emotions is too vast to summarize, but seminal works include William M. Reddy, *The Navigation of Feeling: A Framework for the History of Emotions* (Cambridge: Cambridge University Press, 2001); Peter N. Stearns and Carol Z. Stearns, "Emotionology: Clarifying the History of Emotions and Emotional Standards," *The American Historical Review* 90, no. 4 (1985): 813–836; Barbara H. Rosenwein and Riccardo Cristiani, *What is the History of Emotions?* (New York: John Wiley and Sons, 2017); Peter Burke, "Is there a Cultural History of Emotions?" in *Representing Emotions: New Connections in the Histories of Art, Music, and Medicine*, ed. Helen Hills and Penelope Gouk (Burlington,

VT: Ashgate, 2005), 35–48; Mark D. Steinberg and Valeria Sobol, eds., *Interpreting Emotions in Russia and Eastern Europe* (DeKalb: Northern Illinois Press, 2011).

13. There was a precedent for personalized US-Soviet diplomacy in how Franklin D. Roosevelt and Iosif Stalin drew on "emotional dispositions and sensibilities" to forge their wartime alliance. Frank Costigliola, *Roosevelt's Lost Alliances: How Personal Politics Helped Start the Cold War* (Princeton, NJ: Princeton University Press, 2012), 4.

14. On how the letter mimics oral conversation, see Céline Dauphin, "Letter-Writing Manuals in the Nineteen Century," in *Correspondence: Models of Letter-Writing from the Middle Ages to the Nineteen Century*, ed. Roger Chartier, Alain Boureau, and Céline Dauphin (Princeton, NJ: Princeton University Press, 1997), 132–134.

15. On "emotional communities," see Barbara H. Rosenwein, "Worrying about Emotions in History," *American Historical Review* 107 (2002): 842–845. On textual communities as emotional communities, see Brian Stock, *The Implications of Literacy: Written Language and Models of Interpretation in the Eleventh and Twelfth Centuries* (Princeton, NJ: Princeton University Press, 1983).

16. GARF, f. R7928, op. 2, d. 245, l. 6, dated Sept. 24, 1947.

17. GARF, f. R7928, op. 2, d. 639, l. 60, dated Apr. 9, 1949.

18. GARF, f. R7928, op. 2, d. 245, l. 6, dated Sept. 24, 1947.

19. GARF, f. R7928, op. 2, d. 985, l. 140, dated June 3, 1950; GARF, f. R7928, op. 2, d. 985, l. 77, dated Mar. 18, 1951. The US census listed Englewood's population at 377 in 1940 and 341 in 1950 (https://ipsr.ku.edu/ksdata/ksah/population/2pop33.pdf).

20. GARF, f. R7928, op. 2, d. 361, l. 34, dated Feb. 23, 1948.

21. GARF, f. R7928, op. 2, d. 480, l. 6, dated Dec. 1, 1948; GARF, f. R7928, op. 2, d. 639, ll. 59–60, dated Apr. 9, 1949.

22. GARF, f. R7928, op. 2, d. 483, l. 153, dated Jan. 26, 1949.

23. GARF, f. R7928, op. 2, d. 483, l. 153.

24. GARF, f. R7928, op. 2, d. 361, l. 35, dated Feb. 23, 1948.

25. Letters from men include GARF, f. R7928, op. 2, d. 360, l. 37, dated Feb. 26, 1948; GARF, f. R7928, op. 2, d. 360, l. 7, dated Apr. 26, 1948; GARF, f. R7928, op. 2, d. 361, l. 42, received June 28, 1948; GARF, f. R7928, op. 2, d. 641, l. 12, dated Feb. 1950; GARF, f. R7928, op. 2, d. 481, ll. 27–28, dated Dec. 26, 1948.

26. GARF, f. R7928, op. 2, d. 641, l. 13, dated Feb. 1950.

27. On American and Soviet sentimentalism, see Anne Eakin Moss, *Only Among Women: Philosophies of Community in the Russian and Soviet Imagination, 1860–1940* (Evanston, IL: Northwestern University Press, 2020); Christina Klein, *Cold War Orientalism: Asia in the Middlebrow Imagination*, 1945–1961 (Berkeley: University of California Press, 2003), 23.

28. GARF, f. R7928, op. 2, d. 985, l. 80, dated Mar. 18, 1951; GARF, f. R7928, op. 2, d. 245, ll. 65–66, dated Sept. 24, 1947.

29. GARF, f. R7928, op. 2, d. 639, l. 58, dated Apr. 9, 1949.

30. GARF, f. R7928, op. 2, d. 483, l. 264, dated Oct. 15, 1948.

31. GARF, f. R7928, op. 2, d. 480, l. 4, dated Dec. 1, 1948

32. GARF, f. R7928, op. 2, d. 639, l. 61 dated Apr. 9, 1949.

33. I use Kenneth Osgood's definition of propaganda as "any technique or action that attempts to influence the emotions, attitudes, or behavior of a group, usually to serve the interests of the sponsor." Osgood, *Total Cold War: Eisenhower's Secret Propaganda Battle at Home and Abroad* (Lawrence: University of Kansas Press, 2006), 7.

34. Osgood, *Total Cold War,* 5.

35. Klein, *Cold War Orientalism,* 21.

36. On the assimilation of national myths through letter-writing, see Martin Lyons, *The Writing Culture of Ordinary People in Europe, 1860–1920* (Cambridge: Cambridge University Press, 2013), 9, 17, 60.

37. On nations, see Benedict Anderson, *Imagined Communities: Reflections on the Origin and Spread of Nationalism,* rev. ed. (New York: Verso, 2016). On ideology, see Jochen Hellbeck, *Revolution on My Mind: Writing a Diary under Stalin* (Cambridge, MA: Harvard University Press, 2006); Gábor T. Rittersporn, *Anguish, Anger, and Folkways in Soviet Russia* (Pittsburgh: University of Pittsburgh Press, 2014).

38. GARF, f. R7928, op. 3, d. 483, ll. 153–155, dated Jan. 26, 1949.

39. GARF, f. R7928, op. 3, d. 480, l. 5, dated Dec. 1, 1948.

40. I classify this project as citizen or public diplomacy instead of cultural diplomacy because it exerted influence by establishing relationships rather than showcasing national achievements. Mark Leonard, *Public Diplomacy* (London: The Foreign Policy Centre, 2002), 8; Nicholas J. Cull, "Public Diplomacy before Guillon: The Evolution of a Phrase," in *Routledge Handbook of Public Diplomacy,* ed. Nancy Snow and Philip M. Taylor (New York: Routledge, 2008).

41. The vast literature on correspondence-based political and intellectual networks includes Roger Chartier, *The Cultural Origins of the French Revolution* (Durham, NC: Duke University Press, 1991), 20–66, Gilman M. Ostrander, *Republic of Letters: The American Intellectual Community, 1776–1865* (Madison, WI: Madison House, 1999); Elizabeth Heckendorn Cook, *Epistolary Bodies: Gender and Genre in the Eighteenth-Century Republic of Letters* (Stanford, CA: Stanford University Press, 1996); Peter Burke, "The Republic of Letters as a Communication System: An Essay in Periodization," *Media History* 18, no. 3–4 (2012): 395–407; Dena Goodman, *The Republic of Letters: A Cultural History of the French Enlightenment* (Ithaca, NY: Cornell University Press, 1994). On women's transnational

epistolary networks, see Margaret H. McFadden, *Golden Cables of Sympathy: The Transatlantic Sources of Nineteenth-Century Feminism* (Lexington: University of Kentucky Press, 1999); Mineke Bosch, ed., *Politics and Friendship: Letters from the International Woman Suffrage Alliance, 1902–1942* (Columbus: Ohio State University Press, 1990); Jane Rendall, "Friends of Liberty and Virtue: Women Radicals and Transatlantic Correspondence, 1789–1848," in *Gender and Politics in the Age of Letter-Writing, 1750–2000*, ed. Caroline Bland and Márie Cross (Burlington, VT: Ashgate, 2004), 77–89; Susan Stabile, "Salons and Power in the Era of Revolution: From Literary Coteries to Epistolary Enlightenment," in *Benjamin Franklin and Women*, ed. Larry Tise (Philadelphia: Pennsylvania University Press, 2000), 129–148.

42. Miriam Dobson, "Letters," in *Reading Primary Sources: The Interpretation of Texts from Nineteenth- and Twentieth-Century History*, ed. Miriam Dobson and Benjamin Ziemann (New York: Routledge, 2009), 59; David Henkin, *The Postal Age: The Emergence of Modern Communications in Nineteenth-Century America* (Chicago: University of Chicago Press, 2006), 29, 35, 104, 172–173.

43. Katie Day Good, "From Pen Pals to ePals; Mediated Intercultural Exchange in a Historical Perspective," in *Intercultural Communication, Identity, and Social Movements in the Digital Age*, ed. Margaret U. D'Silva and Ahmet Atay (New York: Taylor and Francis, 2019), 9–14.

44. V. Novikova, *Zdrastvuite tovarishchi!* (Leningrad: leningradskoe oblast'noe izd-vo, 1932); I. I. Khanipova, "Mirovoi pionerii- bratskii privet!" *Gasyrlar-avazy- Ekho vekov*, no. 3–4 (2013): 67–76; Matthias Neumann, "Youthful Internationalism in the Age of 'Socialism in One Country': Komsomol'tsy, Pioneers and 'World Revolution' in the Interwar Period," *Revolutionary Russia* 31, no. 2 (2018): 8–10, 19, 22. The leading study of Soviet cultural diplomacy in the interwar period is Michael David-Fox, *Showcasing the Great Experiment: Cultural Diplomacy and Western Visitors to the Soviet Union, 1921–1941* (New York: Oxford University Press, 2011).

45. On Soviet conventions of letter writing, see Dobson, "Letters," 57–73. On Soviet petitions, see Shelia Fitzpatrick, "Supplicants and Citizens: Public Letter-Writing in Soviet Russia in the 1930s," *Slavic Review* 55 (1996): 78–105; Lewis H. Siegelbaum, "Narratives of Appeal and Appeal of Narratives: Labor Discipline and its Contestation in the Early Soviet Period," *Russian History / Histoire Russe* 24 (1997): 65–87; Miriam Dobson, *Khrushchev's Cold Summer: Gulag Returnees, Crime, and the Fate of Reform After Stalin* (Ithaca, NY: Cornell University Press, 2009), 50–78.

46. Letters from America, Letters to Italy, Letters Abroad, the People-to-People Program, the Girl Scouts of America, and Camp Fire Girls usually sent one-off letters: Jennifer Helgren, *American Girls and Global Responsibility: A New*

Relation to the World During the Early Cold War (New Brunswick: Rutgers University Press, 2017), 66; Osgood, *Total Cold War*, 232–252; Anna Fett, "U.S. People-to-People Programs: Cold War Cultural Diplomacy to Conflict Resolution," *Diplomatic History* 45, no. 4 (Sept. 2021): 715–729; Wendy L. Wall, *Inventing the 'American Way': The Politics of Consensus from the New Deal to the Civil Rights Movement* (New York: Oxford University Press, 2008).

47. David-Fox, *Showcasing*, 319. A slightly higher estimate for 1952–1953 in J. D. Parks, *Culture, Conflict and Coexistence: American-Soviet Cultural Relations, 1917–1958* (Jefferson, NC: McFarland, 1983), 136–139.

48. Works on US-Soviet exchange that downplay the Truman-Stalin era include Yale Richmond, *Cultural Exchange and the Cold War: Raising the Iron Curtain* (University Park: Pennsylvania State University Press, 2003); Osgood, *Total Cold War;* Scott Lucas, *Freedom's War: The American Crusade against the Soviet Union* (New York: New York University Press, 1999); Patryk Babiracki and Kenyon Zimmer, eds., *Cold War Crossings: International Travel and Exchange across the Soviet Bloc, 1940s–1960s* (College Station: University of Texas Press, 2003); Eleonory Gilburd, "The Revival of Soviet Internationalism in the Mid to Late 1950s," in *The Thaw: Soviet Society and Culture during the 1950s and 1960s*, ed. Denis Kozlov and Eleonory Gilburd (Toronto: University of Toronto Press, 2013), 362–399. Research contesting Stalinist isolationism after World War II includes Kiril Tomoff, *Virtuosi Abroad: Soviet Music and Imperial Competition During the Early Cold War, 1945–1958* (Ithaca, NY: Cornell University Press, 2015); Geoffrey Roberts, "Averting Armageddon: The Communist Peace Movement, 1948–1956," in *The Oxford Handbook of the History of Communism*, ed. Stephen A. Smith (Oxford: Oxford University Press, 2014), 322–336; O.S. Nagornaia, *Sovetskaia kul'turnaia diplomatiia v gody Kholodnoi voiny, 1945–1989* (Cheliabinsk: Iuzhno-Ural'skii gosudarstvenyi universitet, 2017).

49. Parks, *Culture*, 116–128; Rósa Magnúsdóttir, "Divided Spouses: Soviet-American Intermarriage and Human Rights Activism during the Cold War," in *Intermarriage from Central Europe to Central Asia: Mixed Families in the Age of Extremes*, ed. Adrienne Edgar and Benjamin Frommer (Lincoln: Nebraska University Press, 2020), 309–332.

50. Ambassador George F. Kennan was declared *persona non grata* in late 1952 (Osgood, *Total Cold War*, 56).

51. "Eisenhower's Inaugural Address to the Geneva Conference," *Documents on American Foreign Relations* (New York: Harper & Brothers, 1956), 183–184. Scholarship arguing that sustained contact between American and Soviet citizens began only after the 1955 Geneva summit, Khrushchev's 1956 "secret speech," or the 1958 Lacy-Zarubin agreement includes Norman E. Saul, "The Program that Shattered the Iron Curtain: The Lacy-Zarubin Agreement," in *New Perspectives on*

Russian-American Relations, ed. William Benton Whisenhunt and Norman E. Saul (New York: Routledge, 2016), 230–231; Günter Bischof and Saki Dockrill, *Cold War Respite: The Geneva Summit of 1955* (Baton Rouge: Louisiana State University Press, 2000); Rósa Magnúsdóttir, *Enemy Number One: The United States of America in Soviet Ideology and Propaganda, 1945–1959* (New York: Oxford University Press, 2018); Richmond, *Cultural Exchange,* 14–15; Vladislav M. Zubok, *A Failed Empire: The Soviet Union in the Cold War from Stalin to Gorbachev* (Chapel Hill: University of North Carolina Press, 2009), 103–120. Scholars challenging the standard periodization and application of "cold war" include Joel Isaac and Duncan Bell, eds., *Uncertain Empire: American History and the Idea of the Cold War* (New York: Oxford University Press, 2012); Holger Nehring, "What was the Cold War?" *The English Historical Review* 127, no. 527 (Aug. 2012): 920–949; Lawrence D. Freedman, "Frostbitten: Decoding the Cold War: 20 Years Later," *Foreign Affairs* 89, no. 2 (Mar.-Apr. 2010): 136–144.

52. Magnúsdóttir, *Enemy Number One;* Kenneth Osgood, "Eisenhower's Dilemma: Talking Peace and Waging War," in *Selling War in a Media Age: The Presidency and Public Opinion in the American Century,* ed. Kenneth Osgood and Andrew K. Frank (Gainesville: University of Florida Press, 2010), 140–169.

53. Osgood, *Total Cold War,* 6; Susan E. Reid, "Cold War in the Kitchen: Gender and the De-Stalinization of Consumer Taste in the Soviet Union under Khrushchev," *Slavic Review* 61, no. 2 (Summer 2002): 212.

54. Examples in GARF, f. R7928, op. 2, d. 361, l. 42, received June 28, 1948; GARF, f. R7928, op. 2, d. 245, ll. 84–85, dated Aug. 27, 1947; GARF, f. R7928, op. 2, d. 482, l. 93, sent July 9, 1948.

55. GARF, f. R7928, op. 2, d. 480, l. 8, dated Dec. 1, 1948; GARF, f. R7928, op. 2, d. 639, l. 62, dated Apr. 9, 1949; GARF, f. R7928, op. 2, d. 483, l. 155, dated Jan. 26, 1949.

56. Dobson, "Letters," 61.

57. "The personal is political" is associated with second-wave feminism but shaped numerous earlier movements. Seminal works on this concept include Carol Hanisch, "The Personal is Political," in *Notes from the Second Year: Women's Liberation,* ed. Shulamith Firestone and Anne Koedt (New York: Radical Feminism, 1970); Claudia Jones, "An End to the Neglect of the Problems of the Negro Woman!" (1949), and bell hooks, "Black Women: Shaping Feminist Theory," in *Words of Fire: An Anthology of African-American Feminist Thought,* ed. Beverly Guy-Sheftall (New York: The New Press, 2011), 107–122, 269–283; C. Wright Mills, *The Sociological Imagination* (New York: Oxford University Press, 1959); Combahee River Collective, "A Black Feminist Statement," *Women's Studies Quarterly* (1981): 42, 210–218; Sara Evans, "The Personal is Political," in *Global Feminisms Since 1945,* ed. Bonnie G. Smith (New York: Routledge, 2000), 141–163.

58. GARF, f. R7928, op. 2, d. 1191, 1. 84, dated Mar. 22, 1952; GARF, f. R7928, op. 2, d. 1191, l. 70, dated Apr. 19, 1952.

59. GARF, f. R7928, op. 2, d. 361, l. 34, dated Feb. 23, 1948; GARF, f. R7928, op. 2, d. 639, l. 60, dated Apr. 9, 1949.

60. Joanne Jahr's direct message sent through Ancestry.com on Dec. 19, 2022.

61. Eleonory Gilburd, *To See Paris and Die: The Soviet Lives of Western Culture* (Cambridge, MA: Belknap Press of Harvard University Press, 2018), 35.

62. Gilburd, *To See Paris,* 45, 39.

63. Dobson, "Letters," 65. "Speaking Bolshevik" is from Stephen Kotkin, *Magnetic Mountain: Stalinism as Civilization* (Berkeley: University of California Press, 1995). On the way cold war activists exercised agency even when not challenging the state, see Jadwiga E. Pieper Mooney and Fabio Lanza, eds., *De-centering Cold War History: Local and Global Change* (London: Routledge, 2013), 4; Laville, *Cold War Women.*

64. Jane Couchman and Ann Crabb, "Form and Persuasion in Women's Letters, 1400–1700," in *Women's Letters across Europe, 1400–1700: Form and Persuasion,* ed. Jane Couchman and Ann Crabb (Burlington, VT: Ashgate, 2005), 5, 11; W. M. Decker, *Epistolary Practices* (Chapel Hill: University of North Carolina Press, 1998), 4.

65. Beverly Fehr, *Friendship Processes* (Thousand Oaks, CA: Sage Publications, 1996), 11, 153–154; Patricia O'Connor, *Friendships between Women: A Critical Review* (New York: Guilford Press, 1992), 49–50, 63–67; Marilyn Friedman, "Feminism and Modern Friendship: Dislocating the Community," in *Feminism and Community,* ed. Penny A. Weiss and Marilyn Friedman (Philadelphia: Temple University Press, 1995), 187–208.

66. GARF, f. R7928, op. 2, d. 985, l. 140, dated June 1, 1950.

67. Lucile Eznack and Simon Koschut, "The Sources of Affect in Interstate Friendship," *Friendship and International Relations* (London: Palgrave Macmillan, 2014), 3–23; Roland Bleiker and Emma Hutchinson, "Fear No More: Emotions and World Politics," *Review of International Studies* 34 (2008): 115–135; Oleg Kharkhordin, "Friendship and Politics in Russia," *Common Knowledge* 22 (March 2016): 225–226, 232–233; Rachel Applebaum, "The Friendship Project: Socialist Internationalism in the Soviet Union and Czechoslovakia in the 1950s and 1960s," *Slavic Review* 74, no. 3 (Fall 2015): 484–507.

68. Eznack and Koschut, "Sources of Affect," 75.

69. Margaretta Jolly, "Corresponding in the Sex and Gender Revolution: Desire, Education, and Feminist Letters, 1970–2000," in *Gender and Politics in the Age of Letter-Writing,* 253–270; Bosch, *Politics and Friendship,* 23; Elizabeth C. Goldsmith, "Authority, Authenticity, and the Publication of Letters by Women," in

Writing the Female Voice: Essays on Epistolary Literature, ed. Goldsmith (Boston: Northeastern University Press 1989). On feminine epistolarity in politics: Eakin Moss, *Only Among Women;* Katherine M. Marino, "Transnational Pan-American Feminism: The Friendship of Bertha Lutz and Mary Wilhelmine Williams, 1926–1944," *Journal of Women's History* 26 no. 2 (Summer 2014): 63–87; Blanche Wiesen Cook, "Female Support Networks and Political Activism: Lillian Wald, Crystal Eastman, and Emma Goldman," in *A Heritage of Her Own: Toward a New Social History of American Women*, ed. Nancy F. Cott and Elizabeth H. Peck (New York: Simon and Schuster, 1979), 412–444; McFadden, *Golden Cables of Sympathy;* Mary Hunt, *Fierce Tenderness: A Feminist Theory of Friendship* (New York: Crossroad, 1992); Alison M. Jaggar, "Love and Knowledge: Emotion in Feminist Epistemology," in *Gender / Body / Knowledge: Feminist Reconstructions of Being and Knowing*, ed. Susan R. Bordo and Alison M. Jaggar (New Brunswick: Rutgers University Press, 1989), 145–171.

70. Bleiker and Hutchison, "Fear No More," 128.

71. Martha C. Nussbaum, "Emotions and Women's Capabilities," in *Women, Culture, and Development*, ed. Jonathan Glover and Martha C. Nussbaum (London: Oxford University Press, 1995), 360–395; Martha C. Nussbaum, *Upheavals of Thought: The Intelligence of Emotions* (Cambridge: Cambridge University Press, 2001); Chris Shilling, "Emotions, Embodiment and the Sensation of Society," *Sociological Review* 45, no. 2 (1997): 195–219; Robert C. Solomon, *Not Passion's Slave: Emotions and Choice* (Oxford: Oxford University Press, 2003).

72. This accusation was infamously articulated by Politburo member Andrei Zhdanov: Andrei Zhdanov, *On Literature, Music, and Philosophy* (London: Lawrence and Wishart, 1950).

1. Dear Sister-Ally

1. Chapter title from GARF, f. R7928, op. 2, d. 50, l. 177, sent Dec. 2, 1944. Shchelogova's letter in GARF, f. R7928, op. 2, d. 146, l. 166, dated Apr. 12, 1945. On ways British mothers used letter writing to grieve and share stories about wartime work, see Jenny Hartley, "'Letters are *Everything* these Days': Mothers and Letters in the Second World War," in *Epistolary Selves: Letters and Letter-Writers, 1600–1945*, ed. Rebecca Earle (Burlington, VT: Ashgate, 1999), 183–195.

2. There is only one book-length study of the Soviet Women's Anti-Fascist Committee, and it makes scant mention of the pen-pal project: G. N. Galkina, *Komitet sovetskikh zhenshchin: stranitsy istorii, 1941–1992* (Moscow: Tonchu, 2013), 19.

3. During the 1930s, a version of the Soviet Women's Anti-Fascist Committee existed inside the Comintern and worked with progressives to fight fascism and promote women's and workers' rights. RGASPI, f. 543, op. 2., dd. 1–3, 39, 42, 43;

Mercedes Yusta, "The Strained Courtship between Antifascism and Feminism: From the Women's World Committee (1934) to the Women's International Democratic Federation (1945)," in *Rethinking Antifascism: History, Memory, and Politics, 1922 to the Present*, ed. Hugo Garcia, Mercedes Yusta, Xavier Tabet, Cristina Clímaco (New York: Berghahn Books, 2016), 167–184.

4. Chris Bellamy, *Absolute War: Soviet Russia in the Second World War* (New York: Alfred A. Knopf, 2007), 206; Geoffrey Roberts, *Stalin's Wars: From World War to Cold War, 1939–1953* (New Haven, CT: Yale University Press, 2006), 85–87.

5. *Zdrastvuite, tovarishchi!* (Leningrad: Leningrad oblastnoe izdatel'stvo, 1932); I. I. Khanipova, "Mirovoi pionerii- bratskii privet!" *Gasyrlar-avazy- Ekho vekov* 3–4 (2013): 67–76; Matthias Neumann, "Youthful Internationalism in the Age of 'Socialism in One Country': Komsomol'tsy, Pioneers and 'World Revolution' in the Interwar Period," *Revolutionary Russia* 31, no. 2 (2018): 8, 22.

6. Michael David-Fox, *Showcasing the Great Experiment: Cultural Diplomacy and Western Visitors to the Soviet Union, 1921–1941* (New York: Oxford University Press, 2011), 318.

7. On stoicism, see Catherine Merridale, *Night of Stone: Death and Memory in Russia* (London: Viking Press, 2000), 312; GARF, f. R7928, op. 2, d. 50, l. 120, dated Mar. 16, 1945.

8. Roberts, *Stalin's Wars,* 87.

9. GARF, f. R7928, op. 2, d. 146, l. 137–139ob., sent May 26, 1945.

10. Jeffrey Brooks, "*Pravda* goes to War," in *Culture and Entertainment in Wartime Russia*, ed. Richard Stites (Bloomington: Indiana University Press, 1995), 9–14. On individual motivations for fighting, see Oleg Budnitskii, "The Intelligentsia meets the Enemy: Educated Soviet Officers in Defeated Germany, 1945," *Kritika* 10, no. 3 (2009): 629–682; Amir Weiner, *Making Sense of War: The Second World War and the Fate of the Bolshevik Revolution* (Princeton, NJ: Princeton University Press, 2001); Lazar Lazarev, "Russian Literature on the War and Historical Truth," in *World War II and the Soviet People*, ed. John Garrard and Carol Garrard (New York: St. Martin's Press, 1993).

11. Lisa A. Kirschenbaum, "'Our City, Our Hearths, Our Families,' Local Loyalties and Private Life in Soviet World War II, Propaganda," *Slavic Review* 59, no. 4 (Winter 2000): 825, 829.

12. N. D. Kozlov, *Obshchestvennoe soznanie v gody velikoi otechestvennoi voiny* (St. Petersburg: Leningradskii Oblastnoi Institut Usovershenstvovaniia Uchitelei,1995), 64–65; Karel C. Berkhoff, *Motherland in Danger: Soviet Propaganda during World War II* (Cambridge, MA: Harvard University Press, 2012), 266; Sarah Davies, "Soviet Perceptions of the Allies during the Great Patriotic

War," in *Russia and the Wider World in Historical Perspective*, ed. C. Brennan and M. Frame (New York: St. Martin's Press, 2000), 168–189.

13. "Doklad Predsedatelia Gosudarstvennogo Komiteta Oborony tovarishcha I. V. Stalina," *Pravda*, Nov. 7, 1942, no. 311, 1.

14. A. V. Golubev and O. S. Porshneva, *Obraz soiuznika v soznanii rossiiskogo obshchestva v kontekste mirovykh voin* (Moscow: Novyi khronograf, 2012), 251–252; V. O. Pechatnov, *Stalin, Roosevelt, Trumen: SSSR i SShA v 1940-xx. Dokumental'nye ocherki* (Moscow: TERRA-Knizhnyi klub, 2006), 36; Berkhoff, *Motherland in Danger*, 261.

15. Il'ia Koldomasov, *Obraz soiuznikov po antigitlerovskoi koalitsiii v SSSR* (Cisnau: Lambert Academic Publishing, 2016), 181; J. D. Parks, *Culture, Conflict and Coexistence: American-Soviet Cultural Relations, 1917–1958* (Jefferson, NC: McFarland, 1983), 84–87.

16. Parks, *Culture*, 77.

17. Golubev and Porshneva, *Obraz soiuznika*, 255, 263–266.

18. Davies, "Soviet Perceptions," 181–185.

19. *Soviet Women to the Women of the World: The Moscow Women's Anti-Nazi Meeting and American Women's Response* (New York: The American Council on Soviet Relations, 1941), 7–8.

20. *Soviet Women to the Women of the World*, 9.

21. GARF, f. R7928, op. 2, d. 4, ll. 92–93. Women's organizations from the British Commonwealth including Canada, Australia, India, and South Africa partnered with the anti-fascist committee. GARF, f. R5283, op. 15, d. 15; Jennifer Anderson, *Propaganda and Persuasion: The Cold War and the Canadian-Soviet Friendship Society* (Winnipeg: University of Manitoba Press, 2017); Olga Kucherenko, "A Fleeting Friendship: Anglo-Soviet Penpalship in the Second World War," *Diplomacy & Statecraft* 32, no. 4 (2021): 692–719; Alexis Peri, "Operation Friendship: Soviet and British Women Discuss War, Work, and Womanhood," *The Russian Review* 82, no. 3 (July 2023): 453–469.

22. GARF, f. R5283, op. 15, d. 15, l. 23, received Dec. 30, 1943.

23. GARF, f. R8581, op. 1, d. 71, ll. 38–39. Emphasis added.

24. GARF, f. R8581, op. 1, d. 71, ll. 2–30b.

25. GARF, f. R8581, op. 1, d. 71, ll. 14.

26. GARF, f. R8581, op. 1, d. 71, ll. 20–23.

27. GARF, f. R8581, op. 1, d. 71, l. 14; GARF, f. R8581, op. 1, d. 107, l. 43.

28. GARF, f. R7928, op. 2, d. 483, l. 75.

29. Kucherenko, "Fleeting Friendship," 696.

30. GARF, f. R8581, op. 1, d. 71, l. 29.

31. GARF, f. R8581, op. 1, d. 71, l. 31.

32. On 1943 as the "peak" of American "enthusiasm" for their Soviet Ally, see Ronald Smelser and Edward J. Davies II, *Myth of the Eastern Front: The Nazi-Soviet War in American Popular Imagination* (Cambridge: Cambridge University Press, 2008), 11; Warren B. Walsh, "What the American People Think of Russia," *Public Opinion Quarterly* 8, no. 4 (Winter 1944): 519.

33. Smelser and Davies, *Myth*, 29; "The World's Number One Army," *Life* 25, Nov. 29, 1943, 25–31.

34. Smelser and Davies, *Myth*, 11; Parks, *Culture*, 62–68.

35. Parks, *Culture*, 9, 25, 28; W. H. Lawrence, "Russia's New Women," *New York Times Magazine*, Nov. 5, 1944, 21, 41, 42. Also see Loy Henderson's remarks in: *The American-Soviet War Exhibit* (New York: National Council of American-Soviet Friendship, 1943), 3–4. National Council of American-Soviet Friendship is hereafter NCASF.

36. "Gettysburg and Stalingrad," *Christian Science Monitor*, Feb. 12, 1942, 12. Quoted in Ralph B. Levering, *American Opinion and the Russian Alliance, 1939–1945* (Chapel Hill: University of North Carolina Press, 1976), 106.

37. One example is *The North Star* (1943).

38. Examples include *Miss V from Moscow* (1942) and *Three Russian Girls* (1943).

39. Michael David-Fox, "From Illusory 'Society to Intellectual 'Public': VOKS, International Travel, and Party: Intelligentsia Relations in the Interwar Period," *Contemporary European History* 11, no. 1 (2002): 7–32; Jean-Francois Fayet, "VOKS, the Third Dimension of Soviet Foreign Policy," in *Searching for a Cultural Diplomacy*, ed. Jessica C. E. Gienow-Hecht and Mark C. Donfried (New York: Berghahn Books, 2010), 33–49.

40. GARF, f. R7928, op. 2, d. 50, ll. 255–255ob., dated June 22, 1943. I refer to the letter writers by the way they rendered their own names.

41. Edward C. Carter, "Russian War Relief," *The Slavonic and East European Review* 3, no. 2 (Aug. 1944), 61–62; "Dear Red," *Time*, June 14, 1943, 27–28; Lois Mattox Miller, "From John Doe to the Russian Front," *Reader's Digest*, May 1942, 122–125; "Russian War Relief—Facts in Figures," *American Review on the Soviet Union* 6, no. 3 (May 1945): 27.

42. Russian War Relief, *Write to Russia: Shake Hands with our Fighting Ally* (Los Angeles: Russian War Relief, Inc., 1942), 3.

43. Laurie R. Cohen, *Smolensk under the Nazis: Everyday Life in Occupied Russia* (Rochester, NY: University of Rochester Press, 2013), 7.

44. GARF, f. R7928, op. 2, d. 50, ll. 254–254ob., dated Nov. 20, 1944.

45. The only major study of NCASF is David Byron Wagner, "Alone Together: Intellectuals in the American-Soviet Friendship Movement" (PhD diss.,

University of California, Riverside, 2016). Accessed through ProQuest. There is some discussion of NCASF in Julia L. Mickenberg, *American Girls in Red Russia: Chasing the Soviet Dream* (Chicago: University of Chicago Press, 2017). Neither work mentions the pen pal project.

46. *National Council of American-Soviet Friendship, Inc.* (New York: NCASF, 1943), TAM 361, box 8, folder 5.

47. Wagner, "Alone Together," 33–36, 51. Some of the members had been in Communist Party-sponsored groups like Friends of Soviet Russia, created in 1921 and revamped as Friends of the Soviet Union in 1929.

48. Wagner, "Alone Together," 18.

49. NCASF, *Stalingrad,* 15, TAM 134, box 6, folder 10; Wagner, "Alone Together," 59.

50. *National Council of American-Soviet Friendship, Inc.*

51. NCASF, *Stalingrad,* 13, TAM 134, box 6, folder 10; NCASF press release (March 5, 1945), 1, TAM 134, box 5, folder 18.

52. *The American-Soviet War Exhibit* (New York: NCASF, 1943), 2–3; TAM 134, box 6, folder 14; Special Agent Peter J. Cattaneo, Report on NCASF, Oct. 21, 1943, 14. FOIA request 1392927-001.

53. House of Representatives Committee on Un-American Activities (hereafter HUAC), "NCASF 1943–1948," box 626, RG233, NARA.

54. William Francis Norton Jr., Report on NCASF, Jan. 31, 1944, file 100–7518, 11. FOIA request 1392927-002.

55. William Henderson, "Plan to Swap Mail with Russians Gets Scrutiny of Army," *New York Daily Mirror,* May 4, 1943, 4; Letter from J. Edgar Hoover to the War Department, May 25, 1944, box 1831, stack 290, row 35, compartment 12, shelf 5, NND 740063, RG 389, NARA.

56. Letter from the FBI's San Francisco Office to the FBI director, Oct. 13, 1943. FOIA request 1392927-001.

57. Letter to Ms. Hannah Dorner, NCASF Publicity Manager, from Ray Atherton, Acting Chief, Bureau of European Affairs, July 5, 1943, A2 00150: 070 / 035 / 02, container 8, RG59, NARA.

58. Letter to J. Edgar Hoover from the Office of Censorship, Washington, J. P. Wolgemuth, Executive Liaison Officer of the US Office of Censorship, Nov. 16, 1943; letter from J. Edgar Hoover to Mr. Ladd, Oct. 28, 1943. FOIA request 3-26-20.

59. The motion for a Committee of Women was made in November 1943 ("The Second Congress of American-Soviet Friendship Report," Nov. 6–8, 1943, TAM 134, box 6, folder 11).

60. Special Agent Peter J. Cattaneo, Report on NCASF, Oct. 22, 1943, 1. FOIA request 1392927-001.

61. Michael S. Sweeney, *Secrets of Victory: The Office of Censorship and the American Press and Radio in World War II* (Chapel Hill: University of North Carolina Press, 2001).

62. Special Agent Peter J. Cattaneo, Report on NCASF, Oct. 22, 1943, 1. FOIA Request 1392927-001.

63. Kucherenko, "Fleeting."

64. Lauren Kessler, *Clever Girl: Elizabeth Bentley, the Spy Who Ushered in the McCarthy Era* (New York: Harper Collins, 2003).

65. GARF, f. R7928, op. 2, d. 146, l. 103–106, sent Nov. 29, 1946.

66. GARF, f. R7928, op. 2, d. 245, l. 210b., dated Oct. 27, 1947.

67. GARF, f. R7928, op. 2, d. 50, l. 77, dated Apr. 14, 1946.

68. GARF, f. R7928, op. 2, d. 50, l. 287, dated Feb. 8, 1944.

69. GARF, f. R7928, op. 2, d. 50, l. 241, dated Mar. 8, 1944.

70. Geraldine Rosenfield, "Overseas Relief and Rehabilitation," *The American Jewish Year Book* 47 (1945–1946): 304–315; Daniel Soyer, "Executed Bundists, Soviet Delegates and the Wartime Jewish Popular Front in New York," *American Communist History* 15, no. 3 (2016): 293–332.

71. GARF, f. R7928, op. 2, d. 50, l. 177, sent Dec. 2, 1944. A handwritten note gives the same first name and patronymic but a different surname for the author.

72. GARF, f. R7928, op. 2, d. 50, l. 73, received May 28, 1946; US Census Bureau, *Sixteenth Census of the United States* (Washington, DC: National Archives and Records Administration, 1940), roll m-t0627-02418, page 7B, enumeration district 25–218.

73. GARF, f. R7928, op. 2, d. 50, l. 259–259ob., dated June 9, 1943.

74. GARF, f. R7928, op. 2, d. 50, l. 152, dated Nov. 20, 1944.

75. GARF, f. R7928, op. 2, d. 245, l. 87 dated Aug. 5, 1947.

76. GARF, f. R7928, op. 2, d. 50, l. 226, dated Jan. 12, 1945. Similar example in GARF, f. R7928, op. 2, d. 50, ll. 162–162ob., dated Oct. 23, 1944.

77. Ten percent of US soldiers in overseas combat were married; five percent were fathers. D'Ann Campbell, *Women at War with America: Private Lives in a Patriotic Era* (Cambridge, MA: Harvard University Press, 1984), 91.

78. GARF, f. R7928, op. 2, d. 50, ll. 171–172, undated, 1944.

79. GARF, f. R7928 op. 2, d. 246, l. 41, dated Feb. 5, 1947.

80. *Second Anti-fascist Women's Meeting* (Moscow: Foreign Languages Publishing House, 1942), 9.

81. GARF, f. R7928, op. 2, d. 75, l. 5.

82. Communist Party members and sympathizers included Elizabeth Moos and Jessica Smith.

83. NCASF executive director Richard Morford called the Committee of Women "the strong right arm" to the National Council and a "vigorous and

successful money-raiser"—complimentary but stereotypical views of women's political work ("Annual Report by the Director to the Members of the NCASF," April 10, 1946, Hoover Institution Library & Archives [HILA], Poole collection 82095).

84. Dorothy Sue Cobble, "More than Sex Equality: Feminism after Suffrage," in *Feminism Unfinished*, ed. Dorothy Sue Cobble, Linda Gordon, and Astrid Henry (New York: W. W. Norton, 2014), 25; Maureen Honey, *Creating Rosie the Riveter: Class, Gender, and Propaganda During World War II* (Boston: University of Massachusetts Press, 1984), 6–7, 25–26, 46–51.

85. GARF, f. R7928, op. 2, d. 146, l. 139, dated June 22, 1945; GARF, f. R7928, op. 2, d. 146, l. 140, sent May 26, 1945; GARF, f. R7928, op. 2, d. 146, l. 143, sent May 26, 1945.

86. GARF, f. R7928, op. 2, d. 50, l. 226, dated Jan. 12, 1945.

87. GARF, f. R7928, op. 2, d. 50, l. 231, dated Dec. 25, 1944.

88. Campbell, *Women at War*, 66; Honey, *Creating Rosie*, 34–35, 19.

89. GARF, f. R7928, op. 2, d. 50, l. 192, dated Mar. 20, but no year; sent in either 1944 or 1945.

90. "Aptos Farmer Dies in S.C.," *Santa Cruz Sentinel*, March 24, 1942, 2.

91. GARF, f. R7928, op. 2, d. 50, l. 274, dated May 27, 1943. Information on Mustanich from *1940 United States Federal Census*, roll m-t0627-00343, page 11B, enumeration district 44–43.

92. David M. Glantz and Jonathan M. House, *The Battle of Kursk* (Lawrence: University of Kansas Press, 1999), 274–276.

93. GARF, f. R7928, op. 2, d. 50, l. 270, dated Oct. 2, 1944.

94. F. Pevnev, "*Sornye travy*," GARF, f. R7928, op. 2, d. 50, l. 271.

95. GARF, f. R7928, op. 2, d. 50, l. 175, dated Feb. 1944.

96. GARF, f. R7928, op. 2, d. 50, l. 173, dated Nov. 28, 1944.

97. GARF, f. R7928, op. 2, d. 50, l. 170, sent Mar. 20, 1944; GARF, f. R7928, op. 2, d. 50, l. 167–167ob., dated Sept. 15, 1944.

98. GARF, f. R7928, op. 2, d. 50, l. 73, dated May 28, 1946.

99. GARF, f. R7928, op. 2, d. 50, l. 177, dated Dec. 2, 1944.

100. Wendy Z. Goldman, *Women at the Gates: Gender and Industry in Stalin's Russia* (Cambridge: Cambridge University Press, 2002), 160, 171, 223; Donald Filtzer, *Soviet Workers and Late Stalinism: Labour and the Restoration of the Stalinist System after World War II* (Cambridge: Cambridge University Press, 2002), 210.

101. "Women against Hitler," 22. Also see "Girls become skilled Coal Miners," *Soviet Information Bulletin*, Apr. 18, 1944.

102. GARF, f. R7928, op. 2, d. 50, l. 284, dated Aug. 8, 1944.

103. GARF, f. R7928, op. 2, d. 50, l. 284ob.

104. GARF, f. R7928, op. 2, d. 50, l. 152, dated Nov. 20, 1944.

105. GARF, f. R7928, op. 2, d. 50, l. 126, dated Mar. 3, 1945.

106. Susan Bridger, *Women in the Soviet Countryside: Women's Roles in Rural Development in the Soviet Union* (Cambridge: Cambridge University Press, 1987), 16.

107. Honey, *Creating Rosie,* 34, 46, 62.

108. "Russian Women Had Place More Important than Most," *Globe and Mail,* Jan. 16, 1942, 13; Edgar Snow, "Meet Mr. and Mrs. Russia at Home," *Saturday Evening Post,* Dec. 22, 1945, 14–15, 65; Oriana Atkinson, "Weaker(?) Sex of Soviet Russia," *New York Times,* March 3, 1946, 15, 51–52; Joseph B. Phillips, "A Typical Woman of Postwar Moscow," *Newsweek,* Nov. 4, 1946, 52; Fannina W. Halle, "Free Women of Russia," *Woman's Home Companion,* Feb. 1943, 30–31; Ralph Parker, "Women Workers of the Russian Miracle," *New York Times Magazine,* Feb. 14, 1943, 18, 34; Maurice Hindus, "The Russian Women," *Woman's Day,* June 1943, 12–13; Rose Maurer, "Those Russian Women," *Survey Graphic,* Feb. 1944, 108–109, 150–157.

109. W. H. Lawrence, "Russia's New Women," *New York Times Magazine,* Nov. 5, 1944, 22, 41–42.

110. GARF, f. R7928, op. 2, d. 50, l. 132, dated Feb. 10, 1945.

111. GARF, f. R7928, op. 2, d. 50, l. 262, dated Mar. 22, 1943. Another example in GARF, f. R7928, op. 2, d. 50, l. 184, dated Nov. 25, 1944.

112. GARF, f. R7928, op. 2, d. 146, l. 94, sent Jan. 1947.

113. GARF, f. R7928, op. 2, d. 146, l. 92, sent Jan. 1947.

2. I Come in Peace!

1. GARF, f. R7928, op. 2, d. 361, l. 29, received July 26, 1948. On the "one world" idea of global interdependence and connectedness, see Samuel Zipp, "When Wendell Willkie Went Visiting: Between Interdependency and Exceptionalism in the Public Feeling for *One World,*" *American Literary History* 26, no. 3 (2014): 484–510.

2. Examples in GARF, f. R7928, op. 2, d. 146, ll. 41, 61, 81, dated Jan. 30, 1947, Feb. 28, 1947, Mar. 29, 1947; GARF, f. R7928, op. 2, d. 359, ll. 24, 28–29, dated May 6, 1947, May 28, 1947, Sept. 5, 1947.

3. Mary Roe Hull, "The Flood of 1881: How it Affected the Roe Property, Lake Rest, and the Lake Rest Summer Resort" (1954), 6, 15, in Wisconsin Historical Society Archive, Roe and Zobel Family Papers, 1911–1960 (M2018–023 MAD 2M / 28 / Q6).

4. Hull, "The Flood of 1881," 2–4.

5. GARF, f. R7928, op. 2, d. 482, l. 55, dated July 26, 1948.

6. GARF, f. R7928, op. 2, d. 480, l. 54, dated Sept. 22, 1948.

7. This chapter focuses on 1945–1946 but follows Hull and Morozova's conversation into 1948 to reconstruct more of it.

8. George H. Gallup, *The Gallup Poll: Public Opinion, 1935–1971* (New York: Random House, 1972), 498. The National Opinion Research Center found 74 percent of Americans blamed the United States and USSR equally for "misunderstandings" between them ("Russia and US Blamed for Strife," *Afro-American*, Nov. 23, 1946, 15).

9. GARF, f. R7928, op. 2, d. 244, l. 36, dated June 21, 1947.

10. GARF, f. R7928, op. 2, d. 50, l. 3, dated Aug. 13, 1946.

11. Petra Goedde, *The Politics of Peace: A Global Cold War History* (New York: Oxford University Press, 2019), 99, 104.

12. On universalism in American liberal capitalism and Soviet socialism, see David C. Engerman, "Ideology and the Origins of the Cold War, 1917–1962," in *Cambridge History of the Cold War, Vol. 1*, ed. Melvyn P. Leffler and Odd Arne Westad (Cambridge: Cambridge University Press, 2010), 20; Thomas Borstelmann, *Just Like Us: The American Struggle to Understand Foreigners* (New York: Columbia University Press, 2020). On universalism in feminist and peace advocacy, see Leila J. Rupp, "Constructing Internationalism: the Case of Transnational Women's Organizations, 1888–1945," *American Historical Review* 99, no. 5 (Dec. 1994): 1571–1600.

13. Goedde, *The Politics*, 17.

14. GARF, f. R7928, op. 2, d. 480, l. 4, dated Jan. 3, 1949. On how the concept of a "cold war" was not widely accepted until summer 1947, see George Gallup, "Term 'Cold War' Unknown to 46%," *Washington Post*, Dec. 3, 1948, 16; Masuda Hajimu, *Cold War Crucible: The Korean Conflict and the Postwar World* (Cambridge, MA: Harvard University Press, 2015), 1–2; Timothy Johnston, *Being Soviet: Identity, Rumor, and Everyday Life under Stalin, 1939–1953* (Oxford: Oxford University Press, 2011), 127.

15. Connie Roe Burtnett's emails of Dec. 20, 2022, and Sept. 8, 2023.

16. Mary Roe Hull, "We Remember" (1960), 57, Wisconsin Historical Society Archive, Roe and Zobel Family Papers, 1911–1960 (M2018–023 MAD 2M / 28 / Q6).

17. Burtnett's email of Sept. 8, 2023; Mary Roe Hull, "The Flood of 1881," 1, 5.

18. GARF, f. R7928, op. 2, d. 483, l. 72, dated July 5, 1949.

19. Yoram Gorlizki and Oleg Khlevniuk, *Cold Peace: Stalin and the Soviet Ruling Circle, 1945–1953* (New York: Oxford University Press, 2004), 87, 31–44.

20. GARF, f. R7928, op. 2, d.146, l. 520b., undated but before Mar. 1947.

21. GARF, f. R7928, op. 2, d. 483, l. 247, dated Oct. 26, 1948.

22. GARF, f. R7928, op. 2, d. 358, l. 250b., undated in Aug. or Sept. 1947.

23. GARF, f. R7928, op. 2, d. 361, l. 48, dated Apr. 16, 1948.

24. GARF, f. R7928, op. 2, d. 481, l. 52, dated Dec. 15, 1948.
25. GARF, f. R7928, op. 2, d. 483, l. 247, dated Oct. 26, 1948.
26. GARF, f. R7928, op. 2, d. 483, l. 74, dated July 5, 1949.
27. GARF, f. R7928, op. 2, d. 361, l. 51, dated Apr. 16, 1948.
28. GARF, f. R7928, op. 2, d. 789, l. 18ob., received Apr. 11, 1950.
29. GARF, f. R7928, op. 2, d. 482, l. 46, dated Aug. 23, 1948.
30. GARF, f. R7928, op. 2, d. 245, l. 11, dated Nov. 19, 1947.
31. GARF, f. R7928, op. 2, d. 146, l. 52ob., undated in Mar. 1947.
32. GARF, f. R7928, op. 2, d. 146, l. 53–54, undated in 1946.
33. GARF, f. R7928, op. 2, d. 244, ll.1–2, dated Nov. 4, 1946; GARF, f. R2798, op. 2, d. 245, l. 12, undated, sent in 1946; GARF, f. R7928, op. 2, d. 359, l. 11, received Mar. 24, 1947.
34. GARF, f. R7928, op. 2, d. 146, l. 133, dated Aug. 15, 1945.
35. Letter, May 10, 1946, box 4809, stack 250, row 37, compartment 9, shelf 2, folder 2, ref. # 811.42761, RG59, NARA.
36. Dispatch from US Embassy to State Dept., June 8, 1946, box 4809, stack 250, row 37, compartment 9, shelf 2, folder 3, ref # 811.42761, RG59, NARA. Also see Embassy reports to US State Dept., box 6641, stack 250, row 38, compartment 11, shelf 4, folder 1, NND760050, ref # 861.00B, RG59, NARA.
37. GARF, f. R7928, op. 2, d. 50, l. 78, dated May 4, 1946.
38. House of Representatives, Committee on Un-American Activities, "Proceedings against Corliss Lamont," 79th Congress, session 2, June 12, 1946, 1, 4.
39. RGASPI, f. 17, op. 128. d. 69, l. 71.
40. RGASPI, f. 17, op. 125, d. 317, ll. 2, 4; Catriona Kelly, "Defending Children's Rights in Defense of Peace," in *Imagining the West in Eastern Europe and the USSR,* ed. Gyorgy Peteri (Pittsburgh: University of Pittsburgh Press, 2010), 76.
41. RGASPI, f. 17, op. 128, d. 69, l. 78.
42. GARF, f. R7928, op. 2, d. 991, l. 69.
43. GARF, f. R7928, op. 2, d. 49, ll. 8–12, dated Oct. 23, 1946, and July 25, 1946; GARF, f. R7928, op. 2, d. 146, l. 101, dated Nov. 29, 1946.
44. Linda Racioppi and Katherine O'Sullivan-See, *Women's Activism in Contemporary Russia* (Philadelphia: Temple University Press, 1997), 72–76; Yana Knopova, "The Soviet Union and the International Domain of Women's Rights and Struggles: A Theoretical Framework and a Case Study of the Soviet Women's Committee (1941–1991)" (master's thesis, Central European University,2001), 92, accessed through ProQuest.
45. Konstantin Azadovskii and Boris Egorov, "From Anti-Westernism to Anti-Semitism: Stalin and the Impact of the 'Anti-Cosmopolitan' Campaigns on Soviet Culture," *Journal of Cold War Studies* 4, no. 1 (Winter 2002): 66–80; Rósa

Magnúsdóttir, *Enemy Number One: The United States of America in Soviet Ideology and Propaganda, 1945–1959* (New York: Oxford University Press, 2018), 10–36.

46. RGASPI, f. 17, op. 128, d. 69, l. 80.

47. Helen Laville, *Cold War Women: The International Activities of America Women's Organizations* (Manchester: Manchester University Press, 2002), 27–33, 54–56, 77–79; Grace Victoria Leslie, "United for a Better World: Internationalism in the U.S. Women's Movement, 1939–1964" (PhD diss., Yale University, 2011), 95–96, 109, 202–203, accessed through ProQuest; Glenda Sluga, *Internationalism in the Age Of Nationalism* (Philadelphia: University of Pennsylvania Press, 2013), 85–87; Akira Iriye, *Cultural Internationalism and World Order* (Baltimore: John Hopkins University Press, 1997).

48. Judy Barrett Litoff and David C. Smith, *What Kind of World Do We Want? American Women Plan for Peace* (Wilmington: Rowman & Littlefield Publishers, 2000), 6–10, 101–131.

49. Helgren, *American Girls*, 57–66.

50. GARF, f. R7928, op. 2, d. 49, l. 23, dated May 16, 1946; GARF, f. R7928, op. 2, d. 49, l. 17, dated June 4, 1946.

51. Emma Bugbee, "Women's Clubs Call off Fight on Communism: Federation Board Meeting backs Full Military and Economic Aid to Russia," *New York Herald Tribune*, Jan. 25, 1942, 17; Mildred White Wells, *Unity in Diversity: The History of the General Federation of Women's Clubs* (Washington, DC: General Federation of Women's Clubs, 1953), 135–137.

52. GARF, f. R7928, op. 2, d. 50, l. 55, dated Apr. 4, 1946.

53. "Visit to Russia: Americans and Soviets can be Friends," *New York Herald Tribune*, Nov. 3, 1946, 20; "In the Soviet Women's Anti-Fascist Committee," *Soviet Woman*, no. 5 (Sept.-Oct. 1946): 56; Also see Lucy J. Dickinson, "Russian Women as I Saw Them," *Redbook*, Feb. 1947, 54.

54. Zipp, "When Wendell Willkie Went Visiting," 484–510.

55. "Visit to Russia," 77–78.

56. GARF, f. R7928, op. 2, d. 244, l. 62, dated Dec. 11, 1946. Other Dickinson-inspired letters in GARF, f. R7928, op. 2, d. 245, ll. 71–72, dated Feb. 1947; GARF, f. R7928, op. 2, d. 50, l. 27, undated from 1946.

57. *Clubwoman of America*, May 1947, 56. This magazine later shortened its name to *Clubwoman*.

58. Oriana Atkinson, "My Life Behind the Iron Curtain," *Woman's Home Companion*, Oct. 1946, 31.

59. GARF, f. R7928, op. 2, d. 246, l. 36–37, dated Dec. 2, 1946.

60. GARF, f. R7928, op. 2., d. 246, ll. 10–10ob., dated Oct. 24, 1947. Atkinson implied Petrova never responded to the letters, but she did: Lidiia Petrova, "Otkrytoe pis'mo moim amerikanskim korrespondentam," *Soviet Woman*, no. 3

(Apr.-May 1947): 41–42; Oriana Atkinson, *Over At Uncle Joe's: Moscow and Me* (Indianapolis: Bobbs-Merrill Company, 1947), 237.

61. GARF, f. R7928, op. 2, d. 482, l. 67; dated July 9, 1948.

62. By contrast, the anti-fascist committee recruited party members to correspond with British and French women whose politics were further to the left (GARF, f. R7928, op. 2, d. 991, ll. 74–75).

63. RGASPI, f. 17, op. 128, d. 246, l. 10. In 1948, chairperson Nina Popova told Mikhail Andreevich Suslov, Secretary of the Central Committee, that her staff censored the letters and advised the letter writers, but there is no evidence of a script or set of instructions.

64. Burtnett's email from Dec. 20, 2022.

65. My interview with Connie Roe Burtnett on Dec. 30, 2022; Burtnett's email of Sept. 8, 2023.

66. GARF, f. R7928, op. 2, d. 245, l. 5, dated Nov. 19, 1947.

67. GARF, f. R7928, op. 2, d. 361, l. 38, dated May 9, 1948.

68. GARF, f. R7928, op. 2, d. 361, l. 26, dated June 12, 1948.

69. GARF, f. R7928, op. 2, d. 245, ll. 5–6, dated Nov. 19, 1947.

70. Susan Lynn, *Progressive Women in Conservative Times: Racial Justice, Peace, and Feminism, 1945 to the 1960s* (New Brunswick: Rutgers University Press, 1992), 18–27; Sylvie Murray, *The Progressive Housewife: Community Activism in Suburban Queens, 1945–1965* (Philadelphia: University of Pennsylvania Press, 2003); A. Lanethea Matthews-Gardner, "From Ladies Aid to NGO: Transformations in Methodist Women's Organizing in Postwar America," in *Breaking the Wave: Women, Their Organizations, and Feminism, 1945–1985,* ed. Kathleen A Laughlin and Jacqueline L. Castledine (New York: Routledge, 2011), 100–102.

71. Consider Dulles's 1947 speech "Ideals, not Deals" and his 1948 tract "Christian Responsibility for Peace," or Kennan's 1953 sermon, "To Be or Not to Be a Christian," *Christianity and Crisis* (May 3, 1954): 51–53. See Mark G. Toulouse, "The Development of a Cold Warrior: John Foster Dulles and the Soviet Union, 1945–1952," *American Presbyterians* 63, no. 3 (Fall 1985): 309–322; Henry P. VanDusen, ed., *The Spiritual Legacy of John Foster Dulles* (Philadelphia: The Westminster Press, 1960); William Charles Inboden III, "'The Soul of American Diplomacy': Religion and Foreign Policy, 1945–1960" (PhD diss., Yale University, 2003), 13–15, accessed through ProQuest; Scott Lucas, "Campaigns of Truth: The Psychological Strategy Board and American Ideology, 1951–1953," *The International History Review* 18, no. 2 (May 1996): 279–302. On Dulles's religious rhetoric under President Eisenhower, see Philip Wander, "The Rhetoric of American Foreign Policy," in *Cold War Rhetoric: Strategy, Metaphor, and Ideology,* ed. Martin J. Medhurst et al. (East Lansing: Michigan State University Press, 1997), 160–163.

72. Inboden III, "'The Soul,'" 38, 156.

73. Robert Donovan, *Conflict and Crisis: the Presidency of Harry S. Truman, 1949–1953* (New York: W. W. Norton, 1982), 358.

74. John Foster Dulles, "Thoughts on Soviet Foreign Policy and What to Do about It," part 1, *Life,* June 3, 1946, 113; Dulles, "Thoughts on Soviet," part 2, June 10, 1946, 119–120, 130.

75. GARF, f. R7928, op. 2, d. 358, l. 26–26ob., undated in Aug. or Sept. 1947.

76. GARF, f. R7928, op. 2, d. 245, l. 24, dated Dec. 12, 1946.

77. GARF, f. R7928, op. 2, d. 244, l. 1–2, dated Nov. 4, 1946.

78. GARF, f. R7928, op. 2, d. 244, l. 5, dated Nov. 21, 1946; "Blanche F. Lamb," *The Post-Star,* Nov. 5, 1991, 12.

79. GARF, f. R7928, op. 2, d. 1191, l. 61–63, dated May 6, 1952.

80. GARF, f. R7928 op. 2, d. 244, ll. 8–10, dated Oct. 20, 1946.

81. GARF, f. R7928 op. 2, d. 244, ll. 13–14, dated Dec. 12, 1946.

82. Daniel Peris, "'God is Now on Our Side': The Religious Revival on Unoccupied Soviet Territory during World War II," *Kritika* 1, no. 1 (Winter 2000): 101–102. The anti-religious campaign resumed after 1953. Victoria Smolkin, *A Sacred Space is Never Empty: A History of Soviet Atheism* (Princeton, NJ: Princeton University Press, 2018), 63–65.

83. David S. Foglesong, *The American Mission and the "Evil Empire": The Crusade for a "Free Russia" since 1881* (Cambridge: Cambridge University Press, 2007).

84. GARF, f. R7928, op. 2, d. 146, 1l. 12–13, dated May 12, 1947.

85. GARF, f. R7928, op. 2, d. 482, l. 56, dated July 26, 1948.

86. GARF, f. R7928, op. 2, d. 482, l. 52, dated July 29, 1948.

87. Catriona Kelly, "Malen'kie grazhdane bol'shoi strany: internatsionalizm, deti, i sovetskaia propaganda," *Novoe literaturnoe obozrenie* 60 (2003): 218–251.

88. Joseph Stalin, *Marxism and the National Question* (Moscow: Foreign Languages Publishing House, 1954), 99–108; Vladimir Il'ich Lenin, *Sotsialisticheskaia revoliutsiia i pravo natsii na samoopredelenie* (Moscow: Partiinoe izdatel'stvo, 1932).

89. Terry Martin, *The Affirmative Action Empire: Nations and Nationalism in the Soviet Union, 1923–1939* (Ithaca: Cornell University Press, 2001); Krista A. Goff, *Nested Nationalism: Making and Unmaking Nations in the Soviet Caucasus* (Ithaca: Cornell University Press, 2021); Adeeb Khalid, *Making Uzbekistan: Nation, Empire, and Revolution in the Early USSR* (Ithaca: Cornell University Press, 2015); Adrienne Lynn Edgar, *Tribal Nation: The Making of Soviet Turkmenistan* (Princeton: Princeton University Press, 2006), 41–69.

90. Matthew J. Payne, *Stalin's Railroad: Turksib and the Building of Socialism* (Pittsburgh: University of Pittsburgh Press, 2001); Sarah I. Cameron, *The Hungry Steppe: Famine, Violence, and the Making of Soviet Kazakhstan* (Ithaca, NY: Cornell

University Press, 2018); Shoshana Keller, *To Moscow, Not Mecca: The Soviet Campaign against Islam in Central Asia, 1917–1941* (Westport: Praeger, 2001), 31–106; Douglas Northrop, *Veiled Empire: Gender and Power in Stalinist Central Asia* (Ithaca, NY: Cornell University Press, 2004).

91. Violetta Hionidou and David Saunders, "Exiles and Pioneers: Oral Histories of Greeks Deported from the Caucasus to Kazakhstan in 1949," *Europe-Asia Studies* 62, no. 9 (2010): 1479–1501; Isaac Scarborough, "An Unwanted Dependence: Chechen and Ingush Deportees and the Development of State-Citizen Relations in Late-Stalinist Kazakhstan (1944–1953)," *Central Asian Survey* 36, no. 1 (2017): 93–112; J. Otto Pohl, *Ethnic Cleansing in the USSR, 1937–1949* (Westport: Praeger, 1999); Pavel Polian, *Against Their Will: The History and Geography of Forced Migrations in the USSR* (Budapest: Central European University Press, 2003).

92. Azadovskii and Egorov, "From Anti-Westernism," 66–80.

93. Joshua Rubenstein and Vladimir P. Naumov, eds., *Stalin's Secret Pogrom: The Postwar Inquisition of the Jewish Anti-Fascist Committee*, trans. Laura Esther Wolfson (New Haven, CT: Yale University Press, 2001).

94. GARF, f. R7928, op. 2, d. 482, l. 46, dated Aug. 23, 1948.

95. Vladislav M. Zubok, *A Failed Empire: The Soviet Union in the Cold War from Stalin to Gorbachev* (Chapel Hill: University of North Carolina Press, 2009).

96. "Russia Protests UN Discussion of Czech Situation," *Medford Mail Tribune*, March 17, 1948, 1.

97. Frank S. Adams, "Gromyko Lauds 'Soviet Stamina': Says No Nation can Rule World," *New York Times*, May 8, 1946, 1. Also see "Gromyko Assails Bloc 'Dominance'," *New York Times*, May 30, 1946, 1, 18; "Gromyko's Little Lecture," *New York Herald Tribune*, May 9, 1946, 26.

98. Carlyle Holt, "Vishinshky adds Byrnes to 'Warmongers' List," *Boston Globe*, Oct. 23, 1947, 1. Also see Vyshinskii, "Za mir i druzhbu narodov, protiv podzhigatelei novoi voiny," *Pravda*, Sept. 19, 1947, no. 247, 3; "Press-konferentsiia u glavy Sovetskoi delegatsii na sessii general'noi Assamblei A. Ia Vyshinskogo," *Pravda*, Sept. 28, 1947, no. 256, 3.

99. NCASF, "Appeal to Reason: A Statement on Foreign Policy" (New York: NCASF Inc., 1947), 1–2, HILA, Alfred Kohlberg Papers 61002, box 130.

100. GARF, f. R7928, op. 2, d. 482, l. 46, dated Aug. 23, 1948.

101. Interview with Burtnett on Dec. 30, 2022.

102. Record for Charles Clarence Hull, case 509, Feb. 9, 1928, Winnebago Asylum for the Chronically Insane, University of Wisconsin Oshkosh Archives and Area Research Center. This information was accessed with permission from Winnebago County Corporation Counsel and publicized with permission from Connie Roe Burtnett.

103. GARF, f. R7928, op. 2, d. 480, l. 54, dated Sept. 22, 1948.

104. GARF, f. R7928, op. 2, d. 483, ll. 246–247, dated Oct. 26, 1948.

105. GARF, f. R7928, op. 2, d. 482, l. 55, dated July 26, 1948.

106. Letter to Helen Westerlund, Oct. 3, 1948, Wisconsin Historical Society Archive, Roe and Zobel Family Papers, 1911–1960 (M2018–023 MAD 2M / 28 / Q6); Burtnett's email of Dec. 21, 2022.

107. GARF, f. R7928, op. 2, d. 481, l. 51, dated Dec. 15, 1948.

108. Interview with Burtnett on Dec. 30, 2022.

109. Email from Burtnett on Dec. 20, 2022.

110. GARF, f. R7928, op. 2, d. 361, l. 39, dated May 9, 1948.

111. GARF, f. R7928, op. 2, d. 361, l. 30, dated July 10, 1948.

112. GARF, f. R7928, op. 2, d. 482, l. 46, dated Aug. 23, 1948.

113. GARF, f. R7928, op. 2, d. 245, l. 26, undated in 1947.

114. Leila J. Rupp, *Worlds of Women: The Making of an International Women's Movement* (Princeton, NJ: Princeton University Press, 1997); Harriet Hyman Alonso, *Peace as a Women's Issue: A History of the US Movement for World Peace and Women's Rights* (Syracuse, NY: Syracuse University Press, 1993), 8. Also see Seth Koven and Sonya Michel, eds., *Mothers of a New World: Maternalist Politics and the Origins of Welfare States* (New York: Routledge, 1993); Molly Ladd-Taylor, *Mother-Work: Women, Child Welfare, and the State, 1890–1930* (Urbana: University of Illinois Press, 1994).

115. Susan Zeiger, "Finding a Cure for War: Women's Politics and the Peace Movement in the 1920s," *Journal of Social History* 24, no. 3, (1990): 73; Anne M. Boylan, *The Origins of Women's Activism: New York and Boston, 1797–1840* (Durham: University of North Carolina Press, 2002).

116. Zeiger, "Finding," 79–81; Celia Donert, "Women's Rights in Cold War Europe: Disentangling Feminist Histories," *Past and Present* 8 (2013): 184.

117. Litoff and Smith, *What Kind*, 3, 15; Erin E Gingrich-Gaylord, "'Every Child my Child, Every Man, My Man': The Ideology and Strategy of the Women's International League for Peace and Freedom in the Beginning of the Nuclear Age, 1945–1965" (master's thesis, University of Kansas, 2007), 50–55, accessed through ProQuest. Also see Sarah Ruddick, *Maternal Thinking: Towards a Politics of Peace* (Boston: Beacon Press, 1989).

118. Rebecca Balmas Neary, "Mothering Socialist Society: The Wife-Activists' Movement and the Soviet Culture of Daily Life, 1934–41," *The Russian Review* 58, no. 3 (July 1999): 400–402.

119. Alexis Peri, "New *Soviet Woman:* The Post-World War II Feminine Ideal at Home and Abroad," *Russian Review* 77, no. 4 (Oct. 2018): 621–644; Kristen Ghodsee, *Second World, Second Sex: Socialist Women's Activism and Global Solidarity during the Cold War* (Durham: Duke University Press, 2018), 9, 23, 66. By

contrast, the leading Soviet women's magazine, *Rabotnitsa,* printed only one article in 1945 and one in 1946 about women in the peace movement.

120. Melanie Ilic, "Soviet Women, Cultural Exchange, and the Women's International Democratic Federation," *Reassessing the Cold War,* ed. Sari Autio-Sarasmo and Katalin Miklossy (New York: Routledge, 2011), 163; Francisca de Haan, "Continuing Cold War Paradigms in Western Historiography of Transnational Women's Organisations: The case of the Women's International Democratic Federation," *Women's History Review* 19, no. 4 (Jan. 2010): 547–573.

121. Alonso, *Peace,* 187; Yulia Gradskova, *The Women's International Democratic Federation, the Global South, and the Cold War: Defending the Rights of Women of the "Whole World"?* (New York: Routledge, 2021), 64–65, 71–73.

122. "Appeal to the Women of the World," *Soviet Woman,* no. 4 (July-Aug. 1946): 11.

123. "To the Women of All Countries," *Soviet Woman,* no. 4 (July-Aug. 1948): 1.

124. Nina Popova, "The Growth of the International Women's Movement," *Soviet Woman,* no. 4 (July-August 1946): 3; Jadwiga E. Pieper Mooney, "Fighting Fascism and Forging New Political Activism: The Women's International Democratic Federation in the Cold War," *De-centering Cold War History: Local and Global Change,* ed. Jadwiga E. Pieper Mooney and Fabio Lanza (London: Routledge, 2013), 62–65.

125. Leslie, "United," 205; Kate Weigand, *Red Feminism: American Communism and the Making of Women's Liberation* (Baltimore: Johns Hopkins University Press, 2001), 56. On similar tactics: Amy Swerdlow, *Women Strike for Peace: Traditional Motherhood and Radical Politics in the 1960s* (Chicago: University of Chicago Press, 1993).

126. "Peace—a Woman's Issue," *Daily Worker,* June 19, 1949, 2.

127. Only one Soviet letter writer evoked maternalism: GARF, f. R7928, op. 2, d. 358, l. 35; undated in Aug.-Sept. 1947.

128. Angelina Checki, "Letter to the Editor," *The Herald-News* (Passaic, NJ), Feb. 3, 1959, 38. Biographic details on Checki from her obituary in *The Herald-News* (Passaic, NJ), Nov. 11, 1977, 36.

129. GARF, f. R7928, op. 2, d. 358, l. 18, dated July 28, 1947. Similar examples in GARF, f. R7928, op. 2, d. 146, ll. 18–19, undated in 1945; GARF, f. R7928, op. 2, d.146, l. 78, undated in 1945–1946.

130. Anna Krylova, *Soviet Women in Combat: A History of Violence on the Eastern Front* (Cambridge: Cambridge University Press, 2010), 12, 168–169.

131. Roger D. Markwick and Euridice Charon Cardona, *Soviet Women on the Frontline in the Second World War* (New York: Palgrave MacMillan, 2012), 1;

Zhenshchiny velikoi otechestvenoi voiny, ed. N. K. Petrova (Moscow: Veche, 2014), 7.

132. GARF, f. R7928, op. 2, d.146, ll. 35–36, undated in 1945. By contrast, Lagunova's memoir, "V lesakh Smolenshchiny," published in *Novyi Mir,* emphasizes her battle heroics, not her desire for peace.

133. On Soviet anti-pacifism, see Vladimir Dobrenko, "Conspiracy of Peace: The Cold War, the International Peace Movement, and the Soviet Peace Campaign, 1945–1956" (PhD diss., London School of Economics and Political Science, 2016), 47–50. Also see: Nina Popova, "Our Women's Movement has Nothing to Do with Pacifism," *Soviet Information Bulletin* 4, no. 41 (Nov.-Dec. 1949). Timothy Johnston argues Soviet citizens reappropriated peace events to express a commitment to pacifism (Johnston, *Being Soviet: Identity, Rumor, and Everyday Life under Stalin, 1939–1953* [Oxford: Oxford University Press, 2011], 157–160). I agree Soviet citizens used discussions about peace to mourn and decry war, but this does not necessarily mean they were pacifists.

134. GARF, f. R7928, op. 2, d. 146, l. 23, sent Apr. 23, 1947.

135. "Letters," *Daily News* (Los Angeles), Dec. 24, 1949, 32.

136. "Letters," *Los Angeles Times,* Aug. 27, 1968, 28.

137. GARF, f. R7928, op. 2, d. 482, l. 56, dated July 26, 1948.

138. Part five, section two, subsection F of President Truman's Executive Order 9835 of Mar. 21, 1947 (https://www.trumanlibrary.gov/library/executive-orders/9835/executive-order-9835, accessed October 2023).

139. David Priestland, "Cold War Mobilisation and Domestic Politics: The Soviet Union," in *Cambridge History of the Cold War, Vol. I: Origins,* ed. Melvyn P. Leffler and Odd Arne Westad (Cambridge: Cambridge University Press, 2010), 454; GARF, f. R7928, op. 2, d. 482, l. 45, dated Aug. 23, 1948; J. D. Parks, *Culture, Conflict and Coexistence: American-Soviet Cultural Relations, 1917–1958* (Jefferson, NC: McFarland, 1983), 105, 116–118; Rósa Magnúsdóttir, "Divided Spouses: Soviet-American Intermarriage and Human Rights Activism during the Cold War," in *Intermarriage from Central Europe to Central Asia: Mixed Families in the Age of Extremes,* ed. Adrienne Edgar and Benjamin Frommer (Lincoln: Nebraska University Press, 2020).

140. RGASPI, f. 17, op. 125, d. 316, l. 110; Nina Konstantinovna Petrova, *Antifashistskie komitety v SSSR, 1941–1945* (Moscow: Institut Istorii, RAN, 1999), 258–266.

141. Rósa Magnúsdóttir, *Enemy Number One: The United States of America in Soviet Ideology and Propaganda, 1945–1959* (New York: Oxford University Press, 2018), 19. Also see Parks, *Culture,* 116–117.

142. GARF, f. R7928, op. 2, d. 356, l. 30, dated Sept. 5, 1947.

143. Matthews-Gardner, "From Ladies Aid to NGO," 99–100.

3. What Do You Do for Work?

1. GARF, f. R7928, op. 2, d. 483, l. 67, dated June 27, 1949.
2. GARF, f. R7928, op. 2, d. 481, ll. 32–33, dated Jan. 4, 1949.
3. GARF, f. R7928, op. 2, d. 483, ll. 55–62, dated June 27, 1949.
4. Joanne Jahr's email of Jan. 9, 2023; Interview with Joanne and Marc Jahr on Jan. 6, 2023.
5. Joanne Jahr's email of Dec. 22, 2022. The Bronx House is now the Bronx House Community Center.
6. GARF, f. R7928, op. 2, d. 481, ll. 32–33, dated Jan. 4, 1949.
7. Joanne Jahr's email of Dec. 22, 2022.
8. GARF, f. R7928, op. 2, d. 483, ll. 55–62, dated June 27, 1949.
9. GARF, f. R7928, op. 2, d. 481, ll. 32–33, dated Jan. 4, 1949.
10. GARF, f. R7928, op. 2, d. 483, ll. 63–67, dated June 27, 1949.
11. GARF, f. R7928, op. 2, d. 483, ll. 55–62.
12. Elena Zdravomyslova and Anna Temkina, "Gosudarstvennoe Konstruirovanie Genders v Sovetskom Obschestve, " *Jurnal Issledovanii Socialnoi Politiki* 1, no. 3–4 (2003): 299–321.
13. A pioneering study of this convergence is Lynne Attwood, "From the 'New Soviet Woman' to the 'New Soviet Housewife': Women in Postwar Russia," in *War-torn Tales: Literature, Film, and Gender in the Aftermath of World War II*, ed. Danielle Hopkins and Gill Plain (Bern: Peter Lang, 2007), 143–162; Also see Alexis Peri, "New *Soviet Woman:* The Post-World War II Feminine Ideal at Home and Abroad," *The Russian Review* 77, no. 4 (Oct. 2018): 621–644. On the influence of Soviet gender policies on progressive American feminists, see Kate Weigand, *Red Feminism: American Communism and the Making of Women's Liberation* (Baltimore: Johns Hopkins University Press, 2001); Julia L. Mickenberg, *American Girls in Red Russia: Chasing the Soviet Dream* (Chicago: University of Chicago Press, 2017).
14. Joanne Meyerowitz demonstrated there were positive postwar models for American women beyond the domestic. See Meyerowitz, "Beyond the Feminine Mystique: A Reassessment of Postwar Mass Culture, 1946–1958," in *Not June Cleaver: Women and Gender in Postwar America, 1945–1960*, ed. Joanne Meyerowitz (Philadelphia: Temple University Press, 1994), 229–262.
15. Linda Gordon, "The Women's Liberation Movement," in *Feminism Unfinished*, ed. Dorothy Sue Cobble, Linda Gordon, and Astrid Henry (New York: W. W. Norton, 2014), 84; Dorothy Sue Cobble, "More than Sex Equality: Feminism after Suffrage," in Cobble et al., *Feminism Unfinished*, 29.
16. Cobble, "More than Sex," 33–43.

17. Greta Bucher, *Women, the Bureaucracy, and Daily Life in Postwar Moscow, 1945–1953* (New York: Columbia University Press, 2006), 47. Working-class American women also demanded the right to work less and stay home more.

18. Laura A. Belmonte, *Selling the American Way: US Propaganda and the Cold War* (Philadelphia: University of Pennsylvania Press, 2010), 32–36.

19. V. Pechatnov, "Exercise in Frustration: Soviet Foreign Propaganda in the Early Cold War, 1945–1947," *Cold War History* 1, no. 2 (Jan. 2001): 20–21, 23.

20. Rósa Magnúsdóttir, *Enemy Number One: The United States of America in Soviet Ideology and Propaganda, 1945–1959* (New York: Oxford University Press, 2018), 24.

21. GARF, f. R7928, op. 2, d. 483, l. 241, dated Oct. 15, 1948. Translation modified. Underlined in original.

22. Interview with Marc and Joanne Jahr on Jan. 6, 2023; GARF, f. R7928, op. 2, d. 790, l. 39, dated May 11, 1950.

23. Joanne Jahr's email of Dec. 22, 2022.

24. Joanne Jahr's email of Jan. 9, 2023; *Seventeenth Census of the United States, 1950,* Bureau of the Census, Washington, DC, record group 29, roll 2197; sheet number 6, enumeration district 3–656; "Facts and Places," *Daily News* (New York City), June 7, 1979, 559.

25. GARF, f. R7928, op. 2, d. 481, l. 32, dated Jan. 4, 1949.

26. Joanne Jahr's email of Dec. 22, 2022; Interview with Marc and Joanne Jahr on Jan. 6, 2023.

27. GARF, f. R7928, op. 2, d. 790, l. 39, dated May 11, 1950.

28. GARF, f. R7928, op. 2, d. 245, l. 2, dated Dec. 2, 1947; GARF, f. R7928, op. 2, d. 146, l. 24, sent Apr. 23, 1947. Another example in GARF, f. R7928, op. 2, d. 50, l. 44, dated Sept. 18, 1946.

29. GARF, f. R7928, op. 2, d. 360, l. 2, dated Apr. 6, 1948; GARF, f. R7928, op. 2, d. 483, l. 211, dated Nov. 10, 1948.

30. GARF, f. R7928, op. 2, d. 360, l. 29, dated Jan. 27, 1948.

31. GARF, f. R7928, op. 2, d. 480, ll. 41–42, dated Nov. 6, 1948.

32. Lizabeth Cohen, *A Consumers' Republic: The Politics of Mass Consumption in Postwar America* (New York: Alfred A. Knopf, 2003), 69.

33. GARF, f. R7928, op. 2, d. 481, ll. 32–33, dated Jan. 4, 1949.

34. Marc Jahr's email of Dec. 23, 2022.

35. On how domestic spaces shape identity, see Erving Goffman, *The Presentation of Self in Everyday Life* (Edinburgh: University of Edinburgh Press, 1956), 17–25; Rachel Hurdely, "Dismantling Mantelpieces: Narrating Identities and Materializing Culture in the Home," *Sociology* 40, no. 4 (Aug. 2006): 717–733.

36. Cohen, *Consumers' Republic;* K. G. Donohue, *Freedom from Want: American Liberalism and the Idea of the Consumer* (Baltimore: Johns Hopkins University Press, 2003); Cheryl Lemus, "The 'Maternity Racket': Medicine, Consumerism, and the Modern American Pregnancy" (PhD diss., Northern Illinois University, 2011).

37. Steven Mintz, *Huck's Raft: A History of American Childhood* (Cambridge, MA: The Belknap Press of Harvard University Press, 2004), 277.

38. Sylvie Murray, *The Progressive Housewife: Community Activism in Suburban Queens, 1945–1965* (Philadelphia: University of Pennsylvania Press, 2003), 40.

39. Belmonte, *Selling,* 137; Elaine Tyler May, *Homeward Bound: American Families in the Cold War Era,* rev. ed. (New York: Basic Books, 2008); J. Edgar Hoover and Frederick L. Collins, "Mothers . . . Our Only Hope," *Woman's Home Companion,* Jan. 20, 1944, 20–21.

40. Only two Soviets asked for descriptions of living space: GARF, f. R7928, op. 2, d. 482, l. 64, sent July 30, 1948; GARF, f. R7928, op. 2, d. 483, ll. 212–214, dated Nov. 15, 1948.

41. Mark Harrison, *Accounting for War: Soviet Production, Employment, and the Defence Burden, 1940–1945* (Cambridge: Cambridge University Press, 1996), 162; Christine Varga-Harris, *Stories of House and Home: Soviet Apartment Life during the Khrushchev Years* (Ithaca, NY: Cornell University Press, 2015), 4.

42. Nicholas Ganson, *The Soviet Famine of 1946–1947 in Global and Historical Perspective* (New York: Palgrave Macmillan, 2009), 7–10, 51–62.

43. GARF, f. R7928, op. 2, d. 483, l. 65, dated June 27, 1949; Donald A. Filtzer, *The Hazards of Urban Life in late Stalinist Russia: Health, Hygiene, and Living Standards, 1943–1953* (New York: Cambridge University Press, 2010), 32. Similar uses of "cozy" in GARF, f. R7928, op. 2, d. 358, l. 2, dated Dec. 3, 1947; GARF, f. R7928, op. 2, d. 146, l. 166, dated Apr. 12, 1945; GARF, f. R7928, op. 2, d. 482, l. 50, dated July 7, 1948.

44. Alex Wilson and Jessica Boehland, "Small is Beautiful: US House Size, Resource Use, and the Environment," *Journal of Industrial Ecology* 9, no. 1–2 (2005): 278.

45. O. N. Mel'nikovskaia, *Sud'ba moia—schastlivitsa,* 2-oe izdanie (Moskva: Rossiiskii universitet druzhby narodov, 2007), 100.

46. GARF, f. R7928, op. 2, d. 483, ll. 176–177, dated Dec. 21, 1948.

47. GARF, f. R7928, op. 2, d. 146, l. 71, dated Feb. 13, 1947. The Soviet state recruited women into industry during the 1930s primarily to advance state interests, not gender equality. Wendy Z. Goldman, *Women at the Gates: Gender and Industry in Stalin's Russia* (Cambridge: Cambridge University Press, 2002), 67.

48. One exception is Margaret E. Faires, whose only letter describes her career as a lawyer: GARF, f. R7928, op. 2, d. 480, ll. 2–3, dated Nov. 22, 1948.

49. Mel'nikovskaia, *Sud'ba moia*, 41, 49.

50. At Nuremberg, Soviet authorities claimed only 632,253 died. Lisa A. Kirschenbaum, *The Legacy of the Siege of Leningrad, 1941–1995: Myth, Memories, and Monuments* (Cambridge: Cambridge University Press, 2006), 122.

51. John Barber and Andrei Dzeniskevich, eds., *Life and Death in Besieged Leningrad, 1941–1944* (London: Palgrave Macmillan, 2005), 1.

52. GARF, f. R7928, op. 2, d. 483, l. 66, dated June 27, 1949.

53. Mel'nikovskaia, *Sud'ba moia*, 76–77.

54. Mel'nikovskaia, *Sud'ba moia*, 75, 79.

55. GARF, f. R7928, op. 2, d. 483, l. 66, dated June 27, 1949.

56. Mel'nikovskaia, *Sud'ba moia*, 22, 79.

57. GARF, f. R7928, op. 2, d. 483, l. 65, dated June 27, 1949.

58. GARF, f. R7928, op. 2, d. 146, l. 77, sent Feb. 1947.

59. GARF, f. R7928, op. 2, d. 361, l. 21, dated July 26, 1948.

60. GARF, f. R7928, op. 2, d. 483, l. 167–168, dated Dec. 12, 1948.

61. GARF, f. R7928, op. 2, d. 638, l. 9, dated Jan. 26, 1949.

62. GARF, f. R7928, op. 2, d. 358, l. 115, dated May 8, 1947; GARF, f. R7928, op. 2, d. 480, ll. 41–42, dated Nov. 6, 1948; GARF, f. R7928, op. 2, d. 246, l. 67, dated Jan. 24, 1947.

63. D'Ann Campbell, *Women at War with America: Private Lives in a Patriotic Era* (Cambridge, MA: Harvard University Press, 1984), 80, 85–86, 232. Seven of eight Americans surveyed in 1946 thought homemaking should be a full-time job.

64. GARF, f. R7928, op. 2, d. 50, l. 65, dated May 14, 1946.

65. Dorothy Sue Cobble, *The Other Women's Movement: Workplace Justice and Social Rights in Modern America* (Princeton, NJ: Princeton University Press, 200), 413–414; Alice Kessler-Harris, *Out to Work: A History of Wage-Earning Women in the United States* (New York: Oxford University Press, 1982), 277; Julia Kirk Blackwelder, *Now Hiring: The Feminization of Work in the United States, 1900–1995* (College Station: Texas A&M University Press, 1997), 123–124.

66. Campbell, *Women at War*, 74.

67. GARF, f. R7928, op. 2, d. 146, l. 124, sent Aug. 14, 1946. Parenthesis in original.

68. Goldman says 42 percent in 1935 and Bucher 38 percent by 1940. Goldman, *Women at the Gates*, 1, 160; Bucher, *Women*, 11.

69. L. N. Zavadskaia, Z. M. Zotova, and A. S. Mikhlin,.*Gendernaia ekspertiza rossiiskogo zakonodatel'stva* (Moscow: BEK, 2001), 105; David L. Hoffman: *Stalinist Values: The Cultural Norms of Soviet Modernity, 1917–1941* (Ithaca, NY: Cornell University Press, 2003), 105.

70. Scholars disagree whether World War II improved women's status. William Chafe argued in favor, Lelia Rupp against, and Karen Anderson and

Susan M. Hartmann claim gender practices changed without altering hierarchies. William Chafe, *The American Woman: Her Changing Social, Economic, and Political Roles, 1920–1970* (New York: Oxford University Press, 1972); Lelia Rupp, *Mobilizing Women for War: German and American Propaganda, 1939–1945* (Princeton, NJ: Princeton University Press, 1978); Susan M. Hartmann, *The Home Front and Beyond: American Women in the 1940s* (Boston: Twayne, 1982); Karen Anderson, *Wartime Women: Sex Roles, Family Relations, and the Status of Women during WWII* (Westport, CT: Greenwood Press, 1981).

71. Bucher, *Women,* 11; Campbell, *Women at War,* 74; As high as 48 percent of American women had worked at some point during the war: Campbell, *Women at War,* 83.

72. Cobble, *The Other Women's Movement,* 13; Maureen Honey, *Creating Rosie the Riveter: Class, Gender, and Propaganda during World War II*, (Amherst: University of Massachusetts Press, 1984), 19.

73. Feiga Blekher, *The Soviet Woman in the Family and in Society* (New York: John Wiley and Sons, 1980), 18, 114–119.

74. GARF F. R7928 op. 2 d. 146, l. 124; sent August 14, 1946.

75. Rupp, *Mobilizing,* 146–152; Honey, *Creating Rosie,* 6; Elena Bondareva, "Moe slovo sovetskim rabotnitsam," *Rabotnitsa* no. 1 (1945): 1–8; Elena Baraban, "The Return of Mother Russia: Representations of Women in Soviet Wartime Cinema," *Aspasia* 4 (2010): 121–138.

76. Honey, *Creating Rosie,* 123.

77. National Manpower Council, *Womanpower. A Statement by the National Manpower Council with Chapters by the Council Staff* (New York: Columbia University Press, 1957), 162.

78. Olga Mishakova, *Sovetskaia zhenshchina v Velikoi Otechestvennoi Voine* (Moscow: Voenizdat 1943), 3.

79. Goldman, *Women at the Gates,* 145, 174; Ruth Milkman, "Redefining 'Women's Work': The Sexual Division of Labor in the Auto Industry during World War II," *Feminist Studies* 8, no. 2, (Summer 1982): 336–338.

80. Donald A. Filtzer, *Soviet Workers and Late Stalinism: Labour and the Restoration of the Stalinist System after World War II* (Cambridge: Cambridge University Press, 2002), 19; Susan Hartmann, "Women's Employment and the Domestic Ideal in the Early Cold War Years," *Not June Cleaver,* 86–87; Joanne Meyerowitz, "Sex, Gender, and the Cold War language of Reform," in *Rethinking Cold War Culture,* ed. Peter J. Kuznick and James Gilbert (Washington, DC: Smithsonian Institute Press, 2001), 106–123.

81. Kessler-Harris, *Out to Work,* 278, 287; Freida Miller, "What's Become of Rosie the Riveter?" *New York Times Magazine,* May 5, 1946, 40.

82. This figure refers to workers between the ages of twenty and forty-four. Bucher, *Women*, 11–12, 67–70; Filtzer, *Soviet Workers*, 210.

83. Honey, *Creating Rosie*, 24.

84. GARF, f. R7928, op. 2, d. 50, ll. 92–93, dated Apr. 17, 1946. The anti-fascist committee quoted Brand's letter as an example of capitalist inequity in a 1946 report to the Central Committee (RGASPI, f. 17, op. 128, d. 69, l. 78).

85. May, *Homeward Bound*, 13–14, 35–37; Anna Krylova, "'Healers of Wounded Souls': The Crisis of Private Life in Soviet Literature, 1944–1946," *Journal of Modern History* 73, no. 2 (June 2001): 326; Anna Loviagina, "Radost' sem'i" and E. Vishniakova, "S materinskoi liubov'iu," *Rabotnitsa*, no. 10 (1945): 10–11.

86. Mie Nakachi, *Replacing the Dead: The Politics of Reproduction in the Postwar Soviet Union* (New York: Oxford University Press, 2021), 2.

87. Mie Nakachi, "N. S. Khrushchev and the 1944 Soviet Family Law: Politics, Reproduction, and Language," *East European Politics and Societies* 20, no. 1 (Feb. 2006): 40–68; Helene Carlbäck, "Lone Motherhood in Soviet Russia in the Mid-20th Century—In a European Context," in *And They Lived Happily Ever After: Norms and Everyday Practices of Family and Parenthood in Russia and Eastern Europe*, ed. Helene Carlbäck, Yulia Gradskova, and Zhanna Kravchenko (Budapest: Central European University Press, 2012), 25–30.

88. GARF, f. R7928, op. 2, d. 50, l. 66, dated May 14, 1946.

89. GARF, f. R7928, op. 2, d. 146, l. 124, sent Aug. 14, 1946.

90. Anderson, *Wartime Women*, 8–11; Hartmann, *The Home Front*, 216; Emily H. Mudd, "Women's Conflicting Values," *Marriage and Family Living* 8, no. 3 (Aug. 1946): 58–61.

91. GARF, f. R7928, op. 2, d. 483, l. 238, dated Oct. 9, 1948. Similar examples in GARF, f. R7928, op. 2, d. 146, l. 14, dated Apr. 1947; GARF, f. R7928, op. 2, d. 482, l. 71, dated July 1, 1948.

92. Honey, *Creating Rosie*, 5–7, 69.

93. GARF, f. R7928, op. 2, d. 244, l. 75, dated Mar. 22, 1947.

94. GARF, f. R7928, op. 2, d. 50, l. 16, dated Nov. 23, 1946; "Maxine Cryder," *Des Moines Register*, Apr. 13, 2007, 7.

95. "Melvin A. Cryder," *Des Moines Register*, Feb. 22, 2007, 8.

96. Cohen, *Consumers' Republic*, 105.

97. GARF, f. R7928, op. 2, d. 244, l. 36, dated June 21, 1947.

98. Honey, *Creating Rosie*, 81.

99. Cobble, "More than Sex," 24–25, 27.

100. Ruth W. Russ, "Report on Committee of Women," Nov. 5, 1945, 1, TAM 134, box 5, folder 18; GARF, f. R7928, op. 2, d. 49, ll. 43, 97.

101. Committee of Women, "Purpose and Program, Fall 1946," 2; and "Minutes of the Committee of Women of NCASF," Jan. 20, 1945, TAM 134, box 15, folder 18. Also see the minutes for May 15, 1944, June 6, 1945, November 5, 1945, TAM 134, box 15, folder 18.

102. Jessica Smith, "What Do the Russians Know of Us?" *Soviet Russia Today,* June 1946, 23.

103. Belmonte, *Selling,* 154.

104. GARF, f. R7928, op. 2, d. 360, l. 5, dated Mar. 17, 1948.

105. GARF, f. R7928, op. 2, d. 483, l. 146, dated Jan. 8, 1949.

106. GARF, f. R7928, op. 2, d. 481, l. 47, dated Dec. 27, 1948.

107. GARF, f. R7928, op. 2, d. 641, l. 18, dated Jan. 30, 1950.

108. GARF, f. R7928, op. 2, d. 358, l. 4, dated Dec. 3, 1947.

109. GARF, f. R7928, op. 2, d. 245, l. 1, dated Feb. 4, 1948.

110. Committee of Women, "Purpose and Program, Fall 1946," 2, TAM 134, NCASF, box 5, folder 18.

111. Helen Ross, "American Kids' Clothing of Medium Prices en Route to Moscow in Exchange Exhibition," *PM (Post Meridien),* July 24, 1944, TAM 134, NCASF, box 5, folder 18.

112. Committee of Women, "Purpose and Program of the Committee of Women, Fall 1944," 1, and "Purpose and Program, Fall 1946," 1, TAM 134, NCASF, box 5, folder 18. I am unable to confirm if the nursery was displayed in Moscow.

113. Committee of Women, "Purpose and Program, Fall 1946," 1, TAM 134, box 5, folder 18.

114. Committee of Women, Meeting Minutes, April 1, 1944, GARF, f. 7928, op. 2, d. 75, l. 28.

115. GARF, f. R7928, op. 2., d. 241, l. 3, dated July 4, 1946.

116. GARF, f. R7928, op. 2, d. 244, l. 37, dated June 21, 1947.

117. GARF, f. R7928, op. 2, d. 360, l. 29, dated Jan. 27, 1948; GARF, f. R7928, op. 2, d. 480, ll. 33–34, dated Oct. 23, 1948.

118. Suellen Hoy, *Chasing Dirt: The American Pursuit of Cleanliness* (Oxford: Oxford University Press, 1996), 152, 156.

119. Diana Cucuz, *Winning Women's Hearts and Minds: Selling Cold War Culture in the US and the USSR* (Toronto: University of Toronto Press, 2023), 35.

120. Susan Frances Dion, "Challenges to Cold War Orthodoxy: Women and Peace, 1945–1963" (PhD diss., Marquette University, 1991), 24–25.

121. Ruth Schwartz Cowan, *More Work for Mother* (New York: Basic Books, 1983), 193–207; Susan Strasser, *Never Done: A History of American Housework* (New York: Pantheon Books, 1982), 275–309.

122. GARF, f. R7928, op. 2, d. 50, ll. 223–224, dated Jan. 12, 1945; GARF, f. R7928, op. 2, d. 358, l. 94, dated May 14, 1947.

123. "Petty housework crushes, strangles, stultifies and degrades her, chains her to the kitchen and the nursery, and she wastes her labor," Lenin famously remarked. V. I. Lenin, "A Great Beginning," June 28, 1919, *Marxist Internet Archive*, https://www.marxists.org/archive/lenin/works/1919/jun/19.htm.

124. Bucher, *Women*, 30.

125. Anatolii Sergeev, "Svetlyi Put'," *Rabotnitsa* no. 2 (1947): 5–6; Elena Kononenko, "Na fabrike i v sem'e," *Rabotnitsa* no. 4 (1947): 8–9.

126. Jessica Enoch, "There's No Place Like the Childcare Center: A Feminist Analysis of <Home> in the World War II Era," *Rhetoric Review* 31, no. 4 (2012): 431–437; Eugenia Kaledin, *Mothers and More: American Women in the 1950s* (Boston: Twayne Publishers, 1984), 70–71.

127. Enoch, "There's No Place," 435; Honey, *Creating Rosie*, 25–27; Kaspar Burger, "A Social History of Ideas Pertaining to Childcare in France and in the United States," *Journal of Social History* 45, no. 4 (Summer 2012): 1010, 1016; Howard Dratch, "The Politics of Child Care in the 1940s," *Science & Society* 38, no. 2 (Summer 1974): 193–198.

128. GARF, f. R7928, op. 2, d. 50, l. 85, dated April 16, 1946.

129. Mickenberg, *American Girls*, 3, 32.

130. GARF, f. R7928, op.2, d. 49, l. 166.

131. GARF, f. R7928, op. 2, d. 49, l. 82.

132. "Mother and Child Care in the Soviet Union," 2, TAM 134, NCASF, box 6, folder 5.

133. "Mother and Child Care in the Soviet Union," 7. See Nakachi, *Replacing*.

134. Russ, "Report on Committee of Women," Nov. 5, 1945, 3–4, and Russ, "Brief Report on Activities of the Committee of Women," Mar. 29, 1946, 1–2, TAM 134, NCASF, box 5, folder 18.

135. GARF, f. R7928, op. 2, d. 146, l. 164, dated Apr. 12, 1945. Similar examples in GARF, f. R7928, op. 2, d. 642, l. 59, sent Sept. 4, 1949; GARF, f. R7928, op. 2, d. 358, l. 16, dated Sept. 8, 1947.

136. Mariia R. Zezina, "Without a Family: Orphans of the Postwar Period," *Russian Studies in History* 48, no. 4 (Spring 2010): 59.

137. GARF, f. R7928, op. 2, d. 358, ll. 31–32, undated, sent in Aug.-Sept. 1947.

138. GARF, f. R7928, op. 2, d. 146, l. 30, dated Apr. 14, 1947.

139. Bucher, *Women*, 57, 89, 105; Nakachi, *Replacing*, 3.

140. Ella Winter, "Soviet's Heroine Seeks Closer Russia-US Bond," *New York Post*, Aug. 8, 1944, 8.

141. GARF, f. R7928, op. 2, d. 483, l. 153, dated Jan. 26, 1949.

142. O. Kozlova, "Nekotorye voprosy povysheniia proizvoditel'nosti truda zhenshchin-rabotnits," *Pravda,* Jan. 24, 1949.

143. GARF, f. R7928, op. 2, d. 245, l. 33, dated Nov. 7. 1947; GARF, f. R7928, op. 2, d. 146, l. 114, sent Nov. 29, 1946.

144. GARF, f. R7928, op. 2, d. 908, ll. 34–35.

145. GARF, f. R7928, op. 2, d. 908, ll. 28–29.

146. GARF, f. R7928, op. 2, d. 908, l. 36.

147. "Call to a Conference on Women of the USA and the USSR in the Postwar World. Saturday November 18," 1944; GARF, f. R7928, op. 2, d. 49, ll. 53–54; Rose Maurer, *Soviet Children and Their Care* (New York: NCASF, 1943); Maurer, *Soviet Women* (New York: NCASF, 1944). On ways Soviet and American gender norms influenced each other at midcentury, see Victoria Vantoch, *The Jet Sex: Airline Stewardesses and the Making of an American Icon* (Philadelphia: University of Pennsylvania Press, 2013), 128–134.

148. See A. Urovsky, "New Homes," *Soviet Woman,* no. 1 (1954): 24–27; R. Chokovskaia, "For the Home," *Soviet Woman,* no. 11 (1954): 45–46. Six articles like this appeared in one issue: *Soviet Woman,* no. 2 (1953): 58–60, 62, 65. On consumerism and Soviet women in the 1950s, see S. E. Reid, "Destalinization and Taste, 1953–1963," *Journal of Design History* 10, no. 2 (1997): 177–201; Susan E. Reid, "Cold War in the Kitchen: Gender and the De-Stalinization of Consumer Taste in the Soviet Union under Khrushchev," *Slavic Review* 61, no. 2 (Summer 2002): 211–252; Nataliia Laas, "Market Research Without a Market: Consumers, the State, and the Economy of Waste in the Soviet Union, 1947–1991" (PhD diss., Brandeis University, 2022).

149. Alexandra Talaver, "Women's Work: The Role of the Soviet Women's Committee in Soviet Policy-Making (1945–1991)," presented at the Summer Research Lab, University of Indiana Urbana-Campaign, July 11, 2021. Cited with the author's permission.

150. Helen Laville, *Cold War Women: The International Activities of America Women's Organizations* (Manchester: Manchester University Press, 2002), 198.

151. "Mrs. Nixon—Ambassadress on her Own," *National Business Woman* 38, no. 9 (Sept. 1959): 5.

152. Studies deemphasizing American and Soviet women's political engagement in the late 1940s in order to emphasize it during later eras include: Linda Racioppi and Katherine O'Sullivan-See, *Women's Activism in Contemporary Russia* (Philadelphia: Temple University Press, 1997); Alice Nichols, *Daring to be Bad: Radical Feminism in America: 1967–1975* (Minneapolis: University of Minnesota Press, 1989); Ruth Rosen, *The World Split Open: How the Modern Women's Movement Changed the World* (New York: Viking, 2000); Stephanie Coontz, *A Strange Stirring: The Feminine Mystique and American Women at the Dawn of the 1960s* (New

York: Basic Books, 2011). Other key works show feminism remained strong in the post–World War II decade: Lelia L. Rupp and Verta Tayor, *Survival in the Doldrums: The American Women's Rights Movement, 1945 to the 1960s* (New York: Oxford University Press, 1987); Meyerowitz, ed., *Not June Cleaver;* Dorothy Sue Cobble, *For the Many: American Feminists and the Global Fight for Democratic Equality* (Princeton, NJ: Princeton University Press, 2021); Helene Carlbäck, "Lone Mothers and Fatherless Children: Public Discourse on Marriage and Family Law," in *Soviet State and Society under Nikita Khrushchev*, ed. Melanie Ilic and Jeremy Smith (New York: Routledge, 2009); Carlbäck, Gradskova, and Kravchenko, eds., *And They Lived Happily Ever After.*

153. Benjamin Spock, *The Common Sense Book of Baby and Child Care* (New York: Duell, Sloan, and Pearce, 1946), 484. Italics in the original. By 1963, Spock softened this stance, telling mothers to consult a counselor before taking a fulltime job: "Dr. Spock Talks with Mothers; Should Mothers Work?" *Ladies' Home Journal*, Jan.-Feb. 1963, 21.

4. How Are You Raising Your Children?

1. GARF, f. R7928, op. 2, d. 146, l. 99, sent Jan. 30, 1947.

2. GARF, f. R7928, op. 2, d. 358, ll. 44–46, dated Sept. 1, 1947. Parentheses in original.

3. GARF, f. R7928 op. 2, d. 358, l. 1, dated Dec. 3, 1947.

4. GARF, f. R7928 op. 2, d. 245, l. 15, dated Oct. 6, 1947.

5. GARF, f. R7928, op. 2, d. 358, l. 1, dated Dec. 3, 1947.

6. GARF, f. R7928 op. 2, d. 482, l. 43, sent Sept. 1948. Deanna Durbin's films, including *His Butler's Sister*, were popular in the postwar USSR. Vladislav M. Zubok, *A Failed Empire: The Soviet Union in the Cold War from Stalin to Gorbachev* (Chapel Hill: University of North Carolina Press, 2009), 171–172.

7. GARF, f. R7928, op. 2, d. 245, dated Oct. 16, 1947.

8. GARF, f. R7928, op. 2, d. 483, l. 276, dated Oct. 26, 1948; GARF, f. R7928, op. 2, d. 358, l. 1, dated Dec. 3, 1947. Marina's father was Andreeva's biological cousin.

9. GARF, f. R7928, op. 2, d. 791, ll. 2–5, sent June 30, 1950.

10. Julia L. Mickenberg, *Learning from the Left: Children's Literature, the Cold War, and Radical Politics in the United States* (New York: Oxford University Press, 2006), 132–133. Also see Margaret Peacock, *Innocent Weapons: The Soviet and American Politics of Childhood in the Cold War* (Chapel Hill: University of North Carolina, 2014); Victoria M. Grieve, *Little Cold Warriors: American Childhood in the 1950s* (Oxford: Oxford University Press, 2018), 120–121; Catriona Kelly, *Children's World, Growing Up in Russia, 1890–1991* (New Haven, CT: Yale University Press, 2007), 110.

11. Steven Mintz, *Huck's Raft: A History of American Childhood* (Cambridge, MA: The Belknap Press of Harvard University, 2004), 257–260, 293; Mariia R. Zezina, "Without a Family: Orphans of the Postwar Period," *Russian Studies in History* 48, no. 4 (Spring 2010): 64–66; James Gilbert, *A Cycle of Outrage: America's Reaction to the Juvenile Delinquent in the 1950s* (New York: Oxford University Press, 1988), 24–41; Rebecca Jo Plant, *Mom: The Transformation of Motherhood in Modern America* (Chicago: University of Chicago Press, 2010), 98–101; G. Khillig, "Kak A. S. Makarenko otkryl sem 'iu: K istorii sozdaniia i vozdeistviia knigi dlia roditelei 1936–1939," *Cahiers du monde russe et sovietique* 33, no. 1 (1992): 84–85; A. S. Makarenko, "O 'knige dlia roditelei,'" *Sem'ia i shkola* 9 (1948): 8–10; A. S. Makarenko, "O 'knige dlia roditelei,'" *Sem'ia i shkola* 11 (1948): 10–14; G. S. Prozorov, "A.S. Makarenko i pedagogicheskom takte v semeinom vospitanii," *Sem'ia i shkola* 8 (1948): 5–8.

12. GARF, f. R7928, op. 2, d. 481, l. 11, dated Jan. 20, 1949. Similar examples in GARF, f. R7928, op. 2, d. 245, l. 77, dated Dec. 7, 1946; GARF, f. R7928, op. 2, d. 483, ll. 119–121, dated Dec. 29, 1948.

13. On the distinction between individuality and individualism as it pertained to Soviet childrearing, see Anton S. Makarenko, *The Collective Family: A Handbook for Russian Parents,* trans. Robert Daglish (New York: Doubleday, 1967), 39.

14. GARF, f. R7928, op. 2, d. 245, l. 16, dated Oct. 16, 1947.

15. GARF, f. R7928, op. 2, d. 480, l. 19, received Dec. 5, 1948.

16. Tomi Knaefler, "The Psychologist Taught Dancing and Other Things," *Honolulu Star-Bulletin,* Oct. 28, 1977, 12.

17. Maurice D. Woolf and Jeanne A. Woolf, *The Student Personnel Program: Its Development and Integration in the High School and College* (New York, McGraw-Hill, 1953).

18. GARF, f. R7928, op. 2, d. 245, l. 15, dated Oct. 16, 1947.

19. GARF, f. R7928, op. 2, d. 358, l. 44, dated Oct. 1, 1947. Anti-fascist committee marginalia indicates Zheliabuzhskaia may have written letters under the pseudonym Ekaterina Germant to Irma Palb, Serena G. Shapleigh, and Althea Somerville Grossman (GARF, f. R7928, op. 2, d. 985, dated Jan. 27, 1950).

20. Central State Archive of Literature and Art, St. Petersburg (TsGALI SPb), f. 2052, op. 1, d. 177, ll. 1–2.

21. GARF, f. R7928, op. 2, d. 146, l. 99, sent Jan. 30, 1947.

22. RGALI, f. 2354, op. 2, d. 7, ll. 2–3, 22–23. Mariia Fedorovna Andreeva helped finance the Bolsheviks during the late tsarist period. After the revolution, she co-led of the Appraisal and Antiquarian Commission, which confiscated valuables from the wealthy.

23. GARF, f. R7928, op. 2, d. 483, ll. 269–274; Zheliabuzhskaia, "O Gor'kom, A.M.," *Sovershenno Sekretno* 11, no. 162 (Nov. 2000).

24. GARF, f. R7928, op. 2, d. 358, l. 1, dated Dec. 3, 1947; GARF, f. R7928, op. 2, d. 483, ll. 107–111, 114, dated Mar. 11, 1949; GARF, f. R7928, op. 2, d. 483, l. 102, dated June 15, 1949; GARF, f. R7928, op. 2, d. 480, l. 26, dated Oct. 23, 1948; GARF, f. R7928, op. 2, d. 480, ll. 17–18, received Dec. 5, 1948.

25. GARF, f. R7928, op. 2, d. 480, l. 20, received Dec. 5, 1948.

26. National Security Council, "Policy on Atomic Warfare," (NSC 30), *Foreign Relations of the United States, 1948, Vol. I,* ed. Ralph R. Goodwin (Washington DC: United States Government Printing Office, 1975), 628.

27. GARF, f. R7928, op. 2, d. 481, l. 57, dated Nov. 30, 1948.

28. GARF, f. R7928, op. 2, d. 245, l. 16, dated Oct. 16, 1947.

29. GARF, f. R7928, op. 2, d. 483, l. 278, dated Oct. 26, 1948.

30. GARF, f. R7928, op. 2, d. 483, l. 113, dated Mar. 11, 1949.

31. GARF, f. R7928, op. 2, d. 483, l. 276, dated Oct. 26, 1948.

32. GARF, f. R7928, op. 2, d. 483, l. 102, dated June 15, 1949.

33. GARF, f. R7928, op. 2, d. 481, ll. 54–60, dated Nov. 30, 1948.

34. GARF, f. R7928, op. 2, d. 244, l. 45, dated June 3, 1947.

35. GARF, f. R7928, op. 2, d. 358, ll. 44–46, dated Sept. 1, 1947.

36. Kelly, *Children's World*, 96–97.

37. GARF, f. R7928, op. 2, d. 245, l. 15, dated Oct. 16, 1947.

38. Ronald D. Cohen, "Schooling Uncle Sam's Children: Education in the USA, 1941–45," in *Education and the Second World War: Studies in Schooling and Social Change*, ed. Roy Lowe (London: Falmer Press, 1992), 50; Gilbert, *Cycle of Outrage*, 20.

39. GARF, f. R7928, op. 2, d. 245, l. 15ob., dated Oct. 16, 1947.

40. GARF, f. R7928, op. 2, d. 480, l. 20, dated Oct. 1948.

41. GARF, f. R7928, op. 2, d. 361, ll. 1–2, dated June 29, 1948.

42. GARF, f. R7928, op. 2, d. 360, ll. 27–28, dated July 29, 1948.

43. Knaefler, "The Psychologist," 12.

44. GARF, f. R7928, op. 2, d. 361, ll. 1–2, dated July 29, 1948.

45. On how individuals transform dominant myths through life writing, see Regenia Gagnier, *Subjectivities: A History of Self-Representation in Britain, 1832–1920* (New York: Oxford University Press, 1991), 9–11.

46. GARF, f. R7928, op. 2, d. 361, l. 2.

47. GARF, f. R7928, op. 2, d. 482, l. 38, dated Sept. 20, 1948. Underlined in original; Ann Livschiz, "Growing Up Soviet: Childhood in the Soviet Union, 1918–1958" (PhD diss., Stanford University, 2007), 691, 697, 718, 746n193. Accessed through ProQuest.

48. GARF, f. R7928, op. 2, d. 482, l. 38, dated Sept. 20, 1948.

49. GARF, f. R7928, op. 2, d. 482, l. 39, dated Sept. 20, 1948.

50. Livschiz, "Growing Up Soviet," 431–436.

51. GARF, f. R7928, op. 2, d. 483, l. 101, dated June 15, 1949.

52. GARF, f. R7928, op. 2, d. 482, l. 39, dated Sept. 20, 1948.

53. GARF, f. R7928, op. 2, d.482, l. 40.

54. GARF, f. R7928, op. 2, d. 360, l. 28, dated Jan. 27, 1948.

55. GARF, f. R7928, op. 2, d. 480, l. 33, dated Oct. 23, 1948.

56. GARF, f. R7928, op. 2, d. 480, l. 19, sent Dec. 5, 1248. Another example in GARF, f. R7928, op. 2, d. 480, l. 33, dated Oct. 23, 1948.

57. GARF, f. R7928, op. 2, d. 244, l. 45, dated June 3, 1947.

58. GARF, f. R7928, op. 2, d. 480, l. 29, dated Oct. 23, 1948.

59. GARF, f. R7928, op. 2, d. 482, ll. 35–37, dated Sept. 20, 1948.

60. Andrew Hartman, *Education and the Cold War: The Battle for the American School* (New York: Palgrave MacMillian, 2008), 69–70.

61. Edna Jan Jacobs, "Zeal for American Democracy: Civic Education and the Cold War, 1947–1954" (PhD diss., Southern Illinois University, 1999). Accessed through ProQuest.

62. *Sovetskaia pedagogika* 10 (Oct. 1943): 2; E. Thomas Ewing, *Separate Schools: Gender, Policy, and Practice in Postwar Soviet Education* (Dekalb: Northern Illinois University Press, 2010), 628–629; Livschiz, "Growing Up Soviet," 631.

63. *Pedagogy* (Moscow: Ministry of Education, RSFSR, 1946), 37–38. Translation from B. P. Esipov and N. K. Goncharov, *I want to be like Stalin*, trans. George S. Counts and Nucia P. Lodge (New York: The John Day Company, 1947), 86, 39. Also see A. I. Sorokina, "Chto takoe khorosho i chto takoe plokho," *Sem'ia i shkola* 7–8 (1946): 27–30.

64. GARF, f. R7928, op. 2, d. 483, l. 100, dated June 15, 1949. Parentheses in original.

65. Sarah Ashwin and Simon Clarke, *Russian Trade Unions and Industrial Relations in Transition* (New York: Palgrave Macmillan, 2003); Wendy Z. Goldman, *Women at the Gates: Gender and Industry in Stalin's Russia* (Cambridge: Cambridge University Press, 2002), 67, 238.

66. TsGALI SPb, f. 2052, op. 1, d.176, ll. 3–6.

67. GARF, f. R7928, op. 2, d. 483, ll. 103–104, dated Apr. 25, 1949.

68. GARF, f. R7928, op. 2, d. 639, l. 63, sent June 9, 1949.

69. On this epistolary pact, see Janet Gurkin Altman, *Epistolarity: Approaches to a Form* (Columbus: Ohio State University Press, 1982), 87–115; Liz Stanley, Andrea Salter, and Helen Dampier, "The Epistolary Pact, Letterness, and the Schreiner Epistolarium," *Auto/Biography Studies* 27, no. 2 (Winter 2012): 264; Peter Goodrich, "Laws of Friendship," *Law and Literature* 15, no. 1 (2003): 23–52

70. GARF, f. R7928, op. 2, d. 483, l. 53, sent July 28, 1949. This should be translated as "building." "Home" gives the false impression Andreeva lived in a big house.

71. GARF, f. R7928, op. 2, d. 483, l. 102, dated June 15, 1949.

72. "One Killed, Four Injured in Three Local Crashes," *Manhattan Mercury* (KS), Nov. 11, 1954, 1; "Maurice C. Woolf," *Manhattan Republic* (KS), Nov. 17, 1954, 4.

73. "Frances Jeanne Austin Woolf," *Manhattan Mercury* (KS), Feb. 8, 1996, 2.

74. Knaefler, "The Psychologist," 12.

75. "Frances Jeanne Austin Woolf," 2.

76. GARF, f. R7928, op. 2, d. 245, ll. 35–36, dated Oct. 17, 1947 (an editor from the Soviet Women's Anti-Fascist Committee crossed out this phrase); my interview with Marguerite Wesle Franklin on July 15, 2022.

77. GARF, f. R7928, op. 2, d. 245, l. 35.

78. Celia Wesle, *Light: Paintings and Poems* (Chatham, IL: Adonis Design Press, 2007).

79. GARF, f. R7928, op. 2, d. 245, ll. 35–36, dated Oct. 17, 1947.

80. GARF, f. R7928, op. 2, d. 245, l. 36, dated Oct. 17. 1947.

81. GARF, f. R7928, op. 2, d. 245, ll. 36–37. Parentheses in original.

82. GARF, f. R7928, op. 2, d. 361, l. 9, dated July 3, 1948.

83. Mosfilm's biographical sketch of Koff: http://www.mosfilm-gsk.ru/1157/1180.

84. GARF, f. R7928, op. 2, d. 245, l. 36, dated Oct. 17, 1947.

85. GARF, f. R7928, op. 2, d. 361, l. 9, dated July 3, 1948.

86. Mintz, *Huck's Raft,* 263. The Supreme Court upheld these laws in 1940 then reversed its ruling in 1943.

87. GARF, f. R7928, op. 2, d. 361, ll. 14–15, dated July 3, 1948.

88. GARF, f. R7928, op. 2, d. 483, ll. 256–257, dated Oct. 19, 1948; Committee of Women, *Dear Unknown Friend* (New York: NCASF, 1949), 29–30. An editor from the Soviet Women's Anti-Fascist Committee crossed out the passage and added the italicized word.

89. Mie Nakachi, "Replacing the Dead: The Politics of Reproduction in the Postwar Soviet Union, 1944–1955" (PhD diss., University of Chicago, 2008), 240–242.

90. GARF, f. R7928, op. 2, d. 483, l. 257, dated Oct. 19, 1948.

91. Elena Bulova, "Lovushka dlia 'kliukvy,'" *Na Zapade Moskvy,* no. 38 / 286, Oct. 18–24, 2013, 13.

92. Elena Bulova, "20 prilozhenie—moe pokolenie," *Moskovskaia Pravda,* no. 270, Dec. 7, 2012.

93. GARF, f. R7928, op. 2, d. 483, ll. 248–255, dated Oct. 19, 1948. Underlining in original.

94. Amir Weiner, "The Making of a Dominant Myth: The Second World War and the Construction of Political Identities within the Soviet Polity," *The Russian Review* 55, no. 4 (Oct. 1996): 638–660.

95. GARF, f. R7928, op. 2, d. 483, l. 258, dated Oct. 19, 1948; Committee of Women, *Dear Unknown Friend*, 31.

96. GARF, f. R7928, op. 2, d. 483, l. 258, dated Oct. 19, 1948. Parentheses and underlining in original.

97. Grieve, *Little Cold Warriors*, 180.

98. GARF, f. R7928, op. 2, d. 50, l. 135, dated Feb. 19. 1945.

99. GARF, f. R7928, op. 2, d. 244, l. 44, dated June 3, 1947.

100. GARF, f. R7928, op. 2, d. 483, l. 259, dated Oct. 19, 1948.

101. GARF, f. R7928, op. 2, d. 358, l. 3, dated Dec. 3, 1947; GARF, f. R7928, op. 2, d. 361, l. 42, received June 28, 1948; GARF, f. R7928, op. 2, d. 50, ll. 87–91, dated May 31, 1946.

102. V. O. Pechatnov, "Exercise in Frustration: Soviet Foreign Propaganda in the Early Cold War, 1945–1947," *Cold War History* 1, no. 2 (Jan. 2001): 19. The directive was given in fall 1946.

103. GARF, f. R7928, op. 2, d. 146, l. 47, dated Sept. 25, 1946.

104. GARF, f. R7928, op. 2, d. 642, ll. 25–26, dated Oct. 24, 1949; GARF, f. R7928, op. 2, d. 244, l. 84, dated Jan. 3, 1946.

105. GARF, f. R7928, op. 2, d. 358, l. 3, dated Dec. 3, 1947; GARF, f. R7928, op. 2, d. 50, l. 141, dated Jan. 9, 1945.

106. Rósa Magnúsdóttir, *Enemy Number One: The United States of America in Soviet Ideology and Propaganda, 1945–1959* (New York: Oxford University Press, 2018), 34.

107. GARF, f. R7928 op. 2, d. 245, l. 16, dated Oct. 16, 1947. Additional example in GARF, f. R7928, op. 2, d. 146, l. 47ob., dated Sept. 25, 1946.

108. GARF, f. R7928, op. 2, d. 358, l. 3, dated Dec. 3, 1947. Parentheses in original.

109. GARF, f. R7928, op. 2, d. 482, ll. 35–37, dated Sept. 20, 1948. Underlined in original.

110. The Soviet Women's Anti-Fascist Committee promoted this novel around the same time. See Galina Osipova, "The Spirit of the Common People," *Soviet Woman*, no. 6 (1946): 53–54.

111. GARF, f. R7928, op. 2, d. 642, l. 78, sent Oct. 25, 1949.

112. GARF, f. R7928, op. 2, d. 482, l. 40, dated Sept. 20. 1948.

113. GARF, f. R7928, op. 2, d. 146, ll. 108–109, sent Nov. 29. 1946; Committee of Women, *Dear Unknown Friend*, 41.

114. Charles Neider, *Mark Twain and the Russians: An Exchange of Views* (New York: Hill and Wang, 1960), 9–10.

115. *Ilf and Petrov's American Road Trip*, ed. and intro. Erika Wolf (New York: Cabinet Books, 2007), 46, xiii.

116. Mintz, *Huck's Raft*, 5.

117. Critics Charles Neider and Yan Bereznitskii argued these interpretations of Twain in 1959: Neider, *Mark Twain.*

118. Albert Parry, "Mark Twain in Russia," *Books Abroad* 15, no. 2 (Spring 1941): 169, 174.

119. Mintz, *Huck's Raft,* 1, 5.

120. GARF, f. R7928, op. 2, d. 361, l. 10, dated July 3, 1948.

121. GARF, f. R7928, op. 2, d. 361, ll.10–11.

122. GARF, f. R7928, op. 2, d. 361, ll. 11–12, dated July 3, 1948.

123. GARF, f. R7928, op. 2, d. 483, ll. 258–259, dated Oct. 19, 1948; Committee of Women, *Dear Unknown Friend,* 32. Parentheses in original.

124. GARF, f. R7928, op. 2, d. 483, ll. 258–259, dated Oct. 19, 1948; Committee of Women, *Dear Unknown Friend,* 30–31.

125. The Soviet Women's Anti-Fascist Committee promoted Fadeev's novel around this time: A. Derman, "Fadeev's *Young Guard,*" *Soviet Woman,* no. 4 (July-Aug. 1946): 55–56; Galina Osipova, "The Spirit of the Common People," *Soviet Woman,* no. 6 (Nov.-Dec. 1946): 53–54.

126. GARF, f. R7928, op. 2, d. 483, l. 259, dated Sept. 19, 1948.

127. Kelly, *Children's World,* 117, 119. Andreeva also recommended *Young Guard* to Woolf: GARF, f. R7928, op. 2, d. 483, l. 183, dated Dec. 31, 1948.

128. GARF, f. R7928, op. 2, d. 641, l. 43, dated Nov. 22, 1949.

129. GARF, f. R7928, op. 2, d. 639, l. 28, dated Sept. 9, 1949.

130. GARF, f. R7928, op. 2, d. 985, l. 135, received Nov. 28, 1950.

131. GARF, f. R7928, op. 2, d. 985, l. 133.

132. Bulova, "20 prilozhenie."

133. Bulova, "'Lovushka,'" 13.

134. Bulova, "20 prilozhenie."

135. RGASPI, f. 17, op. 128, d. 246, l. 10.

5. You May Not Hear from Me Again

1. GARF, f. R7928, op. 2, d. 245, l. 21ob., dated Oct. 27, 1947.

2. GARF, f. R7928, op. 2, d. 244, l. 84, dated Jan. 3, 1946.

3. GARF, f. R7928, op. 2, d. 358, l. 39, undated in 1947.

4. GARF, f. R7928, op. 2, d. 245, l. 21ob., dated Oct. 27, 1947.

5. Committee of Women, *Dear Unknown Friend* (New York: NCASF, 1949), 21.

6. Friday Harbor's population from the United States Census Bureau: https://www2.census.gov/library/publications/decennial/1950/population-volume-1/vol-01-50.pdf.

7. GARF, f. R7928, op. 2, d. 361, l. 19, dated July 4, 1948.

8. GARF, f. R7928, op. 2, d. 245, l. 190b., dated Oct. 27, 1947.

9. Committee of Women, *Dear Unknown Friend*, 18–19.

10. David Brandenberger, "Stalin, the Leningrad Affair, and the Limits of Postwar Russocentrism," *The Russian Review* 63, no. 2 (April 2004): 241–255.

11. GARF, f. R7928, op. 2, d. 985, l. 124, dated Aug. 23, 1950.

12. Commission on CIA Activities in the United States, *Report to the President by the Committee on CIA Activity within the United States* (Washington, DC: Government Printing Office, 1975), 99–116.

13. GARF, f. R7928, op. 2, d. 991, ll. 58–59.

14. Committee on Un-American Activities, *Guide to Subversive Organizations and Publications* (Jan. 2, 1957), 7–8, in Swarthmore College Peace Collection, CDG-A, WILPF Collection DG043, series 1, folder: Elise Boulding. I have no interest in condemning or exonerating the NCASF. I put "communist front" in quotes to underscore that the label was an allegation, not a proven fact. Many scholars apply this term uncritically or use "communist-influenced organization" and "communist front" synonymously, but there is a big difference between supporting communist ideas and conspiring to commit treason. I found no definitive proof NCASF took orders from the Communist Party of the United States or of the Soviet Union in the 1940s or 1950s. According to David Byron Wagner, Soviet authorities contacted the American Communist Party about taking over NCASF later, in 1961: Wagner, "Alone Together: Intellectuals in the American-Soviet Friendship Movement" (PhD diss., University of California, Riverside, 2016), 13, 83. Accessed through ProQuest.

15. Griffin Fariello, *Red Scare: Memories of the American Inquisition: an Oral History* (New York: W.W. Norton, 1995), 19. Legal grounds to prosecute communists came from the 1939 Hatch Act, the 1940 Voorhis and Smith Acts, and the 1954 Communist Control Act.

16. The US House of Representatives' Committee on Un-American Activities, "Proceedings against Corliss Lamont," 79th Congress, Session 2 (June 12, 1946), 1, 4; Morford v. United States, 176 F.2d 54 (D.C. Cir. 1949).

17. The list was based on one compiled in 1942 by the special assistant to the Attorney General Edwin Dickinson under the 1939 Hatch Act.

18. *We Proudly Present: The Story of the NCASF 1943–1953* (New York: NCASF, 1953), 28–29 in US House of Representatives, HUAC, box 626, RG 233, NARA. On the indictments in 1963 and 1989 see Chicago Museum of History, collection: Chicago Council of American-Soviet Friendship, box 2: 2009.0122.1 bib# 65087, folder 3, and box 1: 2009.01221 bib # 65087, folder 1.

19. Elizabeth A. Collins, "Red-Baiting Public Women: Gender, Loyalty, and Red Scare Politics" (PhD diss., University of Illinois, Chicago, 2008), 6. Accessed through ProQuest; Veronica A. Wilson, "'Now You are Alone': Anticommunism, Gender, and the Cold War Myths of Hede Massing and Whittaker Chambers,"

Diplomatic History 36, no. 4 (Sept. 2012): 699–722; Mary C. Brennan, *Wives, Mothers, and the Red Menace: Conservative Women and the Crusade against Communism* (Bolder: University of Colorado Press, 2008), 115–146. Landon R. Y. Storrs argues women were not overlooked when targeted as anti-communists: Storrs, "Attacking the Washington 'Femmocracy': Antifeminism in the Cold War Campaign against 'Communists in Government,'" *Feminist Studies* 33, no. 1 (Spring, 2007): 118–152.

20. Veronica Wilson, "Red Masquerades; Gender and Political Subversion during the Cold War, 1945–1963" (PhD diss., Rutgers University, 2002), 29, 356. Accessed through ProQuest. Critics described Ethel Rosenberg, Mary Van Kleeck, and Anna Louise Strong as masculine and domineering. See Sara L. Knox, "The Genealogy of Treason: Ethel Rosenberg and the Masculinist Discourse of Cold War," *Australasian Journal of American Studies* 12, no. 2 (Dec. 1993): 32–49; Memo, July 27, 1960, FBI File 100-167425, section 2, folder 4, Mary Van Kleeck Papers, Sophia Smith Collection, Smith College (hereafter SSC); "Confidential Source," Anna Louise Strong, Dec. 7, 1970, RG46, NARA.

21. On the femme fatale, see J. B. Matthews, "Operation Women" (Feb. 17, 1951), and George Benson, "Women as Targets of International Communism" (Dec. 1959), HILA, John F. Russell Collection 85015, box 45, folder 4; Lauren Kessler, *Clever Girl: Elizabeth Bentley, the Spy Who Ushered in the McCarthy Era* (New York: Harper Collins, 2003), 159–160. *World Telegram* and *Newsweek* called Bentley a svelte, sexy blonde even though, according to Kessler, she was a "plain-featured brunette."

22. Mary C. Lyne and Dorothy Tuttle, "The Soviet Attack on Women's Minds," *McCall's*, Aug. 1953, 44, 68.

23. Lucille Cardin Crain and Anne Burrows Hamilton, "Packaged Thinking for Women" (Oct. 1948), 3, 14, 23–24, HILA, John F. Russell Collection 85015, box 25, folder 15.

24. "The Committee of Women," HUAC, Organizational Files, box 627, RG233, NARA.

25. NCASF, *We Proudly Present: The Story of the NCASF 1943–1953*, 18: HUAC, box 626, RG 233, NARA; Special Agent William P. Norton, Jr., Report on NCASF, Oct. 30, 1945, File 100–7518, 91–93. FOIA Request 1388746-000.

26. Report on NCASF (May 29, 1946), 2: HUAC, box 626, RG233, NARA. Lamont denied having a communist affiliation but supported the American Labor Party and Independent Socialist Party: Corliss Lamont, *Yes to Life: Memoirs of Corliss Lamont* (New York: Half-Moon Foundation, 1991), 38–39, 47, 50.

27. US Senate Internal Security Subcommittee, *The Communist Party of the United States of America: What it is and How it Works*, Dec. 21, 1955 (Washington, DC: Government Printing Office, 1955), 32–33.

28. Wilson, "'Now You are Alone,'" 714; Lamont, *Yes to Life*, 137, 45–47. Anti-communists also associated communism with so-called "male sexual perversions" like effeminacy and homosexuality. See David K. Johnson, *The Lavender Scare: The Cold War Persecution of Gays and Lesbians in the Federal Government* (Chicago: University of Chicago Press, 2004); K. A. Cuordileone, "Politics in an Age of Anxiety: Cold War Political Culture and the Crisis in American Masculinity, 1949–1960," *Journal of American History* 87, no. 2 (Sept. 2000): 515–545.

29. "Passport Denied to Corliss Lamont," *New York Times*, Oct. 15, 1951, 14; "Lamont Steps out of Columbia Job," *New York Times*, April 29, 1955, 20; Lamont, *Yes to Life*, 133–138, 156.

30. Betsy Fahlman, "The Great Draper Woman: Muriel Draper and the Art of the Salon," *Woman's Art Journal* 26, no. 2 (Autumn 2005-Winter 2006): 33–37.

31. Ellen Schrecker, *Many Are the Crimes: McCarthyism in America*, 147; Michella M. Marino, "Mothers, Spy Queens, and Subversives: Women in the McCarthy Era," in *Cold War and McCarthy Era: People and Perspectives*, ed. Caroline S. Emmons (Santa Barbara: ABC-CLIO, 2010), 135–137; Linn Shapiro, "Red Feminism: American Communism and the Women's Rights Tradition, 1919–1956" (PhD diss., American University, 1996), 27.

32. Draper's FBI file, Report 100–12221 (August 2, 1943), 1. FOIA Request 1379390-000.

33. Committee on Un-American Activities, *Report on the Congress of American Women*, Oct. 23, 1949 (Washington, DC: Government Printing Office, 1950), 3, 67–68.

34. Committee on Un-American Activities, *Report on the Congress of American Women*, 67–68. One of HUAC's sources was Mabel Dodge Luhan, a columnist and associate of Draper's. See Westbrook Pegler, "A Brief Biography of Muriel Draper," *Atlanta Constitution*, Nov. 4, 1949, 21.

35. Ellen Schrecker, *Many Are the Crimes*, 148; Kate Weigand, "The Red Menace, The Feminine Mystique, and the Ohio Un-American Activities Commission: Gender and Anti-Communism in Ohio, 1951–1954," *Journal of Women's History* 3 (Winter 1992): 70–94; Marino, "Mothers," 129–144.

36. RGASPI, f. 17, op. 132, d.228, ll. 3, 67–69; GARF, d. 991, l. 113–115; Draper's letter to the WIDF, Dec. 23, 1949, 1–2, Draper's letter to Patrick M. Malin, Feb. 1950; Draper's letter to Eugenie Cotton, Mar. 3, 1950, 1–2, Muriel Draper Papers, Beinecke Rare Book and Manuscript Library, Yale University, box 24, folder 775, and box 25, folder 801. Conversely, Petra Goedde argues the Congress' members quit because of the WIDF's increasingly anti-American, pro-Soviet stance: Goedde, *The Politics of Peace: A Global Cold War History*, (New York: Oxford University Press, 2019), 137–146.

37. The Commissariat of Internal Affairs' Order no. 486 (Aug. 15, 1937).

38. Conner and Butler called female FBI informants and detectives to testify *against* the National Council.

39. Barbara Ransby, *Eslanda: The Large and Unconventional Life of Mrs. Paul Robeson* (New Haven, CT: Yale University Press, 2013), 224–225. Ransby does not analyze Goode Robeson's work with the National Council of American-Soviet Friendship.

40. Herbert Brownell, Jr., Attorney General of the United States v. National Council of American-Soviet Friendship, Inc., "Report and Order of the Board," docket no. 104–53, decided Feb. 7, 1956, appendix A.

41. TAM 134 box 1, folder 16; Wagner, "Alone Together," 56.

42. "Dr. Kingsbury Sends free Press Biography; Dies Suddenly," *Kingston-Ulster Press* (New York), Aug. 5, 1956, TAM 134 box 1, folder 12.

43. Herbert Brownell Jr., "Official Report of Proceedings Before the Subversive Activities Control Board v. NCASF," docket 104–153, May-June 1954, transcript 37 (July 29, 1954), 2892, 2850–2868, HILA, US Subversive Activities Control Board 71009, box 23.

44. Brownell Jr., "Official Report," (July 22, 1954), 4128, 4215.

45. Brownell Jr., "Official Report," (July 22, 1954), 4220–4221.

46. Brownell Jr., "Official Report," (July 22, 1954), 4280–4281.

47. Brownell Jr., "Official Report," (July 14, 1954), 3279.

48. Brownell Jr., "Official Report," (July 14, 1954), 3283.

49. Brownell, Jr., "Report and Order of the Board," 20–23.

50. Brownell Jr., "Official Report" (July 29, 1954), 4667–4877, HILA US Subversive Activities Control Board 71009, box 23.

51. Brownell Jr., "Report and Order of the Board," 27.

52. Brownell Jr., "Report and Order of the Board," appendix A.

53. Brownell Jr., "Official Report," 4803–4807.

54. Brownell Jr., "Official Report," 4829.

55. GARF, f. R7928, op. 2, d. 477, l. 26, dated Dec. 20, 1948; Special Agent Peter J. Cattaneo, Report on NCASF, Oct. 22, 1943, FOIA Request 1392927-001.

56. Brownell Jr., "Official Report," 4852

57. Mildred White Wells, *Unity in Diversity: The History of the General Federation of Women's Clubs* (Washington, DC: General Federation of Women's Clubs, 1953), 135–137.

58. Brownell Jr., "Official Report," 4780.

59. Brownell Jr., "Official Report," 4777–4778.

60. GARF, f. R7928, op. 2, d. 477, l. 26, dated Dec. 20, 1948; GARF, f. R7928, op. 2, d. 360, l. 7, dated Apr. 26, 1948.

61. Brownell Jr., "Official Report," 4831.

62. Special Agent Peter J. Cattaneo, Report on NCASF, Oct. 21, 1943, FOIA Request 1392927-001. See the National Council's fundraising letters of June 25, 1953 and April 13, 1951, HILA, William T. Poole Collection 82095, box 16, folders 8 and 9.

63. Brownell Jr., "Official Report," 4774, 4784–4785, 4796.

64. Brownell Jr., "Official Report," 4829.

65. Brownell Jr., "Official Report," 4835.

66. Brownell Jr., "Official Report," 4839.

67. Brownell Jr., "Official Report," 4841–4843.

68. Brownell Jr., "Official Report," 4844, 4846–4847.

69. Brownell Jr., "Official Report," 4849.

70. Brownell Jr., "Official Report," 4854–4857. FBI informant Alvera Stone's testimony also linked Smith and Moos to the Committee of Women (Brownell Jr., "Official Report," 314, 323–333).

71. Brownell Jr., "Report and Order of the Board," 55.

72. Herbert Brownell Jr., "Attorney General vs. NCASF, Inc.," *Reports of the Subversive Activities Control Board* (1951–1953), 448, 479–485, 542.

73. Wagner, "Alone Together," 68–69, 139–142.

74. Committee of Women, "Meeting Minutes," Jan. 6, 1949, TAM 134 box 5, folder 18.

75. Committee of Women, "Meeting Minutes," Feb. 2, 1950, 1–2, TAM 134 box 5, folder 18.

76. The FBI stopped watching Epstein in 1955 but resumed surveillance after she visited the USSR in 1957 (Epstein's FBI file, FOIA Request 100-HQ-414233).

77. GARF, f. R7928, op. 2, d. 639, dated Dec. 26, 1949.

78. GARF, f. R7928, op. 2, d. 245, ll. 21–24, dated Oct. 27, 1947.

79. GARF, f. R7928, op. 2, d. 245, l. 22. Kimple's education level from US Census Records for 1940, roll m-t0627-04356, page 1B, enumeration district 28-15.

80. GARF, f. R7928, op. 2, d. 361, l. 18, dated June 4, 1948. Compare to Committee of Women, *Dear Unknown Friend*, 18–21.

81. GARF, f. R7928, op. 2, d. 1191, l. 167, dated Jan. 5, 1952.

82. GARF, f. R7928, op. 2, d. 985, l. 41, received Aug. 28, 1951

83. GARF, f. R7928, op. 2, d. 1365, l. 24, dated Sept. 11, 1953.

84. *Report to the President*, 101–115. I await the release of Kimple's FBI file under FOIA.

85. GARF, f. R7928, op. 2, d. 1365, l. 5, dated Sept. 11, 1953.

86. GARF, f. R7928, op. 2, d. 1191, l. 135; dated Mar. 6, 1952.

87. *Investigation of Communist Activities in the Pacific Northwest Area* (Oct. 1952, March-June 1954) (Washington, DC: Government Printing Office, 1954), 6150, 6163, 6209, 6214.

88. GARF, f. R7928, op. 2, d. 1487, l. 143, dated March 9, 1955.

89. Roy Pearmain's email of Sept. 19, 2022.

90. GARF, f. R7928, op. 2, d. 1192, l. 150b., dated Nov. 7, 1952.

91. GARF, f. R7928, op. 2, d. 1487, l. 31, dated Aug. 6, 1955.

92. GARF, f. R7928, op. 2, d. 1799, l. 123, dated Jan. 16, 1956.

93. GARF, f. R7928, op. 2, d. 991, l. 70.

94. Many American letters from 1952 reference *New World Review* (GARF, f. R7928, op. 2, d. 1191).

95. GARF, f. R7928, op. 2, d. 991, l. 66, 70.

96. RGASPI, f. 17, op. 137, d. 165, l. 37.

97. RGASPI, f. 17, op. 137, d. 165, l. 37.

98. GARF, f. R7928, op. 2, d. 991, d. 991, l. 75

99. GARF, f. R7928, op. 2, d. 991, l. 63.

100. The other two references to the Stockholm Appeal in GARF, f. R7928, op. 2, d. 1191, l. 129, dated Mar. 2, 1952; GARF, f. R7928, op. 2, d. 985, l. 23, dated Aug. 28, 1951.

101. GARF, f. R7928, op. 2, d. 1192, l. 150b., dated Nov. 7, 1952.

102. Most studies of the American and Soviet peace movements during this era focus on conferences and institutions as well as the cultural and scientific elites at their helm: Milton S. Katz, *Ban the Bomb: A History of SANE, the Committee for a Sane Nuclear Policy, 1957–1985* (Westport, CT: Greenwood Press, 1986); Lawrence S. Wittner, *Rebels Against War: The American Peace Movement, 1941–1960* (New York: Columbia University Press, 1969), and Wittner's trilogy from Stanford University Press: *The Struggle Against the Bomb: One World or None* (1993), *Resisting the Bomb: A History of the World Nuclear Disarmament Movement, 1954–1970* (1997), and *Toward Nuclear Abolition: A History of the World Nuclear Disarmament Movement, 1971 to the Present* (2003); Goedde, *The Politics of Peace;* Robbie Lieberman, *The Strangest Dream: Communism, Anticommunism, and the US Peace Movement, 1945–1963* (Syracuse, NY: Syracuse University Press, 2000); Jill Wallis, *Valiant for Peace: A History of the Fellowship of Reconciliation, 1914–1989* (London: Fellowship of Reconciliation, 1991); Amy Swerdlow, *Women Strike for Peace: Traditional Motherhood and Radical Politics in the 1960s* (Chicago: University of Chicago Press, 1993); Vladimir Dobrenko, "Conspiracy of Peace: The Cold War, the International Peace Movement, and the Soviet Peace Campaign, 1946–1956" (PhD diss., London School of Economics and Political Science, 2016). Accessed through ProQuest; Geoffrey Roberts, "Averting Armageddon: The

Communist Peace Movement," in *The Oxford Handbook of the History of Communism*, ed. S. A. Smith (Oxford: Oxford University Press, 2014), 322–338; Jeffrey Brooks, "When the Cold War did not End: The Soviet Peace Offensive of 1953 and the American Response," The Kennan Institute Occasional Papers, no. 278 (August 2000). Alternatively, other scholars have looked at people from all walks of life whose local, grassroots efforts helped shape public opinion in favor of peace. Examples include Timothy Johnston, *Being Soviet: Identity, Rumour, and Everyday Life under Stalin, 1939–1953* (Oxford: Oxford University Press, 2011), 148–166; David Cortright, *Peace Works: The Citizen's Role in Ending the Cold War* (Boulder, CO: Westview Press, 1993).

103. GARF, f. R7928, op. 2, d. 991, l. 64.

104. These criteria are repeated in numerous files: RGASPI, f. 17, op. 137, d. 165, l. 37; GARF, f. R7928, op. 2, d. 991, ll. 42, 53, 58, 59, 62, 71.

105. GARF, f. R7928, op. 2, d. 991, l. 63.

106. E. Iu. Zubkova, L. P. Kosheleva, G. A. Kuznetsova, A. I. Miniuk, L. A. Rogovaia, eds., *Sovetskaia zhizn', 1945–1953* (Moscow: Rosspen, 2003), 361–363; Vera Ivanova, "Friendship of Youth," *Soviet Woman*, no. 3 (1953): 36–37.

107. Maria Vasilyeva, "Pen-Friends," *Soviet Woman*, no. 6 (1956): 22; Maria Dobroselskaya, "The More Often Minds Meet, the Closer Hearts Come Together," *Soviet Woman*, no. 5 (1957): 36; Christine Varga-Harris, "Between National Tradition and Western Modernization: Soviet Woman and Representations of Socialist Gender Equality as a 'Third Way' for Developing Countries, 1956–1964," *Slavic Review* 78, no. 3 (2019): 758–781.

108. GARF, f. R7928, op. 2, d. 991, l. 70.

109. GARF, f. R7928, op. 2, d. 991, ll. 58–59.

110. RGASPI, f. 17, op. 132, d. 228, ll. 372, 370.

111. GARF, f. R7928, op. 2, dd. 1191, 1365.

112. GARF, f. R7928, op. 2, d. 991, ll. 74–75.

113. GARF, f. R7928, op. 2, d. 991, l. 43. Also see RGASPI, f. 17, op. 132, d.228, l. 364.

114. Melanie Ilic, "Soviet Women, Cultural Exchange, and the Women's International Democratic Federation," in *Reassessing the Cold War*, ed. Sari Autio-Sarasmo and Katalin Miklossy (New York: Routledge, 2011), 163; Francisca de Haan, "Continuing Cold War Paradigms in Western Historiography of Transnational Women's Organisations: The Case of the Women's International Democratic Federation," *Women's History Review* 19, no. 4 (Jan. 2010): 547–573.

115. GARF, f. R7928, op. 2, d. 991, ll. 26, 30–35.

116. Helen Laville, *Cold War Women: The International Activities of America Women's Organizations* (Manchester: Manchester University Press, 2002), 113–115; Gradskova, *The Women's International Democratic Federation, the Global South,*

and the Cold War: Defending the Rights of Women of the "Whole World"? (New York: Routledge, 2021), 66. For examples of when the WIDF did not rubber-stamp Soviet proposals, see Francisca De Haan, "The Women's International Democratic Federation: History, Main Agenda, and Contributions, 1945–1991," *Women and Social Movements Online Archive*, ed. Thomas Dublin and Kathryn Kish Sklar (Oct. 2012), 6, http://alexanderstreet.com/products/women-and-social-movements-international; Yana Knopova, "The Soviet Union and the International Domain of Women's Rights and Struggles: A Theoretical Framework and a Case Study of the Soviet Women's Committee (1941–1991)" (master's thesis, Central European University, 2001), 115–125; Gradskova, *Women's International Democratic Federation*, 34–37.

117. Laville, *Cold War Women*, 117.

118. GARF, f. R7928, op. 2, d. 991, l. 137; GARF, f. R7928, op. 2, d. 1668, l. 75; Devaki Jain and Amartya K. Sen, *Women, Development, and the UN: A Sixty-Year Quest for Equality and Justice* (Bloomington: Indiana University Press, 2005), 15–20.

119. On clashes between American and Soviet delegates during the late 1940s, see Dorothy Sue Cobble, *For the Many: American Feminists and the Global Fight for Democratic Equality* (Princeton, NJ: Princeton University Press), 268–270; during the mid-1950s, see Laville, *Cold War Women*, 115.

120. Jacqueline Van Voris, *The Committee of Correspondence: Women with a World Vision* (Northampton, MA: Sophia Smith Collection, 1989), 5–6; "Origin of the Committees of Correspondence," 1–2: SSC, MS 340, box 1, folder 1.

121. "Correspondence," and "Correspondence and Field Work," SSC, MS 340, boxes 28–29, 32–33; "Training, Evaluation and Toolkits," and "Training Materials," SSC, MS 340, box 5, folders 13, 15.

122. Hugh Wilford, *The Mighty Wurlitzer: How the CIA Played America* (Cambridge, MA: Harvard University Press, 2009), 149–154.

123. "Committee of Correspondence Annual Report," April 1, 1954–March 31, 1955, 8: SSC box 1, folder 2; "Committee of Correspondence Minutes of Meeting," Dec. 9, 1958, 1: SSC box 4, folder 3; Victoria A. Smallegan, "Cross-Gender Cooperation in the Cold War: The Committee of Correspondence and the Central Intelligence Agency, 1953–1967" (master's thesis, Ball State University, 2015), cited with the author's permission; Wilford, *Mighty Wurlitzer*, 159.

124. "Foundations Linked to CIA are Found to Subsidize 4 Other Youth Organizations," *New York Times*, Feb. 16, 1967, 26; Wilford, *Mighty Wurlitzer*, 158, 161, 163.

125. On the power of physical affection in Soviet citizen diplomacy, see Eleonory Gilburd, *To See Paris and Die: The Soviet Lives of Western Culture* (Cambridge, MA: Belknap Press of Harvard University Press, 2018), 84–91; Vladislav

Zubok, *Zhivago's Children: The Last Russian Intelligentsia* (Cambridge, MA: Belknap Press of Harvard University Press, 2009), 109; Anne E. Gorsuch, "'Cuba, My Love': The Romance of Revolutionary Cuba in the Soviet Sixties," *American Historical Review* 120, no. 2 (April 2015): 510–514.

126. Michael David-Fox, *Showcasing the Great Experiment: Cultural Diplomacy and Western Visitors to the Soviet Union, 1921–1941* (New York: Oxford University Press, 2011), 319.

127. On this phenomenon, see David-Fox, *Showcasing.*

128. GARF, f. R7928, op. 2, d. 1487, l. 161, dated Dec. 17, 1954.

129. GARF, f. R7928, op. 2, d. 1487, l. 161.

130. *Hearings before the Committee on Un-American Activities* (Washington, DC: US Government Printing Office, 1957), 6023–6033.

131. Dayo F. Gore, *Radicalism at the Crossroads: African American Women Activists in the Cold War* (New York: New York University Press, 2011), 81, 86.

132. GARF, f. R7928, op. 2, d. 991, l. 64.

133. GARF, f. R7928, op. 2, d. 1364, l. 1, dated Aug. 6, 1953.

134. GARF, f. R7928, op. 2, d. 1364, l. 15, dated Aug. 4, 1953.

135. GARF, f. R7928, op. 2, d. 1364, l. 24, dated Nov. 14, 1953.

136. GARF, f. R7928, op. 2, d. 1798, l. 15, dated May 13, 1956. Yulia Gradovska observed the same in letters between WIDF officers, including members of the Soviet Women's Anti-Fascist Committee (Gradskova, *Women's International Democratic Federation,* 38).

137. GARF, f. R7928, op. 2, d. 1364.

138. This marginalia appears atop most letters in GARF, f. R7928, op. 2, dd. 985, 1486, 1487.

139. GARF, op. 2, dd. 1799–1800.

140. GARF, f. R7928, op. 2, d. 1365, l. 14, dated Oct. 20, 1953; GARF, op. 2, d. 1485, l. 75, dated July 28, 1955; GARF, f. R7928, op. 2, d. 1798, l. 19, dated July 2, 1956; GARF, f. R7928, op. 2, d. 1800, l. 8, dated Oct. 30, 1957.

141. GARF, f. R5283, op. 14, d. 577, ll. 169–171.

142. GARF, f. R7928, op. 2 d. 1668, l. 7.

143. GARF, f. R7928, op. 2 d. 1668, l. 57.

144. GARF, f. R7928, op. 2 d. 1668, ll. 1–17.

145. GARF, f. R7928, op. 2 d. 1668, ll. 77–78.

146. Knopova, "The Soviet Union," 97–98.

Closing

1. GARF, f. R7928, op. 2, d. 985, l. 146, dated Oct. 10, 1950.

2. Norman E. Saul, "The Program that Shattered the Iron Curtain: The Lacy-Zarubin Agreement," in *New Perspectives on Russian-American Relations,* ed.

William Benton Whisenhunt and Norman E. Saul (New York: Routledge, 2016), 230–236.

3. GARF, f. R8581, op. 1, d. 71, l. 31.

4. Walter Winchell, "Howz about Calling the Russians our Frenemies?" *Nevada State Journal*, May 19, 1953, 4.

5. Special to the *New York Times*, "Text of the Joint Communique of U. S. and Soviet Union on Cultural Exchanges." *New York Times*, Jan. 28, 1958, https://www.nytimes.com/1958/01/28/archives/text-of-the-joint-communique-of-u-s-and-soviet-union-on-cultural.html.

6. GARF, f. R7928, op. 2, d. 1191, 1. 27, dated Nov. 1, 1952. Parentheses in the original.

7. This information from the Russian State Archive of the Economy's catalogue: http://opisi.rgae.ru/scripts/uis/rgae_any.php?base=mysql:rgae&list=17409&idObj=9333008.

8. GARF, f. R7928, op. 2, d. 789, l. 20, dated Mar. 13, 1950; GARF, f. R7928, op. 2, d. 985, l. 58, dated July 8, 1951.

9. GARF, f. R7928, op. 2, d. 791, l. 12, dated May 26, 1950.

10. GARF, f. R7928, op. 2, d. 1365, l.74, dated Mar. 26, 1953.

11. GARF, f. R7928, op. 2, d. 791, ll. 11–12, dated May 26, 1950.

12. GARF, f. R7928, op. 2, d. 985, l. 144, dated Oct. 10, 1950.

13. GARF, f. R7928, op. 2, d. 985, l. 146.

14. GARF, f. R7928, op. 2, d. 985, l. 51, dated Aug. 7, 1951.

15. GARF, f. R7928, op. 2, d. 1365, ll. 75–76, dated Mar. 26, 1953.

16. GARF, f. R7928, op. 2, d. 985, l. 61, dated Aug. 7, 1951.

17. Studies probing the effectiveness of public diplomacy include Justin Hart, *Empire of Ideas: The Origins of Public Diplomacy and the Transformation of American Foreign Policy* (Oxford: Oxford University Press, 2013), 13–14; Efe Sevin, "Pathways of Connection: An Analytical Approach to the Impacts of Public Diplomacy," *Public Relations Review* 41, no. 4 (Nov. 2015): 562–568; Pierre Pahlavi, "Evaluating Public Diplomacy Programmes," *Hague Journal of Diplomacy* 2, no. 3 (Jan. 2007): 255–281; Joe Johnson, "How Does Public Diplomacy Measure Up?" *Foreign Service Journal* (Oct. 2006): 44–52; Eyton Gilbao, "Searching for a Theory of Public Diplomacy," *The Annals of the American Academy of Political and Social Science* 57 (2008): 63–66. Positive assessments of citizen diplomacy's efficacy in David Scott Foglesong, "When the Russians really were Coming: Citizen Diplomacy and the end of Cold War Enmity in America," *Cold War History* 20, no. 4 (2020): 419–440; Jan Melissen, ed., *The New Public Diplomacy: Soft Power in International Relations* (New York: Palgrave Macmillan, 2007); Alan K. Henrikson, *What Can Public Diplomacy Achieve?* (Clingendael: Netherlands Institute of International Relations, 2006); Robert Banks, "Public Diplomacy Evaluation" in *Routledge*

Handbook of Public Diplomacy, ed. Nancy Snow and Nicholas J. Cull (New York: Routledge, 2020), 64–76.

18. *Amerika* was pulled from circulation in 1952. It resumed in 1956, produced by the United States Information Agency.

19. Roy Pearmain's email of Sept. 19, 2022.

20. Roy Pearmain's email of Sept. 19, 2022.

21. "Dinner in a Few Minutes," *Soviet Woman*, no. 2 (1955): 46.

22. "Sunday Dinner," *Soviet Woman*, no. 11 (1954): 47.

23. The Committee of Women's (reduced) activities are summarized in the minutes of the annual meetings of NCASF's Board of Directors and its "director's reports" from 1950–1961: TAM 134 box 1, folders 37–41, 72–75.

24. "List More Pen Pals," *Friendship* 3, no. 11–12 (June-Oct. 1959): 2, HILA, John F. Russell Collection 85015, box 23, folder 2; Student Exchange and Correspondence in HILA, United States National Student Association International Commission Call Number 68011, box 142, folders 2–5. On the Soviet Youth Committee and the US National Student Association, see Chicago Council of American-Soviet Relations, "For Friendly Co-Existence, Trade, Travel, Exchange" (Sept.-Oct. 1955), 1, Chicago Museum of History, folder "NCASF."

25. On peace rallies: TAM 134 box 7, folders 20–22; on delegations: TAM 134 box 7, folders 26, 30, 38, 40, 44; on youth letter exchanges: TAM 134 box 7, folders 84, 90, 96–99; on Artek: TAM 134 box 8, folders 8–40.

26. TAM 134 box 5, folders 17–19.

27. Linda Racioppi and Katherine O'Sullivan See, "Organizing Women Before and After the Fall: Women's Politics in the USSR and post-Soviet Russia," *Global Feminisms since 1945*, ed. Bonnie G. Smith (New York: Routledge, 2000), 215.

28. Linda Racioppi and Katherine O'Sullivan See, *Women's Activism in Contemporary Russia* (Philadelphia: Temple University Press, 1997).

29. It won 8.1 percent of the vote in 1993, enough to hold parliamentary seats, but only 4.6 percent in 1995. Mary Buckley, "Adaptation of the Soviet Women's Committee: Deputies' Voices from 'Women of Russia,'" in *Post-Soviet Women from the Baltic to Central Asia*, ed. Mary Buckley (Cambridge: Cambridge University Press, 1997), 158; Racioppi and O'Sullivan See, "Organizing Women," 215–217.

30. Alexandra Talaver, "Nina Vasilievna Popova (1908–1994): 'Woman in the Land of Socialism,'" in *The Palgrave Handbook of Communist Women Activists*, ed. Fransisca de Haan (London: Palgrave Macmillan, 2023), 245–250. There are two biographies of Popova: N. V. Borisova, *Nina Popova: Zhizn' kak soizdanie* (Yelets: Eletskii gosudarstvennyi universitet, 2005); Renita Grigorieva, ed., *Golub' mira Niny Popovoi* (Moscow: Tonchu, 2010).

31. Alexandra Talaver, "Women's Work: The Role of the Soviet Women's Committee in Soviet Policy-Making (1945–1991)," 9. This paper was presented at the Summer Research Lab, University of Indiana Urbana-Campaign, July 11, 2021. Cited with the author's permission.

32. Nina Popova, *Ob Izmenenii v Ustave Professional'nykh Soiuzov SSSR* (Moscow: Profizdat, 1954),16–17; Talaver, "Nina Vasilievna Popova," 252.

33. Yana Knopova, "The Soviet Union and the International Domain of Women's Rights and Struggles: A Theoretical Framework and a Case Study of the Soviet Women's Committee (1941–1991)" (master's thesis, Central European University, 2001), 68; Talaver, "Women's Work," 4.

34. Talaver, "Nina Vasilievna Popova," 256, 251–252.

35. Alix Holt, "The First Soviet Feminists," in *Soviet Sisterhood*, ed. Barbara Holland (Bloomington: Indiana University Press, 1986), 237–250. Scholarship defending state-socialist organizations' commitment to women's rights includes Wang Zheng, *Finding Women in the State. A Socialist Feminist Revolution in the People's Republic of China, 1949–1964* (Oakland: University of California Press, 2017); Kristen Ghodsee, *Second World, Second Sex: Socialist Women's Activism and Global Solidarity during the Cold War* (Durham, NC: Duke University Press, 2018); Francisca de Haan, "Continuing Cold War Paradigms in Western Historiography of Transnational Women's Organisations: The case of the Women's International Democratic Federation," *Women's History Review* 19, no. 4 (Jan. 2010): 547–573.

36. Racioppi and O'Sullivan See, *Women's Activism*, 73–64; Mary Buckley, *Perestroika and Soviet Women* (Cambridge: Cambridge University Press, 1992).

37. Talaver, "Women's Work," 2–3.

38. GARF, f. R7928, op. 2, d. 1823, ll. 127, 123–124, 28.

39. GARF, f. R7928, op. 2, d. 1823, ll. 8–9.

40. GARF, f. R7928, op. 2, d. 1823, l. 95.

41. Alexandra Talaver, "Women Should be Given the Right to Decide for Themselves: The Role of the Soviet Women's Committee in Gender Policy-making in the Soviet Union (1945–1991)" (PhD diss., Central European University, forthcoming), chapter 4. Cited with the author's permission.

42. Talaver, "Women Should be Given," chapter 4.

43. Mie Nakachi, "Replacing the Dead: The Politics of Reproduction in the Postwar Soviet Union, 1944–1955" (PhD diss., University of Chicago, 2008), 540.

44. Mie Nakachi, *Replacing the Dead: The Politics of Reproduction in the Postwar Soviet Union* (New York: Oxford University Press, 2021), 167–180. Samples of letters in Talaver, "Women Should be Given"; Nakachi, "Replacing the Dead," 542–546. On how Soviet women's letters helped decriminalize abortion, see Helene Carlbäck, "Lone Mothers and Fatherless Children: Public Discourse on

Marriage and Family Law," in *Soviet State and Society under Nikita Khrushchev*, ed. Melanie Ilic and Jeremy Smith (New York: Routledge, 2009), 97.

45. Knopova, "The Soviet Union," 87–89.

46. Eleonory Gilburd, *To See Paris and Die: The Soviet Lives of Western Culture* (Cambridge, MA: Belknap Press of Harvard University Press, 2018), 26, 35.

47. Gilburd, *To See Paris*, 39–41.

48. Gilburd, *To See Paris*, 40–42.

49. Gilburd, *To See Paris*, 42.

50. Rachel Applebaum, "The Friendship Project: Socialist Internationalism in the Soviet Union and Czechoslovakia in the 1950s and 1960s," *Slavic Review* 74, no. 3 (Fall 2015): 491–500; A. N. Tregubov, "Organizatsionnaia transformatsiia sovetskoi kul'turnoi diplomatii v gody 'khrushchevskoi ottepeli," *Nauka IuUrGU* (2018): 233–235; N. S. Savel'ev, "'Narodnaia diplomatia' kak element 'ottepeli' na primere severo-zapadnykh oblastei sovetskogo soiuza," *Vestik novgorodskogo gosudarstvennogo universiteta*, no. 73, t. 1 (2013): 100–103; Nigel Gould-Davies, "The Logic of Soviet Cultural Diplomacy," *Diplomatic History* 27, no. 2 (April 2003): 193–214.

51. SSOD's charter quoted in Serevyan Dyakonov, "Soviet Cultural Diplomacy in India, 1955–1963" (master's thesis, Concordia University, 2015), 18.

52. Katie Day Good, "From Pen Pals to ePals; Mediated Intercultural Exchange in a Historical Perspective," in *Intercultural Communication, Identity, and Social Movements in the Digital Age*, ed. Margaret U. D'Silva and Ahmet Atay (New York: Taylor and Francis, 2019), 21–23.

53. Applebaum, "The Friendship Project," 484–507; Belova, "Kontsept 'internatsional'naia druzhba'," 4–19; A. V. Belova, "Kontsept 'internatsional'naia druzhba' v ideologii i povsednevosti pozdnesotsialisticheskikh obshchestv GDR i SSSR," *Vestnik TvGU, Seriia 'Istoriia,'* 2 (2017): 4–19; A. A. Kritskii, "Obshchestva druzhby v sovetsko-kanadskom dialoge epokhi razriadki," *Kanadskie ezhegodnik* 20 (2016): 197–229; S. B. Makeeva, "Deiatel'nost' zabaikal'skikh molodezhnykh organizatsii v razvitii sovetsko-kitaiskogo kul'turnogo sotrudnichestva v 50-e gody XX veka," *Vestnik Cheliabinskogo gosudarstvennogo universiteta* 34, no. 249 (2011): 40–45; Vera Ivanova, "Friendship of Youth," *Soviet Woman*, no. 3 (1953):36–37; Yuriy Boyko, "International Friendship Club," *Soviet Woman*, no. 6 (1961): 30–31; E. Indrikson, "Sverdlovsk-Birmingham," *Moscow News* 15 (1959): 8; "School has World Friendship Club," *Moscow News* 11 (1957): 8.

54. Walter L. Hixson, *Parting the Curtain: Propaganda, Culture, and the Cold War, 1945–1962* (New York: Palgrave Macmillan, 1997), 6–8.

55. David Scott Foglesong, "When the Russians Really Were Coming: Citizen Diplomacy and the End of Cold War Enmity in America," *Cold War History* 20, no. 4 (2020): 420–425.

56. David Foglesong, "How American and Soviet Women Transcended the Cold War," *Diplomatic History* 46, no. 3 (2022): 545, 544.

57. GARF, f. R7928, op. 2, d. 985, l. 19, dated Sept. 25, 1951.

58. GARF, f. R7928, op. 2, d. 985, l. 83, dated Feb. 25, 1951.

59. GARF, f. R7928, op. 2, d. 985, l. 61, dated Aug. 7, 1951.

60. Elena Bulova, "20 prilozhenie Moe pokolenie," *Moskovskaia Pravda*, no. 270, Dec. 7, 2012.

61. Linda Gordon, "The Women's Liberation Movement," in *Feminism Unfinished*, ed. Dorothy Sue Cobble, Linda Gordon, and Astrid Henry (New York: W. W. Norton, 2014), 90–91; Holt, "First Soviet Feminists," 237–250.

62. Natalia Vinokurova, "Reprivatising Women's Lives: From Khrushchev to Brezhnev," in *Gender, Equality and Difference During and After State Socialism*, ed. Rebecca Kay (Palgrave Macmillan, 2007), 65; Feiga Blekher, *The Soviet Woman in the Family and in Society* (New York: John Wiley and Sons, 1980), 84.

63. O. N. Mel'nikovskaia, *Sud'ba moia—schastlivitsa* (Moscow: Rossiiskii universitet druzhby narodov, 2007), 97.

64. Mel'nikovskaia, *Sud'ba*, 100.

65. Mel'nikovskaia, *Sud'ba*, 103.

66. Mel'nikovskaia, *Sud'ba*, 111–112.

67. Mel'nikovskaia, *Sud'ba*, 141–142.

68. Susan M. Hartmann, "Women's Employment and the Domestic Ideal in the Early Cold War Years," in *Not June Cleaver: Women and Gender in Postwar America, 1945–1960*, ed. Joanne Meyerowitz (Philadelphia: Temple University Press, 1994), 86.

69. Dorothy Sue Cobble, "More than Sex Equality: Feminism after Suffrage," in *Feminism Unfinished*, ed. Dorothy Sue Cobble, Linda Gordon, and Astrid Henry (New York: W. W. Norton, 2014), 28; Alice Kessler-Harris, *Out to Work: A History of Wage-Earning Women in the United States* (New York: Oxford University Press, 1982), 312.

70. Marc Jahr's email of Dec. 22, 2022.

71. Kessler-Harris, *Out to Work*, 302–303.

72. Hartmann, "Women's Employment," 86.

73. Joanne Jahr's email of Dec. 22, 2022.

74. Marc Jahr's email of Dec. 22, 2022.

75. Interview with Marc and Joanne Jahr on Jan. 6, 2023.

76. Letter from Jean Jahr to Joanne Jahr from Nov. 10, 1967.

77. Letter to Joanne and Marc Jahr from March 15, 1968.

78. Marc Jahr's email of Dec. 22, 2022.

79. These demands varied by class, not just by country. Poorer American women wanted more time at home but could not afford it, while Soviet women laid

off in the late 1970s and 1980s demanded more work. See Cobble, "More than Sex Equality," 29; Judith Shapiro, "The Industrial Labour Force," in *Perestroika and Soviet Women*, ed. Mary Buckley (Cambridge: Cambridge University Press, 1992), 21–25.

80. Louise Roach, "Families Say 'Yes' to Casual Social Life," *The Pantagraph* (Bloomington, IL), March 4, 1956, 9; "Illinois Family Plus its Baby Sitter Attends Art Association Parley Here," *The Courier-Journal* (Jacksonville, IL), April 3, 1958, 12.

81. Information from my interview with Marguerite Wesle Franklin on July 15, 2022.

82. "Her Activities Change with her Daughters," *The Pantagraph* (Bloomington, IL), Dec. 24, 1961, 16.

83. Interview with Franklin on July 15, 2022.

84. *The Pantagraph* (Bloomington, IL), July 10, 1965, 15.

85. Marguerite Wesle Franklin's email of July 25, 2022.

86. Interview with Franklin on July 15, 2022; "Cicero Workshop," *Berwyn Life* (IL), May 7, 1975, 3.

87. Cobble, "More than Sex Equality," 62; Gordon, "Women's Liberation Movement," 71.

88. Interview with Franklin on July 15, 2022.

89. Nicole Ziegler, "Brainchild gives Women in Springfield a Forum for Their Writing and Thoughts," *St. Louis Dispatch*, Jan. 29, 1998, 110.

90. Gordon, "Women's Liberation Movement," 84.

91. Celia Wesle, *Light: Paintings and Poems* (Chatham, IL: Adonis Design Press, 2007).

Acknowledgments

The power of human connection has been much more than an object of study for me; it has been my lifeline throughout this process. I leaned heavily on colleagues, friends, and family during the years spent working on this book, which were filled with big life changes, a global pandemic, Russia's invasion of Ukraine, and the deterioration of US-Russia relations. My heartfelt thanks to friends in Russia who supported me during difficult times and inspired this project. I am using their first names only to protect their anonymity. My deepest thanks to Anya, Masha, Aleksandr, and Nadia. To Tamara, Ol'ga, and Tetia Anya, whom we lost to COVID-19, I miss and love you. And Tania, I cherish our friendship. Your generous spirit and intellectual acumen have nourished my soul for the last fifteen years.

I owe an enormous debt to Anna, Alex, Darya, and Ivan, who helped me complete aspects of my research. Ethel Gershengorin, Sijie Jiang, Daria Lugina, Zaim Radoncic, and Brett Shagoury were among the undergraduates at Boston University who helped with my research process. Natalie Belsky and Mirjam Voerkelius gave invaluable assistance with archivists from afar. My sincere thanks to Wendy E. Chmielewski, Jennifer Bumann, Joshua Ranger, Amy Fels, Savannah Winkler, Meryl Roepke, James N. Gregory, Ben Snyder, and other archivists who graciously lent their expertise and help. The Russian Academy of Sciences, the Darwin Museum in Moscow, and George Lee at the *Honolulu Star-Advertiser* kindly assisted with permissions. Thanks to Roe Nurseries, Inc., for sharing genealogical documents.

On the winding road of writing a book, many individuals propelled me forward with their insight and picked me up when I stumbled. Victoria Smallegan, Alexandra Talaver, Eleonory Gilburd, Lanethea Matthews-Schultz, Aiko Watanbe, and Francisca De Haan shared their scholarship (published and unpublished) with me. I got regular energy bursts from brainstorming and laughing with dear Catherine Ashcraft and the incomparable Dina Fainberg. I owe an insurmountable debt to Frank Costigliola, Erik Scott, Christine Evans, and Christine Varga-Harris, who slogged through draft sections and offered feedback. Rivi Handler-Spitz, Julian Bourg, Des Fitz-Gibbon, Margaret Litvin, and Penny Ismay all generously read sections despite having no vested interest in US or Soviet history. Rivi, it is a joy exchanging materials with you and learning from you. Penny, thanks for believing in me and reminding me of the power of friendship.

I was truly privileged to have shared early iterations of my work at the *kruzhki* run by Ethan Pollock and Bathsheba Demuth at Brown, by Michael David-Fox at Georgetown, and by Terry Martin and Serhii Plokhy at Harvard. Those groups made excellent recommendations. Then there are those generous souls who read the entire manuscript. Kate Brown, Michael David-Fox, David Engerman, and David Foglesong (who read everything twice!) braved January in Boston and a new COVID-19 surge to spend six hours in a room, masked, poring over my rough draft with me. Just the memory of it overwhelms me with gratitude. Thanks to Rachel Weiser for taking copious notes and adding good cheer on that frigid day. I am grateful to the anonymous reviewers who made incisive suggestions for revision to my manuscript. Finally, there is my support team, the Boston area "brain trust," who read everything, offered invaluable advice, and helped me laugh along the way. Rachel Applebaum, Nicole Eaton, Johanna Conterio, Rhiannon Dowling, Nataliia Laas, Erina Megowan, Yana Skorobogatov, and Anna Whittington, I simply could not have done this without you. I also owe a debt of thanks to Christine Worobec, Chris Ruane, Wendy Goldman, Kate Brown, Sarah Phillips, and Brooke Blower, who have mentored me and helped me with this project and numerous other professional challenges. Thank you for inspiring me with who you are, as women and as scholars.

There are no adequate words to thank the grandchildren, grand-nieces, daughters, and sons who shared their family photos, documents, and stories so generously. To Constance Roe Burtnett, Joanne Jahr, Marc Jahr, Marguerite Wesle Franklin, Roy Pearmain, and Rebecca Kimple, thank you. It is a great honor to have gotten to know your mothers, grandmothers, and great-grand aunts through their letters and then to have gotten to know you a bit as well. You showed me the same grace and generosity that your letter-writing relatives showed to their pen pals. Thank you for the fascinating conversations and for permission to share your words and photographs.

Every effort has been made to identify copyright holders and obtain their permission for the use of copyrighted material. Notification of any additions or corrections that should be incorporated in future reprints or editions of this book would be greatly appreciated.

I could not have brought this project to life without the beautiful maps from Gregory Wooltson, as well as the steadfast support of Kathleen McDermott and the editorial eye of Katrina Vassallo at Harvard University Press. Generous financial support from the Kennan Institute, the American Philosophical Society, the Boston University Center for the Humanities, and Boston University's Department of History made this project possible by providing funding and time to write.

While studying friendship, I was reminded every day of my sister, Amiee, my brother, Bobby, and my parents, Bob and Teri, who surround me with love, wisdom, and encouragement. To my son, Caleb, you are a miraculous gift. You brought light and beauty to the isolation of pandemic life. I love you all my ketchups. And to Hanns, my partner in everything, who has been there to celebrate every high and endure every low, you are the love of my life. I am infinitely grateful that we are on this journey together.

Any mistakes that may appear in this book are entirely my own.

Index